OUT OF CHARACTER

OUT OF CHARACTER

Modernism, Vitalism, Psychic Life

OMRI MOSES

Stanford University Press
Stanford, California

Stanford University Press
Stanford, California

Printed in the United States of America on acid-free, archival-quality paper

Library of Congress Cataloging-in-Publication Data

Moses, Omri, author.
Out of character : modernism, vitalism, psychic life / Omri Moses.
pages cm
Includes bibliographical references and index.
ISBN 978-0-8047-8914-1 (cloth : alk. paper)
1. American literature—20th century—History and criticism. 2. Characters and characteristics in literature. 3.Vitalism in literature. 4. James, Henry, 1843-1916—Characters. 5. Stein, Gertrude, 1874-1946—Characters. 6. Eliot, T. S. (Thomas Stearns), 1888-1965—Characters. 7. Modernism (Literature)—United States.I. Title.
PS228.C47M67 2014
809'.927—dc23
2013038502

ISBN 978-0-8047-9123-6 (electronic)

Typeset by Bruce Lundquist in 10/15 Minion

To Daniel, Edna, and Tally Moses, with love.

CONTENTS

Acknowledgments ix

Introduction 1

1 Personhood beyond Personality 29

2 Novel Interests: Henry James 73

3 Lively Habits: Gertrude Stein 117

4 Intoning Voice: T. S. Eliot 153

Afterword: Vital Signs 199

Notes 215

Bibliography 261

Index 277

ACKNOWLEDGMENTS

This book has gone through many phases, and with each phase the thinking behind it has undergone incremental shifts and reorganizations. In this sense, its character has evolved (like that of the fictive individuals chronicled within these pages). Each period of its composition has added something new and significant to the argument. Many of the subtler adjustments have taken place without my being in a position to understand how or why, except in retrospect (and then only partially). I do know this much: the book would not have been possible in conception or in completion without the help of many individuals and institutions. I cannot discharge these debts, but I am delighted to acknowledge them.

First and foremost, I would like to thank Kaja Silverman and Charles Altieri. They have been a continual support to me, and the book has been enriched immeasurably by their way of thinking and by their flood of particular advice. Kaja has greeted our divergences as well as stretches of intellectual sympathy with the greatest generosity and interest, and she has also stepped in at times of difficulty to help this book along. Charlie has offered me precious feedback and counsel over the years. Timothy J. Clark made some compelling suggestions at crucial early moments in this book's development. I also have to thank many of my early interlocutors and conversational partners: Paul Stasi, Daniel Grausam, Huey Copeland, Samuel Liebhaber, Jami Bartlett, Naomi Beckwith, and Charles Sumner.

I spent a year at Cornell University as a Mellon Postdoctoral Fellow. During that time, I had the privilege of circulating parts of the book to members of the faculty seminar in which I was participating. I received many encouragements from them. I have particularly to thank my host in the English department, Douglas Mao, as well as Leslie Adelson, Cymene Howe, and separately, Anne-Lise François.

When I arrived at Concordia University, I began an enriching intellectual and emotional existence. Over the course of several years in Montreal, I have found myself in an engrossing dialogue with numerous colleagues and friends. In this category, I have to give special mention to Jonathan Sachs who read almost anything I threw his way and who has given me cartloads of practical advice. Likewise, Mary Esteve has read my work and supported me through good times and bad, and I have had long, engaging tête-à-têtes with her that have forced me to sharpen and defend commitments quite different from hers. Several other people in Montreal have read and commented on portions of the manuscript: Andrew Piper, Meredith Evans, and Danielle Bobker. From far away, Bibi Obler fedexed me her blessed comments on one of my chapters. I have had the fortune of a very gifted research assistant in Rachel Kyne. Catherine Skeen has given me exceptional editorial advice. As my copyeditor, Carolyn Brown has also sharpened this book's prose at innumerable points.

This book has required many conspiratorial planning sessions with some of my dearest friends in Montreal who have helped me with all the messy details of book planning, titling, worrying, as well as with the niggling matters of life beyond work. No one has endured more than Ara Osterweil, who will occasionally get through to me about what matters. Anya Zilberstein has offered me her inimitable perspective. David Baumfleck, Cecily Hilsdale, and François Furstenberg have also helped me celebrate successes when they come. Many other colleagues gave me guidance and assistance: Jason Camlot, Marcie Frank, Jill Didur, Nicola Nixon, and Andre Furlani. Sharon Frank smoothed away many administrative hurdles.

In response to the articles of mine that were parlayed into segments of this book, I received meticulous counsel from Justus Nieland, Jonathan Greenberg, and Lisa Ruddick, as well as unstinting advice from my anonymous readers who pushed me to engage more deeply with the current field of scholarship. Portions of this book have appeared in "Henry James's Suspended Situations," *Modern Philology* 108:1 (2010), and "Gertrude Stein's Lively Habits," *Twentieth-Century Literature* 55:4 (2009).

I reserve special gratitude for the readers of the full book manuscript whose advice sustained me over many months of revision. Emily-Jane Cohen at Stanford University Press supported this book project generously, though I did not make it easy on her. I also wish to thank several friends who have helped me present my work: Joseph Jeon, Charles Tung, and Benjamin Widiss, as well as Taiwo Osinubi, who invited me to give a talk at the University of Montreal.

I am obliged to Cornell University, Concordia University, and Canada's Social Science and Humanities Research Council (which awarded me their Standard Research Grant) for funds to conduct the research in this book.

Finally, to my family, who expect to understand very little of my recondite prose, I can only say that their love and encouragement have been, to me, a vital lifeline and a means to further thought.

OUT OF CHARACTER

INTRODUCTION

Nature hates calculators; her methods are saltatory and impulsive. Man lives by pulses; our organic movements are such; and the chemical and ethereal agents are undulatory and alternate; and the mind goes antagonizing on, and never prospers but by fits.

—Ralph Waldo Emerson, "Experience"

This book offers a series of case studies that challenge the axiom that moral integrity requires faithfulness to one's established beliefs and ideals. We are often told that we fail to be true to ourselves if we violate our convictions. The schemas connecting our organic coherence as individuals and our moral agency to the bonds we have established with a determining past are everywhere present in our culture. Thus, when individuals depart from a set of avowed principles or act out of harmony with an established demeanor, they risk censure or, at a minimum, misunderstanding. Indeed, the very concept of character has encouraged us to accept that people have an identity and a dominant set of traits whose core structures they violate not only at their peril but also at the peril of the social order at large. In literary terms, the word "character" carries many of these assumptions, conjuring up fictive beings in novels whose presumed regularity and occasional flights of unpredictability allow us to assess them as people.[1] At least as long as there has been such a thing as literary character, and increasingly in the contractual and legal stipulations of modern commercial culture, people's personal commitments and their organic coherence have been seen as an index of their moral integrity.[2] What is behind this esteem for consistency? What is it meant to protect us from? It may be a strategy of resistance to a world in flux, but one that has tended to consolidate against any necessary risk of change. This ideal of consistency has built into it a certain obstructive hostility to relationality itself. And the ideal has infiltrated literary and moral conceptions of character to such a degree that it is quite difficult to disentangle assumptions about reliability and constancy from our methodological approaches to character.

A number of the most significant, exigent, and formally innovative writers in the early twentieth century sensed these limitations in the concept of character and set about reinventing the means of depicting people in fiction and poetry. They did so by upending our culture's faith in unwavering consistency. Modernists such as Henry James, Gertrude Stein, and T. S. Eliot thought that such consistency left no room for people to respond ably to each other. The tendency to valorize the coherence of one's personality had a harmful effect: it insisted that people firm up their character by conforming their actions to already announced dispositions without paying much heed to shifting circumstances. These writers felt that overemphasis on personality limited the possibilities for imagining human beings because it prevented self-invention and enforced critical paradigms that looked for secret unmovable centers guiding and motivating behavior. To counter this, James, Stein, and Eliot tended to avoid ascribing to individuals any psychological quality that would encourage an act of interpretive penetration into a person's underlying character. They were sometimes perceived for this reason (erroneously, I would say) as taking a stand against character as such, so pervasive were—and are—the accounts that equate consistency with character. But modernist writers were not as antipsychological as critics have thought.[3] In this introduction, I call attention to the situational and relational understandings of character that these writers developed, partly as an antidote to older moralistic models of character they wished to contest.

Once modernist writers succeeded in freeing morality from characterological consistency over time, they were in a position, I will argue, to present a richer, more intricate, and more socially satisfying conception of ethical life. They focused on creating individuals who set store by their openness to circumstance. These characters think and act on the basis of attitudes that are not shaped in advance. In so doing, such characters make decisions that transform *themselves* as well as the objects of their actions. Among the branches of late nineteenth- and early twentieth-century philosophy, an influential movement called "vitalism" emerged, which did most to treat character as a complex of changing impulses. Rather than grounding ethics on prescribed rules or principles, vitalists tend to promote a capacity to improvise and adapt to a world that is mutable. James, Stein, and Eliot learned from vitalism to pay attention to moment-by-moment alterations in relationships that define the self. Consequently, this book theorizes modernist character through a vitalist prism.

At the turn of the century, vitalism labeled a rather loose camp of thinkers who sought to identify broad trends that strengthen living systems.[4] The term "vitalism" refers to a range of nonmechanistic philosophies that regard life as a conjunction of these unique systems that unfold by operations that are self-determining rather than wholly constrained by physical or chemical laws.[5] Vitalist philosophies focus on emergent processes that develop in unpredictable ways and sustain themselves by means of their own internal logic. My account brings the work of Henri Bergson, William James, and Friedrich Nietzsche into closer alignment with each other as well as with the evolutionary theories of Charles Darwin, capitalizing on the recent critical "return" to vitalism. Each of these figures examined life itself and used it as a model for understanding how complex changes come about.

The modernist writers in the Anglo-American tradition who were most influenced by a vitalist style of thought insisted on bringing people—their activities and modes of conduct—into greater continuity with the mutable world of which they are a part. Rather than treating character as a bulwark against the shifting tides of circumstance, James, Stein, and Eliot thought that our ethical existence consists in forming vigorous social relationships, which are themselves dynamic and capable of changing over time. Indeed, I will be suggesting that modernist concern with literary character is dominated by the question of how to think about life. What are the capacities and values that let life flourish, and conversely, what are the ones that pose an impediment to life? As we will see, this is not a trivial matter to ascertain, in part because community formations vary so much and gain strength from so many shifting conditions on the ground. Vitalists also make it clear that there is not one form or ideal direction maximally suited to life. At best, life exists as a set of tendencies that are subject to swings of direction. Therefore, vitalists prefer to keep as an open question what qualities are life affirming, embracing values that are supple, experimental, and tailored specifically to unfolding events. It may be true, as Elizabeth Grosz argues, that Bergson and Darwin, unlike Nietzsche, do not advance "an ethical and evaluative project" (Grosz, *Nick of Time*, 157), at least not one that explicitly interrogates "the value of value," but their ontology specifies by implication a set of salutary inclinations of character, which is not necessarily the same as a set of standards or prescriptions. The literary texts I examine in the following pages are likewise concerned with the advancement of values that strengthen individual and community life. Their depictions teach us what life looks like at its most intricate, complex, and unpredictable.

It is no accident that the writers to whom I attribute a substantial innovation in the representation of character were also interested in exploring aesthetic experience specifically because that experience gave them a model for an alert, open, unscripted attitude to the world, one that does not rely on special rules or programmatic principles, either cognitive or practical, for specifying how to react. The aesthetic offers a calculated disengagement from instrumental modes of response, leaving individuals at liberty to improvise rejoinders to each other that follow no hard-and-fast rules of comportment. These responses proceed by feeling-based intuitions and judgments rather than by concepts. To understand the inner workings of these distinctive responses and their place in ethical life, I will need to put affect front and center in my account.

Vitalists thought that people's affective responses—as they entwine with other psychological powers, such as will, habit, and intuition—help them navigate circumstance. Vitalists distrusted strictly cognitive explanations for behaviors as well as the rational and intellectual biases that produce them. Nietzsche, James, and Bergson, for example, are concerned with the ways that agents react to events when they do not possess a fixed grasp of them or ready-made categories for dealing with them. They presume that agents are left to feel their way through the potential extenuations and possibilities of their situation. Darwin, for his part, focuses on small-scale changes within the habits of organisms that point to processes of adaptation and self-organization. Life evolves through a dynamic series of repetitions. Bergson and James had their quarrels with Darwin's ideas, but all three share a concern with evolving living processes that takes complexity and open-endedness of life as a conceptual starting point.[6] By exploring their commonalities, I will excavate an ignored, or rather largely disavowed, vitalist strain of Darwinian science.

In the theoretical chapter that follows, I spell out in detail modernism's vitalist-inspired conception of character. I do so by putting modernism and vitalism in dialogue with a number of other intellectual disciplines and critical methodologies: from behaviorism and empirical social psychology to psychoanalysis and ego psychology; from character criticism to narratology and poststructural criticism; and from aesthetic theory and pragmatist criticism to evolutionary science and certain "naturalist" strands of virtue ethics. Together, these theoretical encounters allow me to rethink what it means to have a character, or, in the literary case, what it means to be one.

Although this theoretical chapter will serve as an extended philosophical primer to the subject of this book, I commence with a more literary-historical approach. I aim to clarify what is so distinctive about the models of character that modernists invented. To understand the literary backstory, it will be necessary to contrast the modernists' approaches to those of important nineteenth-century predecessors or contemporaries. I offer three lengthy investigations taken from the writings of George Eliot, Herman Melville, and Joseph Conrad. Modernist innovations in characterization did not, however, emerge in the isolation of purely literary concerns. To grasp the impact that vitalism had on modernist character techniques, we will do well to trace some of the historical ties that bound James, Stein, and T. S. Eliot to vitalists. This will help us assess the importance of vitalism as a discourse specifically about psychic life.

PRECURSORS

Substantialist Models of Character

Most descriptions of character start from the idea that people have fixed, intractable, and repetitive psychological content that is not readily responsive to the immediate conditions imposed by a situation. This contention is far more pervasive than any single moralistic equation would lead one to suppose. In the business of interpreting novels and plays, readers and audiences are called upon to dig into characters' desires or motivations to understand them, even in the absence of their overt coherence. As we will see, psychoanalysis has been a chief propagator of such readings, but the practice extends equally, although with some variation, to the sort of character criticism we associate with F. R. Leavis, F. O. Matthiessen, and Lionel Trilling. Such analyses of anterior motives have also been central to many philosophical dissections of ethical agency. I would argue that a parallel can be drawn between the moralism of character criticism (with its inherited ethical schemas) and the psychological formulas of psychoanalysis in that both seek to make immutable psychological verities the basis of subjectivity.

James, Stein, and Eliot refused to submit to this morally recalcitrant conception of people. They focused on the fluid identifications, emotive capacities, and ad hoc reactions that allow subjects to adjust to their circumstances rather than on the behaviors that tie them to a fixed and dominating past. But to do this—to counter the gamut of interpretive norms that would predetermine identity—they had to question the organizing structures that define a person's consistency. This necessarily meant developing sophisticated formal strategies that left character unrecognizable from the standpoint of older representational paradigms. Modernists felt that individuals can change themselves while engineering their own affirmed forms of continuity with the past without falling back on a substantive underlying sameness at their core.

In other words, writers such as James, Stein, and Eliot imagined character as a process, not a substance, and gave singular attention to the manner in which that process unfolds. In doing so, they were in a position to recast nineteenth-century models of character. Nineteenth-century literature—and realist fiction in particular—tends to find ever more complicated ways of enforcing the interpretive protocols that look for persevering structures within characters, even if this literature did not invent those protocols. Of course, the nineteenth century had its own share of writers who appeal to twentieth-century tastes for open-ended, psychologically involved fiction, and each has a distinctive way of staging psychic life. Figures as eclectic as Melville, George Eliot, and Conrad do not offer an easy-to-describe formula for their handling of character, and yet on the whole they present an instructive contrast to the modernists on whom this study is focused. George Eliot and Conrad can be seen as promoting critical paradigms that search for the metaphorical patterns of repetition within character and disguised structures that guide and motivate behavior. Melville, however, pleaded for inconsistency as a defining motif of character. Unlike writers who fall more squarely in the nineteenth-century realist tradition, he serves as a different kind of touchstone for my argument. By choosing not to present sustained relationships, Melville renders his characters' futures intangible and therefore abstract. The key to the contrasts lies in the interactive definitions of character to which James, Stein, and T. S. Eliot adhere and the emergent and therefore unfinished relations that constitute social life.

George Eliot's Centered Selves

Gertrude Stein titled her first (rather conventional) effort at short story writing by alluding to one of George Eliot's chapter headings, "In the Red Deeps."[7] T. S. Eliot said of George Eliot's character Rosamond Vincy in *Middlemarch*: she "frightens me far more than Goneril or Regan" ("The Three Voices of Poetry," 93). As one of the preeminent Victorians, George Eliot served a significant role in James's tutelage as a writer. It is revealing, then, that James, Stein, and T. S. Eliot ended up pushing against her methods of characterization. Stein ranked her as one of "those" nineteenth-century writers who inspired such an interest in their characters that "people lived and died" by them, taking "violent interest in them," finding them more real to the average human being than the people they knew" ("Transatlantic Interview," 21). She contrasted Eliot and her brand of realism with Henry James, whom she considered the first twentieth-century writer because he is less attentive to characters as individuals and much more attentive to an "ensemble [that] lives" (21). At first sight, Stein's comments may be taken to elevate literary form above character, but I would argue that she is criticizing a specific mode of nineteenth-century characterization.

To understand this mode, we could jump straight to a passage from *Middlemarch* (1871–1872) in which George Eliot ratchets up the novel's central conflict between the ingenuous Dorothea, whose morally uncalculating nature leads her to grandiose marital misreckoning, and the brittle, stony Mr. Casaubon:

> We are all of us born in moral stupidity, taking the world as an udder to feed our supreme selves: Dorothea had early begun to emerge from that stupidity, but yet it had been easier to her to imagine how she would devote herself to Mr. Casaubon, and become wise and strong in his strength and wisdom, than to conceive with that distinctness which is no longer reflection but feeling—an idea wrought back to the directness of sense, like the solidity of objects—that he had an equivalent centre of self, whence the lights and shadows must always fall with a certain difference. (208)

The "certain difference" of which Eliot speaks is the unequivocal division that separates one person from another, and it presumes a certain persistency with which each goes on being who he or she is. Characters, in her terms, enjoy solidity. They are capable of casting shadows and are subject, emotionally and physically, to the laws pertaining to things that endure in their own separate nature. Eliot's protagonists are ranked as separate—and equivalent—centers, but what makes them a center is not a point of view or a specific responsibility all their own, formed by virtue of their present position in a social configuration. Rather, they are centers on the basis of their abstract status as moral beings, with obligations accruing to them accordingly, or else because they are subject to the constraints of their appointed nature. Dorothea's bright expectancy, Eliot implies, cannot long withstand the erosions of an incompatible alliance, which reveal to her only the massive outline of her husband's shadowy difference from her.

The passage describes Dorothea's slow-awakening feeling that she and her husband are mismatched, and it does so by describing both the awareness of being separate from him and the recognition that she has hitherto blurred essential differences from him and thus has not acknowledged his distinctness because of her own narcissistic overinvestment. In his reading of this passage, Neil Hertz suggests that Dorothea's emergence from moral "stupidity" is unavoidably incomplete, rejecting the implication that this moment of awakening is the novel's final say. As he remarks, "to be born in moral stupidity is to be born imaginative; and it is against the inertia of this mode of imaginative activity, the narcissistic dwelling on and in an image, that the moral imagination has both to define itself and defend itself" (*George Eliot's Pulse*, 29). Hertz's argument seems to be that for Eliot moral life requires that we recognize other people's differences but without allowing ourselves to remain wholly detached from them, lest we lose sight of the very principles that draw us into human community with them. In effect, he thinks, people are not quite so disconnected from each other as Dorothea wishes to believe at this moment in the novel. Therefore, "the difference between the two kinds of imagination [Dorothea's and Casaubon's] may not, under scrutiny, be all that clear" (30). Dorothea cannot simply "cast out" Casaubon as a narcissist because he is not simply "an exteriorized embodiment of a mode of imagination threateningly antithetical to hers" (29). He also stands as a figure of emotional illegibility, which the moral imagination can never fully ignore or triumph over.

For Hertz, identification tends to blur boundaries and erode capacities for differentiation between self and other. Eliot's characters have permeability in their social lineaments, and I would argue that it is this quality of permeability that has also confounded readers of James's late fiction and T. S. Eliot's poetic personae. The difference is not that George Eliot fails to account for complex identifications by conceding a premature contrast between Dorothea and Casaubon. It is that her decided belief in the ultimate goodness of human connection seems to weather all possible conditions and to triumph over any possible check, almost before relationships have a chance to fail. It is no accident that Hertz spends most of his book focusing on Eliot's marginal characters, because it is through them that the author risks an exploration of social failure. Still, that risk is not taken as far as it might, and one generally sees Eliot edging toward a vague recovery process for the characters she has not banished from the narrative.[8]

The problem with Eliot's approach to characterization, as James described it, is that "she proceeds from the abstract to the concrete; that her figures and situations are evolved, as the phrase is, from her moral consciousness, and are only indirectly the products of observation. . . . The world was, first and foremost, for George Eliot, the moral, the intellectual world; the personal spectacle came after" (*Critical Muse* 208). This does not mean that Eliot simply dresses up abstract moral qualities and calls them people; it is more that her characters cannot but reveal within their own "unique" desires the orderly nature of a society that refuses social and moral fragmentation.

Middlemarch's "diffuseness," as James labeled it, stems from its author's conception of society: in the novel, relations themselves are diffuse and undefined, evidently existent, but lacking proof of what they accomplish or what they lead to. Eliot simply insists on them as a precondition of her sometimes anxious moral idealism. We have to assume that Dorothea's kindness or Lydgate's liberality has eventual, although dispersed, effects. In other words, we must assume a structured social world of interlocking relationships. As Leo Bersani argues, Eliot "won't abandon the dream of structured significance"—a society whose idealized unity and orderliness are already preserved for it in advance—"even if she has to sustain it by the vague doctrine of individual goodness finally, in some way, affecting the course of history, or by the more desperate move of showing how the very subversion of her protagonists' dreams is itself a proof of the interconnectedness in life" (*Future for Astyanax*, 64). The desires of characters are themselves structured by and mirrored in a tissue of already fashioned communities. If characters change, it is because they come up against this matrix of preexisting relationships and find themselves needing to adjust. The power of human connection is the seed of communal life, which remains even when specific communities totter and threaten to founder.

In contrast to George Eliot, writers such as James, Stein, and T. S. Eliot wish to show not only how individuals change as they confront social reality but—because reality itself is only the sum of what we make of it—how the social sphere is open to change as individual agents access and modify it. Change cannot be understood as existing outside or independent of the ways that people steer a course through a situation. Nor do the imaginative connections that draw people, traditions, and histories together exist separately from the mental maps that they are constantly constructing or adapting. For such modernists, then, change is a constant. And if we call James and Stein situational novelists, then, it is because they rely on the contingencies and possibilities of everyday relationships—not on faith in a unifying, underlying social fabric that is merely conjectural—to anchor the ethical lives of their characters. Likewise, for T. S. Eliot, entry points to the "tradition" that help to ground social life (not just literary history) are constantly in motion.

Transcendental Subjectivity in Conrad

Although George Eliot thinks that inescapable social ties hold her characters' lives together, Conrad does not. Nevertheless, I would argue that this does not stop Conrad from searching for veiled sources of consistency within his characters. This emphasis on predetermined attributes or effects aligns him with Eliot and other nineteenth-century writers. Despite occupying a joint position with James in the transition to modernism, his modes of characterization differ markedly from James's, as they do from Stein's and Eliot's.[9] Focusing on *Lord Jim* (1900), I would like to argue that Conrad's narrative assumptions have their roots in moral Romanticism.

Like James and Stein, Conrad presents us with characters driven by impulse. Conrad's Jim is not nearly as refined as James's protagonists, whose impulses are not visceral but products of alert, open, agile minds. The rudimentary drives that motivate his characters seem to have more in common with Stein's habit-bound characters. Conrad, however, is more concerned with the templates that the past provides for action than either Stein or James. His character Jim establishes himself in the narrative as something of a puzzle. In his capacity as first mate of the Patna, the British officer disregards his duty to inform some 800 variously dark-skinned travelers on board that he believes the vessel is in imminent danger of sinking. He and other officers abandon ship, avoiding the melee awaiting the passengers when they realize there are too few boats to accommodate everyone. This cowardly but confounding act, which "cuts himself off from the rest of his kind" (*Lord Jim*, 19), turns out to be a symptom of a cause hidden in the depths of Jim's character. And yet nothing adds up to a coherent picture. Attempts to interpret the motivation for Jim's impulsive ethical lapse never achieve a seamless fit with the willful idiosyncrasy of his acts: "The views [Jim] let me have of himself were like those glimpses through the shifting rents in a thick fog—bits of vivid and vanishing detail, giving no connected idea of the general aspect of a country" (48). Excavating the grounds and motives of Jim's action becomes Conrad's focus for the rest of the novel.

While Conrad treats his characters' impulses as part of a pattern rooted in a disguised "interior" source, James and Stein regard their characters' exertions as a productive series of improvisations whose implications the narrative hopes to work out or fine-tune. A subtle line separates the two versions of character. In Conrad's case, character is subject to an intense hermeneutic demand. Marlow, the narrator, obsesses over the degree to which Jim's puzzling, impetuous actions can be linked to an essential facet of his personality. The appalling nature of the surface becomes an invitation to analyze buried motives or deep structures of the self. Marlow follows a logic of substitution whereby any manifestation of an act refers itself to an earlier act and to the psychological design "behind" it that makes it readable. Ultimately, analysis stalls, unable to bridge the divide between the surface action and the unfathomable subjectivity that sets it in motion. In the meantime, though, Conrad's novel foregrounds the insistent questioning of the interpreter—in this case, Marlow, who is a proxy for the reader. The impression of Jim that Conrad registers through Marlow—like any impressionist's "bid for immediacy"—ends up, in Jesse Matz's terms, "featuring the byproducts of the failure to get it" (*Literary Impressionism and Modernist Aesthetics*, 11).

Tzvetan Todorov in 1975 suggested that the psychological and moral center that Marlow journeys to find in *Heart of Darkness* is "empty" (*Genres in Discourse*, 111). Various deconstructionist readings have taken up the idea, suggesting that the novel resists plumbing its characters for meaning or explanation, dramatizing instead an intrinsic perplexity about character itself.[10] Geoffrey Harpham proposes that Conrad's twentieth-century critics assimilated him too quickly "to Freud and the general notion of the unconscious" ("Beyond Mastery," 33). However that may be, I would argue that Conradian character demands to be interpreted, and that the resistance it poses to interpretation makes us feel the charge of the demand. It is worth connecting the solicitation to interpret—and the investments entailed therein—with the failing results.

I would contend, for example, that in *Lord Jim* readers are made to feel that surface demonstrations of character do not adequately present or encapsulate the moral basis of action, the "supersensible" freedom that Kant claimed to be at the core of agency. Character exceeds all attempts to resolve or grasp it and retains a transcendental aura of sublimity that makes of all empirical facts a deceiving or impossible measure of the force of the person. If Conrad fails to discover a coherent structure of desire that organizes identity, he insists on a higher definition of human integrity, namely, the capacity to act autonomously, a power that he posits apart from any specific circumstance. In this sense, Conrad's account of moral life is exactly the opposite of the one Michael Levenson attributes to him when he suggests that the author's language is bent on collapsing fact and value, empirical description and moral appraisal.[11] In the case of *Lord Jim*, Marlow's contingent understanding of Jim's motives may suffice as a local claim to knowledge, but it leaves the sensible unity of Jim's character unresolved. Conrad aims for a "total" account of character: this is why he privileges last words and final acts. Yet an inquiry into character so total would require giving up on empirical corroboration of sensibility as a means of achieving it: "Are not our lives too short for that full utterance which through all our stammerings is of course our only and abiding intention" (*Lord Jim*, 145)? Like less metaphorical forms of utterance—Kurtz's "The Horror! the Horror!," for instance—language signals or gestures at something beyond linguistic competence, dissolving at key moments into a cry or stutter, "no more than a breath" (*Heart of Darkness*, 69), at the vanishing point of reference. In the vein of his Romantic counterparts, Conrad must use language to evoke what cannot be directly represented: a transcendental capacity for freedom that commonsense understandings cannot grasp directly.

Conrad's protagonists tend to shirk any possibility of completing their ventures by acting. As William Bonney points out, it is as if "all attempts to act against status quo imperial capitalism are systematically disallowed, suspended, in a paralyzing miasma of existential and psychological confusions" ("Suspended," 175). Often, as with Jim, the intentions that give rise to actions crumble and perish before they ever rise from the bosom of their agents, swallowed up by the immense range and formlessness of these possibilities, a range too great to define the personality of the character concerned. Conrad's uncertainties about the consequences of human acts often have to do with the contradictions he sees between human freedom in all of its moral ambiguity and ruinous (because deluded) idealizations of integrity spawned by ideology.

In this way, Conrad differs from James, Stein, and T. S. Eliot in his understanding of character and in his conception of what ensures or awakens ethical conduct. As a sign of this, one might note that Conrad searches for meaning in the past much more persistently than in the present or future. James, however, depicts characters' motives and desires as embryonic distillations of some quite definite process of coming to an insight or an understanding. For James, such understandings are not cognitive or intellectual in nature but rather in the first instance permissions to respond to a situation differently. An action and its possible meaning may be suspended, but only to give characters time to clarify or anchor the meaning through further actions, whose range of implications is still in progress. Stein develops a narrative style that she calls the "continuous present" to track the ongoing alterations that occur within characters' habitual responses. T. S. Eliot, like Conrad, seeks to gather disparate social facts that define characters as a totality, but for Eliot the connections that give these facts their meaning are themselves ad hoc. Rather than presuming that such connections are either immutable or nonexistent, as Conrad does, Eliot thinks they trace a shifting pattern within time. Conrad still has a residually transcendental belief in the integrity of person. He teases readers with the possibility of discovering the antecedents of a character's intentions (the unity of personality underneath the veil) or, barring that possibility, of inferring the invisible essence as it is refracted in the situation, illuminated only indirectly—as the glow of moonshine (itself an indirect source of light) illuminates mists (this being one of Conrad's most celebrated metaphors in *Heart of Darkness*).

George Eliot and Conrad rely on separate standards of consistency as a basis for defining character, but both point to a fixed quality that James, Stein, and T. S. Eliot do not accept or recognize. For George Eliot, complicated entanglements exist to prove that personal destiny, inscribed in desire itself, is commensurable with, or at least bound to, the rigid necessity of structured human relations. Conrad, by contrast, sets out to expose the ideology that would presume such a necessity. One cannot take for granted that communal norms establish a coherent foundation for ethical life, not when the social body is composed of highly variable and conflictual interests. Yet in their intentions Conrad's heroic characters are just as likely to be disinterested as self-interested—their motives issuing from some ground of freedom that diminishes the psychological claim to inevitability. At the same time, Conrad draws attention to the kernel of autonomy that bears fruit in his characters' surprising, erratic behaviors. This autonomy guarantees, if not consistent action, then a mysterious dignity of action.

Inconsistency without a Future in Melville

Although James and Stein do not assume that there is a preconceived unity to character, they think it is possible to fashion a consistent or continuous ground for action. Human freedom, for them, is less about being erratic than it is about being interactive. Rather than seek a constant set of characteristics or capacities that defines a self across different environments, they examine selfhood as a series of contacts, relations, and tensions with those environments. In this regard, their representations of character seem closer to Melville's (if we can overlook Melville's flirtation with allegory). He, like James, Stein, and T. S. Eliot, present encounters between individuals whose unpredictable affective force compels them to improvise new, less familiar identities. Indeed, in his last novel, *The Confidence-Man: His Masquerade* (1857), he would seem to abandon the metaphysical impulse to unlock the obsessive kernel of desire expressed within character. In this respect, and also because his depictions of character are less narratively and more scenically organized, Melville is a revealing antecedent to modernism. It does not matter that Melville precedes Conrad. As vitalists observe, the impetuses for change are multiple, indirect, and not necessarily sequential. For this reason, I am not taking a chronological literary-historical approach to questions of precedence. It is enough to note how little Melville was known even in the latter phase of James's career as a writer.[12] He also forsakes a realist framework for his fiction without encouraging investment in an alternate brand of realism. Consequently, he cannot sustain the richer vision of social life that James and Stein insist on, which depends on their characters having a future. What is more, Melville's vision of slippery, ersatz social relations in the public sphere dramatizes why modernist writers turned to the domain of intimate relations to carve out their conceptions of character.

Melville's characters are not quite the solitary outcasts that earlier critics imagined: people whose motives rest on undisclosed sources buried within their own unmapped interiors.[13] Ahab, his most famous protagonist, gave him that reputation. This man's mysterious motives are tied to an unconquerable fantasy of hunting down Moby Dick, the whale that has harmed him. But Ahab's stubborn will is administered through violence, and *Moby-Dick* treats the interpretations that lead him down the path of such consistency as an imposition, one that Melville does not necessarily endorse.[14] Like the protagonist in "Bartleby, the Scrivener," Ahab's apparently unchanging attitude may be less important for what it expresses about his personality than for what it reveals in the surrounding society's reaction to him. For Gilles Deleuze, Melville's founding act as an American novelist is to "give birth to characters who exist in nothingness, survive only in the void, defy logic and psychology and keep their mystery until the end" ("Bartleby; or, the Formula," 81).

The refusal to supply characters with reasons for their actions allows Melville to displace the forms of psychological rationalism that the Western reader expects. Ahab's soliloquys and Bartleby's formulaic response, "I prefer not to," isolate these characters. As Deleuze notes, Bartleby is "a man without references, without possessions, without properties, without qualities, without particularities" (74), and hence a kind of fixture within the office in which he works who thwarts all common forms of relationality. But his fixity merely proves the inconsistency of those around him. The ripples of affective discomfort that he, like many of Melville's characters, radiates create a circuit of reactions that intensify until they provoke a crisis.[15] Thus, while his heroes' unsocialized proclivities and stalwart defiance seem far removed from the tractability of James, Stein, or Eliot's characters, all four are attentive to the changes in social climate that their characters effect.

The Confidence-Man would seem to give even more of a sweeping look into the affective susceptibilities that lend variability to characters, now reckoned within a heterogeneous social field. It presents a fluid federation of loosely linked individuals—passengers on the steamship *La Fidèle*—who, however grotesquely and comically, defy the pretense of consistency that they are enjoined to display by the confidence men who hit them up for money. An herb doctor, one of the many dubious operators in the novel, insists that a miser reluctant to part with his money must have "unquestioning confidence" in the medicine he is selling, without which the medicine will not work. But in the novel's atmosphere of lawlessness and public skepticism, the confidence he preaches is liable at any moment of interaction to weaken and miscarry, as when the same miser, yielding to another "strange caprice," suddenly presents "the aspect of the most calamitous dejection" (89). This bewildering impulse (rooted in obscure affective grounds) obstructs the smooth running of the con man's repertoire of manipulations. By the same token, the confidence men rely on the lability of their auditors, their perviousness to affective suggestion, to bring their dupes around. What this proves is that inconstancy is a psychological fact of life, though one not easily mobilized for any programmatic aim, good or bad.

The vagaries of whim and paranoid eruptions of doubt that define the encounters among the ship's strangers, though hardly conducive to public intimacy, do give rise to one of its effects: they present great range and variability of response. What undermines sympathy in this human comedy is the nature of the encounters, at once repetitive and illegible. *The Confidence-Man* follows a series of characters in the position of "operator" (the word itself suggestive of interchangeability) who sidle up to their fellow passengers or otherwise hail them. The con men and the dupes, while individually eccentric in a particular way, are also equally inscrutable and therefore barely differentiated from each other. The narrative's attentiveness to particularity is swallowed up by its schematic, iterative structure—by the characters' erratic responses, which are too pervasive and overwhelming for us to track any reliable, unifying features of self. The con men exacerbate each dupe's brand of inconsistency, spurring it on and one-upping it.

As the narrator says, in an aside, "in real life, a consistent character is a rara avis [rare bird]," and fictions that take consistency for granted are likely to be "very untrue to reality" (75).

One reading would maintain that Melville is less interested in a situation-by-situation assessment of the ethical effects of inconsistency than he is in gauging the disturbing breakdown of transcendental principles that guide ethical behavior. From this standpoint, Melville's worry concerns the higher unity of personhood that guides free choice, enforcing—or failing to enforce—respect for the ongoing dependencies of selves on each other. This would make some sense of Melville's savage treatment of Emersonian optimism, which requires that one ignore evil intent by adopting a different—more cheerful—set of initial premises. Melville encourages conjectural interest in what motivates the swindles of the con men. At the same time, he refuses to provide plausible motivations that are commensurate with their situations—something as banal as the appetite for money, for instance—which ultimately prompts speculation as to whether these are agents of diabolical power, literally or metaphorically. One of the distrustful misanthropes aboard the ship, the Missourian, reflects on the success that a confidence man has just met with in getting him to "waive, in his exceptional case, that general law of distrust systematically applied to the race" (135). He observes to himself: "Was the man a trickster, it must be more for the love than the lucre. Two or three dirty dollars the motive to so many nice wiles?" (135). The con game appears to have no object save the reckless pleasure of undermining the moral foundation of human decision-making. Such a reading would make Melville into an allegorist very different from James, Stein, or Eliot in that he is not invested in the situation-specific responses and calibrated attitudes that make for an intricate moral psychology.

But there are indications that Melville's dark, impenetrable comedy has no great investment in such rigid transcendental principles of justice. For instance, any consistent application of moral purpose would have to be erected at the cost of more elastic and personalized means of brokering confidence. Of course, the attempt to earn such confidence specifically in the public sphere has its dangers. During a time of Western expansion and displacement, when community status and concrete ties of intimacy no longer established trust (an affect that enables one to cope with the contingency of the future), social systems placed new and more categorical emphasis on rules and imperatives for enforcing the predictability of agents, administering constraints on their capacity to change their mind or behavior even if circumstances demand it.[16] Melville explores anxieties about trust that emerge at a moment when ways of guaranteeing it are both more tenuous and more abstract, geared toward the specific risks and uncertainties that animate an emergent antebellum commercial culture, with its perennial worries about rampant speculation and lawlessness.

This suggests that Melville is less interested in supporting the characterological assumptions that back a metaphysical foundation for moral behavior than he is in attacking consistency for normalizing the forms of variability possible in social life. The unreliable responses hang over the strangers as so many possibilities of sensitive realignment, and the con men themselves, like James's most perceptive improvisers, perform marvelous feats of social adjustment, saying just what is necessary to bring their dupes along. Yet they do so, we infer, with the same monotonous end of extracting financial gain, which ultimately damages any noninstrumental appreciation of their fellow men as well as flattening the differences among them. Inconsistency has as its affirmative ideal a sensitive, impersonal brand of contact, eroticized in *The Confidence-Man* and in *Moby-Dick*,[17] although appearing in *The Confidence-Man* chiefly in a negative or degraded form as unreliable talk. Melville thus offers a particularly roundabout satire of those social forces that would diminish the pleasures involved in sustaining roving public intimacy.

The inferred malevolence of the con men would seem to be intentionally nonrealistic, a campy psychological exaggeration of a rather more ordinary form of inconsistency. To the degree that the con men are mirrorlike projections of the dupes—the distorted versions of their own fears—the satirical target is not inconsistency per se but rather the profit-making logic that homogenizes it.[18] I would argue that Melville is probing and playing with the naturalistic frameworks that allow one to interpret character. If he diminishes the glamour and psychological complexity of his con men's driving aims, he cannily allows for the possibility that this affective flattening has more to do with the workings of impersonal systems to which these figures belong than with any preposterous threat that they personify. Indeed, the novel presents not a single unequivocal instance of harm or fraud enacted. In this respect, it merely proves that the "con men" are not so much villains or bogeymen as they are, in Deleuze's terms, "a comic version of authentic brothers, such as *overly suspicious* Americans see them, or rather have already become incapable of seeing them" (*Essays Critical and Clinical*, 89; emphasis in original[19]). The near strangers who make up this "piebald parliament" (*Confidence-Man*, 16), displaced from their customary social networks and environments, would seem to be granted unprecedented opportunities for self-invention. By the same token, the anonymous relations that define the public sphere limit the forms of entanglement and intimacy that are possible in it.

If the writers I have selected to examine in this book give broad attention to intimate relationships that are less anonymous, it is not because they give up on public experience as a staging ground for imagining human togetherness or because they ignore the ethical responsibilities that belong to public life. As Jessica Berman points out, "the intimate, ethical domain [is] also important for the political development of matters of justice, community, and citizenship" (*Modernist Commitments*, 15). As Melville serves to remind us, the intimate is not the same thing as the private. Nevertheless, many modernist writers are attracted by the greater intensity or complexity of relationships that sustain themselves across time and by the immediacy of social interaction on a local scale. In vitalistic fashion, they recognize that change is predicated on the nature of time itself, which does not proceed in sequential fashion but in a dynamic, prospective way that introduces unpredictable, nondeterministic effects into both material and living systems.

Melville's negative vision acknowledges the power of inconsistency, especially as resistance to regulative ideals of commercial culture, but he also explores its several unavoidable downsides. Without antecedent knowledge of the persons around them, for example, the novel's individuals participate in a rather impoverished and abstract conception of civic life. In addition, the protean capacity to improvise new identities threatens to divest the self of its own thread of continuity. Melville's work shows that inconsistency tends to become sterile when lived as a series of synchronic moments that repudiate any faith in a futurity. Although it is possible that Melville sought to treat such degraded forms of inconsistency satirically, the satirical targets—pervasive yet fleeting—point toward another way of escaping the confines of a fixed outlook without showing how one establishes new commitments.

VITALISTIC MODERNISM

A Theory of Psychic Life

Of the three writers just surveyed, Melville most clearly departs from the modus operandi of realist characterization. His con men glide from one form to another, revealing a degree of hectic uncertainty about the very possibility of maintaining an identity; the other characters in *The Confidence-Man* fare little better. Although James, Stein, and Eliot might have taken inspiration from Melville's fitful characters, their writings are far more sensitive to the adjustments that characters make to their situation. As they act on what is inchoate and unformed, characters are eventually in a position to take responsibility for their changes of heart or perspective—that is, for what they become in the process of change. Modernists' insistence that people can be discontinuous with their past instantiations does not mean that such individuals are fickle, mercurial, or simply unstable. The writers on whom I focus understand that continuity over time includes variation.

In their "vitalist" psychologies, Bergson, William James, and Nietzsche helped to redescribe the individual in ways that account for such psychic continuity, while also giving ethical standing to the self that is suspended in a state of transition. They did so by doing away with definitions of personhood that rely too much on personality or bare ego. It is not often acknowledged that William James offered his famous formulation of a stream of thought to account for "mutations of the self" that nonetheless allow one to conceive of oneself as continuous without positing a transcendental ego, soul-substance, or any consistent attribute other than a special orientation or set of responsibilities ("relating," "owning," "affirming") toward the particular experience or behavior at issue. This formulation of stream of thought bears close resemblance to Bergson's idea of *durée* and to Nietzsche's understanding of will as that which requires that one undo all false assumptions about an underlying ego as agent, cause, or executor of orders. For Nietzsche, will is not a summatory act but a process.[20]

The influence of vitalism as a discourse on modernism was enormous, as a wave of recent scholarship has acknowledged. Not only was William James the brother of Henry James, he was a crucial early mentor to Gertrude Stein. Critics have drawn attention to Stein's early training as an empirical psychologist as well as her scientific interests in Darwinian biology, which she continued to reference with some regularity throughout her life. Meanwhile, Eliot moved to Paris in 1910 (a year before commencing his graduate coursework in the philosophy department at Harvard), motivated in large part by his desire to hear Bergson's celebrated lectures in person.[21] He declared himself a Bergsonian for the period that led up to the writing of such lyrics as "The Love Song of J. Alfred Prufrock" and "Portrait of a Lady," after which he rejected the affiliation.[22] Many other modernists benefited directly or indirectly from vitalist ideas and a vitalist sensibility, including James Joyce, Wallace Stevens, Wyndham Lewis, D. H. Lawrence, and an array of visual artists.[23] The writer and critic T. E. Hulme, fraternizing with Pound and other imagists, wrote extended meditations on the relevance of Bergson to literature that helped popularize the philosopher in Britain.[24] William Faulkner imbibed Bergson solemnly, incorporating allusions to the philosopher's concept of lived time in his fiction.[25] Scholars have explored Virginia Woolf's Bergsonian depiction of flux and fluidity in human experience and have turned recent attention to her anxieties about evolutionary change, which she inherited from Darwin and uses to reflect on the futurity of human life.[26] And these are just the Anglo-American lines of connection. Marcel Proust and Bergson are related by marriage. When Bergson wedded Proust's cousin, Proust served as best man at the ceremony, and his intellectual identification with the time philosopher is well known.[27]

Although scholars have recognized the intellectual influence of the vitalist movement, they have not taken global account of its significance for writers' approaches to characterization. I will argue that vitalism allows us to repsychologize character and thus avoid approaching it in formalist terms—for example, as a matrix of symbolic functions, thematic significance, or narrative sequencing. By examining modernist representations of fictional people (in some cases, simple representations of voices or perspectives) as they react or are shaped by shifting circumstances, we are in a position to treat them as a set of test cases for rethinking humanist psychological paradigms. Rather than presenting characters in ways that imply the global integration of personality across contexts, such modernists as James, Stein, and Eliot, on whom this study is focused, but also others, such as Woolf and Stevens, insisted that character should be thought of as a two-way interaction between situations and the individuals who are responsive to them. In other words, modernism's reimagining of character coincided with an ethical vision of a highly responsive subject able to enter into compelling new relations with others.

We may be in a better position to gauge the ethical lessons of vitalism because of its striking prestige in contemporary cultural theory. As Lisa Blackman surveys the field, current vitalists address "issues of change and transformation through a recognition that materiality is governed by relations of indeterminacy, contingency and openness" ("Affect, Relationality and the 'Problem of Personality,'" 25). The "new materialisms," as they have come to be known, promise to redefine human life by breaking down the boundaries that separate us from all other things.[28] They present a picture of the world in constant movement, where human and nonhuman powers work in an interwoven configuration to effect change. The consequences of these accounts are exceptionally useful in revealing how much our will and very sense of self are contingent on the environment and material forces beyond us. Yet the emphasis on novelty and change do not immediately lead to prescriptive demands: transmutation is not a value in itself. We have to appreciate that what counts as "good" or "bad" is only meaningful in the context of life.[29] The new materialisms remain attractive for many critics because of their psychophysiological orientation, which offers continuity between scientific and cultural domains, and because the imperatives of survival and augmentation of life revisit the concerns of the "old" materialisms, but with a less deterministic stance.[30] Nonetheless, the highlighting of a materialist framework has led them to pay less attention to the specificities of psychic life than did modernists and their vitalist contemporaries.

This book will be interested in correcting that balance: I aim to show how rich and varied are the consequences of vitalists' ways of approaching the psyche. To accomplish this, I underscore the importance of psychological relations (recollections, thoughts, mental connections) in the business of coping with experience. More than this, I think it is important to recognize that life is a system that creates its own constraints, priorities, and urgencies. At all levels of complexity, it is concerned with the dynamic continuation of life (in its innumerable competing structures). At higher levels, however, this process of experimentation and consolidation is felt as a psychological imperative. Nineteenth- and twentieth-century vitalisms help us to appreciate modernists' concern with what we might call the intensification of modes of living. What matters to modernists is not simply that people can change or reinvent themselves but that such reinvention is felt to be experientially self-justifying: it increases their capacity to act and adjust to their situation, specifically by creating an opening onto a future compatible with human interactivity, the mutually dependent and broadly social character of communal life.

A Literary-Conceptual Genealogy

I have chosen to focus on Henry James, Stein, and Eliot as exemplars of vitalist modernism because of their wide-ranging concern with the psychological experience of change. They offer a genealogy of far-reaching efforts to model alternatives to the available traditions in the English-speaking world for presenting character. We could make a comparable case for the "fitful" nature of character in a number of other writers, as I have intimated, but the impulses of James, Stein, and Eliot are in my opinion more resolutely vitalistic and attest to the significance of their encounters with vitalistic intellectual and philosophical currents of thought. Also relevant is their having each in their own way stood as spokespersons for the theory and practice of modernism. Critics have often discounted their commitment to presenting distinct, recognizable individuals under any program of apparent realism. But in my judgment the forms of fluidity and transitive experience that they explore do not diminish the viability of their conceptions of psychic life, however counterintuitive their paradigms of character may appear to critics used to more conventional representational models. In fact, they offer something that postmodern metafiction often does not, despite its emphasis on fluidity: a set of immensely serious efforts to examine human capacities for alteration without dispensing with the essential contours of personhood itself.

I begin this book with James because his work stages forms of intimacy that engage and require the lively emotional impulses of the self. This is the side of human agency that leaves behind calculated intentions, predetermined motives—anything that prevents an individual from adjusting to another person within a constantly changing situation. He shares with Nietzsche a desire to restore innocence to the process of "becoming" by refusing to impose a psychology of blame that would trace each act of will to a prior motive, thus presuming that every discharged action has a conclusive measure of its moral rightness at hand.[31] Stein allows us to reflect on people's repetitive behaviors, the habits that combine to shape their character. She captures the reiterative, slow-moving, and idiosyncratic dimensions of psychological change. Recursive action, rather than replicating exact behavioral repertoires, consolidates new changes of direction into older patterns of conduct. Her attentiveness to psychic change makes her one of the genuine heirs to James. The choice of Eliot might seem less obvious, given his lyric commitments. But of modernist poets he is perhaps most clearly interested in presenting characters. He also inaugurated the discourse of impersonality—or, rather, institutionalized it—and, as we will see, his antagonism to what he calls "personality" helps us identify some of the revisionary claims that modernists make about character.

James, Stein, and Eliot are all early modernists, and their experimental urges play out in specific response to nineteenth-century models of character. James offers the clearest case, as he was significantly older than Stein or Eliot, and he straddles periods. In fact, certain critics may be unaccustomed to considering him as a modernist at all. But his late work furnished many first-generation modernists with a signal example of artistic experimentation.[32] I would argue that the contrast between James's early and late fiction reveals the effects of his own vitalistic process as he comes to rely less on narrative pressures for presenting psychological change.[33] Stein and Eliot learn from him to give attention to actions, scenes, and events whose meanings ramify or multiply in ways that upend the causal basis of narrative reasoning. In the novels of James's "great phase," characters begin to act in ways that depend on an unfinished future to understand what they are doing because the implications of their improvised responses have yet to be worked out or fine-tuned. James thus expresses a commitment, shared with Stein and Eliot, to drawing out what we might, exploiting Bergson's conceptual vocabulary, call the "virtuality" of situations.

Bergson's view is extraordinarily hard to summarize, containing as it does a complete rethinking of how we understand possibilities entering our world. "Virtuality" refers to relations between things that are potential rather than actual. These real but immaterial elements hover, so Bergson thinks, as an "after-image" (*Matter and Memory*, 102) projected from objects and things that traces their prospective movement or transformation. Because such potentials have not been consummated and may never be fully actualized, they remain indistinct, yet we are capable of discerning, discovering, or activating them through our powers of perception and intuition. Bergson conceives of the body not principally as a physical barrier or as the mantle of sensuous life but as a temporal axis, a suspended interval between the past and a future that has yet to present itself. Therefore, people immersed in time cannot be understood in the manner of objects present in themselves, complete and fully located in the immediate moment.

I intend to clarify the importance of virtuality and other vitalist concepts in shaping modernist conceptions of character. That some of these concerns have not come to the fore in accounts of modernist character has a lot to do with the influence of other continental intellectual theories that had a decisive influence on Anglo-American literary history. Psychoanalysis, the most prominent psychological discourse to emerge out of the fin de siècle, had a large hand in obscuring vitalist ideas and its rich conceptual legacy. I deal with some of the historical reasons for this in this book's afterword, in which I explore the intellectual fortunes of vitalism after its moment of cresting. For now, we might simply note some of the old-fashioned conceptual biases of psychoanalysis as well as the methodological limitations of the discourses that emerged as a countercurrent to it. As I argue in Chapter 2, psychoanalysis is heir to a nineteenth-century view of character as a persevering structure and, mutatis mutandis, continues to insist on a sedimented, repetitive personality shaped by certain formative events in personal life. Its complex picture of the unconscious offers a twist on a more general belief in characterological consistency. Of course, psychoanalysis leaves room for psychic variability and "free-flowing" desire, but it tends to see such possibilities as caught within, or set up against, a prescribed normative order. It posits an elaborate narrative arc in which reckless and uncontrolled "infantile" desires succumb—or else, fail to succumb—to the territorialized oedipal map of adult sexuality, one that coincides with the social teleology of marriage. As with the nineteenth-century novel, the collective voices of social order do not necessarily prevail over the unruly individual, nor, for that matter, does the successfully evolved person rid herself of remnants of an older emotional economy underlying the newer formations of her desire. But in those cases psychoanalysis still insists on measuring departures against prevailing psychic patterns.[34]

Because these (admittedly qualified) estimations of human integrity have been with us for a long time, articulated through multiple critical approaches, it will not do simply to claim that James, Stein, or Eliot's texts "resist" psychoanalytic readings. Resistance is built into psychoanalytic interpretive operations. If one wishes to argue against psychoanalysis, one has to locate particular cases in which psychoanalytic descriptions fail to be convincing. Such a task is not the main focus of this study, although I do hope that my reading of James's *Golden Bowl* in particular is taken as a propaedeutic for such an endeavor. I will note my quarrels with psychoanalysis as they arise. My main concern, however, as we consider the indirections of James's *Golden Bowl* and the recursive style of Stein's "Melanctha," will be to demonstrate that a more general concern with psychic consistency—or, equally, with the warding-off of inconsistency (which is in some sense the real issue for psychoanalysis)—overlooks the ethical aims of these fictions.

At other points—in the chapter on James and the chapter on Eliot—I will consider how to avoid the opposite critical impulse, felt chiefly in the approach to characterization born of postwar French theory, with its emphasis on the "play" of textuality and the deep-down unreadability of all signifying processes. It aggrandizes the indeterminate, the free-flowing, and the decentered in questions of human action, rendering individual agency open to wholesale redefinition. In place of consistency, poststructuralism describes anarchic, disorderly, but ultimately jubilant displays of variability within character, which it celebrates as a liberating swerve from expected modes of self-understanding.

We may consider ourselves beyond the point where these fraught debates, with their dreams of release or deliverance from structured life, have taken hold of us, but the discourse about character remains heavily under their sway. Thus, if James's, Stein's, or Eliot's characters are not consistent and internally coherent, then they must be contradictory, undecidable, spectral, purely textual, and so on. These pairs of alternatives—between the consistent and the in-flux—seem to me equally dubious. Both fail to take into consideration modernist allegiance to a fully material account of psychic life, with all its limits and irrefutable social boundary-points.

James is not the author of limitless self-expansion—as some of the repossessors of his late work see it[35]—precisely because he insists on presenting identities as informed by social expectation and profoundly contingent. And despite Stein's obvious interest in grammatical and stylistic experimentation, her characters are not merely grammatical functions. In Chapter 3, I examine the unusual kind of character that emerges out of her repetitious compositional process in *Three Lives*, in which she tracks habits that paradoxically enable psychological change. In Chapter 4, I pursue elements of Eliot's presentation of character that emerge through tone and through subtle shifts of perspective rather than through elaborate structures of personality that require self-protective masks and personae. By regulating their tone in a dramatic context, his characters adjust to the emotional climate of a situation. Although Eliot's representations are not set up as narratively sustained fictional individuals, they do dramatize aspects of voice and tone that reveal an everyday mobility connected to individual perspective. I argue that Eliot develops his account of character in active engagement with Bergson's vitalist philosophy, which he eventually integrates with his reading of F. H. Bradley; together, Bergson and Bradley offer a novel theory of voice, which Eliot begins exploring in his early and minor poetry. Character is an irreducible category for each of the aforementioned writers, and no amount of agitating on behalf of textuality can take away from the psychological commitments or indeed the social ones that come to define the horizon of human alteration and amendment.

In fact, throughout this book, I aim to explore the social repercussions of this belief that the self is capable of affirming (and therefore amplifying) its own variability. For instance, in Chapter 2, I focus on the unpredictable nature of the interests that are asserted by such selves. Despite what many social scientists think about people's social interests, James does not treat them as fixed or transparent, a given that we can take for granted on the basis of people's identity-based positions. Interests develop and change in response to what others do and say and in this way cut across the boundaries between people. The capacity to change personal interests and fold them into social interests is for James at the very core of ethical life. Likewise, Stein does not treat the habits that she explores exclusively as conservative social instruments but rather as behaviors that enable flexibility in social life. I argue that we can better understand such flexibility by noticing the virtuality operating within our habits and interests. Our body allows us to perceive and project potential actions, which, at different scales or distances measured from the immediate point of need, enable degrees of latitude to depart from the scripts of the past.

James, Stein, and Eliot create texts that present an astonishing desire to fashion a social order that is open-ended to the degree that characters can alter it, and do so in makeshift ways. Their alterations and recreations are not the intentional acts of sovereign agents, with a fixed image of what they want inscribed onto their consciousness. But neither are they "undecidable" or "indeterminate" agitations. In place of the familiar store of expressions marshaled by deconstructionists, I propose that we come to see their presentation of characters' feeling as inchoate, which is to say, not yet determined or worked out, linked to a will which does not wish to foreclose on experience. The inchoate speaks to the unsettled state of things that allows change to happen.

The chapters, as described, demonstrate the adaptive behaviors and attitudes of characters who struggle to keep pace with the changes occurring around them. The alterations they undergo are the result of temporal processes that are indeterminate and future-oriented. To track the gossamer quality of such changes, one cannot simply attend to narrative or plot, or describe a character by the states of mind or endpoints she or he reaches. This is because they are subject to ongoing serial modifications that define departures from a provisional character template. The ever-changing nature of the psyche makes itself felt on the level of modernist compositional practice in the juxtapositions, shifts, modifications, conjunctions, and leaps from one temporary resting place to another, one thought or movement or attitude to another. We normally regard people as substantial entities that have a defined identity. How does one systematically rethink them as a set of mental transitions that create but do not complete the individuals concerned? This question was once posed by a figure who had a significant impact on late nineteenth- and twentieth-century vitalism: Ralph Waldo Emerson. Along with Baruch Spinoza, Emerson crops up in this book as an important antecedent to vitalism. As Jonathan Levin reminds us, Emerson validates a constantly mutable and therefore not yet attained self: "Transition and abandonment figure a power that at once supports and shatters the self" (*The Poetics of Transition*, 3). James, Stein, and Eliot inherit from Emerson and his vitalist heirs a paradoxical commitment to personal autonomy or self-reliance, but one that requires people to forsake or vacate settled instantiations of themselves to live properly.

Thus, we return to life itself as the measuring stick through which modernists validate our endeavors. Till now, modernism has often been saddled with a reputation for impersonal writing, formalism, and a commitment to ruthless purification of experience. I would argue instead that we might see it as offering new ways of thinking about relationality and community life.

1 PERSONHOOD BEYOND PERSONALITY

On the face of it, literary modernism is not the most promising movement on which to ground a study of character. As I indicated in the introduction, it rises at a moment when realist commitment to the representation of sustained structures of personality wanes as a guiding principle of characterization. With such waning comes a loss of credibility that its writers are anywhere especially interested in rendering the lives or experiences of specific individuals, or at least in upholding the value of such experiences in personal terms. Depending on the text, these claims may be exaggerated. Yet the impression remains that the fragmented perspectives, blurred subjectivities, and dispersed identities that are so often said to define modernist character do not maintain their coherence long enough or with enough force and distinctiveness to merit the status of full personhood.

In this chapter, I will be working to uncover some of the assumptions that underlie these judgments. This will lead me to reexamine what establishes or expresses people's psychological contours and relations to the social world, and thus to give more credence to modernist strategies of characterization, particularly the modernism of Henry James, Gertrude Stein, and T. S. Eliot. But we must recognize that the prevailing critical wisdom that such figures were not particularly friendly or responsive to the claims of discrete and separate psychological beings has its roots in the discourse around "impersonality" that Eliot and other modernists used to describe their work and literary values. Many early critics and promulgators of modernism understood "impersonality" to refer to a specific aesthetic attitude in the work, one that took precedence over the psychological perspective being rendered. They aligned the text's "impersonality" with its formal imperatives, its complexity, purity, and attention to materials and medium. To a certain degree, modernists themselves were complicit in this. Was it not to escape the realm of the muddy, the idiosyncratic, the subjective, the personally prejudiced, and the inartistic that a range of modernists adopted the rhetoric of impersonality to begin with? Yes and no. Certainly, the discourse gave modernist writers a chance to emphasize the tough-minded aesthetic protocols of the artistic product. But I will argue that the literary practices it named offered them something more: the chance to devise new ways of staging the psychological experiences of individuals. As the best critics of modernism have recognized, these writers had a larger ethical and social agenda in mind when they invoked the impersonality of their work, one that in certain ways was belied by the expression they chose to stand in for the principal features of their practice.

Impersonality and correlative terms served polemical needs of the moment. These needs—to give objective status to their work, translate its appeal, and assert its authority[1]—were sometimes at odds with the prevailing presentational approach of their art and were too easily assimilated to the empirical values that their work was in other ways criticizing: the strictly third-person ideals of clinical objectivity, neutrality, and cold detachment in judgment. We therefore have to gauge talk of impersonality with an ear to the prevailing understandings of "personality" that they were criticizing as well as to the novels and poems in which they pursued their ideas. The remaining chapters set about doing this. In this chapter I confine myself to examining the concept of personality and articulating some alternative ways of understanding character (helped on by vitalist psychology) that make modernist psychological depictions more legible.

PERSONALITY AND CHARACTER

In the early twentieth century as now, the term "personality" was used to refer to "the unique combination of psychophysical qualities or traits, inherent and acquired" (*Oxford English Dictionary*) that define an individual's character, usually signified by adjectives: kind-hearted, witty, aloof, thoughtless, dull, and so forth. But while the concept was thought to identify people's attributes and dispositional tendencies, it was never expected to cover all the features or dimensions of character. Rather, it describes in very general terms a person's preferences, demeanor, and temperament. Talk of people's personalities serves a specific set of uses: to describe them, judge them, or predict their behavior. We are meant to identify a typifying attitude or manner and treat it as a substantive feature of an individual without taking into account his or her personal commitments or ongoing reactions. In so doing, we ignore any occurrent reactions, by which I mean passing thoughts, responses, or gusts of feeling that transpire, which are too specific to the occasion to be treated as epiphenomenal signs of enduring dispositions. Meanwhile, as modernists sensed, the failure to take into account these elements, which include ways that people reflect on their values as they shift or evolve in the moment, make it unlikely that we characterize them with any complexity.

Such characterizations also tend to leave out deliberative responsibilities that address an individual's power to reason or legislate over decisions. For this reason, Peter Goldie insists that "a character trait is deeper than a personality trait" because it concerns a human being's "moral worth as a person" (*On Personality*, 4). I do not think that modernists commit themselves to this distinction, which requires that one exclude from character any of the seemingly superficial features that I described as occurrent reactions—responses that are fleeting and situation-specific. Nonetheless we must recognize the historical grounds for this division. As the cultural historian Warren Susman contends, the weight given to the moral qualities of "character" in the eighteenth and nineteenth centuries reflected the ethos of a Puritan-republican culture; its emphasis on the productive power of the individual prized firm standards of conduct, moral fortitude, and self-control, features "felt to be essential for the maintenance of the social order" (*Culture as History*, 273). In Susman's account, this was displaced by a "culture of personality" that arose in the middle of the first decade of the twentieth century and asserted "another vision of self-development and mastery, another method of the presentation of self in society" (274), one that emphasized "being liked and admired" (xxii). The shift followed a commensurate change from "a producer to a consumer society, an order of economic accumulation to one of disaccumulation, industrial capitalism to finance capitalism, scarcity to abundance" (275). The culture of personality betrayed an increasing concern with "individual idiosyncrasies, personal needs and interests" (276), exchanging a vision of self-sacrifice for one of self-fulfillment.

We need not view such distinctions as absolute, because both periods clearly retain the value of "character" and "personality." The expressivist accounts of the self that Susman associates with a culture of personality begin, arguably, with the Romantics. Yet for him the two cultures signal differences of discursive emphasis, reflected, for example, in the advice manuals or self-help books of each era and the key words that crop up in them. To the degree that the term "personality" captures the dreams of "gratification," "leisure," "play," and the "self-definition" of an individualist culture rather than obligations of "citizenship," "work," "honor," or "duty," it defines the self as a consumer entity. Although a culture of personality has a high regard for being a "somebody" and commanding attention, it does so not through self-exertion. Thus, it is no wonder that, for modernists, personality came to be associated with the passive elements of self. They understood the very contradiction that Susman identifies: throngs of people are told to "be themselves" and not follow the direction of others "at the same time that specific directions are provided for achieving just those ends" (*Culture as History*, 277–278). The more the value of personality extols internal self-definition, the more it requires an unacknowledged ideal imported from without.

When modernists rejected personality for its increasingly heteronomous definition of self, they did so not on the grounds of a return to something called "character," understood as bourgeois industriousness and staunchness (which also reverences fixity or consistency). In redefining character—now used in its more neutral and global sense—they applied the term "impersonality" to the set of evaluative ideals that they adopted, and they did so partly to signal their opposition to expressivist accounts of the self that were dear to middle-class popular culture. By voicing these ideals as a negation, they sparked an ongoing debate about the extent of their refutation or dismissal of personal experience.[2]

I do not believe, as some grosser formulations have put it, that the modernist concept of impersonality is an attempt to expunge all components of a personal psychology. The task of a critic is not to set impersonality in relation to what it represses or to scrutinize that which it allows by the back door but bars from the front.[3] This way of seeing things avoids asking why modernists made efforts to undermine certain cognitive and humanistic constructions of psychology, and it fails to recognize the sophistication of the psychological models that they took up. Even a critic as sensitive to minute differences as Sharon Cameron, for instance, still habitually treats Eliot's poems as if they represent "experience and affect as independent of any person or entity to whom experience and affect could be referred" (*Impersonality*, 145). Touching on Eliot's late poem *Four Quartets*, she turns a blind eye to the modernist concern with the textures of psychological depiction by considering poetic utterance "outside the parameters of an individual life" (146). As my study unfolds, we will repeatedly come up against this kind of critical indifference or hostility toward modernism as a realist psychological enterprise committed to characterization that has reference to the lifeworld of specific individuals.

What I see at stake in the term "impersonality" is a particular way of attuning to circumstances as an embodied being that lays people open to their social predicament. Thus, impersonality might be described as an attitude or orientation to the world. Granted in Eliot's case, it may seem at first to refer to an aesthetic strategy of presentation, reflecting "the relation of the poem to its author" (T. S. Eliot, "Tradition and the Individual Talent," *Selected Essays*, 7).[4] Eliot protests against Shakespeare's treatment of Hamlet, in which the author's relationship to his character implicitly offers an example of excessive personalization. Shakespeare's failure to find an "objective correlative" reveals that there is "some stuff that the writer could not drag to light, contemplate, or manipulate into art" ("Hamlet and His Problems," *Selected Essays*, 124). The play fails to present "a set of objects, a situation, a chain of events which shall be the formula" for the emotions it evokes, thus giving an emotion "in *excess* of the facts as they appear" (124–125). Eliot hints vaguely at Shakespeare's buried psychic content, which on one reading may simply not be conducive to making good art. He offers a prescriptive claim that refers to its aesthetic effects. But I will argue in Chapter 4 that the criticism is rooted in a psychological account of people. And if, as I believe he did, Eliot tended to see such buried psychic content as a misguided or flawed interpretation of how the psyche is structured, then the deficiency that Shakespeare transmits to his character Hamlet, the feeling of excessive response without an adequate emotional reason, is not only too personal to qualify as successful art; it fails to represent the situational correlates that are capable of expressing such a character.[5]

Thus, to be impersonal is not (as commonly thought) to betray a negative capacity such as irony, which allows one to distance oneself from others and maintain personal boundaries that define one's identity in advance, as though separate from any specific experience or context. Eliot's term "impersonality" names a relationship to a scene, situation, set of objects, or events that defines one precisely because one is altered by the interaction with it. Conversely, to find in a work the remnants of a personality behind it requires one to have an account of the writer's own intransigence in the face of context per se. Of course, such an account happens to be one that individuals, especially artists of sensibility, sporadically gravitate toward. For example, Eliot undoes half of his argument in these famous lines of his essay "Tradition and the Individual Talent":

> Poetry is not a turning loose of emotion, but an escape from emotion; it is not the expression of personality, but an escape from personality. But, of course, only those who have personality and emotions know what it means to want to escape from these things. (*Selected Essays*, 10–11)

Eliot would seem to imply that there is a substantive core to character, even if one is supposed to break out of it.

Maud Ellmann suggests that Eliot "rehabilitates . . . personality" (*The Poetics of Impersonality*, 40) in the latter half of "Tradition and the Individual Talent," where his "terms relentlessly contaminate their own antitheses" (56). She argues that Eliot's attack on expressivism, however contradictory, aims to rid the poet of any individual agency across the board, whereas I am suggesting that his account is directed against a set of intractable psychological schemas that pathologize individuals by placing them under the sway of static, compulsive, highly predictable impulses. In his literary-critical writings, Eliot is more ambiguous than in his dissertation on F. H. Bradley about the utility of defining core structures of individuals apart from their changing contextual relations, but his hostility to such psychological interpretations is clear.

We do not need to accept Eliot's aversion to models of character that ascribe global elements of personality to individuals. Clearly, there are essential structures of human cognition and behavior that are "hardwired" and others that are inherited or are the outcome of strong genetic tendencies, even if they are not entirely determined. As Eliot seems to grant, we have long-standing dispositions that may be hard to change. The point is not that people are "blank slates," as J. B. Watson and B. F. Skinner (the most famous behaviorist psychologists of the period) would have it; rather, these structural consistencies within the self, when viewed in their isolation, can obscure the situational parameters that activate them. For Eliot, the implied privacy of the interior states of personality does not acknowledge the interconnected cultural contexts through which we interpret such experiences. It is only by adopting external points of view that we can discover the analogies and reference points that generalize our experiences, though the way that we bring such shifting analogies to bear are themselves situation-specific, part of the dramatistic ground of any sufficiently rich scene in which we are to participate. Although these contexts are sometimes only potential within a situation, such as the mythical frameworks that Eliot mobilizes in *The Waste Land*, they are nevertheless capable of exerting a powerful role in helping us to understand the psyche under consideration. "Impersonality" names a way of inhabiting a scene otherwise than under the sway of merely private associations and reactions.

I will outline an ideal of personhood beyond personality as a rhetorical corrective to the more polemical notion of impersonality touted by Eliot. But even for Eliot, we must be clear, impersonality is a form of relationality. Incidents and situations create forms of identification and communal associations that allow us to connect with each other, and they prevent us from consolidating into monadic individuals. My claims center around the ethical implications of refusing to define agency on the basis of an antecedent personality; at the same time, I propose that there are good philosophical and psychological reasons to be skeptical of models that aim to find integral, consistent psychic patterns that determine behavior. Such models tend to define individuality based on what a person *is* (and has been) rather than on what she or he *does* over time.

"Personality" implies that there is something inert and recurrent within us that is a direct threat to our autonomy and that this very thing is supposed to shape our identity. Historically, the concept fit in with the commitments of personality psychology, which came on the scene at almost the same moment as modernism itself. As practiced by Carl Jung and Gordon Allport, among others, personality psychology offered assessments of the stable set of characteristics possessed by individuals that uniquely influence feelings, motivations, and their impetus in behaviors.[6] Jung's *Personality Types* (1921) specified paired combinations of traits that individuals exhibit on a continuum, such as thinking/feeling or sensation/judgment (6–7). Although personality psychologists contested Freud's explanatory account of the role of psychosexual development within early childhood and debated among themselves the relative force of heredity and environment, they shared a faith in the unique constellation of experiences and dispositional differences of individuals that shapes and restricts outcomes and that, for this reason, is subject to prediction. Modernists took it upon themselves to purge their characters of "personality" because it located singularity in the wrong place, in the interior of the subject. Not only did it present character as something with "accidental" but predictable uniqueness, it tended to comport with a view of the subject as in need of regulation and discipline. Empirical particularity and subjective idiosyncrasy, at every point, reduce the real force of disposition or tendency to more or less static appurtenances, amenable to the labor disciplining associated with Taylorization, the tonic of therapy, and other forms of rationalized endeavor.

The promise of therapy, however, implies a concept of personality that does not require immunity from change.[7] Indeed, most accounts of personality offer some hope of dynamic development. Ego-psychology, for example, sees reality testing as a personality function that impacts an individual's negotiation with the external world. Since Aristotle, explanations of character development have regarded ethical agency in terms of one's power to legislate through self-control or strength of will, thereby redirecting one's impulsive desires. These accounts celebrate the deliberative capacities of the self as a means of overcoming its passivity.[8]

Peter Goldie helps to flesh out some of the assumptions behind these psychological accounts. He sees personality as having an important evaluative dimension that he correlates with a narrative sense of self. To make decisions about our pattern of actions, we have to integrate our life into "a satisfying narrative" (*On Personality*, 118), meaning one that can specify the causal grounds for our actions, which puts us "in a position to take an evaluative perspective on our past or future selves, . . . and to arrive at a correlative emotional response. 'Damn it, I'm such a fool! . . . I see now what I did, although it seemed right at the time, was mean and thoughtless'" (117). Goldie refers to this as a desire for emotional closure. I would suggest, however that his commitment to personality reduces the rich emotional life—the "myriad impressions" (Woolf, "Modern Fiction," 149) that modernists such as Woolf aimed to capture in their works—to only the most instrumental forms of decision-making, those that correspond to reason-bearing assessments.[9] The various scenarios of self-mastery or defeat that Goldie, like ego psychologists, projects have implicit teleologies, which tend to define resistance to or deviation from a social ideal as pathological. In part, writers such as Eliot were reacting against the pernicious normative assumptions built into models of personality and the therapeutic culture they spawned.

Ego psychology's models of change are too predictably based in fantasies of self-command. The writers I examine, James, Stein, and Eliot, present in their fictive characters forms of sensitivity to changing circumstance that alter them in ways that narratives cannot adequately represent—for one, because narratives sculpt lives by placing them into generalized patterns, evacuated of contingent circumstantial specificity and, for another, because these same narratives tend to depict characters as heroic subjects capable of defining their behavior and avowing their destiny. This does not mean, however, that James, Stein, and Eliot imagine characters who are determined by contingencies. Instead, their characters improvise their responses to circumstance by creating open-ended patterns that reverberate on and adjust to their milieu in so many different respects that any simple causal account of their own motivation or intention ("I did X because Y") fails to describe its nature. Again, I am not suggesting that these imagined characters are not constrained by recurrent patterns. What matters is not the nature of the patterns but the powers of will, attention, and intuition that allow each character to compose moment-by-moment variations through an almost "artistic" sensibility.

Nietzsche, for whom art was a form of life (*Will to Power*, 453), speaks of the artistic feeling as "the free ordering, placing, disposing, giving form in the moment of 'inspiration,'" in which the artist "obeys thousandfold laws . . . that precisely on account of their hardness and determination defy all formulation through concepts" (*Beyond Good and Evil*, 100). The forms of agency he has in mind—and which I am here calling upon to explain ordinary ethical response—are not motivated by a specifically formulated purpose and, even retrospectively, cannot claim to be following one, but nevertheless they display harmonies or connections that one can construct and grasp in an ad hoc way.[10]

ETHICS AND PSYCHOLOGY

The alternative to psychological accounts that insist on an antecedent personality are situation-specific accounts of behavioral response, which need not refer to any special quality within the self that subsists across time. Personality psychology coincided with the historical development of a contrasting science of psychology, behaviorism, which played down the antecedent role of personality and instead showed the influence of classical and operant conditioning on behavioral response. Superficially invested in situational accounts of behavior, behaviorists, such as Ivan Pavlov and B. F. Skinner, focused on the environmental determinants that modify sequences of response by an organism. At the same time, they tended to regard situations as a class of structurally distinct but functionally equivalent environments for producing equally decomposable behavioral units.[11] In so doing, they ignored slight differences among repetitive situations, differences that manifest themselves in a creature's sense of connection to its tasks and such intangibles (for them) as its feelings of duration or awareness of relation to other situations. Behaviorists, interested in a causal account of behavioral response, offered modernists no better alternative than personality psychologists because they tended to see the self as deprived of all independent force, impetus, or agency.[12] Antecedent dispositional differences among individuals were practically irrelevant to them. They flattened differences between individuals by placing them into line along statistical averages. The power that situations possess to determine learning responses tended in their models to silence individuality. Ivan Pavlov and B. F. Skinner may differ in the way that they understand adaptive responses and learning patterns, but they both start from a notoriously reductive standpoint: they consider all introspective motivations of thought or feeling irrelevant to behavior.

In the world of psychology, the more significant challenge to ethical accounts anchored in an idea of stable character has come from the experimental social psychology that emerged in the wake of behaviorism. Since the 1960s, much research in social psychology has suggested that character and behavior are much more situationally sensitive than we are inclined to think. From Stanley Milgram's famous experiments testing obedience and authority in the 1960s and 1970s, to Alice Isen and Paul Levin's experiments testing the relation between feeling good and helping behavior, to Philip Zimbardo's prison experiments testing the power of socially assigned roles, to John Darley and Daniel Batson's "Good Samaritan" experiments, the results show that people are liable to react based on circumstantial contexts much more than on situation-independent values, character traits, or moral sensibilities. The relevant cases include high percentages of people who obey instructions from authority figures to shock others with an electric shock even when the act appears to cause harm;[13] test subjects who are much more predictably disposed to help someone fumbling papers on the street if they find a dime in a payphone;[14] students with no history of crime, emotional disability, or predisposition to violence who display sadistic behaviors as guards in an extended prison role-play exercise;[15] and seminarians whose inclination to assist someone in distress is more reliably calculated on the basis of whether they are in a hurry than any intrinsic measure of their commitments or predispositions.[16]

John Doris has argued that such empirical evidence ought to shape our sense of the limitations of character as a determinant of behavior. The "old saw," as he puts it, that character is destiny requires considerable rethinking. The principle that character "decides the moral texture of a life," that "the person of good character will do well, even under substantial pressure to moral failure" (*Lack of Character*, 1) is foundational for Aristotelian accounts of moral life and more recent philosophy within the "virtue ethics" tradition, but such an ethical claim turns out to be more problematic than at first appears. Underlying such "globalist" accounts of personality are three theses: (1) that character and personality traits are consistent—that is, "reliably manifested in trait-relevant behavior across a diversity of trait-relevant eliciting conditions" (22); (2) that these traits are stable over time given the same eliciting conditions; and (3) that they are coordinated or evaluatively integrated with like traits. But because the substantial body of empirical data Doris brings to bear appears to contradict all three counts, he concludes that people "lack character," at least to a substantial enough degree that they need to consider the "situational liabilities" (151) to which they are prone as a basic concern of ethical deliberation.

For all the enormous appeal of his argument, Doris tends to assume that were it possible, human beings would benefit from having more globally consistent characters, even as he makes it clear that such consistency is not likely to emerge. At least, this is what his account implies when he insists on accommodating the revisionary picture of character that social psychology imposes on ethical thought by himself problematizing "only particular, and dispensable, features of ethical thought associated with characterological moral psychology" (108) rather than attempting, like Nietzsche, the accused "amoralist," to rethink the "institutions of morality" (108). Although I take inspiration from his careful accounting of the empirical evidence about character and agree that descriptive claims about the nature of people ought to have direct bearing on prescriptive ethical paradigms, I would argue that his measured accounting has not gone far enough in contesting the value of consistency itself. If one takes accommodation to change as a basic feature of life, then perhaps it would not be wholly unexpected that situations alter people and affect behavior in profound ways—that individuals take on social roles and attitudes befitting their situation (as the prison role-play exercise suggests); that they are enormously responsive to slight mood-altering situational changes (as the payphone experiment suggests); that circumstantial factors such as being late might affect people's decision-making in somewhat ambiguous situations when they lack previously formed bonds with the individuals who request help from them (as the "Good Samaritan" experiment suggests); and even—this one is perhaps most alarming—that as social creatures human beings are subject to pernicious influence or pressure from figures who convey authority to them, even when this authority is nominal (as the Milgram experiments suggest). I do not deny that the results of the experiments are surprising, but I think we have to learn different lessons from them, lessons about how to value the situational sensitivities that they highlight and how to understand some of the complexities of moral life on the basis of them, despite the obvious moral hazards that they are designed to reveal.

For a variety of reasons, including the experiments' short duration, the fixed conditions that were imposed on the experimental frameworks, and the bracketed setting in which some of them unfolded (decontextualized from the subject groups' ordinary lives), the researchers in each case diminished the situation's complexity and eliminated the errant influences that could make the elicited responses more dynamic and variable.[17] Consequently, they produced a high degree of statistical predictability within the behavior of their subject group. It seems possible that less narrowly tailored situations could have generated more complicated and unpredictable reactions and outcomes. All the same, their findings are remarkable: they show just how malleable individuals are to their circumstance, how little inclined they are to assert agency at cross-purposes to their situation. The Milgram and "Good Samaritan" experiments in particular also reveal how reluctant people are to break up the situational continuum of action with independent ethical reflection. In later chapters, I will suggest some reasons why malleability as such might benefit ethical life, especially when it coincides with special efforts to accommodate events rather than to intervene against them. Vitalist philosophy teaches us that we act before we think, that thinking is a late developmental capacity that is imperfectly differentiated from more primitive "doing."[18] This means that our capacity to reflect, when it does happen, is likelier to follow on a situation or embed itself in specific situation-defined actions than to rationally precede response to events and structure our reaction to them.

Like the social psychologists just examined, writers such as James and Stein offer a series of situations that test character, though their fictional frameworks allow them the luxury of giving individuals extended temporal attention. The prolonged duration of their imagined scenarios reveals more complicated bidirectional relays and interactions between the individuals represented and the situations that they face than any evinced by the social psychology experiments. In particular, my chapter on James seeks to account for characters who obtain their consistency from their unfolding social environments rather than from any fixed quality within them. But James also shows how people alter and remake their situation as a means of accommodating it. And I argue that he presents situationally defined characters whose improvised adjustments over time offer them ways of coping with their dependencies on others. Like Stein and Eliot, James insists that the self is not a discrete entity but a temporal ecosystem. In this respect, my account centers on his and other modernists' redefinition of character, not on an attempt to bypass it. The imperative is not to minimize character as an arbitrating force within prescriptive ethical paradigms, as Doris attempts, but to understand the necessity of circumstantial alteration as basic to what character *is*.

To be clear, Doris does not insist that consistency by itself is enough to evaluate ethical conduct.[19] According to Bernard Williams, whom he invokes, one has to ask how and to what end one is being consistent, or what one takes as one's "supposed *criterion* of action" (Williams, "Replies," 212). This suggests that holistic integration of behavior is not in and of itself good or bad. But to the extent that Doris sets up his own argument by taking cues from philosophers working within the Aristotelian tradition—even as he is working against them—he accepts the argument that consistency is a necessary but insufficient condition for ethical virtue: it "is necessary for executing one's projects in the face of obstacles" and without it, "it is only by luck that one's values will come to pass" (*Lack of Character*, 18). It seems to me, however, that one needs a more sensitive account of the forms of consistency and firmness or, in my preferred term, "continuity," that define a self without giving up what is most important: the plastic capacity to maintain commitments while allowing for life-sustaining "give" within circumstance. Stein represents such malleability through small departures that individuals make from a provisional, but typifying, character template. James and Eliot insist that individuals take on shifting points of view that encapsulate the perspectives of others, perspectives that reciprocally define and alter those who adopt them.

Part of the problem with empirical psychology, whatever the specific orientation, is the premise that if any concept of character or personality were really useful in ethical life, it would be predictive. It would be capable of establishing consistency over time. But this raises the question: how and in what form does one have the freedom to depart from a previous behavioral repertoire without accepting an alternative situational account of character that renders response equally predicable? For a person to be of truly singular character, she or he would have to be in some degree autonomous, capable of adhering to situations or making departures from them in a variety of distinct ways. Yet modernists rejected the categorical logic of Kant's ethics—even though he presupposed such autonomy—because his principles subordinated all individual differences to a universal equivalence between people premised on their putative free will, which in turn set in motion abstract rational imperatives. As J. M. Bernstein argues, Kantian rationalism cannot bridge the reasons that justify norms of behavior and the personal motivating grounds, "the reasons why any particular agent should act on that norm" (*Adorno*, 11). In this sense, Kant's account is not psychological enough; it does not give us a sharp sense of the passions and varied commitments that get us to act. The imperatives that Kant specifies "appear increasingly irrational" (10) because their "agent-neutral" validity is without appeal and detached from the motivational set provided by agent- and community-specific practices.

Another, perhaps better, way to allow ethical life a measure of choice is to turn from top-down rational premises to bottom-up sociological descriptions. To understand a person's motivations, one would pay attention to the rich network of "thick" descriptive and evaluative concepts to which agents resort, which pass between ethical and nonethical predicates and rely on a grammar that one inherits from a community, from its notions of a good life. Philosophers call this an "internalist" position, meaning one that regards moral reasons as intrinsically motivating.[20] The idea is that we obtain a range of choices to act from values that are embedded in ordinary accounts of situations and people, which are available to us as members of a given community. In its simplest form, we could consider a vocabulary of descriptions, such as vicious, rude, selfish, helpful, and courageous. These discriminations would have prescriptive force, even as we are given room to disagree about the descriptions, granting us discretion. Some critics, such as Lee Oser, propose that modernists regained a foundation for their "moral project" (*The Ethics of Modernism*, 1) that "stays closer to the concrete actuality of moral life" (5) by putting such practical discriminations to work within a teleology, relying on the precepts that "motivate people to realize their best potential" (4). Modernists would thus avoid the opposing dangers of relativism and overweening metaphysical claims. With a kind of rearward wistfulness, Oser argues that modernists espoused a nearly Aristotelian belief in the enduring but meliorative capacities of a universal human nature, despite their biting irony and apparent contradictions. Even if one discounts or plays down the teleology, the problem with such accounts is that it is not clear how individuals can depart, more than minimally, from the norms of their community or how unprecedented cases fit into the system of values, let alone how individuals create or cope with surprising or wide scale shifts in the social customs and standards that constitute that system of values (an issue that modernists confronted directly).[21]

For all their obvious interest in presenting the intricate texture of social life, modernists cast a skeptical eye on the normative power that any description or judgment of a situation might comprehensively hold. There is simply no guarantee that prevailing values and concepts can put together a satisfactory account of moral agency in the most complex and evolving situations, either because such situations outpace and overwhelm the social grammars and ethical frameworks that individuals bring to bear to understand them or because events, inherently dynamic, run in so many different directions that one has to suspend definitive judgment about them and instead fall back on improvised, provisional responses.

I have already suggested that ethical life on this level might be understood by analogy to an artistic or aesthetic enterprise. Indeed, for modernists such as James and Eliot, the capacity to evolve along with a situation rather than be overrun by it calls for a creative aptitude for altering circumstance over time and altering oneself in accord with it. For ethical deliberation at its richest does not just change outcomes, it also alters the deliberating self.[22]

SOCIALLY FRAGMENTED SELVES: HISTORICAL CONSIDERATIONS

James, Stein, and Eliot saw individuals as collections of incomplete and half-formed desires who respond to events without necessarily having a firm idea of what counts as "right" or decent on the level of conduct or sensibility. These writers presented imagination as an engine of self-fashioning, a way of aggregating a character's powers of will and attention, connecting facts and observations in unexpected configurations. The aesthetic life, as they understood it, dangled the promise of finding vagrant satisfactions in situations experienced at a distance from moral prescription. Many commentators, especially those influenced by the Frankfurt school, have assumed that the inability to depend on social agreement over ethical matters says something about the historical condition of modernity and the damaged state of the institutions and authorities that give guidance and aspirational ambition to individuals. They lament the systemic impoverishment of modernity's own dwindling community standards. If, as Max Weber and Jürgen Habermas suggest, modernity tends to splinter into autonomous spheres—modern science and technology, private morality, law and politics—each with its own commensurate forms of practice, definitions of value, and modes of "knowing," it becomes increasingly difficult to find a common vantage point for ethical reflection. The result is social fragmentation. According to this now familiar critique, modernists took refuge in private affairs or in aesthetic experience, unable to resuscitate a shared or public language for ethics; however, the escape they imagined for themselves merely exacerbates the state of affairs to which they were reacting because the attempt to live a life apart from the reified demands of economic rationality or consumer culture only continues the processes of fragmentation and rationalization. Other, more recent historicist critics remain unconvinced that modernists ever lived or worked very far apart from economic institutions in the first place, however much they professed to withdraw into the rarified precincts of high culture.

Either way, such perspectives have made their way into accounts of the self, which is thought to be pervaded by the structures of capitalist modernity. Contemporary historicists and older materialist critics—broadly construed—share a common assumption that the socioeconomic sphere structures and, crucially, limits the creative lives of individuals. To be sure, adherents of each persuasion have disagreements among themselves and neither necessarily treats the economic foundations of social life as the determining horizon for modern existence. For reasons, good and bad, they rarely espouse such explicit positions.[23] It is enough that they cast doubt on modernist claims to autonomy of thought or action. I will return to those who subscribe to the mixed bag of historicist methodologies a bit later. For now I want to focus on the argument, made most forcefully by Theodor Adorno, that the compartmentalization of everyday life under capital puts into relief the marginal role that imagination and reflective judgment have as a way of confronting social fragmentation and the dominance of means-ends rationality.[24] I will suggest that Adorno capitulates too much to the causal power of capitalism. More generally, I argue that modernists—who gained so much from vitalist psychological theories—grant more faith than either their historicist or materialist critics in people's mental aptitudes, their capacity to devise new and unpredictable ways of thinking, behaving, performing, and acting in situations.

Adorno holds that aesthetic experience establishes compelling powers of attention that have the potential to reintegrate modern life, otherwise under the threat of dissociation, erasure, or elimination by the violence of wartime assault (*Minima Moralia*, 54–55) as well as by the fault lines of everyday existence. Thus, he says that modern art radiates "deep into the zones of subjective experience" (*Aesthetic Theory*, 34) and that "by its force artworks wrest themselves free from fatal disintegration" (186). In this respect, Adorno gives voice to a modernist outlook, formulating the writers' intuition that the aesthetic arena (whether in art or, as I would also argue, more generally in experience) may be the place where the mind can bring together its impressions of the world without submitting them to instrumental goals or preestablished ethical valuations. Although Adorno revels in such freedom, he claims that it is already deformed because it is the reserve of such a narrow range of times and spaces and, more important, because the experience it expresses is illegible to the prevailing ways of valuing that our "bottom line"-obsessed culture understands. The experience is already defanged: the sensory and affective level at which it might make itself felt does not have any authority over the cognitive and practical understandings that tend to rule social life. For this reason, Adorno speaks of the unity or reconciliation that aesthetic experience offers as "illusory," "ephemeral," a mere "semblance" (186).[25]

Though Adorno does not specifically treat the affective negotiations of aesthetic experience as a model for ethical action, it would not be hard to conceive of this. J. M. Bernstein, Adorno's most relentless contemporary critic, extends Adorno's defense of nondiscursive cognition to assert the practical value of aesthetic reasoning.[26] At the same time, ethical philosophy of a more analytic orientation is strewn with critical and deeply antagonistic accounts of such reasoning, as when Alasdair MacIntyre singles out Henry James for glorying in aestheticized models of ethical life, which he reads as a form of moral perspectivism. He asserts that James's emotivist commitments partake of a tradition in which "the social world is nothing but a meeting place for individual wills, each with its own set of attitudes and preferences," and those who see the world in this way treat it "as a series of opportunities for their own enjoyment . . . for whom the last enemy is boredom" (*After Virtue*, 24). Although I consider this a manifestly inadequate description of James—as I will make clear in the next chapter—it is also true that the very immunity that his apparent aestheticism asserts from discursive reasons and principles has a tendency to withdraw aesthetic taste and its expression in action from the discourses of value that could specify its raison d'être. Although Adorno would take much more seriously modernist claims to staking ethical behavior on the particularities of a social world without immediately imposing preconceived moral concepts, he would argue that the appearance of "solipsism"—however specious—means that aesthetic life is already damaged, suffering from its own form of "disenchantment" (*Aesthetic Theory*, 259).

Certainly, modernist writers worried about the hieroglyphic nature of their own ethical gestures. They were well aware that the negotiations of the social world they presented could not rely on an obvious framework to make their social or ethical significance clear. The deep obscurity of the mythic context and structure of Eliot's *Waste Land* would be an obvious example to cite, but in less dramatic form much the same can be said for most modernist texts. Although these works variously display anxieties about the vagueness, twilight, or messiness of the ethical frameworks they deploy, I would argue that they also relish the creative opportunities such vagueness affords them. Indeed, the beauty of these works resides in the provisional and situationally embedded character of the voices and perspectives they construct. It is not that our social language of values can be appraised as a historical whole and then assumed to be inadequate. All histories—all forms of the past—are inadequate. This is because the self is characteristically incomplete. The voices in *The Waste Land*, like the characters in James's and Stein's novels, do not know what they desire or how to live with the situations and histories they confront, and neither do we. Thus, we are left to fall back on what Bergson would call our "intuition" to devise new ways of expanding and integrating our perspectives—and finding momentary pleasures, satisfactions, and points of ethical affirmation in the process. Such mental adjustments require pragmatic experimentation, an ability to think and act without having the guidance of advanced moral prescription. The open-endedness of these texts gives these characters or voices and us the space to do this: to struggle and clarify the connections that help us to affirm our own relationally defined identities. These creative acts cannot rely on some myth of unity from the past to do this. As I will argue in Chapter 4, the tradition that Eliot acclaims, for instance, is not a set of fixed values—with their own latent truths—but virtual resources in the individual's ongoing attempt to devise new ways of thinking in and acting on a situation.

Adorno's theorizing does not necessarily refute such novelty of response, but he insists on containing it to the point that it has little historical efficacy in the face of modern capitalism. In this respect, he treats capitalism as an institution whose explanatory power exists in its enormous scale and pervasive reach. I will not go into the specifics, but it is clear that Adorno's speculative philosophy proceeds on the assumption that history is penetrated by an immanent teleology from which human beings struggle to break free.[27] Because there is genuine but sporadic freedom to be had, his pessimism may reduce one to squabbling about emphasis. But I would argue on more basic grounds: what looks like an immanent logic is really just a contingent historical formation, which always only partially elucidates the frictions, conflicts, and scope for remedy in ethical life (and only as one imposing context among others). Also, the aesthetic reasoning that Adorno vaunts is not valuable principally for its critical function but rather because it has the potential for improvising new values.[28] And I would propose, pace Adorno, that such engagements with particularity are not limited to encounters with autonomous art. James, Stein, and Eliot prove that they can be felt in ordinary social interactions.

Obviously, modernist writers created works that appear to be strategically closed off from—or else in tension with—the more legalistic, political, and utilitarian corners of the social world. Their novelistic and poetic subject matter is opaque, often resistant to interpretation, precisely because it is presented with an eye to making conventional ethical judgments as difficult as possible. For this reason, their forms had to be different from writing that has an instrumental communicative function. But it does not follow that the experience they presented is "contained" in art alone or that it has no relation to the sequences of thought and patterns of judgment that occur to individuals in daily life. Rather, it was designed to recreate very particular milieus and to orchestrate the encounter with those milieus, in which the weight of public morality does not necessarily intervene. James, Stein, and Eliot gravitated to the intimate sphere, which tends to bring about affective attachments that stand the best chance of surmounting the inducements to treating other people instrumentally. The intensity and mutability of such attachments also arguably flesh out the relations that most directly express the social basis of character.

Such accounts of modernism have—to certain ears—made its writers sound un-civic-minded. There were plenty of writers in the period, even very ambitious experimental writers, whose creative output gives voice to larger political commitments and who were, to varying degrees, at home in the heated skirmishing grounds of political self-formulation and positioning (Berthold Brecht is Adorno's favorite). And even among the writers I have chosen, James has *The Princess Casamassima*, a novel about an international terrorist in the making, and Eliot, his *Idea of a Christian Society*. In recent years, scholars such as Jessica Berman and Rebecca Walkowitz have insisted that modernists allowed for greater fluidity between the sphere of intimate ethical relations and larger political commitments. Moving outside the local context in which such relations unfold, they set about tracing modernist attitudes toward transnational community. This is their way of arguing against one kind of isolation or political fragmentation. They have been less content to frame modernists' political commitments in Adorno's critical or oppositional terms.[29]

Berman explores disjunctive frames of reference, the intimate problems of both subaltern actors and metropolitan elites as their fictional lives intersect intermittently with larger political histories and social causes, even when they may be inattentive or insensitive to them or fail to understand their import. She makes the "critical disjunction between ethics and politics" (*Modernist Commitments*, 15) a constitutive—and thematized—feature of modernist political and historical thinking. Walkowitz does something similar when she suggests that "the ethical pitfalls and aesthetic opportunities of diverting or withholding attention are central topics for modernist art" because modernists' self-conscious depiction of their characters' failures to be interested in "the conditions of imperialism" prepares the ground for self-reflection (*Cosmopolitan Style*, 19). She observes that modernist styles—as they express themselves in "patterns of attentiveness, relevance, perception, and recognition" (6)—help define their cosmopolitan commitments, even as their embrace of the trivial or the transient destroys the agreed-upon "order and proportion" (10) of wartime values, for instance, which are in the service of strident nationalism.

Theirs is a reasonable suggestion. The problem is that one cannot be sure that such criticism does not reflect our obsession with the reasonableness, the "order and proportion," of our own political urgencies, not modernists'. With all the horror, violence, disappointment, routinization, and stupidity of political life, who is to say that some modernists did not find it a relief to turn back to the intimate? It is not worth generalizing too much or prejudging modernist attitudes when they do not interrogate empire. The moments of negligence or absentmindedness that Berman and Walkowitz describe often simply reflect modernist puzzlement over what counts as an "appropriate" response to political disappointment or frustration, or how best to let characters play out their identifications and disidentifications with people continents away or living under very different conditions. In any case, modernist appreciation for what is unaccountable or narrow in human feeling is bound up with a larger matter: the need to promote the forms of variability in response that make social and political freedom a value in the first place. Such swings away from the "really important" to the seemingly trifling reveal the effect that small relations have in orienting one to the local conditions in which ethical response takes place. I will be focusing on tiny as well as substantial alterations that characters carry out in their domestic and erotic lives. For some, I might be stacking the deck in favor of what are easier ethical problems to address. In one sense, this is probably true because ethical agency is always most pointed and effective in the situations and locations that are most proximate. In another sense, this is certainly false if it implies that the domestic relations are relatively trouble-free or undemanding because one is already disposed to goodwill. In fact, the stakes are often higher for getting what one wants as well as for rearticulating the structures of one's desires.

In all this, I do not mean to discount modernist cosmopolitan and political commitments as tangential to other, staple commitments. By and large, I am simply observing that, for modernists, the experimental nature of modern lives would require some shelter from the explicitness and consistency of attitude generally demanded of figures in public. As Justus Nieland points out, however, there may be ambiguous public figures and public spaces that generate and sustain the forms of intensity and intricacy that I am interested in tracking.[30] In any case, even political commitments or "globalist" anxieties are "intimate" if they are felt to be intimate to the self. I would only argue that if we want to grant improvisational complexity to people's political responses (T. E. Lawrence would be a historical example), we may not wish to anticipate how the local intersects with international political commitments by presuming that the relations between these spheres are congruent, easy to characterize and frame, or continuous at all points, let alone that the commitments can rely on available norms or ideas of the good life to give the terms for, or ground the validity of, the person's political thinking. We have to extend the same suspensions and incompleteness that I am arguing occur in the intimate domain to the individual's encounters with the political sphere.

At any rate, Walkowitz and Berman are right that attention was a vital instrument in the modernist repertoire of psychological functions. This is because it helped to frame and arrange relations between fact and value, between what happens and what matters. Modernists thought that special kinds of attention aid in the task of modifying and restructuring available public languages of value. Such attentions work by finding purposive patterns in details and particulars, the accumulation of which leads individuals to draw provisional connections, otherwise neglected, that influence how they think and act. (I am speaking about relations that fall outside the bounds of very clear-cut imperatives that regulate ethical behavior.)

This modernist valorization of attention came at the expense of other psychological powers that modernists tended to dismiss, such as habit (associated, for them, with instrumental routine). As Athena Vrettos suggests, "Theories of habit conceptualized the mind as a closed system, driven to repetitive, automatic behaviors in order to conserve energy for more difficult or novel tasks" ("Defining Habits," 3). The eccentricities, psychological ticks, and "hardened 'images' of habit" that Dickens, for example, continually returns to stamp his characters as "superficial" or "flat."[31] For Eliot, habit might be ranked along with all the other passive ingredients of "personality" that he wished to deemphasize: the compulsive but unnamed propensities that he acknowledges in himself in "Tradition and the Individual Talent." Like James before him, Eliot tended to stress the person's active orientation to circumstance and raw inventiveness at the expense of any empirical feature that could be described as given or intransigent or untransmutable. James and Eliot saw the routines and regularities that fix selves as unhealthy and deterministic because they work contrary to the individual's free exercise of imagination. Thus, Eliot appeals for the separation of "the man who suffers and the mind which creates" ("Tradition and the Individual Talent" in *Selected Essays*, 8). The freedom he and James crave tends to make itself felt, they thought, outside workaday life. It would seem that modernists pressed for certain distinctions, not only between private and public spaces, but, relatedly, between those psychological powers that were better equipped and less well equipped to foster dynamic improvisational lives. To devise a means of combat against passivity, aimless drift, and docility, they split the self in two.

Eliot and James insisted on presenting the most complex and socially irreducible elements of character. By relegating unthinking habits, predilections, and eccentric traits to the periphery of character, they ratified a categorical separation that has long existed in aesthetic as well as ethical discourses between unreflective inclinations (which are "pathological" when allowed to ride roughshod) and those expressions of taste and character that are effortful and controllable, that require special mental exertions.[32] By attempting to eliminate personality in this way, however, they ended up creating characters artificially purified of all "dumb" idiosyncrasies. James (especially in his late phase) and Eliot tend to do away with adjectival descriptions of their characters that impute robust traits (for example, referring to them as charming, greedy, or irascible), but in the process their privative schema also gives up some of the grist of ordinary social and empirical limitations. The weight James gives to psychological complexity also threatens to render his depictions illegible. His subtle and unusually sensitive characters are so diffused within their situation that elemental contours of their character are blurred. In some respects, their characters seem as regimented, sanitized, and socially disciplined as the passive or therapeutically "improved" subjects that the writers would otherwise spurn.

For Jonathan Crary, the claim that modernists could preserve autonomy for individuals through a practice of attentiveness is derisory, not least because the assumed separation between aestheticized attention and other kinds of attention could not be maintained.[33] There is something all too familiar about the desire to escape habit and smarten up character that all appeals to attentiveness share. They speak to the undaunted capitalist urge to remain productive: "What is important to institutional power, since the late nineteenth century, is simply that perception function in a way that insures a subject is productive, manageable, and predictable, and is able to be socially integrated and adaptive" (*Suspensions of Perception*, 4). Crary explores the "larger disciplinary and administrative apparatuses" that organize attention and make it a key ingredient in the "management and control of human subjects" (45). In his account, one cannot secure any superior value to attention because the phenomenon or practice cannot maintain its integrity: it coexists with habit, automation, and distraction in all the arenas of social life in which it is prized, from the factory and the office to the artist's studio and museum: "Attention always contained within itself the conditions for its own disintegration" and undoing; "it was haunted by the possibility of its own excess" (45). The more such writers and artists as Rainer Maria Rilke and Paul Cézanne insist on "authentic attention" and "artisanal absorption . . . now exiled to the margins of a mechanized and routinized world" (49), the more such attention breaks down and blurs its boundaries with other kinds of attention.

Despite the breathtaking range of discourses that Crary examines and the useful historical context he provides—especially on nineteenth- and twentieth-century psychological discourses that impinge on modernist methods and procedures—his work shares many of the limitations that beset historicist critics of modernism working in literary studies (though he is an art historian). His confidence in the explanatory value of such context leads him to underrate any possibility of genuinely constructive novelty in people's responses to the predominant forms of regulation that govern daily life. By his own reckoning, Crary marries a Foucaultian-inspired concern with how subjectivity is constructed by power and a deconstructive critique of the coherence of the self. He differs from Frankfurt School theorists such as Adorno and Walter Benjamin only by being more skeptical of the possibility of any absorbed form of contemplation that can remain intact and different from the kinds of attention promoted in industrial culture.

One sign of Crary's faith in social context is that he thinks that a survey of the available discourses on a complex phenomenon such as attention is capable of determining the phenomenon's scope and manner of operation. He presumes that some distillation, perhaps even some common thread, can be found in all the various discourses or "field of . . . statements" (*Suspensions of Perception*, 23) on the subject. He prefers such canvassing to a philosophical or psychological account of the phenomenon as such. This assumption leaves him with a model deeply fixed on and limited by the dominant conceptions of the way attention works. Crary refuses to make qualitative distinctions between different kinds and organizations of attention, and he offers only a binary model in which attention and distraction are opposites on an abstract continuum. Because attention is continuous with "states of distraction, reverie, dissociation, and trance" (46), he argues that an artist like Cézanne could lay bare its instability.[34] Cezanne's fascination with the self-deconstructing workings of attention, for instance, allowed him to treat it as an oppositional force, breaking the back of the instrumentality placed on it by commodity culture. But I would argue that this negative work that attention enables does not leave Crary with a very forceful account of modernist resistance to instrumental culture. The imperatives of his project, which are entirely historical and political, end up reading as "thin" precisely because what matters to him are not the qualities or powers derived from attention but only a historical description of the constellation of a discourse or the "network of effects which [it] produced" (23).

I will be pursuing a different strategy, which requires giving more consideration to the potential unpredictability harnessed by people's psychological powers. With such emphasis comes a different view of history, more open, uncertain, provisional, and in-progress. As I have suggested, modernists sought to reorganize attention and exercise it within an articulated configuration that included other psychic powers, such as will, perception, and feeling, expecting that such efforts would allow them to connect their experiences in various ways that are not dictated by the patterns of the past. Yet by casting out habit as an impediment to such attention—deeming it a contributor to the instrumentalizing forces that regiment daily life—they participated in the fragmentation and splintering of experience. They also backed those same forces that discipline modern subjects.[35]

This aggressive reimagining of the individual, purged of habits and other predictable touchstones of the self, is not a historical inevitability for modernism at large but rather a contingent strategy for navigating the social, technological, and economic rationalization of people whose contours we will confront in the coming pages. Such strategies had its dissenters. As I argue in Chapter 3, Stein's construction of character is obsessed with the idea that habit is an engine of creative alteration. For her, patterns of behavior that merely repeat, such as habits, cannot be readily divorced from creative impulses, not because they accompany intelligent activity but because habits generate self-organizing changes among themselves. Other modernists too were not able to strip off all passive or given aspects of a person, if indeed they ever wished to. Even Eliot, who separates the empirical dimensions of a person from those elements of imagination that appear active and dynamic, refuses to make an absolute distinction between them. The "man who suffers" and the "mind which creates" are the same entity conceived of from separate points of view, the difference between them depending on the context in which these aspects are viewed or voiced. To be "impersonal" is not to be wholly self-creating. Impersonality requires only that one align one's will with the impulses and circumstance that from another point of view appear uncontrollable or predetermining. As I will explore in later chapters, this understanding of impulse accords with the vitalist psychologies of Bergson and William James. They usefully call into question the rationalist model of psychology that would divorce the passive from the productive in expressions of character.[36] In Bergson's terms, "élan vital" may be better viewed as a plastic and malleable tendency or disposition, neither self-acting nor unconditioned.

In *Matter and Memory*, Bergson offers a fine-grained account of the workings of attention that accords with this more malleable depiction of the self. His account influenced a significant number of writers of the period. He begins by asking what attention as a phenomenon does, what the process of selection and emphasis is in the service of:

> There are then, in short, divers *tones* of mental life, or, in other words, our psychic life may be lived at different heights, now nearer to action, now further removed from it, according to the degree of our *attention to life*. . . . That which is usually held to be a greater complexity of the psychic state appears to us, from our point of view, to be a greater dilatation of the whole personality, which, normally narrowed down by action, expands with the unscrewing of the vice in which it has allowed itself to be squeezed, and, always whole and undivided, spreads itself over a wider and wider surface. (*Matter and Memory*, 14).

For Bergson, attention can be lived at different levels. When nearer to action, it conforms to something like habit and when further removed from action, it becomes more and more total and dreamlike, a network of interconnected, singular nodal memories. Bergson calls the experience of such a complex in its unalloyed form "pure memory." But mental life remains attentive so long as it accesses but succumbs to neither of these poles, which are in fact forms of the past, hardened and static. Properly defined, the self is at its most singular not when it is absorbed in memory (in its past instantiations) but rather when it puts those memories to work as part of a bodily practice or sensory-motor development that incorporates habits.[37] In those moments, the self is in process and the body the site of production.

Crary does refer at length to Bergson, but his readings tend to glide over much of the delicacy and provocation of the philosopher's distinctions—his insistence, for instance, on accounting for diverse kinds of action, which, especially in their higher or more complex form, are never in the service of predetermined instrumental goals.[38] For Bergson, attention is bound up with all the individualizing forces and powers of the self because it speaks to the qualitative character of any individual's interest in things. Our attention to life is bound up with the reflection of ourselves stamped on the things we do. Bergson calls this "personality," but he does not mean either the empirical basis of a person's character or a fixed disposition, as I have been using the term.[39] Rather, personality is a sense of self that is undivided, owned, and felt—our individuality revealed within our activity.

Bergson's work challenges Frankfurt School–inspired theorists and historicist critics to be materialists without the one-way causal arguments that give special or exclusive efficacy to the economic foundations of cultural practices and experiences. Indeed, I would maintain that vitalism promotes and sustains historical reflection on the transformations within Western society and demonstrates an attachment to historical argument. Without being able to rely on basic codes or determinants for showing how social processes unfold, vitalists must turn to history as a record of contingent pathways of innovation. The future is not decided in advance by mechanical or teleological principles, and therefore one can only reconstruct its directionality retrospectively. Individuals are historical agents who intervene in an intricately embedded but rationally unpredictable way in the circumstances of their moment. To do history in the manner I am proposing, we have to avoid the illusion that the small-scale level in which individuals think and act can be reduced to the large-scale operations of power; we cannot be confident that we can isolate the levels or even the interactions between the scales. Lack of confidence does not preclude us from trying. I would argue, however, that we need to be more skeptical of methodologies that inadvertently reproduce expectations of finding homogeneous or higher-order explanations for those interactions. Often, as well, such methodologies presume commensurability between different kinds of discourse (for example, self-help manuals, scientific studies examining how to maximize people's performance aptitudes, modernist novels and poems, and philosophical psychologies), treating them as "statements" or data points that can be collated in the same way. When they do so, they risk flattening the rhetorical, situational, and material specificity of these discourses as well as the specificity of the practices that led to them.

For vitalists, to be properly historical, we have to grant specific kinds of situations and people their incompleteness. We cannot take for granted that they evolve or change because of the latent effects of certain forces or determinants that an analysis of the past would reveal. Rather, existing in time, they react to events, forces, and effects that converge in ways that are improbable, accidental, and contingent as well as probable, repetitive, and obvious. Sometimes, the one becomes the other. At points of emergence, there is something about situations and historical actors that have yet to resolve themselves or finish sculpting the contours of their identity and definition. Contingent on future events, these situations and people are suspended in history, awaiting events in a manner that renders them ongoing and unfinished in character. Therefore, how it is to feel incomplete is a historical factor of the highest interest.

REPSYCHOLOGIZING CHARACTER

I have just been arguing that social fragmentation—the dizzying feeling of lost direction, social isolation, aesthetic marginality, political inwardness, sensory and experiential specialization—is one set of historical descriptions, on the whole too broad and totalizing in their scope, for portraying the tensions and conflicts that individuals experienced in the midst of modern economic life, as well as the correlative freedoms and constraints it presented. To arrive at a less totalizing view, we need to take into account lower levels of analysis. As we historicize mental powers such as attention, situating the phenomena within a complex of social and ideological practices, we should make sure to clarify what the allocation of processing resources accomplishes as a psychological and pragmatic matter. Approaching character by way of vitalist psychology allows me to ask a question hitherto at the margins of literary studies: What do the imagined personages in exceptionally complex (in this case, modernist) novels and poems tell us about what it means to be a person? Since the 1950s, critics interested in characterization have tended to approach character as a fictive element within a structure. Long after narratologists started referring to characters as "actants" and "existents," classable by the range of predictable roles, types, and actions they represent in a narrative, literary critics have remained committed to formal or structural analysis. In practice, this has often meant a theoretical indifference to character in critical methodologies ranging from structuralist to poststructuralist. As Thomas Petruso argues, these methodologies display elaborate formalisms that displace issues of characterization, not as L. C. Knights did by favoring "literary" concerns with metaphor and imagery, but by focusing on the "tensions" and "anxieties" of the text itself rather than the people within it (*Life Made Real*, 3–5). Otherwise, character is a source of merely thematic interest. For instance, James Phelan combines these several approaches, marking out character as a complex of mimetic, thematic, and synthetic—that is, artificial or constructed—elements within the developing structure of a text (*Reading People, Reading Plots*, 3).

Reviewing the sources of this "critical prejudice" against character, Baruch Hochman points out that "the case against character has been made from a great many vantage points: textual, historical, literary-critical, ideological, metaphysical, and theoretical" (*Character in Literature*, 14). In explicit opposition to such perspectives, he insists: "there is a profound congruity between the ways in which we apprehend characters in literature, documented figures in history, and people of whom we have what we think of as direct knowledge in life" (36). Yet Hochman sounds a very traditional humanistic note by wishing "to construct our images of character in terms of our own knowledge and experience" (56)—without perceiving in an exposition of character a challenge to such experience. The approach, though it is obviously intended as a corrective, remains both undertheorized and essentially static in its view of human beings.

When it is considered at all these days, character tends to be treated as an epiphenomenon of economic forces or narrative demands and expectations.[40] But its status continues to be equivocal. More recently, Alex Woloch has attempted to chart a sophisticated middle pathway between structuralist views of character as codes or allegorical features within a "distributional matrix" and an earlier character criticism that focused on individual psychologies irrespective of placement within the narrative. His "synthetic" theory of literary character prefers to speak about character-spaces and character-systems—that is to say, about how fictive individuals get positioned within a narrative frame and how their positionings intersect to create social configurations (*The One vs. the Many*, 17). The way that narrative attention is distributed to characters in a narrative field fleshes out a figural development that has at once formal and extraformal implications about the standing of the "implied person." Thus, for instance, the Victorian novelist Anthony Trollope refuses to introduce an important character at the end of a chapter, which says something both about the status of the specific character and about the conventions that the author is adapting.

It seems to me, however, that the experience of depth or complexity in a character cannot simply be accorded to it by a quantity of narrative attention or by the number of minor characters that are sacrificed on that character's behalf. It is created by a presentation of specific individuating qualities that emerge as these "implied people" respond to each other. Obviously, such psychological negotiations cannot happen in the absence of rigorous formal arrangements, but the interpretive dictates emerge out of something besides narrative imperatives alone. Focusing on characters' makeshift and extemporized acts, this study describes modes of characterization that cannot be classified or explicated in terms of plot functions and structural tensions. I offer, therefore, an alternative to narratology with its predictability ratios and its interest in the structural positions of characters in narrative spaces.

I suggest that modernist fascination with psychic variability can have serious consequences for our conception of what a person is. In this way, I insist on repsychologizing character. I mean that we must imagine characters as having a psychological presence that is different in kind from merely asking how they comport with predictions of real people's behavior within a certain range of experience or how they flesh out thematic issues. To the degree that character deserves a psychological rather than a formal or logical account of its workings, it will be necessary to focus on emotional responses that we experience within texts. This entails a shift in concern from what characters know or believe—and what we as readers know or believe about them—to a focus on what characters make us feel or what they show us about how it is like to feel, to react to an extremely specific situation that at every point has the capacity to change them.

As Blakey Vermeule has recently suggested, "the tendency to think of literary characters as if they were real people is a habit lodged deep in the human psyche, and no amount of literary-critical sophistication is likely to cure people of it" (*Why Do We Care about Literary Characters?*, 176). I can only sanction her observation. As she points out, literary fiction has always been well positioned to reflect on moral conceptions of conduct and to give a "feel" for moral life. Nevertheless, her account of why we care about literary characters relies too much on cognitive science for its defense. She regards character as a form of play that stimulates our "inference systems" (17), allows us to hone our social expertise as mind-readers and test our judgment through make-believe "without risking too much" (41), when the cost of error is not great to ourselves. This suggests that our investment in character is largely a question of predicting people's intentions, striving to represent to ourselves their mental stance "under conditions of imperfect access to relevant information" (55). Thus, experiencing character is a kind of "algorithm" (89), a Machiavellian game of odds and evens, which requires anticipating the next thought of one's opponent. Vermeule thinks that the conceits of detective fiction, for instance, make this calculation literal. Her account of mind-reading implies, however, that what we do in such practices is to train ourselves to find rules or concepts that help us to predict other people's behavior, which we can then import into our actual social lives. In this respect, her explanation is quite functionalist. But if, as I have been suggesting, behavioral impulses at their finest and most complex are unpredictable, then perhaps what we feel, imaginatively speaking, when we observe characters engaging in such behavior, is the pleasure of experiencing what is new and unexpected in them. By observing the behavioral patterns unfolding over time, we harmonize our own reasoning capacities, our reflective judgment, with the social world whose utter novelty and particularity we are taking in. The rules we discover are not about characters per se but about the mind's capacity to engage with them and ultimately about people's way of expressing changes of attitude and feeling that evoke our own capacity to intuit change.[41]

In any case, fiction does not simply tell us what social life is like for us, or what it would be like if we existed in the world summoned up by the fiction. It unfolds at a distance from questions of practical import to ourselves. Its distance promotes a reflective attitude, a propensity to explore feelings and reactions that we might have toward others when our own instrumental calculations are not at issue. This is perhaps why modernist fiction so compulsively and self-reflexively reminds us that it is fiction: to enforce an attitude of noninstrumentality toward its invented worlds, by means of which readers allow themselves the leeway to react in unexpected ways in turn. Such gestures are not necessarily intended to flatten our response to characters as real people but at least sometimes to extend the range of our possible response.

Vermeule thinks that we enter into scenarios that we know to be fictional because we have certain cognitive biases that push us to attribute agency to anything that moves or might be treated as a self. We also have mental preferences for forms of information that we might regard as social information. Though she relies on very recent cognitive experimental findings, her account is in some ways quite traditional. She treats fiction as an epistemic conundrum: Why does fiction work us up even as our beliefs tell us that it is not real? Answer: Make-believe allows us to simulate reality by quarantining the fictional copy as a metarepresentation. We treat fictive worlds as though they were real, even as we learn to "decouple" hypothetical and counterfactual situations from real ones that concern us more directly. But as Richard Moran observes, people do not always, or even usually, have an emotional reaction to a fictional case that is different in kind from that of an everyday setting: one is not necessarily more second-order than another. Even nonfictional emotions are vicarious, as when one winces at someone else's pain. We experience empathetic emotions on behalf of others, whether fictive or otherwise.[42] In their ordinary range, "comparatively little of one's emotional attention" concerns beliefs about what is here and now (Moran, "Expression of Feeling in Imagination," 78); we have emotions about what might be or what could have been in ordinary life, not just in fiction. Many aesthetically relevant feelings "such as pleasure, boredom, disgust, anxiety, or suspense [are not] conceptually dependent on any beliefs about the real existence of their objects" (81). These emotions move fluidly between reactions to the fictional content or *matter* and reactions to the *manner* in which the fiction is depicted on the level of representation.

Vermeule would like to think of feelings evoked by fiction as honing our reasoning capacities by helping us navigate beliefs about other people's intentions. But for Moran they promote a certain kind of receptiveness to others—a receptiveness to a state of mind that one attributes to characters in a work of fiction—rather than training us to negotiate comparable behaviors in real-world settings. "What is vivid about some representations," he thinks, "is that they provoke the mind to *do* various things (relating, contrasting, calling up thoughts)" ("Expression of Feeling in Imagination," 89); this is not a reaction to a work's verisimilitude. Nor do we have to treat these representations primarily as a training ground for practical judgment. Emotions in fiction model emotions in life; they dispose us in a certain way to the world, hone our attitudes, reveal connections between different intentional states, and, if at all as a practical matter, conjure up possibilities of response, lending us examples of how to react to a changing situation.

Richard Wollheim makes the case that emotions ought to be granted a psychological reality that cannot be subordinated to their functional or explanatory value (*On the Emotions*, 3–6). They are not simply dispositional patterns that allow us to predict what people will do within certain logical entailments (for example, if desire P is satisfied, then emotion Q is terminated); they have a specific intentionality. The mental states or feelings that emerge from them demand a phenomenology, the experience of "what it is like" (*On the Emotions*, 6) to have them. Emotions originate out of a person's history and should not be treated as behavioral responses that follow propositional structure or that are triggered by logical criteria, by specified, generic equations that determine their emergence or satisfaction. Part of their mysterious appeal is that we do not know a priori what triggers them; they emerge in experience and can only be figured out after the fact. Like Wollheim, I insist that emotions accumulate force out of historical circumstances within the life of an individual rather than out of an appeal to their rational or cognitive grounds. But departing somewhat from his psychoanalytically inflected perspective, I emphasize the conative dimensions of emotions and feelings more than he does—the way that they put possibilities of action in view and help steer a course through varying kinds of possibility.[43]

Emotions do not simply enable anticipations on the basis of an assumed pattern, nor do they simply provide us with reasons for what we do. They help reveal to us what we become as we do a thing and as our doing suggests to us new possibilities for action that are for the most part tentative and not yet developed.

AFFECTIVE LIFE

Let me clarify why I think it is so important to consider the nature of feeling, or, as it is variously termed, "affection" or "affect," as an axis point in modernist writing about character. In what way, for instance is it bound up with Jamesian indirection, Steinian habit, or the intonations of Eliot's poetic voice? One of the most consequential premises of nineteenth- and early twentieth-century vitalist psychology as well as evolutionary science—the work of Darwin, Nietzsche, William James, and Bergson may be invoked together—revolves around the idea that feeling is at once the way we prepare ourselves to take in change and the way we experience that change as related to ourselves. Because a great deal of my argument hinges on the work of affect, a few clarifying remarks may be in order.

The genealogy of the term "feeling," as of its not-quite synonyms, "passion," "affection," "sentiment," "mood," and "emotion," is extraordinarily complex. In ordinary language, each of these terms makes reference to a slightly different set of psychological phenomena, even though we also tend to use the terms somewhat interchangeably. "Feelings" tend to be cued to a momentary experience, and they refer often, but not exclusively, to psychological phenomena that are eventlike and situation bound. Thus, we might say that someone has a feeling of pain or a feeling of rapture, but we do not say that a person's general fear of heights is a feeling. The more general or long-term mental response is an emotional disposition, something that may be discussed apart from an actual trigger. Still, emotions (love, hate, jealousy, etc.) have an intimacy with the specific objects that set them off, and in this sense they are inseparable from the situations in which they form or express themselves. As they flash up, we might as easily refer to them as feelings as emotions. As Philip Fisher argues, "We need to notice first the difference between the eruptive momentary impassioned state and the more enduring underlying states of which we sometimes speak when thinking of the passions" (*The Vehement Passions*, 18); he gives the contrast "between anger (eruptive moment) and hatred (abiding state), or between falling in love (eruptive moment) and love (abiding state)" (19). Wollheim relies on a similar distinction. He regards emotions as abiding mental dispositions or patterns of behavior that manifest themselves occasionally in transient states of mind or feelings, at which point they betray the quality of subjectivity or "coloring" associated with an experience (*On the Emotions*, 6–9). Such distinctions are clearly useful for anatomizing the different temporal arcs or life cycles of feelings and emotions. But in other respects, they are less useful and even misleading.

Wollheim and Fisher tend to privilege emotions because they entail long-term attitudes and commitments of the self that help to clarify people's identities. Vitalists such as Bergson and William James, however, pay much more attention to what Wollheim would call "feelings" because they reveal a link between global dispositions and the occurrent thoughts and situation-specific reactions in which these dispositions manifest themselves. In other words, vitalists tend to see these emotional dispositions as inseparable from feelings. For example, in the case of guilt we cannot recognize the emotion in ourselves without feeling guilty. Likewise, we cannot hate someone but be unable to feel or manifest anger either directly or indirectly. The disposition means nothing apart from the way it shapes thoughts, even if we are not burning with rage in any given moment. Bergson remarks that even durable emotions such as love may be estimated by "the number and nature of the peripheral sensations which accompany them" and which give way to effects on "our ideas, our memories, our states of consciousness of every description, which will turn in larger or smaller numbers in a definite direction" (*Time and Free Will*, 31). Emotions always have an experiential aspect that expresses itself across time in specific situations, a good sign that states and dispositions are not wholly distinguishable to begin with. Indeed, Bergson and James tend to treat feelings and emotions as circumstantial in their very nature. As vitalists, they shy away from describing them as a free-floating impetus contained within the mind, existing latently apart from the situations that give rise to them, such as a latent agitation, pressure, or inward sensation.

Unlike Wollheim, Bergson and James do not simply equate feelings with states of mind, because every state prolongs itself, has duration, and tends toward a new state.[44] Wollheim's mistake, which he shares with so many philosophers of the current moment, is to conceive of feelings as mental contents with particular mind-stuff or properties (in his case, intentionality, subjectivity, grades of consciousness) rather than to treat them as total orientations of the self that are expressed in particular actions. He wants feelings and the beliefs in which they are grounded to have a causal effect on emotional response. In this respect, he can establish a qualified form of rationality for the emotions. Emotions are manifest in feelings, which present attitudes that incite impulses. But this account makes it hard for him to understand emotional responses that do not have a discrete or isolable "precipitating factor."

To adhere to his logical sequence, Wollheim insists on altering much of what is unacceptable to him in William James's famous formula for emotional response in *The Principles of Psychology*, which states that we "feel sorry because we cry, angry because we strike, afraid because we tremble" (2:450). The gist of James's thought is that we have an impulse or bodily reaction to what he terms an "exciting fact," which causes physiological changes that express the emotion and embody it. He thus reverses the cognitive schema that presumes that we have the attitude first and then the response. For James, emotions are not physiological accompaniments to beliefs and attitudes. They are expressions or precipitates of action in situ that help to determine attitudes belatedly. Feelings come after the fact as a way to register how we have experienced our situation and to orient us to possible response. This is why James calls the body a "sounding-board" betraying "indefinitely numerous and subtle" (2:450) changes that take place in reaction to an overall situation. When Wollheim disagrees with James, he does so using James's account of fear as an example (*On the Emotions*, 120) because the affect has such a strong and obvious intentional component: one sees a bear and runs. But in fact we can imagine any number of scenarios that cause fear, which are the result not of an obvious imperiling object but of passing alignments of a state of mind (for instance, one has just seen a scary movie and therefore tends to find other things scary) or subtle situational triggers that work in concert (for instance, a certain slant of light brokers an atmosphere that is slightly "off," forcing one to negotiate what one is reacting to or how one is feeling). As a rule, if we do not treat emotions as the dispositional extension of preformed attitudes or orientations to the world, then we are in a better position to appreciate their potential disclosive power, their capacity to unveil new situations and new ways of looking at things.

James and Bergson both give great prominence to aesthetic feelings in their overall account of affects, in part because they wish to emphasize the intense particularity and even novelty of the range of possible responses.[45] These feelings involve indeterminate judgments about resonant objects that make the process of clarifying how we feel central to the experience. Bergson's use of the word "affection" harkens back to the philosophical vocabulary of Augustine and Aquinas ("the affections of the soul"), but removed from the theological context. To have a feeling is to be affected by a thing, to have it work on us in a certain way. In this sense, it approximates an older usage of the word "passion." Passion (*passio*) does not first and foremost imply passivity in the face of an object or circumstance, that is to say, an intrinsic weakness to something not under our control. Instead, it refers to the fact that a situation *acts on us*, irritates or frightens or worries or pleases us. In fact, I will argue that for vitalists, feelings and emotions are ways of registering these impingements on the self while at the same time registering how they alter one's capacity to act. Of course, we can misattribute the cause or quality of our feeling, but this is because things act on us in indirect ways. As critics, we do not need to presume that individuals are repressed to grant that they can be insufficiently attuned to the relations around them.

Sigmund Freud obviously thought otherwise, but his models of affective functioning tend to separate the emotion's impetus from its situational manifestation. Rather than treating emotions as total orientations of the self, he regards them as discrete excitations that can attach to or detach from specific ideas, subject only to the vicissitudes of the desire that underlies them. Thus, for instance, when a traumatic memory undergoes repression, the unpleasant affect is severed from the memory itself, and each follows a separate pathway. The idea, which is the content, thought, or image that precipitates the affect, is shunted into the unconscious, while the affect itself is transformed, displaced onto another object, or left unattached in the form of generalized anxiety.[46] As Eve Sedgwick has observed, Freud treats an emotion as a vehicle or manifestation of an underlying libidinal drive. Libido tends to take on some of the same functions as an affect system because it shapes important relationships that a person has, but with this difference: libido does not care what precise expression or character it takes. "Excitement, rage, even indifference, are seen as more or less equivalent transformations of desire" (*Touching Feeling*, 18). Sedgwick warns that Freud's reduction of affect to drive "permits a diagrammatic sharpness that may, however, be too impoverishing in qualitative terms" (18).[47] Freud does not grant emotions any direct value as end-directed dispositions that are capable of affecting or reorienting behavior. Instead, he subordinates them to drive and makes them a contingent expression of it.

Bergson and William James, like Freud, treat an affect as a sensible alteration in a person's state, mental as well as somatic. Collectively, their theories of affect emerge from the materialist investments of the late nineteenth century, which Darwin helped to create with his *Expression of the Emotions*. But the approach that vitalists take to theorizing affective functioning is distinctively different in ways that have direct relevance to modernist approaches to character. Vitalists show how much expressions of character depend on situationally bounded forms of affective self-reflection. And as we will in subsequent chapters, their account of affects also brings to bear a broadly relational understanding of the self. Affects dispose us in a particular way to a situation, but the "me" or "you" that emerges is the product of a qualitatively new relation.

PRAGMATISM AND VITALISM

Although more than one hundred years have passed since Bergson published *Matter and Memory*, the novelty of his ideas still makes them liable to frequent misunderstandings, and Bergsonism has only begun to enjoy the efflorescence of critical interest that an intellectual movement of its historical and conceptual significance deserves. Bergson's work does not stand alone but is part of an active dialogue with the work of a number of nineteenth-century figures.[48] These include Nietzsche, William James, and Darwin, as I have already noted, as well as Ralph Waldo Emerson, and, more distantly, Baruch Spinoza. Emerson paid tribute to the value of the unsettled in character formation, and his writings exercised eloquent sway over members of the James family, to whom he was a particular friend, and Stein. Together with the others, he allows for a refashioning of some of the prevailing approaches toward modernism and its psychology. What all the aforementioned figures have in common is not only the prominence they accord to the modes of change within the world, including changes to character itself, but also an investment in affective transmission that blurs boundaries between self and other,[49] and a psychology that prioritizes action over thought or cognition whose processes bypass intellectual and rational calculation.

It may not be immediately obvious why Emerson, William James, or Darwin, each enormously significant in a number of intellectual and scientific spheres of concern, ought to be treated under the vitalist moniker. Emerson described himself as a transcendentalist. According to many critics, James made his mark on Anglo-American literature mostly, though not exclusively, through his self-branded philosophy of pragmatism, with a self-consciously American pedigree that shelters it from the cosmopolitan commitments and milieu of vitalism. Darwin's evolutionary biology is capable of expressing great hostility in response to the imputation that an unexplained vital principle fuels evolutionary change. Of the other figures, Nietzsche's individualist philosophy has eclectic roots, though he does insist that human value concerns the extent to which it is "life-promoting, life-preserving, species-preserving, perhaps even species-cultivating" (*Beyond Good and Evil*, 11). Bergson used the term "vitalism" with cautious approbation, but the imputation, right or wrong, that he subscribed to a mysterious creative force at the bottom of all things—an untestable metaphysical supposition—probably contributed to the diminished fortunes of his once enormously influential philosophy. As John Mularkey observes, "His theory of the *élan vital* has little of the *anima sensitiva*, *archeus*, *entelechy*, or vital fluid of classical vitalisms" ("Life, Movement and the Fabulation of the Event," 53). I would argue that Emerson, James, Darwin, Nietzsche, and Bergson are vitalists in the sense that they accord specific explanatory attention to biological processes, which are not coextensive with deterministic physical and chemical ones, and trace intricate systems that develop and organize themselves in purposeful ways in response to changing environments.

Critics have not ignored the connections among the writers central to this study, but they have described them within a lineage of American pragmatism, not vitalism, at the cost of ignoring or minimizing Bergson's particular drawing power.[50] This allows scholars in American Studies, for instance, to stay within more recognizable disciplinary boundaries. Yet obviously there are compelling continuities between these two powerful conceptual assemblies, and their principal intellectual formulators were more apt than not to emphasize their overlap.[51] Jonathan Levin offers a précis of pragmatist concerns: "pragmatists emphasize the constant need to adjust and readjust knowledge and belief about the world. Instead of asking whether the content of a thought or perception is right, pragmatists typically ask how a thought or perception effects particular consequences in experiences, and how those consequences lead to further adjustments in thought or perception" (*The Poetics of Transition*, 4). This stress on adjustments in experience and on change might remind us of Emerson, whom numerous contemporary pragmatist critics take as a point of origin for the discourse. Emerson states in a famous epigram that "a foolish consistency is the hobgoblin of little minds" and asserts that a "reverence for our past act or word" prevents us from trusting our flexible nature ("Self-Reliance" in *Emerson's Prose and Poetry*, 125). Nonetheless, pragmatism and vitalism have important differences of emphasis. And there are reasons why vitalism might be a more useful or encompassing classification.

First off, pragmatism emerged as a means of countering philosophical skepticism. As William James puts it, it is "primarily a method of settling metaphysical disputes that otherwise might be interminable" (*Pragmatism*, 506). Stated on this level, it remains a kind of practice, "a new name for some old ways of thinking," as James terms it in the subtitle to his volume of lectures on the subject. As such, it often takes the form of an epistemological inquiry, even as it circumvents the usual procedures for such inquiry, "*looking away from first things, principles, 'categories,' supposed necessities; and of looking towards last things, fruits, consequences, facts*" (*Pragmatism*, 510). According to Bergson, who sets out to correct readings of Jamesian pragmatism that impoverish or falsify it, James regards "every truth [as] a path traced through reality" (*Creative Mind*, 217), understood as a set of new relations that are constantly being created by the mind. Reality is open-ended, filled with redundancies, superabundant, perpetually recomposing itself as an "indefinite series of objects and events" (209); therefore, although "we ordinarily define the true by its conformity to what already exists," James "defines it by its relation to what does not yet exist" (215). Bergson insists on grounding James's pragmatism in a more encompassing ontology. James himself refers to this ontology as his "radical empiricism," in which the methodological aims of pragmatism remain subordinate to his account of how, as he puts it, "the parts of our universe *hang together*" (*Pragmatism*, 544).

Pragmatism's recent proponents tend to focus more narrowly than James on how to resolve conflicts over truth and falsity. They give central weight to the beliefs that people harbor, thus perpetuating a cognitivist bias, sometimes ignoring vaguer but equally important ways of responding to or acting on experience through intuition or feeling. Neopragmatist philosopher Richard Rorty, for instance, wishes to discard intuition altogether as a means of accessing reality (*Consequences of Pragmatism*, xvi). His conception of pragmatism is not only averse to talk of "reality" as a mind-independent ground for our truth claims but also rejects any perception of it or contact with it that is not culturally contingent and linguistically mediated. Rorty disregards the vitalistic grounding of James's thought, which makes no distinction between realism and pragmatism.[52]

James, however, insists that intuitions exist prior to belief. As Bergson puts it, for James "those truths it is most important for us to know, are truths which have been felt and experienced before being thought" (*Creative Mind*, 213). Emerson makes a similar point when he says, "character teaches above our wills" (125), guiding our thoughts and actions without our necessarily understanding why. Thus, as Emerson declares, "we cannot spend the day in explanation" (123). Like Nietzsche, Emerson implies that too much thinking retards living processes: "If a man should consider the nicety of the passage of a piece of bread down his throat, he would starve" ("Experience" in *Emerson's Prose and Poetry*, 203).

Some pragmatist literary critics find Rorty appealing;[53] others, such as Patricia Rae, prefer James's cautious "epistemological optimism" (*The Practical Muse*, 30) to Rorty's "radical skepticism" (11). Rae, like Richard Poirier and other critics attuned to the literary artifact, pays closer attention to the workings of feeling and intuition within the texts of the pragmatist tradition. Yet she, like Rorty, treats pragmatism as a theory of truth concerned with methods of verification. Modernist texts draw the reader "into an ongoing process of hypothesis-testing, in which an ordered world is a possibility under constant review" (13). Although Rae is adamant that neither she nor James falls "back on a simple 'correspondence' or 'copy' theory of truth" (30), her aim to establish or authenticate truth still betrays an epistemic bias, a concern with knowledge rather than the experience of agency as it manifests in impulse, drive, tendency, or feeling. As Emerson defines action, it is "the *preamble* of thought, the transition through which it passes from the unconscious to the conscious" ("The American Scholar" in *Emerson's Prose and Poetry*, 61; emphasis mine). Emerson is indicating that beliefs, like other constituents of thought, are the belated products of certain tendencies or vectors of action rather than the guiding instrument of them.

Poirier, one of pragmatism's most sensitive critics, calls attention to this "naggingly suggestive" (*Poetry and Pragmatism*, 25) sentence of Emerson's because, I think, it raises a question about how Emerson understands action's connection to practice, if as an emergent force it precedes consciously understood conceptions of usefulness. Emerson's account of action withstands easy recruitment "in the service of blustering athleticism and worldly enterprise" (25). Indeed, pragmatists give such central weight to the utility of statements, to the practical effect of beliefs and actions, that they have a lot to explain when it comes to thoughts or stances deemed useless or impractical, the kind most often associated with aesthetic experience. At the outer perimeter of a thought process, how does one shape, redefine, or settle on what counts as useful? Emerson's language, like Henry James's, Stein's, or Eliot's, retains an opacity that skeptically undermines its own claims.

This restless skepticism and concern for the impractical are part of the reason for Stanley Cavell's preferring to treat Emerson as a transcendentalist rather than assimilating him "to pragmatism [which] unfailingly blunts the particularity, the achievement, of Emerson's language" (*Emerson's Transcendental Etudes*, 7). Pragmatism does not pay enough attention to the pauses in speech and to the silences that surround it—moments when language's usefulness inevitably hangs in suspension, in opposition to conceptions of use and practicality as they stand. "What calls for thinking in Emerson," Cavell presses, "occurs before—or as—our life of perplexities and aspirations and depressions and desperations and manifestations of destiny resolve themselves into practical problems" (9). Like the Wittgensteinian silence to which Cavell refers, which attends the "recognition that all invocable practices have been canvassed," such moments prepare us, "providing words, for suffering, awaiting, an inevitable crossroads" (219). From a vitalist point of view, these moments of pause or suspension reveal language at work not just when it conveys meaning but also when it withholds and modifies previous uses of the words at issue. These are affecting moments for both speaker and audience. The work they reveal language performing has to do with its effect on the individuals who use it. Such instances of cessation, interruption, or breakdown help condition an appreciation for the value of the words, while rejecting any predetermining sense of their pragmatic effect. I am less committed than Cavell to preserving definite differences between the thinking of William James and Emerson in both sound and consequence.[54] It may be true that James is "uncontentiously" a pragmatist, while Emerson is "only contentiously so" (216), but both figures reveal their common ground as vitalists; that is, they do not take for granted what the usefulness of words may be in advance of their imperfectly determined effect, partly unconscious, on the agents who employ them.

There is one other, perhaps overriding, reason why scholars of modernism might wish to give special precedence to vitalism. This has to do with the familiar complaint, leveled first and foremost against Emerson but making its way to other pragmatist-identified figures: that they are wanting in tragic sensibility. As Henry James says of Emerson, his "eyes were thickly bandaged" to the "evil and sin" ("Emerson," 627) of the world, and "we feel that his first impressions were gathered in a community from which misery and extravagance, and either extreme, of any sort, were equally absent" (617). Whether James's accusation is fair to Emerson's thinking, it is a reaction, I think, to the enormous reverence Emerson held for the working power of nature, the perfection of its means of growth and its compensatory processes. In his essay "Compensation," Emerson winds up with the following: "A fever, a mutilation, a cruel disappointment, a loss of wealth, a loss of friends seems at the moment unpaid loss, and unpayable. But the sure years reveal the deep remedial force that underlies all facts," which he maintains are "friendly to the growth of character" (*Emerson's Prose and Poetry*, 149). Partly on pragmatic grounds, Emerson insists on cleaving to the generative forces of nature because the optimism there spawned has a healing effect. As we will see, however, for Henry James, Stein, and Eliot, such voluble sanguinity does not create the happiest of emphases, especially when stated as a predictable law. For them, the neuroses and contingencies of social life require greater attentiveness to the psychological and ethical consequences of loss.

Nevertheless, Emerson has another side to him that agrees more closely with Henry James's tragic muse, Stein's feeling for naturalist depletion, and Eliot's incursion into anarchic disarray, insofar as these elements of their work display the decreative power of nature and hence the possibilities of existential loss. And this side aligns better with Emerson's vitalism. For while he believed that the compositions of nature *as a whole* are constructive, he also believed that its local constituents—human beings included—are vulnerable to failure and dissolution. "All nature," he writes, "is the rapid efflux of goodness executing and organizing itself" ("Circles" in *Emerson's Prose and Poetry*, 177), but the book of nature is beyond our view. As David Jacobson puts it, it becomes "the book of fate, illegible and dictatorially eloquent" (*Emerson's Pragmatic Vision*, 8). Like Darwin and Bergson,

Emerson yields to the notion that living entities are in competition with each other, "race living at the expense of race" ("Fate" in *Emerson's Prose and Poetry*, 263), despite the concealment of the slaughterhouse. Hence, any human life is always liable to the loss of its own power. Such diminishment casts its shadow over much of Emerson's writings, even as he struggles to articulate ways of conjoining individual agency with the larger workings of what he calls the "over-soul," the actively changing and constructive unity within nature.

Arguably, the complaint that pragmatism does not appreciate the tragic applies less to primary figures such as William James or Emerson—because their pragmatism was just one element of their thinking—than to the subsequent criticism they spawned.[55] Indeed, for Emerson, the individual man or woman not only suffers from the bombardments and misadventures of a destiny that emerges from without but from the "vice and contumacy" ("Compensation" in *Emerson's Prose and Poetry*, 148) that marks his or her own character. Such malice may not present its negative effects in easily observable outcomes. Emerson thinks, however, that character is a sensitive instrument of its own diminishment, its decrease from nature. It expresses itself in the very quality of the person, regardless of the visible consequences: the man who does evil acts "carries the malignity and the lie within him" (148). Nonetheless, Emerson's optimism does not allow him to tarry long on such natures, which are simply the product of their lesser being. Henry James, Stein, and Eliot are better anatomists of those who get caught in relations that weaken their capacity for action. Such individuals reveal their incapacity as an overfastidious attention to their own trapped consciousnesses, as a recalcitrance within their characters, or as an inability to sense their effect on others. To account for these variously unproductive states, one needs the resources of a discourse that does not take pragmatic action as its starting point but rather, like Nietzschean *ressentiment*, can research the manifestations and effects of impotence and negative agency within the very site of character itself.

In broad strokes, how some characters evade the inducements to negative agency, while others do not, is the theme of this book. To track how characters express vital relations and increase their ethical sensitivities will require specific—and of necessity, very intricate—examples. Because the vitalist models of psychology toward which modernists gravitated tell us that we are situationally and relationally defined, it would seem of no small importance that modernists set out to unwind their thoughts about character through situation-specific imaginings of human interactivity. It should be clear by now that they present exceedingly ambitious claims about what constitutes personhood, claims that, till now, we have not well understood. To keep faith with their thoughts on the matter, we will have to attend in detail and at length to the process that demonstrates ethical thinking in action.

2 NOVEL INTERESTS
Henry James

In *The Ambassadors*, Henry James gives us Lambert Strether, a protagonist so immersed in the web of connections, real and potential, that draw him into his situation that he positively neglects to pursue any previously observed economic interests of his own. By contrast, in *The Wings of the Dove*, James offers a spectacular demonstration of self-interestedness: Kate Croy concocts a plan to marry off Merton Densher, her lover, to a wealthy heiress whom she knows to be mortally ill. But after setting up this double-dealing plot design, James proceeds to dismantle its conventions. To remain alive to the world, Densher must stray from his scripted part. In *The Golden Bowl*, the third novel of the triptych that is usually thought to constitute James's "great phase," Maggie Verver holds off responding to her husband's affair. Rather than taking her assumed interests in hand, she seems to discover her intentions only after acting.

What is odd in each case is not that the characters manage to shift course or even that they are capable of improvising as events unfold. It is the impression these characters present of being so attuned to their situations that they give up any fixed set of motives and therefore any sense of self that can be said to exist apart from their engagements with each other. Meanwhile, each of their circumstances is constantly in flux and demands responses of them before they have a chance to process unfolding events. They thus have to make do without the usual guideposts for action. Rather than pursuing predetermined intentions and motives according to a scale of understood interests, they seek to discover them among the various possibilities that hang before them in a flickering half-light. In this respect, Maggie, Densher, and Strether begin their endeavors by improvising new selves, constructed through the emotional adjustments to the situations they find so unaccountably interesting.

By refusing to equip these characters with fixed motives or interests, James, I argue, takes away the armature we normally ascribe to selves, the core properties that are said to give people a consistent outline. His characters are so profoundly relational that they cannot be bound to any independent—which is to say, pre-established and recurring—form of being. Suspended in their own situations, these individuals have identities that seem contingent on a future that is yet to resolve itself. Without having an already codified identity on which to rely, James's characters are at greater liberty to extend and alter their own sense of advantage and to define themselves on the basis of their constantly developing interests.

The idea that certain kinds of desire and interest are an achievement of the self rather than a starting point for its activities strains against the cognitive models that we tend to use when picturing psychic life. Specifically, we assume that people have desires that give rise to intentions and in turn lead to action. But, more often than not, in James's last novels intentions seem belated or halfhearted, expressing only a tendency to act in a certain way or to pursue a specific direction of thought; they are not purposes underwritten by fully formed interests. To understand this, we would do well to turn to James's contemporary, Henri Bergson, who described the cognitive picture of the mind that reduces impulses (or what he calls "élan vital") into preordained rationales as a psychological fallacy to which we succumb when we grant future-directed action a clarity that we gain only retrospectively. Bergson suggests that we are apt to confuse the end with the road itself, but "the road has been created *pari passu* with the act of traveling over it, being nothing but the direction of this act itself" (*Creative Evolution*, 51). For Bergson, the attempt to assign a preexisting order to actions and events may suit a certain practical psychological need for predictability, but it distorts the way an action unfolds in any given situation.

James takes this Bergsonian idea one step further: he uses considerations of form to develop characters in dramatic interaction with circumstances, and he arrives at a "situational self" that changes or develops moment-by-moment.[1] The resulting psychology carefully frustrates the models of personhood that hold high currency in our culture. We tend to assume that people derive psychological consistency from a set of dominant traits and interests that, whether visible or not, provides them with an identity that cannot easily be surmounted or swept away. And as long as we assume the stability of their desires and the underlying interests that confirm them, we look, sooner or later, for linkages to the formative events of their lives or to their inherited traits. We might call these substantialist models of character. However much one model varies from another in its details, they all presuppose that people make large-scale adjustments to their situation, adjustments that are regulated by intractable preferences and fixed patterns that emerge from outside the situation at hand and transcend it. James, however, gives us characters who have desires and interests that depend much more profoundly on the successive social environments with which they are obliged to interact. I do not mean to suggest that their interests can be bent whichever way the situation blows, and certainly some interests remain pressing across a range of situations. I am simply proposing that these projected individuals are caught in the process of redefining the self for whom a variety of interests are relevant. These characters are not less robustly realistic because of the malleability of their interests. On the contrary, their reactions have real repercussions for themselves and others around them, and the powers of perception and willpower that they wield shape them in meaningful ways. James insists that their capacity to defer previously held conceptions of advantage and take an increasingly detached attitude to their circumstances allows them a richer perspective and set of responsibilities than would otherwise be available to them.

These individuals never free themselves entirely from self-interested calculation. Indeed, James's narratives are each in their own way about conflicts of interest, and, contrary to any number of ethical commonplaces, he does not insist that ethical life consists in abjuring calculations of personal advantage. As a matter of fact, life—and therefore ethics—demands that we pursue our interests. Yet when conflicts arise, James compels us to see the reconfiguration and alteration of those interests as an indispensable social value and (at least sometimes) as a means of mending relationships and dampening threats of rancor and rivalry. Because James celebrated aesthetic experience, he understood better than most writers that interests are not givens, fixed by our biological and material needs, but rather relations capable of wide flexibility. As he presented it, aesthetic experience does not negate interest but proliferates interests, and it emphasizes the capacity to solicit investment without having a fixed grasp of what the nature or quality of the advantage is.

To theorize such formations of interest, I will turn to vitalist models. Vitalism does not posit fixed constraints or standards for what regulates an agent's pursuit of action. I would suggest, moreover, that vitalism captures the improvisational side of Jamesian values better than pragmatism, which has served for the last two decades as the predominant prism through which critics have examined James's novels and especially their extemporized flourishes and open-endedness.[2] Although pragmatists in the contemporary mold do not insist that specific ideas are inherently pragmatic, apart from the consequences they impose on experience, they tend nonetheless to favor claims that are biased toward what seems strictly practical.[3] Vitalists, by contrast, are concerned with behaviors that demonstrate complexity without presenting immediate practical objectives—that is, behaviors that suspend or keep open the criteria or considerations that define the value of what is "practical." In this respect, they are better equipped to investigate characters' own sense of personal advantage.[4]

In contrast to James's recent pragmatist critics, his commentators in the years before and just after the Second World War were quicker to locate gestures of melancholy renunciation in his work, seeing either a perverse *im*practicality on the part of the author and his characters or a morally triumphant asceticism.[5] These perspectives imply that the supposed "disinterest" professed by James's characters amounts to self-denial and excludes all possible motivation on grounds of self-interest. The ideal of disinterestedness that lent dignity to their vision of moral life has disparate religious and philosophical genealogies, but it draws on a rationalist tradition that believes that one is doing service to others by renouncing personal interests on higher grounds (according to reason's own stable imperatives).[6] Because it denies individual desires, this potentially ascetic vision vies with a tradition of social thought that we might describe as "realist" in the political sense and that is often aligned with certain strands of pragmatism. It cautions against disinterested action and promotes self-interest (defined from Machiavelli to Adam Smith largely in economic terms) because the narrow range of motivations allows for a predictability that can regulate social life.[7] Despite their differences, both positions share an orthodox assumption that James appears to challenge: that consistency—whether disinterested or interested—can best satisfy the urges and concerns of social life. Instead, James celebrates moments when individuals depart from the template of choices and desires that mark their past, at least when such plasticity grants them more power to adjust to events and, with the procured autonomy, a greater range and variety of responses. He does not assume, prima facie, that an invocation of interests can rally consensus on what is personally or socially advantageous. As we will see, James shows that individuals are best able to alter their conceptions of self-interest and increase the scope of their actions when they are not made to feel instantly accountable for their actions or responses.

As a discourse, vitalism is sensitive to the ways individuals can backslide from pragmatic agency to impotence; it also celebrates forms of action that expand the scope of what is deemed useful, nascently valuable, or at least interesting. Like Friedrich Nietzsche and the vitalistic "sage" who inspired him, Baruch Spinoza, James is invested in turning the experience of vulnerability, helplessness, and loss into a more life-affirming existence, recuperating these expressions of contingency, when possible, as a means to further action. In this respect, vitalism encompasses both visions of James (as pragmatist and as melancholy ascetic), mediating between them. In his last novels, which are the focus of this chapter, James is concerned with the psychic conditions and the forms of relationality that allow one to transition from negative agency to power. To understand how this vitalistic transition happens, we need to pay attention to the central role that affects play in defining and underwriting interests. Emotions secure the motivation that gives an interest its force while also helping us negotiate among different orders of interests. I argue, then, that interests are a species of affect, and one must grant them the same indeterminacy and flexibility that other affects demand.[8]

Typically, philosophers, social theorists, and political analysts do not concede a large role to affective self-examination when considering how people come to formulate their interests. For example, rights-based political discourses and other liberal projects of emancipation start from the presumption that interests ought to be secured in advance as a condition of entrance into the community. Other materialist discourses suppose that interests are to a great extent fixed by inalterable human needs. In enforcing such perspectives, they tend to discount all but prevailing economic values as a basis for social life, allowing little margin for people's creativity and inventiveness in fashioning or retailoring their interests. Although James presumes that individuals are circumscribed by a rich variety of material and social relations that exist prior to any specific exchange or conversation into which they enter, he holds out the possibility that conversation and interaction may in fact help to restructure the nature of the self in the community and thus the nature of the community to which the self belongs. Meanwhile, James parts company with communitarians who value legibility in all communal stances.[9] He imagines forms of responsibility that expect interests not to be explicit, public, or universal but rather open-ended, situation-specific, and subject to highly contextual forms of judgment. At the end of this chapter, I will explore the implications of James's conception of self-interest for liberal social thought. What matters now is to understand what the ramifications are of such interests for ethical life and how they are nurtured and enriched by the novel's formal parameters.

James's late novels present interests across a spectrum: from Strether's commitment, ultimately, to gain nothing in *The Ambassadors* to Kate Croy's excessive interestedness in *The Wings of the Dove*. Through these novels, which we will consider in turn, James demonstrates the crucial entanglement of various kinds of interest. The complex affective responses of his characters model for readers how to fashion new accommodating interests that traverse social and economic registers, adapting creatively to situational exigencies that emerge over time. Finally, in the last third of this chapter, we will consider *The Golden Bowl*, in which Maggie Verver's love of Prince Amerigo and her resolve to fight for him demonstrate the social value of remaining interested while also offering an appealing middle ground between extremes, and thus a way to assess and test the social—as opposed to personal—advantages of such interests. My aim throughout the chapter is to discover the affective process that leads to the alignment and reconstruction of interests. I argue that James represents characterization through complex theatrical metaphors that flesh out how people adopt a public mask that allows them to "try on" a range of possible interests, resulting in self-consciously provisional ways of being in the world. These performed, yet unscripted, responses enable individuals to orchestrate common interests, allowing them to adapt to changing circumstances while giving them refuge from public modes of accountability. Psychoanalytic accounts of James tend, however, to treat characters' desires as scripted, thereby misrepresenting the improvisational nature of these roles, an understanding of which is crucial to grasping James's vision of ethical life. Therefore, I will also explore the limitations of psychoanalytic conceptions of social interests.

THE INTERESTING NOVEL

Before examining some of the conflicts of interest that James dramatizes in his late novels, it may be helpful to ask: Why is it that questions about interests arise so specifically and, as it were, persuasively, in relation to the novel, and what do the novel's own preoccupations tell us about interests and the people who have them? In his essay "The Art of Fiction," James introduces a single criterion as the basis for defining a successful novel: "The only obligation to which in advance we may hold a novel, without incurring the accusation of being arbitrary, is that it be interesting" (191). It would seem that as a form, the novel is tasked with eliciting and brokering diverse kinds of interest. Keeping this in mind, we might reflect that conflicts of interest tend naturally to engage our attention. Furthermore, because he is so attentive to character, James connects interest *in* the novel to the interested individuals within it. In the broadest sense, interests are the relations to things—objects, people, social standards, or goals and ideas—

judged to be somehow beneficial to us. The benefit itself, however, might be quite indeterminate. Treated broadly enough, James's dictum implies, *anything* might fall under the category of an interest. Indeed, he refuses to predetermine what sets of concerns or staked claims count as relevant.

James's approach to interests reverses the approach taken by an economist or social scientist: rather than focus on advantages that are secure in value, thus privileging narrowly instrumental motives, he emphasizes the vague concern that attends interest formation (the preliminary feeling that something is "interesting"). He regards the capacity to solicit investment as basic to an interest, whatever the strength or variety of the investment. By this measure, aesthetic "interests" are not weak examples but paradigmatic in their open-endedness. Yet they are even more complicated than other kinds of interest because investment in them is inseparable from the capacity to reflect on the interest itself. The novel in general, and James's late novels in particular, are not simply a staging ground for vying personal interests of a settled order; they present conflicts about what counts as an interest.

In *The Ambassadors*, *The Wings of the Dove*, and *The Golden Bowl*, James presents characters who make use of an aesthetic attitude to extend the range of possible interests in their fellows. By hesitating to pursue private economic advantage, these characters attain a wider perspective than would otherwise be available to them. Meanwhile, the complex identifications into which they enter change how they conceive of their interests. They show a capacity to experiment, revealing to us the malleability and unpredictability of their possible interests. James, by refusing to tether his characters' sense of advantage to an already encoded identity or to a particular set of characteristics, demonstrates the extent to which the self is an improvised product of its own constantly developing interests.

James's characters are not just objects of interest, then, but proxies for readers: they model what it is like to remain responsive to others without a precise set of goals at hand. And the novel, as a genre, is a successful staging ground for this improvisational self in part because its own generic aims are indeterminate. It facilitates the activity of imagining the lives of others without demanding any specific sort of recompense other than the cultivation of certain powers of mind. Of course, James's characters are assumed to be more directly interested in their circumstances, by which I mean that they are supposed to have a greater range of agency over the situations they contemplate than do readers tarrying over the pages of a novel. Yet often these same characters suspend action or adopt a wait-and-see attitude, in part because they do not quite know how to respond. They confront an unprecedented, because highly particular, constellation of relations that yields no stable interpretive framework with which to judge it. Each strand of the situation is dependent on reciprocated understandings that have yet to firm up. A character's motives are tied to future relations that have not yet formed or hardened. Rather than settling the meaning of a gesture or a thought, these characters and their fellows prefer to leave them suspended while they track the possible directions they may take or actions they may pursue. For James, the novel affords an opportunity to observe conflicts that are embedded in unfinished or imperfectly formed situations that pose an unusual challenge to ethical judgment.

In this respect, we might regard James as a realist, though in his characterizations he foregoes the presumption of a preexisting personality that is typically evoked in the nineteenth-century realist novel. As I clarify in the next section, he formulates alternative parameters of characterization. Again, I am not saying that James sweeps away all "interior" content from his characters, all desires or consistent intentions. There are many examples of characters' desires remaining constant and unquestioned even as circumstances change. Maggie's love for Prince Amerigo, for instance, does not change. But whatever elements of character James fixes from the start are neither a sufficient basis for his fiction nor a satisfactory representation of character itself. The expressed desires are preliminary: they do not "signify" of themselves, and they come to mean something important about the characters who harbor them only when placed in a dynamic context. Unlike Joseph Conrad, for example, James does not invite readers to interpret or excavate the causes underlying a character's actions. We are left to gather that patterns of causes are taken for granted and are therefore uninteresting apart from the situation in which those determinants are deployed or tested. In James's fictions, characters come alive when, in response to a situation, a vital hesitation suspends or transforms an initial intention or interest.

RELATIONAL BEING

James's characters are strangely "superficial." The self that is open-ended requires different standards for defining its "consistency" or continuity with itself because it can no longer rely on core structures or the machinery of a preexisting personality for determining its desires or interests. The superficialness I describe does not refer to a tendency toward triviality but to the responsiveness of James's characters to the surface of social life and its webs of signification.[10] Vitalism, I have suggested, helps provide a psychological model that makes allowances for a character's self-inventive capacity while still pegging selfhood to nontrivial forms of material and social constraint.

James's depicted selves are in some ways so unlike the standard substantialist conceptions of character that they have led critics to dispute their reality as selves or at least to dispute their reality as distinct psychological agents with contingent interests. Instead, they assume that James's protagonists are formal devices that James deploys for his own compositional priorities. At best, this leaves James's novelistic resolutions as avoidance strategies or substitutes for full engagement with human problems. In what follows, I question this view, which puts a wedge between the novel's aesthetic interests and its psychological ones and deposes character from being the ultimate seat of reckoning for negotiations of conflict in James. Instead, I argue that James adheres to the novelistic law that solutions to social conflicts and dilemmas have to be legible to the principal characters concerned; indeed, we would have to imagine that such solutions are experienced by them. Again, James can be seen as a realist in this regard. He may dissolve the standard of consistency traditionally applied to moral entities, but he refashions their modes of unity and individuation in ways that are unexpected yet ultimately psychologically and ethically compelling.

The challenges that critics mount to Jamesian character have tended to veer in contrary directions, which one could label "arelational" and "hyperrelational" accounts of consciousness. Leo Bersani offers an influential version of the former; Sharon Cameron, the latter. Yet where they diverge is ultimately less revealing than where they converge. Both critics end up claiming that James's solutions do not obey realist strictures, whereas I would argue that he breaks ground for a new kind of realism.

According to Bersani, James "dramatizes the possibility of an intentionality unsupported by motive, that is, of a desiring self so responsive and so indefinite that it is created entirely (but never limited) by the responses to its performances" (*A Future for Astyanax*, 137). Bersani suggests that this desiring self diffuses itself into what amounts to a set of linguistic performances detached from psychology.[11] His argument contributes to a critical inclination, evident already from the time of character criticism, that either celebrates or decries—but in any case, insists on—James's subordination of any single fictive personage's interest or point of view to a larger aesthetic order.[12] Language in James "would no longer reveal character or refer to desires 'behind' words" (137); the "I" merely becomes a "neutral territory" that is "by nature always 'outside' any particular self" (146).[13]

Cameron contends instead that consciousness is given the power to define rather than attune itself to the situation around it. Jamesian consciousness is so all-encompassing and domineering that it swallows up any opposing perspective or interest.[14] In *The Golden Bowl*, argues Cameron, Maggie imposes the terms of her vision, projecting her own understandings while denying anyone the capacity to share in the vision (*Thinking in Henry James*, 102). Because James's characters do not obey limits, they do not amount to plausible psychological agents. Cameron thus sees herself as working "against the traditional account of consciousness as psychologized" (170–171). She prefers a poststructuralist methodology.[15] But her assumption that a psychologized consciousness is necessarily understood as "internal, centered, circumscribed, [and] fixed" (170) ignores many alternative psychological theories of the period, including William James's. Like other critics, she presumes that such characters as Maggie know exactly what they want and proceed to get it. I would suggest that in fact Maggie has only makeshift knowledge and must learn how to accommodate the reality of the affair she confronts rather than force reality to be conceived in such a way as to accommodate her.

Having already proposed that personality is not the only means of generating psychic consistency, I would add that another, indeed suppler, means is revealed by vitalist psychology. Bergson famously argues that mental states "continually [swell] with duration" (*Creative Evolution*, 2) and that there is no substratum to reality, no "impassive ego" (4), to unite separate phenomenal manifestations of the same self. His claim bears obvious relation to William James's original formulation of the "stream of consciousness," a metaphor that describes what is continuous and "without breach, crack, or division" (*Principles of Psychology* 1:237) in psychic life. Instead of positing an abstract sameness at the core of identity, William James, like Bergson, propounds psychic models grounded only in continuity. Indeed, such connections help clarify the mutual affinities that each felt for the other. They suggest a common vitalistic orientation.[16] For his part, Bergson suggests that "an ego which does not change does not *endure*" (*Creative Evolution*, 4), playing on the etymological propinquity to the term "duration" and suggesting that only things with a plastic quality can survive the test of time.

Less often cited, though integral to understanding what William James means by "stream of thought, of consciousness, or of subjective life" (1:239), is this passage in which he explains the form of coordination among thoughts:

> Each pulse of cognitive consciousness, each Thought, dies away and is replaced by another. The other, among the things it knows, knows its own predecessor, greets it, saying: "Thou art *mine*, and part of the same self with me." Each later Thought, knowing and including thus the Thoughts which went before, is the final receptacle—and appropriating them is the final owner—of all that they contain and own. Each Thought is thus born an owner, and dies owned, transmitting whatever it realized as its Self to its own later proprietor. (*Principles of Psychology* 1.339)

In a sense, what William James makes central is the interested relationship that thoughts have to their objects. Consciousness is not an "entity" or private content of a subject's experience but an orientation or interest-conferring function, as James clarifies in a subsequent essay ("Does 'Consciousness' Exist?" in *Essays, Comments, and Reviews*, 3–4). As such, it resists objectification. As Robert D. Richardson glosses William James, "We should have our eye on the process as well as—perhaps more than—the product, on the path as well as the goal" (*William James*, 235). A stream of thought, then, is a method of relating or "owning" in which a thought directs itself to its object, appropriates it, and in turn becomes appropriated. First in a position of structuring experience and framing objects in the world, a thought later dies and becomes an object to be framed.

A stream of thought is nothing but a circuit of relations within the world, through which thoughts gain their coherence. For this reason, consciousness is not an interior condition. As a proto-phenomenologist, William James moves from an eighteenth- and nineteenth-century picture of the psyche as a self-contained receptacle for mental content (ideas) toward a model of consciousness whose consistency comes from being directed onto objects in the world.[17] He understands intentionality not as a one-way process but as a reciprocal activity that does as much to determine what conscious agents are as it does to construct and give shape to what they take in. Transcendental notions of subjectivity take for granted that one has a core of unchanging structures that underlies and gives shape to one's activity, while James sees activity, particularly the activity of a thinking process, as the basis from which one arrives at structures (including, I would argue, structures of interest and desire).

William and Henry James share a conception of reality built on the insistence, in Jonathan Levin's terms, "that nothing has its identity in itself. Everything is instead what its dynamic web of relations constitutes it as" (*Poetics of Transition*, 122). Thus, Henry James remarked to Hugh Walpole shortly after finishing *The Ambassadors* that "the whole thing . . . is a picture of relations" (*Letters of Henry James* 2:245)—relations, I would add, that are principally created and maintained in thought. Despite their disagreements, both brothers understand thought to be a reality-producing event.[18] Agents are not left passive in the face of a priori structures that determine their capacity to think (as Kantian transcendentalists maintain) or passive in the face of a world of objects whose structures organize their experience (the assertion of Lockean empiricism). Consciousness involves a whole series of receptive tendencies—effort, attention, perception, and imagination—the activity of which seems to promote an active attunement to things. In *The Golden Bowl*, when Maggie breathes to her friend Fanny her astonishing knowledge of the affair between her husband and Charlotte, James remarks that "the situation had changed . . . by the outbreak of the definite" (346). This banal evidence of the power of thought gains considerable poignancy, however, when we realize that even definite knowledge is merely a preliminary to establishing new and as yet undefined relations. Thus, Maggie and Fanny have to keep up a thought process in which possibilities are encompassed, absorbed, and followed up on. Knowledge is not the endpoint of this process but an invitation to think further and eventually to act. James emphasizes that the world is not given but made, fashioned.

One consciousness is differentiated from another in William James's account by the particular responsibility that we each have for our own thoughts and deeds—that is, the particular ownership that we take of thoughts and deeds, the feeling of warmth this imparts, the range of special responsibilities entailed by reflective self-consciousness, and the deliberative commitments entailed therein. Oddly, his brother's fiction tests the validity of these principles by presenting characters who refuse to express interests altogether detached from those of their intimates, who suspend action, and who even decline to accept explicit or public responsibility for their offenses and deeds. According to the philosopher Robert Pippin, the blurred character of psychic life—the feeling that mental activities are "somewhere 'between' and not 'in' persons" (*Henry James and Modern Moral Life*, 64)—causes James's characters to lose their psychological and moral sense of orientation.

Pippin's description of James is in many ways apt, and his charge turns out to be a hard one to dispose of outright. Of course, one could argue, as I already have, that open-ended and flexible interests may be able to accommodate other people's interests without breaking into conflict, but this seems to settle too quickly the points where overlap is not immediately possible and not even welcome (such as when one marries on behalf of the interests of a third person, as Adam Verver arguably does in *The Golden Bowl*). Though Pippin does not deny that James delivers a plausible moral psychology, he worries that his characters are insufficiently individuated. The open-ended nature of their attitudes makes them too dependent on others for the meaning of their identities and interests, threatening "to dissolve the integrity of any self into its social constitution" (*Henry James and Modern Moral Life*, 126). In the modern world where social norms are increasingly unstable and unable to generate confidence in their authority, Pippin thinks such extravagantly interconnected interests lead to a "great moral crash" (77). This is particularly true when these socially negotiated identities are deferred, as they are in James, to some indeterminate future when characters can finally settle on a discrete conception of their own well-being.[19] According to Pippin, such moments never seem to arrive.

Pippin stresses the need for clear guideposts for enabling social exchange.[20] But for James, I would suggest, such clarity fixes interests and forecloses on the possibility that these interests can be made to change so as to accommodate the interests of other parties. The changes that James explores in his fiction may prevent protagonists from falling back on convenient interpretations and preconceived attitudes, but they do not stop them from taking a directed course of action or, once they have understood their situation, from drawing fine distinctions between their own interests and responsibilities and those of others. In other words, it is easy to overstate the degree to which his characters are unbounded and in flux. James is not the author of limitless self-expansion, as Bersani and Cameron would have us think. James simply insists that all interests are social in nature, although "social" does not necessarily mean symmetrically apportioned among parties. Sometimes James's characters go too far in the direction of suspending their own initial interests and responsibilities, but their stances represent the extreme edge of a psychology that upends so many truisms about American individualism.

I want to suggest, then, that deferral of responsibility is not tantamount to an abdication of it. To appreciate this, we need to understand better the nature of the suspensions that James explores in his fiction. As the next section, on *The Ambassadors*, will show, the process that allows agents to change to accommodate new interests is not immediate. It takes place through an affective process that helps teach characters what activates their agency, and on a basic level this practical sense is what defines their interests. Vitalist philosophers have paid special attention to the elasticity of this process, and James's conception of agency is broadly vitalistic. Bergson, for example, does not restrict personal interest to a subset of immediate and predictable needs. Because life has no single teleology, its trajectory is not logically predetermining and leads to a great variety of transforming ends.[21] Human beings "have the power to value the useless," Bergson writes, which enables us to withdraw "from the action of the moment" (*Matter and Memory*, 83). In so doing, we bring to bear a much wider range of psychic resources, which in turn proliferates the interests we are capable of pursuing. Bergson is thinking specifically of attitudes of heightened detachment that are associated with aesthetic life, but I find that his theoretical models can be applied usefully to ethical life as well. In the coming section I discuss how James offers an intricate characterological basis from which to understand how formulations of self-interest emerge affectively and how they may be assessed ethically.

AESTHETIC INTERESTS AND CHARACTER FORMATION

In *The Ambassadors* and *The Wings of the Dove*, James presents characters who variously defer, delay, and at crucial moments renounce direct pursuit of economic gain. On the surface, such gestures might seem to reflect a wholesale abnegation of their interests on moral-theoretical grounds. But we can view these acts as instances of shifting interests. In this section, I look at *The Ambassadors*, whose protagonist, Lambert Strether, struggles to define and enlarge his conception of self-interest in a way that is character forming. (In the next section, I contrast Strether's enlarged conception of self-interest with Kate Croy's self-conscious attempt to narrow or contract her self-interest in *The Wings of the Dove.*)

Strether, who is tasked with the repatriation of Chad Newsome, his potential son-in-law, spends a great deal of time in *The Ambassadors* preventing himself from drawing his ambassadorial mission to a too hasty close, even though his potential marriage and therefore his financial interest encourage urgency. Before deciding conclusively what his own interests are in the matter, he sets about discovering what Chad's interests are in Europe and by extension what his own interests might be there. It is not that he relinquishes all personal motives (an impossible task). But his motives—or perhaps one might say his inclinations—are influenced less by any instrumental object at hand (the attainment of which he has deferred) than by his calculation of the kind of person he would be if he did not allow Chad the space to decide for himself how to proceed. James suggests that an individual cannot resolve an ethical dilemma solely by considering the consequences of an act, unless she or he also treats as one of those consequences the self that is created or expressed in the action. Thus, the narrator asserts that Strether "had often enough wondered to what degree his interference might pass for interested; so that there was no want of luxury in letting it be seen whenever he could that he didn't interfere" (113). Strether attempts to project disinterestedness and to articulate its significance for himself, and the attempt gives shape to the decisions he has made or is making. This character squirms away from any identity that might classify him and by extension classify how he sees. His resulting detachment allows him multiple possible relations to the world on the condition that he must withdraw from the subset of relations most likely to dominate: the relations defined by use, practical necessity, and considerations of public benefit and social good (or at least by what generally counts as good).

The distinctive course of development that Strether undergoes as he generates new interests brings into play his entire affective life. As James declares in his preface to *The Ambassadors*, Strether is "a belated man of the world" whose moral scheme is bound to "break down on any approach to vivid facts" (7). The process that James sets in motion for Strether—by having him go to Europe to rescue Chad, only to find that his image of wicked Paris is different from the one he actually encounters—is a process that reorients his scheme of values and causes him to act in ways that are unprecedented for him. And yet Strether's capacity to change is predicated on his having a discriminating imagination. Just as important, Strether needs privacy: sanctuary from public life and the attitudes and modes of judgment that belong to it. In other words, Strether does not abandon *all* conception of what is of paramount moral concern. Rather, he enters a situation whose range of considerations is so large and indeterminate that it overwhelms his sense of cause and consequence and therefore overturns the social grammars of moral calculation or means-ends rationality.

Initially, Strether is preoccupied with how to regard Chad as the object of his custodial attention. At first, he is astounded "in every throb of his consciousness" by the impression that Chad is "so totally different" (95) from what he had expected. He finds himself unable to answer Chad's question as to whether he looks improved because with "an absolutely *new* quantity to deal with one simply couldn't know" (95). "There was," he thinks, "no computing at all what the young man before him would think or feel or say on any subject whatever" (96). Given enough time, one might think that Strether's new impressions would sink in, whereupon he would be in a position to decide whether to renew his appeal to remove Chad from the maleficent ambiance of Paris or to give up the effort. But even after an extended period has elapsed, Strether finds that his impressions are too intricate to be grouped into one overbalancing consideration: he "took [Chad] in again—he was always taking him in and yet finding that parts of him still remained out; though even thus his image showed through a mist of other things" (186).

We might wonder why Strether cannot rely on a determined set of ethical norms to appraise the situation, especially because the novel's tacit worry—that Chad is engaging in adultery—ranks as a cliché, not exactly "unprecedented." Indeed, James frets about the platitudes of his theme in the novel's preface. The treatment of Paris as a tempting ground for Americans seeking temptation, he remarks, is "one of the vulgarest in the world" (7). What spares his novel such a verdict is the "complexity of relations" (8) in it, he claims. After all, Strether's interest extends not only to himself and to Mrs. Newsome (Chad's dowager mother and Strether's ostensible fiancée) but to Chad and his friend Little Bilham as well as to Mlle de Vionnet and Mme de Vionnet (once Strether surmises the nature of Chad's affair). But these relations are not static, and Strether has trouble keeping pace with the changes. The evolving makeup of these relations constantly changes his sense of the picture at hand. He ends up being concerned for the welfare of each according to a separate standard of imaginative investment. Even as Strether attempts to size up Chad, he is forced to find ways of marking salient points of interest for himself out of an ambient background of never-ending relations. He must also contemplate the note of warning intended for him in his recent telegram from Mrs. Newsome.

Strether struggles to maintain a pragmatic handhold on his situation: he "didn't, as he talked, absolutely follow himself; he only knew he was clutching his thread and that he held it from moment to moment a little tighter" (164). James's presumption is that people are guided by impulses and thrust into action before they have a chance to register cognitively all the relations forming around them. He seems particularly attuned to moments of incipience, to the way characters come to focus on a thing before they know exactly what they are focusing on, or why. How characters seize on certain kinds of salience, how they settle on one set of approximate possibilities at the expense of another, and finally how they orient or adhere to their choices as they attempt to reconfigure their current situation—this is what matters to James. He is preoccupied by a character's manner of attending to a thing rather than the strictly theoretical question of what the character knows or believes. In this respect, James reminds us of Bergson, who prefers action-oriented criteria to epistemic criteria for gauging situations.[22] James and Bergson would agree, I think, that to give primacy to people's beliefs or to fixed assessments of a situation is to live at an intellectual distance from the world.

It may be odd to emphasize that James values action when Strether, who spends most of the novel doing nothing so much as observing others, seems to resort mainly to his faculty of perception. But for James, perceptions are much closer to actions than to mental representations. And they are intimately entwined with a person's interests. For Bergson, the evolutionary trace of our practical relation to the world is evident in our faculty of perception. What one does when one perceives is to project onto objects that surround oneself the shadow of the body's "eventual or possible actions" (*Matter and Memory*, 22) on them. In this view, a perception is always halfway toward an intention or a tendency toward action, or something clarified by an intention or tendency. For Bergson, the emphasis is on how people interrogate their interests by inclining to act in a particular way and thus alighting on intentions or working them out. Perceptions isolate and simplify experience, putting complicated relations into useful shorthand that allows one to make difficult decisions. If Strether relies on his affectively shaped interests to help him sort through his perceptions, Bergson's theoretical models may assist us in understanding the precise nature of this sorting function that interests have.[23] We can clarify how what Strether finds "interesting" might make possible the advantages that we refer to as "interests."

As an organism grows increasingly capable of delaying the interval between stimulus (or perception) and response, its agency expands, and it is "subject to more and more distant influences" (*Matter and Memory*, 32). Our affects help us negotiate among our interests: they dispose us to a range of possibilities and suggest an attitude proper to our aims. An affect (pain, in Bergson's example) turns an "indifferent spectator" into someone who acquires "a vital interest" (55).[24] Feeling guides a person toward certain ends above others. Out of the endless variety of merely possible things to do, an affect makes an individual attentive to one set of possibilities over another and thus gives force or efficacy to an interest.

As we have seen, James tends to present changing interests as a process that takes place during intervals of suspended agency. These intervals allow individuals to reinvent themselves. What does this look like? *The Ambassadors* provides an example about halfway through, when in a strange turn Strether asks Chad to stay in Paris (hitherto he had been asking him to return to America), although doing so threatens to bring Mrs. Newsome's ultimatum down on him (either he returns, with or without Chad, or she sends Chad's sister to the rescue). He is apparently willing to court her mistrust over how he manages the situation. Of course, if Chad returns, as he now seems ready to do, then Strether must return. Suddenly, Strether wants Chad to help him delay, and Chad does not understand why. He asks whether Strether has sent a response to his mother's telegram and to the ultimatum:

> "No, I've done nothing yet."
>
> "Were you waiting to see me?"
>
> "No, not that."
>
> "Only waiting"—and Chad, with this, had a smile for him—"to see Miss Gostrey?"
>
> "No—not even Miss Gostrey. I wasn't waiting to see any one. I had only waited, till now, to make up my mind—in complete solitude. . . . Have therefore a little more patience with me. Remember," Strether went on, "that that's what you originally asked *me* to have. I've had it, you see, and you see what has come of it. Stay on with me."
>
> Chad looked grave. "How much longer?"
>
> "Well, till I make you a sign." (189–190)

Chad is feeling Strether out, as it were, looking to discover the reason for his abrupt "change of position" (190)—whether it may be himself (Chad), romantic affection for Maria Gostrey, or something else. With respect to Maria Gostrey, Strether's interests become clearer as he begins to exclude considerations not immediately relevant to him. Meanwhile, Strether pleads patience. He has felt "the charm of life" in Paris too "immensely": "You've helped me so to feel it that that surely needn't surprise you" (190). Ambivalently, Chad agrees to wait. Strether reports to Miss Gostrey: "That I wanted to stay seemed to *interest* him, and he acted on that" (194; emphasis mine). It is not any strong affect that binds them. Indeed, the very weakness and indeterminacy of the interests at issue are what preserve the freedom of each to make choices according to their own particular calculus of benefits.

As Strether questions his original mission to Paris and struggles to figure out how to proceed, he buys time to work out his new interests. He has to delay to determine which of his interests engage his attention most decisively. There are, he knows, more people at issue than Chad and himself—including the unnamed but not unthought-of Mme de Vionnet, who so concerns (and intrigues) Strether that he hardly dares to speak her name. The world of relations that Chad opens up for him offers many new considerations, and Strether relies on his own feeling to help him weigh them. It is worth noting how much narrative energy James grants to this process of mental negotiation and adjustment, which conveys emotional response in a much more intricate way than by description alone. Strether feels it necessary to enter into a proper understanding with Chad. In this case as elsewhere, James's characters measure the parameters of their standing with respect to each other: they deflect and absorb each other's solicitations, and they refer their companions' assertions and demands—as well as the silences, bridling, and exasperation—back to the possible actions at their disposal. Their feelings allow them to navigate and amplify points of interest.

At such moments affects trigger specific modifications in the individuals undergoing them. They allow people to refine their inchoate interests. For Bergson, an affection is a specialized kind of movement that precedes and readies the body for its executions. Before an action comes about as an effort directed at things in the world and meant to influence them, an affection occurs as the body's "actual effort upon itself" (*Matter and Memory*, 57)—effort being the body's way of adjusting to possibilities, aligning its powers with them.[25] "Consciousness means virtual action" (50). When people become immersed in a thing, they attune their attention; they translate attitudes and tendencies into movements, working themselves up to the furtherances and hindrances to which a situation gives way, yielding and resisting, circling around, "impress[ing] particular attitudes upon the body" (13–14). For Bergson, the body is a locus of agency, capable of sensing the effect of the things around it. An affection represents the body's "power to absorb" (56) those effects, which are not so distant as to be experienced out there "in the world" (subject to the "reflecting" power of perception), nor so immediate as to demand action. Positioned midway between a perception and an action, an affection represents a postponement of response long enough for the individual to alter or fine-tune a sense of his or her nascent interests.

We have seen that Bergson and James grant adjustments of the self an affective dimension, but to understand why these adjustments are seen as intimately linked to an individual's psychological identity, we need to turn to James's brother, William. Though he does not talk about interests at large, William James returns again and again in *The Principles of Psychology* to what I would call a feeling of personal concern, seen as a basic dimension of psychological experience:

> If we divide all possible physiological acts into *adjustments* and *executions*, the nuclear self would be the adjustments collectively considered. . . . In the midst of psychic change they are the permanent core of turnings-towards and turnings-from, of yieldings and arrests, which naturally seem central and interior in comparison with the foreign matters, *apropos* to which they occur. (1:302)

"Executions" are more distant from the self because they are in some sense detachable. They achieve a kind of separateness from the body or the person, and they are more immediately correlated to purposes outside the acts themselves. "Adjustments," however, are the felt activity of the self-in-process as it goes about perceiving, sensing, or discerning other centers of interest.

Henry James may be one of the most cerebral novelists, but he shares with William James, with Bergson, and, as I will suggest, with Nietzsche a conception of the body as an intimate site of affective regulation and hence of the production of interests, using corporeal metaphors to describe the calibrations and upsurges in his characters' thought or speech. Michael Levenson provides some examples, phrases from *The Ambassadors* such as "she liked to get it all out of him," and he "took her up." These metaphors that pop up in the midst of dialogue evoke "bold physical gesture" and occasionally a latent sexual connotation, exposing "the shadows which the physical world casts upon the smooth plane of polite discourse" (*Modernism and the Fate of Individuality*, 16). For Levenson, James's metaphors do not actually displace the body; rather, they harbor a residual trace of the "bodily world" that is otherwise "neglected, suppressed, tamed or concealed" (17). Indeed, I would argue that in these instances James gives corporeal weight to the emotional adjustments that his characters make in thought or speech. "He fell back" (*The Ambassadors*, 26), "she took it in" (40), "she threw out" (47), or from *The Golden Bowl*, "she wound up" (179), "he fell in" (182), "he brought out" (183). These phrasal verbs, so conspicuous a feature of James's late style, leave their prepositions to dangle. Technically, the terminal words are not prepositions at all but particles, conventional signs that alter the meaning of the verbs to which they are conjoined. But in James they assume a conspicuous physicality. The phrases almost literalize by means of gesture the relation between an action indicated and the position, course, or approach to it (the "pre-position"). They function as signs of affective access or direction. Grammatically, the verbs are not wholly intransitive. The quotations they introduce function as implied indirect objects (he came out *with* the statement; she wound up *with* the idea). At the same time, they do not refer with specificity but leave open the object of reference. As utterances, they seem very purposely not to complete themselves, merely pointing out or pointing to. In so doing, they tie what are in essence physical attitudes to the mental adjustments of characters whose bodies serve as a resonating structures, absorbing and reflecting their perceived relations to other characters. Feeling in this instance gives direction to the body's possible actions and therefore helps to hone its ongoing interests. Like James's syntax, the feeling that is presented signals a leap into the indeterminate.

Nietzsche refers to the will itself as an affect or feeling because it expresses a certain tendency or vector of action: it is composed of "a plurality of sensations, namely, the sensation of the state '*away from which*,' the sensation of the state '*towards which*,' the sensations of this 'from' and 'towards' themselves," each complex accompanied by muscular activity (*Beyond Good and Evil*, 25). Rather than treating the will as a monolithic edifice, Nietzsche regards it as a composite of permeable forces. Human beings affected (influenced, touched, impinged upon) by some order of circumstance are not fully individuated, are not in a settled relation to what is around them. Indeed, insofar as affect entails an open-ended relation, it pulls agents in a direction away from themselves, renegotiating the very boundaries of selfhood with each new exposure. Feeling is the way in which we register and give place to all that diverts us from ourselves. Indeed, the body, around whose contours one's selfhood emerges, is not a self-contained image, but a fluid synthesis of relations to the world, whose promises it must compass and absorb, and whose threats it must dodge and reflect in order to function. As Bergson puts it, this body has a virtual character: it occupies a "zone of indetermination," compassing many possible actions before actualizing one of them. This elasticity increases the power of individual agency.

In *The Ambassadors*, Strether's capacity to prolong the moment before he must act on his interests allows him new, more expansive ways of relating to others. The weakness and relative open-endedness of his interests turn out to strengthen his hand, not weaken it, inasmuch as they increase the virtual repertoire of his actions. Only superficially does the diffuseness of his interests diminish his agency. His affective adjustments correspond to an effort exerted on himself to alter the range of his choices. As I have already indicated, James models Strether's ethical response on an aesthetic attitude. Kant might have labeled it a "disinterested" reaction, but the vocabulary is misleading if thought to denote an evacuation of all interest. Nietzsche objected to Kant's terminology because it emphasized the negative. He referred to "contemplation without interest" as a "nonsensical absurdity" (*On the Genealogy of Morals*, 119). Ever cautious about the ascetic impulse within philosophy, Nietzsche insisted on *more*: "The *more* affects we allow to speak about one thing, the *more* eyes, different eyes, we can use to observe one thing, the more complete will our 'concept' of this thing, our 'objectivity,' be" (119). Strether's capacity to connect his own interests to other people's interests without losing focus or tripping up on the complexities of his situation increases his receptivity to the range of contingencies that shape and influence his capacity to act.

The discriminations that Strether develops as part of his ethically oriented response have a specific affinity with aesthetic judgment. Strether cannot come to an appreciation of his interests without having an affective reaction that precedes and guides his actions. His calculations do not take place in the abstract but emerge out of the specific constellation of circumstances that call forth a response in him. J. M. Bernstein brings attention to the parallel between moral insight and "the familiar aesthetic pattern of an imposing perception finding approval in a felt response" (*Adorno*, 23). What the two forms of insight have in common is an experience of passivity before an event that precedes any theoretical determination of it. I would add that this experience of passivity is not passivity itself. Verging on the contemplative polarity, it bleeds into action, allowing one to adapt to an environment through ad hoc adjustments and, crucially, to change oneself so as to reach a richer range and power of action. Nonetheless, as Bernstein insists, the response does involve a self that is the product of an unprompted but directly felt judgment, which then orients the self: "Approval is a 'spontaneous achievement of the self' in that the self that does the approving is in part a product of its act of approval" (*Adorno*, 26). In Bergsonian terms, the interests or possibilities of action perceived by Strether remain strictly virtual, lifeless, except as they make their urgency felt within his situation as the outgrowth of his rapport with others.

The judgments at stake are not felt so immediately as to be compulsive. Like the exclamation "this is interesting" that Sianne Ngai considers a preliminary expression of aesthetic judgment—one that "toggles" between aesthetic and nonaesthetic categories—these judgments involve a feeling whose low intensity makes it hard "to say whether it counts as satisfaction or dissatisfaction, feels good or bad to feel (and in contrast to the unequivocal feelings of pleasure/displeasure that give rise to judgments of the beautiful/disgusting)" ("Merely Interesting," 788). The interests described by Ngai as particular intensities that are not yet qualified afford one only a vague feeling as a corroborating reason for the judgment; in other words, they engage aesthetic response but do not allow one to make a strong distinction between aesthetic judgment and other forms of judgment.

For James, the aesthetic attitude is not simply a matter of enjoying one's sensations or contemplating beautiful things.[26] In the first place, it concerns a way of seeing or approaching the world beyond any specific object under consideration. In the second place, it requires disengagement from instrumentalized pursuits, which leaves a person free to exercise his or her imagination in fresh ways, to draw connections among sensuously understood particulars. This is exactly what James emphasizes in his preface to *The Ambassadors*, when he describes Strether's awakening to the question of whether he has, in his working life, squandered his chances to really *live*: "*Would* there yet perhaps be time for reparation?—reparation, that is, for the injury done his character . . . ? The answer to which is that he now at all events *sees*; so that the business of my tale and the march of my action . . . is just my demonstration of this process of vision" (34). James thinks that Strether's eventual disengagement from his ambassadorial role accords him a measure of freedom—a difficult, uncertain freedom—because it also obliges him to give up the values that he has hitherto relied on and to relinquish any hope of the economic gain he might have achieved. The freedom to "see" in this way comes for Strether at tremendous personal cost, though it also affords him the chance to transform himself, to reconceive his idea of what it means to make a life.

Even Kant thought that aesthetic reflective judgment, though it might take its occasion from an object or a scene from nature, refers itself to the "*free lawfulness* of the imagination" whose harmony or "free play" gives rise to the experience of beauty (*Critique of Judgment*, 1.22.240). He considered it a mistake to connect aesthetic judgment to a quality within the object rather than to the mental state it provokes. Aesthetic experience, which is feeling-based, is therefore ultimately about the self, the form its cognitive powers assume when it refuses to integrate things under any preestablished prism. The freedom to which Kant refers pushes one to improvise a train of thought or, if one is an artist, a train of action, which in Kant's terms is "purposive." These actions or reactions do not follow a definite plan or specify their own ends. Rather, they are capable of modifying the self by modifying the self's intentionality. "Kantian aesthetics," remarks Charles Altieri, "affords crucial resources for developing an expressivist psychology" (*Subjective Agency*, 104) by shaping "a conative sense that is more abstract and persistent than any of the specific contents it attracts" (108).

The novel ends with Strether's return to Woollett. He neither consents to enjoy Paris, carrying on as he has been, nor does he yield to Maria Gostrey's romantic solicitations or make up with Mrs. Newsome. He abjures all *apparent* interests in order, as he says, "[t]o be right" (*The Ambassadors*, 346). He does not wish to be seen as having benefited materially or erotically from his sojourn, which would then cast his benevolent counsel toward Chad in the wrong light. He insists on his autonomy to act without regard for his personal advantage, but it is an autonomy that does not finally make a distinction between "personal" desires and "social" interests. The former merges with the latter as his influence over others extends to include relations that have a weak relation to his individual needs. Strether's final act of renunciation, significant as it is, is not the determining measure of his freedom but the final phase of a long process. The culminating act of his "process of vision" is not to abjure all interest but to take account of his experience by constructing new "disinterested" interests, new second-order relations to the world. Strether thus creates a self whose multiplied consciousness is intensified in the act of renunciation.

Strether's attitude verges on being self-negating, but he skirts that danger in a way that makes him, I think, a fitting representative of vitalist agency. He preserves his interests even as he denies himself personal benefits enormously important to him. It is crucial to the psychology that James presents that Strether not shy away from his interests on abstract moral grounds. Indeed, my contention is that according to James there are no purely moral motivations (that is, rational imperatives separate from personal motivating grounds) because the self acting or sacrificing is always one of the products of the action and not an irrelevant side concern.[27] Any attempt at self-abnegation would express only a reactive tendency, one that would dangerously deny the self the exercise of its powers. This in essence is what Nietzsche calls "slave morality," whereby one searches for extrinsic but unacknowledged approval for one's deeds as a form of consolation for powerlessness and therefore "separates strength from expressions of strength" (*Genealogy of Morals*, 45). What prevents Strether's actions from being a form of masochistic asceticism is that he thinks that ultimately his self-exertions will augment his powers (he remains clear-eyed about the constraints involved, however).

WILL TO CONSISTENCY

Strether's peculiarly vicarious forms of interest are not for everyone: his diffuse conception of what defines advantage is bound to an old man's comparative indifference to material accumulation and sexual need. Therefore, it is worth turning to *The Wings of the Dove* to see how far two youthful protagonists, Kate Croy and Merton Densher, can go in deferring or suspending their judgments of right and wrong, giving them time to assimilate what is good for others into what is good for themselves without diminishing their character. James sets up a scenario in which the two pledge their commitment to each other and concoct a plan for Densher to marry Milly Theale. Because Kate is certain that Milly is dying, she assumes that this arrangement will be temporary. Kate's intentions may be quite definite in themselves, but James is concerned with them only insofar as they are activated and modified by their placement in a complex situation that shapes them across time. Kate's persisting in her intention becomes a reflection of a wondrously opportunistic will that we see crystallizing in the midst of her experience. Before the couple completes their plan, James sets the two of them at odds, contrasting the inflexibility of Kate's pursuit of self-interest with Densher's urge to alter those interests when confronted with profound human dependencies. James reveals through Densher's eyes the disastrous effect of Kate's will to consistency. *The Ambassadors* and *The Wings of the Dove*, perched on either side of an extreme, have at least this in common: both involve characters who insist on the plasticity of their interests once they enter into the perspectives of others.

In *The Wings of the Dove*, as elsewhere, James suggests that individuals and communities prioritize their interests in a way that is extraordinarily sensitive to local situational differences. Further, he implies that, when people are interdependent, their interests, freely pursued, extend in both directions. In his preface to *The Wings of the Dove*, James emphasizes the intersecting interests of Kate and Densher on one side and Milly Theale on the other. James tells us that we see Milly "through the successive windows of other people's interest in her" (*The Wings of the Dove*, 16). Perhaps surprisingly, however, James goes out of his way to underscore Milly's agency rather than her victimhood, highlighting her own role in the drama that ensues. Densher and Kate are entangled in her reciprocal interest in them: they are "tempted and charmed; bribed away, it may even be, from more prescribed and natural orbits, inheriting from their connexion with her strange difficulties and still stranger opportunities, confronted with rare questions and called upon for new discriminations" (preface to *The Wings of the Dove*, 5). And Milly the sick heiress is not wholly unaware of the attention she inspires. Indeed, she appeals to Kate and Densher—even coerces them—on the grounds of "particular human interests" (5). She therefore bears some responsibility by virtue of her own profound needs and the power she holds over others.

As his narrative proceeds and Kate's assumptions are tested, James postpones the finality of moral conclusions. The intelligence with which she and Densher pursue their rather sensational stratagem would seem to validate their aims, for they accommodate Milly's needs in ways that enable more inclusive social benefits—at least, up to a point. And they exercise their power of agency in a manner that demonstrates their self-inventiveness. We note Kate's "pure talent for life, as distinguished from [Densher's] own, a poor weak thing of the occasion" (*The Wings of the Dove*, 281). She seems to view her flamboyant pursuit of her own self-interest as somehow serving Milly. She remarks that Milly will live out her last days lifted up by Densher's kindness and then entrusts the rest of the affair to Milly. "Leave the rest to *her*" (239), she tells Densher, thus effacing her own part in the affair. Kate implies that Milly does not *want* to see the tie or bond between her and Densher, that Milly has an interest in not seeing that she cannot acknowledge to herself. Kate's view is that she is simply helping Milly do something she otherwise would not: take a risk whose unprecedented nature will intensify the remainder of her life. Rather than exempt themselves from the social logic of accepted ethical prescription, Kate and Densher bring to bear a wide range of calculations that are social in nature, but whose specificity and interconnection are unique to their circumstance, giving them license to validate their mutual undertaking.

Densher's attitude is much less assured than Kate's, but he seems open to the possibility that marrying Milly would not be a bad thing if it succeeded in bestowing on her something that she intensely wants. We might note that Kate seems from the outset more willing than Densher to risk Milly's potential injury. Densher remains passive, becoming the agent-representative of the narrative's suspensions as he submits to Kate's superior will. Kate instrumentalizes Milly on self-interested grounds and does not claim otherwise, but she does insist that her special efforts to accommodate Milly's interests over time, understood on *separate* terms, might compensate, allowing her and Densher to keep their self-respect. Kate's interests are not open-ended. In this sense her attitude is the opposite of Strether's open-ended self-interestedness as he expresses it in *The Ambassadors*. By persisting till the bitter end with her strategic design, Kate tries to fix the world in the image of what she wants, inuring herself to change rather than accommodating herself to it. At the moment when her powers seem most confident, assertive, and self-assured, they threaten to shut her up within herself, blocking all influences capable of possessing her.

On the question of how to understand this fixity in Kate's desire, there is some critical disagreement. Although Slavoj Žižek recognizes Kate's immovable doggedness, he refuses to fault her for it. Indeed, he celebrates her demystified attitude to the extent that it enables her to void all fantasies of fulfillment and emotional plenitude. In his terms, James "is a true antipode . . . to Proust's 'Bergsonism'" insofar as Kate's emptiness refuses to respect the process of "becoming" over "being" ("Kate's Choice, or the Materialism of Henry James," 289). To my mind, however, Žižek's willfully counterintuitive reading—he celebrates Kate as the "only ethical figure in the novel" (306)[28]—fails to recognize the nature of the harm that Kate creates.

Densher becomes the focus of the novel when he can no longer repress his doubts about Kate's characterization of the situation, because at this point he becomes "interesting" to himself and therefore to the narrative: "In default of being right with himself he had meanwhile, for one thing, the interest of seeing—and quite for the first time in his life—whether, on a given occasion, that might be quite so necessary to happiness as was commonly assumed and as he had up to his moment never doubted" (*The Wings of the Dove*, 285). The interest that Densher experiences at this moment—ill-defined as it is—opens up an affective process that allows him to reassess the coherence of his values—that is, the advantages and patterns of significance that have guided him hitherto. In this moment of suspension, he has not yet determined how the situation affects him except by advancing several lines of consideration. The development that James traces is expressly connected to Densher's character because the worry Densher has begun to feel directly impinges on his sense of himself.[29] As James points out, Densher's wonder at his predicament coincides with a sense that his "general plasticity" (284) of feeling is jeopardized. Later, when Densher considers whether he is afraid of having to explain to others his compromised role as

Milly's suitor, he realizes "soon enough that it was of himself he was afraid, and that even, if he didn't take care, he should infallibly be more so" (338).

Ultimately, Densher breaks company with Kate. His attempt at "stillness" or self-effacement in Kate's plan grows more absurd to him each time he renews the effort and says to himself "that he was not *there*" (286); by deciding to let Milly take over, he only reminds himself that his own interested motives cannot be disentangled from hers. He cannot accept Kate's interpretation that he is acting disinterestedly in denying Milly knowledge of his relationship to Kate. He recognizes—to a degree that Kate cannot—that interests are interconnected. Kate refuses to concede that what Milly wants is not just happiness but a love that is freely conferred on her. Kate gives herself the freedom to do more by *not* recognizing Milly's claims, but this freedom comes at the expense of being able to see the situation as a whole. Kate cannot claim not to see this ethical truth without distorting what she takes the situation to be. Thus, her contention at the end of the novel—that before she died, Milly "realized her passion" (364), and that Densher allowed Milly to express her generosity, even her intensity of love, in a manner that cannot now be denied her—reveals, at least to Densher, the desperate nature of her self-interested interpretation, for once again she fails to acknowledge the injury done to Milly. Kate ignores the range of specifications and provisos internal to any interest. By contrast, Densher insists on appreciating the nature of Milly's interests with respect to himself.

It is significant that Densher chooses ultimately not to lie to Milly by denying what Lord Mark has revealed to her: that he and Kate are engaged. Some critics see his about-face as a "call of conscience" that dictates his action without regard for his interests or happiness.[30] But the familiar moral claim, which separates rational freedom from personal desire (and which has its genealogy in Kant's philosophy[31]), does not in fact account for Densher's personal interest in coming clean and renouncing the wealth within his grasp. He discovers how difficult it is to keep separate his devotion to personal gain from other kinds of social interest to which he is affectively attached, in part because his regard for others infringes on his sense of himself (another vital interest). Densher begins to redefine his sense of what it takes to live well. His treatment of Milly as an instrumental object produces in himself a feeling of profound personal depletion and unease. He sees that by regarding Milly as an advantage to himself, he instrumentalizes her and is in danger of instrumentalizing his own life too if he fails to admit claims that do not fit into narrow means-ends satisfactions.

Densher's overwhelming reaction against his and Kate's mutual pursuit of narrow self-interestedness emerges as an affective compulsion. He now understands that he cannot approach the world or have any hope of maintaining receptiveness to it without utterly demolishing his own self-interested arrangements and course of action. He will not perjure himself; he cannot tell Milly that he loves her when his love has been cast elsewhere. He can no more permit Milly to instrumentalize him than he can instrumentalize her. Densher's decision at the end to renounce Milly's bequest and Kate in the process (Kate cannot agree to the tenets of his conviction) is not an attempt to rectify the situation he has created—Milly is dead—but to acknowledge the impossibility of rectifying it.

What seems to be at stake, ethically, for James is the need to preserve the capacity to be receptive to the world as it changes and to align oneself with change, for it is through such striving that one most fully lives, that life most fully exemplifies itself. Densher is not seeking a particular outcome, whether to salvage his love for Kate or to regain the power over himself that he has surrendered to her. He forsakes immediate gain to preserve his capacity to create new interests, upholding a plastic relation to things whose benefit cannot be prescribed in advance. James demonstrates that people's interests in other people's interests are basic to them as selves. Because of the centrality of such relationships, any restriction they place on how they treat such interests has the effect of limiting their affective response to the world as a whole.

FROM LESSER TO GREATER AGENCY

The Ambassadors and *The Wings of the Dove* present characters whose final act is a renunciation of economic interest. These repeated renunciations in James's work have left some critics with the impression that James understands his protagonists' hard-won disinterestedness as an exclusion of interest of all kinds. I have suggested that, on the contrary, the gesture is not a negative or ascetic one. And yet there are times when his characters abandon important personal investments on grounds that weaken them or put them into contradiction with themselves. Hyacinth Robinson, James's accidental revolutionary in *The Princess Casamassima*, is one dramatized instance of this. His suicide at the novel's close resolves his conflict with himself by hastening his dissolution as a self. He reacts to a set of causes that, in Spinozan terms, "so dispose his imagination, and so affect his body, that it takes on another nature, contrary to the former [i.e., the nature of something dead]" (Spinoza, *Ethics* in *A Spinoza Reader* IV.II.225).

Unlike Spinoza, however, James seems to think that Hyacinth can have an interest in his self-diminishment, even perhaps an interest in his cessation of interest, which is all the more complicated because it springs from a conflicted "sense of everything that might hold one to the world, of the sweetness of not dying, the fascination of great cities, the charm of travel and discovery, the generosity of admiration" (*The Princess Casamassima*, 377).[32]

Hyacinth's renunciation expresses an extreme form of negative agency akin to disinvestment. This "disinvestment" is not a nullification so much as a change in the nature of the interests. All forms of renunciation in James, no matter how positive or liberating, convey some ambiguity about whether they undermine agency. It is interesting then, that in *The Golden Bowl* James seems to present a case—as Maggie exercises her imagination to contrive to keep the Prince—that advocates the promotion of personal interests. And yet Maggie's personal pursuit is as contingent and vulnerable as any. Because all forms of power or agency are relationally defined, her aims must by necessity appeal to the investments of those around her; she must widen her interests.

Maggie becomes vital as a character when, in response to a situation, a hesitation suspends or transforms her initial interests. *The Golden Bowl* thus gives full ethical attention to the unfinished impulses that define her and allow her to reinvent herself. During much of the novel, Maggie hardly acts at all. Her nascent recognitions about the compromised state of her marriage take the form of "instinctive postponements of reflection" (245). She feels as though she is being passed around like a "dressed doll" (274) while another drama is unfolding out of her sight. Her forestalled thought and action on this score might lead one to think that she is avoiding knowledge or wallowing in self-defeat. But James presents something much stranger. Maggie grants her husband the same incompleteness that she feels, knowing that his affair, like any liaison, depends on elaborate understandings that alter with time. She treats her situation as one susceptible to different forms of anchoring, to different ways of suiting and arranging implications, and thus open to and waiting for future relations that have not yet formed or hardened.

Before she does anything, she must discover the contours of the Prince's affair with Charlotte, who is married to her father. As one of James's prototypical heroines, she is not looking for something as simple as the means or instrument of realizing her intentions. Critics have tended to exaggerate both her power and her forethought,[33] but when Maggie responds it is not with anything so complete as a plan of action. Like many of James's characters, she does not simply fail to have preconceived intentions; rather, she actively resists having them. These characters embrace the indistinctness of their own and other people's conduct, discovering finer and more generous interpretive possibilities. The "instinctive postponements" are recognized and mutually felt between Maggie and the Prince: "What befell, however, was that even while [Maggie] thus waited she felt herself present at a process taking place rather deeper within [Amerigo] than the occasion on the whole, appeared to require—a process of weighing something in the balance, of considering, deciding, dismissing" (260). Maggie sees that her conscious sense of herself interests the Prince, and he in turn is given the space to be interested precisely because Maggie does not attempt to qualify or define his relationship to Charlotte on her terms.

To rectify matters, Maggie has to put off determining exactly what she desires. Her suspensions are the most significant in the book because she is best placed to recognize the mutually entangled interests that have brought about her predicament, for which she has to take some responsibility. This suspension of direct engagement does not diminish Maggie's capacity to act but is an extraordinary augmentation of it. Through a form of "obstructed agency" and "impassivity," her stillness does not give rise to the "ugly feelings" that Sianne Ngai has explored. Ngai sets out to study "ambivalent situations of suspended agency" (*Ugly Feelings*, 1), but her paradigmatic examples, such as Melville's "Bartleby, the Scrivener" (1853), tend to represent forms of equivocation that are not positive or liberating. James also offers "a non-cathartic aesthetic" (9) and seems to parade characters before us who fit Ngai's description of having "relatively weak intentionality" (22). That is, they have emotions that "destabilize our sense of the boundary between the psyche and the world" and superficially at least disclaim autonomy (20). And yet they do not necessarily give way to resentment or betray negative emotion, which would diminish their agency.

Maggie combines Strether's vicarious sensibility with Kate's self-regarding aims. She represents the confluence of interests in her person, expressing a form of curiosity that for Ross Posnock stands as a third term, troubling any simple binary between "blind practicality" and "perceptive uselessness" (*The Trial of Curiosity*, 32). Thus, through Maggie, James illustrates diverse interests that preserve continuity with each other and that operate across a vitalist spectrum of mental functions (from immediate reactions and impulses that rely on means-ends rationality to more elaborate musings and thought processes spurred by indeterminate calculations of interest).

By invoking Jamesian vitalism rather than pragmatism, I wish to suggest more than that "the 'self' is merely another transitional agency, a progressive unfolding that is at the same time an ongoing reflection on that unfolding" (Levin, *The Poetics of Transition*, 118). Jonathan Levin's quasi-Spinozan formulation emphasizes Henry James's interest in process, in the "drama of transition," over any substantive conclusion afforded us as readers but says little about why transitions in experience are meaningful or what aspects of agency they liberate. In other words, Levin misses an opportunity to place these transitions within a larger account of grounds for ethical comportment in James's novels.[34] By contrast, I emphasize how transitions and the suspensions that enable them bring about ethical responsiveness by allowing people to rethink their interests while maintaining the psychological plausibility of their own accounts and thought processes.

In his retrospective review of James's collective works, T. S. Eliot remarks that "the real hero, in any of James's stories is a social entity of which men and women are constituents" (*Critical Assessments* 1:304). I would suggest that if James elevates a "social entity," he does so not in the abstract but through individual characters whose experimental attitudes allow them to test and modify the tidy communal arrangements previously set in place.[35] Picking out a central protagonist for narrative focus, James is less concerned with epistemological access than with the character's entanglement in a wider variety of interests. First, the Prince takes the starring role in *The Golden Bowl*: "We see Charlotte also at first, and we see Adam Verver, let alone our seeing Mrs. Assingham, and every one and every thing else, but as they are visible in the Prince's interest, so to speak—by which I mean of course in the interest of his being himself handed over to us" (*Art of the Novel*, 330). Then the narrative turns to Maggie when she contributes to the "economy" of affective speculation, outlay, and investment.[36] She begins yielding dividends and proving her worth by devising novel conceptions of advantage that recognize people's different interests while aligning their various stakes in the outcome.

The idea that Maggie's emergent values are experimental, I acknowledge, cuts against the grain of the conventional view of her. Her conspiracy to silence Charlotte and restore the Prince's loyalty has invited mistrust from a rung of critics who regard her "power grab" as serving preestablished and rather conservative interests. Jonathan Freedman's analysis, for example, which is Foucaultian in inspiration, centers on the disciplinary practices that Maggie embodies and reproduces.[37] She enforces her interest, says Freedman, under a veil of ambiguity and knowledge that is not verifiable.[38] This ambiguity prevents Charlotte from protesting or maneuvering, allowing Maggie to maintain family integrity while cutting Charlotte off from the Prince and thus preserving Maggie's undivided tie to him. Freedman agrees with Mark Seltzer in faulting Maggie for taking advantage of power asymmetries—based on her position as guardian of the family—that block Charlotte from contesting or resisting Maggie's proprietary conjugal interests.[39]

I would counter, however, that such accounts do not give enough weight to the reluctant but freely given consent of the stakeholders in the collective compact. James plays up the messiness of the situation, but he also shows how each of the parties derives vital advantages from the deal. Maggie, for example, adapts to the constraints of her situation by figuring out how to accommodate the independent claims of others in her intimate circle; furthermore, she identifies exclusive and irreconcilable interests that allow her and Charlotte to take separate responsibility for their lives. As we will see, James gives a great deal of attention to the process that leads up to this feat, which does not occur by personal fiat or through Maggie's imagination. It occurs, rather, through an elaborate form of playacting: Maggie and Charlotte try out roles that allow them to experiment with a range of possible interests. James shows that such playacting unfolds in mutually orchestrated theaters and is a shared social enterprise.

THEATER OF AFFIRMATION

Scholars have long focused on the theatrical values and forms of masking that structure the relationships among characters in James's novels.[40] Psychoanalytic theorists who have attended to this aspect of his work worry that the ritualized scripts that his characters enact reproduce prescribed forms of subjectivity, thus consolidating dominant—and rather coercive—social interests. In particular, they have turned their attention to scenes, often highly theatrical ones, in which characters restage what theorists see as their phantasmatic desires. Even the most sophisticated among these critics assume that James's characters are inhibited by the precedents of the past, which encourage either repetition or destabilization of certain power structures associated with family life. In either scenario it seems to me that psychoanalytic theories impose an excessively rigid architecture for understanding how marriage as a prescribed interest might be socially reproduced. On the contrary, the performed parts that James depicts in *The Golden Bowl* are improvised productions that allow Maggie and Charlotte to define and negotiate their social responsibilities. They provide these characters with room to maneuver: they can accept accountability for their actions or perspectives without having to take a guarded public stance.

As I noted previously, Maggie does not, at first, know how to act in the face of her marital difficulties. She catches a glimpse of Charlotte and the Prince together on a balcony at Portland Place and sustains a traumatic impression of their intimacy. While she suspends reaction, she adopts a mask of equivocal ignorance, not to shield herself from unwelcome facts, but to insulate herself from exposure. As James puts it, she falls "into a succession of moments that were *watchable*," each like a "scene on the stage" (249). In fact, Maggie does not long remain a spectator but soon takes the lead on that stage, thus establishing the roles that others are to take in her domestic drama. Joseph Litvak, who has explored the nature of such performances in James's novels, disputes Seltzer's and Freedman's assertion that Maggie acts out the part of a surrogate author, claiming the principal position of power. Instead, he suggests, Maggie toggles unstably between that position and the position of spectator. Her unpredictable reversals prevent her from dwelling in any one position of dominance.[41] Yet even if, by his account, power does not take on a uniform structural form, Litvak worries that its dominating arrangements get socially reproduced in ways that unthinkingly repeat anterior social interests. And so he sees as a counterweight to this possibility James's use of role-playing individuals, which allows him to "unpack subjectivity as performance and to denaturalize—to read as a *scene*—the whole encompassing space in which that subjectivity gets constituted" (*Caught in the Act*, xii). Litvak takes his cue from gender theory that celebrates gestures of gay spectacle or masquerade that risk violations of social decorum, thus disrupting the "patriarchal, heterosexualizing pressure of narrative linearity" (xiii).

It is worth noting how much Litvak's theater of desire borrows from psychoanalysis. He makes this clear by identifying a "primal scene" and by regarding such scenes from the past as key scripts that consolidate and reproduce, or else stymie, particular patterns of subjectivity. For Litvak, a theatrical performance can be a subversive political act precisely because it takes aim at the ur-scenarios that shape people's desires, which we know to be essential from their obsessive rehashing of them. Yet Litvak's investments in psychoanalysis force him to treat the performances of James's characters as primarily reproductive or disruptive "acts" rather than as inherently productive ones. He downplays the potential novelty in characters' ways of managing and expressing their social interests.

By contrast, I suggest that the theatrical roles that Maggie adopts offer her an unscripted refuge from the performative precedents already at her disposal.

In *The Golden Bowl*, the topic of theater comes up explicitly at a number of significant moments. In one, James depicts Maggie standing on the terrace, looking in as Charlotte, the Prince, Maggie's father, and their family friend Fanny Assingham, play a game of cards. The scene reprises the aforementioned moment when Maggie observes Charlotte and the Prince together on a balcony and would seem to count as yet another of the primal scenes to which Litvak alludes. The picture is one of tableaulike immobility. Maggie has been systematically avoiding Charlotte, keeping matters cold between them, and at the same time avoiding a confrontation. Charlotte wants to catch her alone to precipitate an encounter. She hopes to put to an end to her conjectures as to whether Maggie has found out about her affair with the Prince. Right before Charlotte catches a glimpse of Maggie outside watching them, which affords her the opportunity she has been looking for, James makes us privy to Maggie's thoughts: her family circle "might have been figures rehearsing some play of which [Maggie] herself was the author" (385). A bit later, in her peripatetic agitation she passes by another room, which, though empty, reminds her of the smoking room she has just left and "seeming to speak the more, in its own voice, of all the possibilities she controlled. Spacious and splendid, like a stage again awaiting a drama, it was a scene she might people, by the press of her spring, either with serenities and dignities and decencies, or with terrors and shames and ruins" (385). The very emptiness of the space invites her to impose her imagination on the scene or stage, to fill out the relations, which remain uncertain, "of the whole group, individually and collectively, to herself" (383). The question that hangs on this scene is how she will improvise with the different potential roles she has been handed.

Maggie's glimpse of this scene of domestic tranquility has left her with the shocked sense of threat to her family life. In this respect, the episode only seems to confirm Kaja Silverman's assertion that *The Golden Bowl* "is in many ways an extended primal scene" (*Male Subjectivity at the Margins*, 169). It presents Maggie caught between two powerful attachments, one to her father and another to her husband. From a psychoanalytic point of view, such moments back up Leo Bersani's suggestion that Maggie has to choose between a fluid, fragmented (pre-Oedipal) form of desire (associated with her childhood identification with her father) and the sanction of marriage that prepares Maggie for the "goal of post-Oedipal, genital heterosexuality" (*The Freudian Body*, 85). By this measure,

Maggie can either opt for a narrative teleology that trumps marriage as a conventional social interest or undermine that interest by holding to her vestigial (unconscious) identifications, which impede the formation of adult sexual identities. Although Bersani's psychoanalytic readings of *The Golden Bowl* do not commit him to a single narrative teleology expressing a monolithic communal interest, he does think that the burdens of Maggie's past limit her potential options to these broad trajectories. It seems to me, however, that James, who is a canny anatomist of marital relations, treats marriage not as a single edifice representing prescribed social interests but as a template of complicated, interconnected, occasionally improvised social arrangements, some of which may include tolerated forms of infidelity under highly managed situations. Bersani's schematic either/or argument seems to discount the specifically circumstantial understandings of marriage in *The Golden Bowl.*[42]

By convention the marital bond pledges sexual exclusivity, and this affords James dramatic grounds for exploring how people depart from their commitments for certain ends that are to them risk-worthy. Because marriage expresses profound forms of interdependence, its safekeeping occupies a high place within social life; its violation is therefore an ideal locus of dramatistic investment. Maggie's love for her husband eventually moves her to sacrifice her father—not, however, before brokering a tolerable parting and securing Adam Verver's assent to it. Thus, it is not a simple matter to decide whether James is a socially conservative writer for upholding marriage at the end of *The Golden Bowl.* First, we have to decide what kind of marriage he presents.

In the sequence of scenes previously recounted, Maggie contemplates the choices before her. She could rend the fiction of family unity, accuse Charlotte of violating her trust, and show herself to be a woman derided. This prospect momentarily opens up for her as "that fascination of the monstrous, that temptation of the horribly possible" (383). Or she could acquiesce to the state of affairs as it stands. Another option, admittedly not fully worked out, would continue the severe logic of her husband's example, denying comprehension of the situation, shutting Charlotte out (this is already in some manner a victory for her), meanwhile slowly accommodating herself to the conditions of an alternative family ordering. We might note that initially she is mentally rehearsing various scenarios that implicate her and is simultaneously scripting those scenarios. (This activity is part and parcel of the suspensions I previously examined, in which she projects possible futures.)

The elaborate struggle with Charlotte that Maggie pictures in her mind might tempt us to think that she is not scripting the potential directions of a future scene in an ad hoc fashion but rather relying on an anterior script, which in turn lends support to the idea that she is playing out the fantasy structure of the primal scene. Maggie imagines herself as the inevitable loser of any battle with Charlotte. She also pictures her father looking up from the card table and, perfectly understanding her internal drama, rescuing her from the exertions she takes up on his behalf, choosing her above his wife: "He might make some sign—she scarce knew what—that would save *her*; save her from being the one, this way, to pay all. He might somehow show a preference—distinguishing between them; might, out of pity for her, signal to her that this extremity of her effort for him was more than he asked" (390). Maggie's triangulated fantasy restages her vulnerability and marginality, conforming to the masochistic structure that Silverman identifies with the primal scene.[43] It has Maggie confronting unwanted knowledge at the very point when it threatens to overtake her "preferred self-image" (Silverman, *Male Subjectivity at the Margins*, 161). Also, Maggie's fantasy gives us yet another indication of her ardently cathected relationship to her father. In Silverman's account, the primal scene does not simply shut the door on the labile desires and boundary-defying identifications of infantile sexuality. While it reenacts the moment when the child confronts adult sexuality, it also offers a degree of unconscious access to the experiences of early life.[44] Dangling between two painful temporalities, the primal scene renders her both "too early" and "too late" in Silverman's account. The marital bond encroaches on the daughter's childlike affection, demanding that love take an exclusionary form—in this way constantly threatening loss and with it a belated feeling of disillusionment. At the same time, the primal scene brings her back to a moment of unreadiness, when the child feels overwhelmed and unprepared for adult sexuality. On its deepest level, argues Silverman, the primal scene has the capacity to disrupt the steady march toward marital submission and concession, alternating as it does between a feeling of disappointment in love and a more malleable capacity for identification that accepts positions and perspectives in fantasy otherwise foreclosed by an individual's socially sanctioned gender role.[45]

Silverman's intricate account captures beautifully the forms of heteropathic identification that James's characters display, thus confirming the ethical value that James places in relationships that do not aggress other people's perspectives. She is right to suggest that such patterns of identification are at antipodes to normative heterosexual masculinity. At the same time, the psychoanalytic framework on which she and Bersani rely does not make it a priority to explore the ways that individuals confront an uncreated future reality. In the "outside-looking-in" scene Maggie is not simply fantasizing but virtualizing, which is to say, projecting possibilities of action that have the potential to shake up her social world. "Projection" in this sense does not refer to an expulsion or displacement of feelings and wishes from one object to another.[46] Tapping into Bergson's notion of virtuality, I want to point toward a more phenomenological kind of projection that includes anticipating, waiting, holding oneself open, and casting possibilities that radiate from the world of things.[47]

Ultimately, Maggie concludes that, if she were to reveal her knowledge of her husband's betrayal, her father would not necessarily support her side. This line of thought indicates a complicated intuition on Maggie's part, one that demonstrates her vitalistic powers.[48] This intuition weighs several outcomes, exploring how her perspectives and accompanying interests might differ from her father's. Psychoanalytic conceptions of projection are insufficient to describe the exceptionally complex forms of hunch and presentiment that guide Maggie's judgment; they underdescribe, they say too little about the extent and range of her awareness. Rather than see Maggie as passive, prey to unwanted knowledge, or as someone unconsciously interested in reorchestrating an identification with the various participants of her primal scene, we might think of her as a character who is especially attuned to how others might react and in a dissimilar manner to her. Psychoanalytic models of identification tend to ignore or collapse positional differences in a relational field to underscore the underlying mental equivalences among the perspectives and attitudes.[49] But Maggie does not see her father as a stand-in for herself; ultimately, she grants him his own separate status as a stakeholder.[50]

Maggie's intuitions enable her to improvise more successfully, and so they allow her to seek out new social interests when old ones only increase resentment and conflict. Following the scene on the terrace, Charlotte succeeds in catching up with Maggie. Once caught, Maggie refuses to clarify matters for her, claiming no grievance, even going so far as to bestow on Charlotte a reconciling kiss, even if coldly delivered. Significantly, this is followed by a second scene in which the pair convenes alone. They exchange roles: pursuer becomes pursued. Again, James frames the situation through a theatrical metaphor: Maggie sees Charlotte "driven in a kind of flight" and recalls "some echo of an ancient fable—some vision of Io goaded by the gadfly or of Ariadne roaming the lone sea-strand. It brought with it all the sense of her own intention and desire; she too might have been, for the hour, some far-off harassed heroine—only with *a part to play for which she knew, exactly, no inspiring precedent*" (427–428; emphasis mine). Maggie cannot rely on a prescripted part for herself, partly because she so unexpectedly identifies with Charlotte. Therefore, she must write a new one that is unrehearsed, formulating interests as she goes along. She approaches Charlotte with the sense that she has already secured her solution to the impasse in the two marriages (a parting between the couples is in the works): "She knew [Charlotte] doomed, doomed to a separation that was like a knife in her heart" (430). But then Maggie does something unexpected, outside the bounds of narrow self-interest: she lays herself open to Charlotte's rebukes and accusations and sacrifices her cold supremacy. In this way, she seems to strike with Charlotte a different kind of exalted bargain from the one she strikes with the Prince. The two give up certain interests to exact new claims of responsibility from one another.

When Maggie ventriloquizes Charlotte as remarking, "It's her lie, it's her lie that has mortally disagreed with her; she can keep down no longer her rebellion at it, and she has come to retract it, to disown it and denounce it—to give me full in my face the truth instead" (429), it appears that she knows that Charlotte knows, or at least suspects, that she is lying and perhaps that Charlotte is a willing party to the deception and has an investment in it. Maggie does not break with the performance; she lets herself look the absurd naïf, opening herself up to Charlotte's burning reproaches when Maggie herself has the right to reproach. In this way, Maggie accepts her portion of responsibility for a collective failure. Charlotte's complaint, in turn, gives her a basis for confirming a decision to separate, a decision she does not choose.

What follows, therefore, is a kind of playacting. The two don masks that are not simply false: "Charlotte flamed aloft—might truly have been believing in her passionate parade" (433). Charlotte lies about her involvement with the Prince but is not exposed. Her lie allows her to take a measure of responsibility for the aggravated crisis she has had a part in creating. There is candor even in her lie: she *is* a kind of victim. Her desire to have her husband "at last a little to myself" (432) seems to express a lately felt, or perhaps unearthed, commitment to Adam Verver on terms different from those on which their marriage was founded. Charlotte has the space to protest and admit fault at the same time. James bows to

Maggie's gentleness, extolling a number of her unaccountable feelings that allow her to give Charlotte this space, in turn enabling both to embrace new interests rather than force their fluid mixture of attitudes to harden by being exclaimed publicly in a reifying and corrosive way.

The pair's role-playing is neither wholly conscious nor wholly intentional. It requires self-forgetfulness, that "positive faculty of repression" that Nietzsche thinks is an indispensable ameliorant to a bad conscience (*Genealogy of Morals*, 57). Rather than think of such failed recall in psychoanalytic terms, we might describe it as a kind of suspension or bracketing that allows Charlotte and Maggie to lose themselves in their roles.[51] Nietzsche, who thinks "[e]very profound spirit needs a mask," does not consider it a means of suppressing truth but a way of structuring and consolidating appearance. A man who conceals his shame

> *wants* and sees to it that a mask of him roams in his place through the hearts and heads of his friends. And supposing he did not want it, he would still realize some day that in spite of that a mask of him is there—and that this is well. . . . Around every profound spirit a mask is growing continually, owing to the constantly false, namely *shallow*, interpretation of every word, every step, every sign of life he gives. (*Beyond Good and Evil*, 51).

By esteeming the shallow, Nietzsche undercuts the distinction between reality and exterior manifestation. Well aware that the word "person" derives from the Greek word for mask, he insists on a pervasive shallowness of character that offers no recoverable or at least representable psychological depth. Masks may "falsify" the forces that define any underlying will, but only by offering a simplifying front that makes greater agency possible.

Critics in recent years have turned to the concept of performance as a way of rescuing James's characters from fixed subject positions, though they sometimes overemphasize one element, the potential distance characters take from their roles, to the exclusion of another, the fact that performances require endorsements of those same roles.[52] After all, performances require people to choose among disparate interests. In their two theatrically framed scenes, Maggie and Charlotte project their powers of will through creative playacting, which implies an improvised but coordinated effort, an achievement of dexterous self-positioning. Although their performances may allow them to defer making final choices on the basis of a predefined social or sexual identity, as Leland Person argues, these performances do not stave off their need to submit to limitations inherent in their roles.[53]

The two episodes underscore how decisively James departs from the fantasy of exposure that Blakey Vermeule cites as one of the early preoccupations of the novel as a form, which encourages one to regard the psychology of characters in terms of "surface/depth relationships, with true motives lying deeper than merely social ones" (*Why Do We Care About Literary Characters?*, 110). He contravenes the moralistic impulse to uncover their "secret cache of self-interest" (108).[54] Indeed, Maggie's and Charlotte's performances enable them to pursue their conceptions of advantage by offering them a set of social permissions—a performative front or façade—that augments their agency.

One strand of liberal politics that James contests by sweeping away its moral vernacular is the idea that people need to be protected from the interests of others. As Wendy Brown argues, liberalism and the identity politics it spawns encourage a climate in which people have to avenge themselves against injury by "reproach[ing] power rather than aspir[ing] to it" (*States of Injury*, 55), in this way shielding themselves from others' naked pursuit of interest. For her, this is a recipe for *ressentiment* in Nietzsche's sense. The seething desire for public recognition for injury emerges as "an effect of domination that reiterates impotence, a substitute for action, for power, for self-affirmation that reinscribes incapacity, powerlessness, and rejection" (69). By turning the injured into fortified social identities, the resentful often cast "suffering as the measure of social virtue" (70). But this form of politicized identity fails to imagine or desire any ideal except that from which it is excluded. Part of Brown's point is that while the resentful see themselves as contesting the social order, in fact they unconsciously fix and install it as an ideal.

Identity-based struggles of the current moment take it as more or less axiomatic that the political starting point of any emancipatory project must be the specifying and apportioning of a set of interests to distinct identity positions that in the aggregate form a constituency. Of course, such politicized movements aim to expand such constituencies, but they do so by encouraging identification with interested groups whose defined boundaries strengthen their claim to be recognized disputants. The claim to public recognition that such groups demand tends to require explicitness on interests that confine individuals to settled positions. Even theorists such as Charles Taylor, who promotes a "politics of recognition" based on a processual notion of identity formed and refined through dialogue with others, tend to "limit our community identities," according to Jessica Berman, "to those that may be expressed as externally coherent and stable wholes" (*Modernist Fiction, Cosmopolitanism and the Politics of Community*, 11). For Berman, a politics grounded on such claims to recognition "falters when it does not account for differences *within* publically recognized groupings or for the provisional quality of those groupings" (12). Berman herself treats the avoidance of definiteness and explicitness on the part of characters such as Strether and (to a lesser extent) Maggie Verver as a triumph, at least to the degree that such avoidance renders "a declarative statement of identity impossible" (66). Although she celebrates Jean-Luc Nancy's deconstructive account of the "inoperative community" that "never resolves into an entity that has an identity or performs tasks" (14), Berman, like Nancy, tends to regard the resulting pluralism and resistance to consensus as a value in itself. I would argue, however, that the chief worth of such open-endedness is that it allows people to suspend their interests long enough to help them define new provisional communities and a set of interests appropriate to them.

James may be a cosmopolitan writer, but he refuses to ground political interests on abstract social imperatives (especially ones that privilege detachment or context-blind judgments), and he is acutely aware of the layered allegiances that define community life. For instance, Maggie may have loyalties to her family that are different, say, from her identification with her Americanness or the American nation and the imperatives of cultural negotiation (a running side theme in *The Golden Bowl*), but even within her family, her loyalty to the Prince, to her father, and to Charlotte overlap and disaggregate depending on the matter in question. In this respect, James anticipates the anthropological tradition that supports late twentieth-century theories of cosmopolitanism, which, as Rebecca Walkowitz describes it, emphasize "multiple or flexible *attachments* . . . , resisting conceptions of allegiance that presuppose consistency and uncritical enthusiasm" (*Cosmopolitan Style*, 9). As James shows, some forms of agreement are so contingent that they cannot take place in public, where values are enforced by public transparency.[55] This is because individuals need a space or interval for suspended judgment, which offers them shelter from the accusatory perspectives of others. Like Wendy Brown, James would seem to insist on finding ways for people to share interests when possible by refusing the "defensive closure on identity, its insistence on the fixity of position, its equation of social with moral positioning" (*States of Injury*, 75). For Brown, this entails supplanting "the language of 'I am' . . . with the language of 'I want this for us,'" thereby constituting a temporal identity in motion "rather than fixed interests or experiences" (75).

Maggie's virtuoso feat in *The Golden Bowl* is to discover collective interests, however imperfect or compromised, capable of appealing to Charlotte and to her husband, as well as to herself. She avoids the pitfalls of obstructed agency that Brown anatomizes by refusing to take on the identity of an aggrieved wife. Her marital success depends on her abandoning the character template that James establishes for her at the outset. She becomes wonderfully inconsistent. She makes no small concession by "giving [her father] up" (442), considering how deeply entrenched her attachment to him is. Despite such definitive compromises, she continues to embrace an air of tentativeness, avoiding attitudes that fortify or retrench psychic life. Maggie finally quells any expectation that she might demand her husband's confession. She does not require a declaration of guilt from him (the possibility of which would only serve, Maggie is aware, to defame Charlotte at the moment of her supreme sacrifice). She knows that her own delays and circumventions give the Prince resources to make his own adjustments, and she invites him to take his cues from her: "It had operated within her now to the last intensity, her glimpse of the precious truth that by her helping [the Prince], helping him to help himself, as it were, she should help him to help *her*" (357). In this statement, her postponements, which are proffered almost as a gift on her part, also allow her to fold her own interests into those of the Prince and, indeed, into those of other characters as well.

In Judith Butler's terms, Maggie engages in an "ethics of capacity" ("Capacity," 118), by which Butler means that she need not disavow Charlotte to sustain her love of the Prince. But Butler grounds this capacity on identifications undergirt by a form of "queer" desire (theorized by recourse to psychoanalytic models). This desire does not demand exclusivity, an either/or choice: theirs "is not a love based in repudiation, for even though Charlotte must go, she remains between them, the token by which their exchange is opened, the basis of their new bond" (118).[56] I would interject, however, that conflict and competition are irreducible realities of human life. Any ethics based on the form of desire that Butler anatomizes is not terribly meaningful if it does not acknowledge the needs and demands that make one party's interests discontinuous with another's. Conceptions of advantage, I have suggested throughout, oblige one to create order among one's desires, recognizing relative merits and giving priority to some forms of advantage over others on the basis of situational contingencies. Insofar as Maggie's newly devised interests structure her desire, she in effect chooses her husband over either Charlotte or her father. Although Charlotte is renounced, her newly won autonomy and her sacrifice, which have changed her, are not. The successful implementation of these transformations stands as the real ethical triumph for a novel that steadfastly refuses to flinch from life's storied conflicts of interest. James invents a justly "interesting" novel that asks us to reject an ethical lexicon wedded to fixed conceptions of advantage.

3 LIVELY HABITS
Gertrude Stein

In the writing of *Three Lives*, Gertrude Stein seems excited by the material that other novelists discard. Avoiding values of craftsmanship as well as stylishness, she goes about fashioning and then repeating crude, makeshift descriptions of people and their characters. When she has them talk, they produce an incessant, recurring palaver of the sort that we may tolerate in others but do not necessarily celebrate. Wyndham Lewis, no fan of Stein's, said of her work (he had read *Three Lives*), "Cut it at any point, it is the same thing; the same heavy, sticky, opaque mass all through. . . . It is mournful and monstrous, composed of dead and inanimate material. It is all fat without nerve" (*Time and Western Man*, 59). But Stein does not accept the charge that the habits, temperaments, and forms of decency that incline people toward their particular brand of unthinking sociability are dead. For her, the inner movement of repetition is the very principle of liveliness: "And if this vitality [of movement within repetition] is lively enough is there in that clarity any confusion is there in that clarity any repetition?" ("Lectures in America," 292). I will argue that habit, as Stein understands it, is not a fixed, rigid, and permanent part of the person and that it never repeats in the same way twice. It certainly defines us, as much as anything does, but she thinks that it does so without indicating a set character that underlies our behaviors. For this reason, habit attests to the fact that we do not have a preordained seed of personality that makes us consistent from the start. We are regular beings because we accumulate manners and behaviors and because that accumulation has a history that allows us simultaneously to recognize ourselves and to depart from ourselves.

In other words, in Stein's conception habits do not immunize us from change. Nor do they promote precipitous self-transformation. As Lisi Schoenbach suggests, Stein's celebration of routines, habits, and middle-class customs are calculated to affront avant-garde theories of art that advocate shock as a way of jolting people from staid, conventional patterns of perception and response.[1] Yet critics who have examined Steinian habit invariably think that it is mixed up with inert and conservative social functions. Schoenbach and Liesl Olson, for instance, worry that habit leads to servile reproduction of behavioral response, mindlessly delivering individuals into the hands of the Vichy occupier and the social engineer. At the same time, they celebrate habit for its capacity to transmit and bind elements of experience and limber up the higher faculties.[2] They follow Walter Benjamin in presenting habit as a buffer against the "shock experience [that] has become the norm" (*Illuminations*, 162) of modern life and that threatens to obliterate psychic stability.

I would propose that Stein accords habit a more active range of functions. To understand Steinian habit as a character-shaping force capable of emotional variety, we need to turn to an intellectual lineage that cast a wide shadow over Stein's early intellectual life. Charles Darwin is perhaps the great arbiter standing behind her conception of habit. She elaborates on an undercurrent of his argument—that repetition is a useful, indeed a necessary, part of human sociality—and explores its reach and consequence. Like Darwin, Stein concentrates attention on the emergence of variants that alter earlier precedents. But what we will find is that, because of her particular sensitivity to questions of habit (as a result of the vitalist optic she had developed under the influence of William James, her mentor at Harvard), she picks up on a side of Darwin that rarely receives attention: his claim that variations within a repetitive sequence are not always arbitrary but sometimes involve choice.

Stein learned from Darwin that habits arise out of and modify biological systems. Darwin's late treatise, *The Expression of the Emotions in Man and Animals* (1872), is less concerned with the randomly inherited physiological variations discussed in *On the Origin of Species* (1859) than with behaviors at the vanishing point between psychology and biology. We are accustomed to treating the majority of human choices—when they are purposeful and novel—under the rubric of culture, where all of our intellectual strivings are focused, and where we generally locate the creative potential of human lives otherwise restricted by genes and environment. We reserve biology for the more deterministic undercurrent of life. But Darwin's and Stein's fascination with the dynamic relation between repetitive processes and innovation rubs out any hard-and-fast dividing line between nature and culture. This means not only that they understand culture to have biological determinants (a view shared by evolutionary psychologists for the last several decades); Stein and Darwin also wish to import some of the characteristics of culture into the biological realm.

In this chapter I read biological discourses alongside literary and philosophical ones to demonstrate the nonexclusivity of scientific models while using humanistic frameworks to recontextualize scientific thought, thus reframing biological concepts in a new way or in what we might term a "nonnative" environment. Through Stein I aim to draw attention to strands of Darwin's thinking that do not feature prominently either in contemporary biological discourses or in the sociopolitical ones that initially succeeded in claiming his legacy. Indeed, Stein's work brings us back to a moment when science was renegotiating its relations to culture, particularly to humanistic endeavor, following in the wake of Darwin's turbulent ideas. I will highlight in her work what appears to be a startling continuum between biology and culture, one that contests both biological essentialism and social constructionism.

For Stein, habit permits novel forms of attention to happen. Reiterations turn potential experiences—what we might call "virtual" impressions and tacit connections—into actual ones. In other words, recursive action consolidates possible behavioral responses, galvanizing or motivating them in a particular direction. I am borrowing this language of virtuality from Bergson, who, like William James, wished to account for life processes through nondeterministic principles and to explain psychological phenomena by considering how thresholds of potentiality repercuss on behavior. James and Bergson, and Ralph Waldo Emerson before them, explored the strange agreement or unpredictable interactions among multiple habits, behaviors, and events that, in combination, decide the fate of individual lives. I would argue that their vitalist affinities are a useful intellectual basis from which to understand Stein's work and her relation to Darwinism. The vitalist camp shared an emphasis on the liveliness, malleability, and ever-changing nature of biological process. Indeed, James and Bergson both used Darwinian theory as a point of entry into their own conceptual projects.[3]

I will establish in some detail how Stein put ideas inspired by Darwin into operation in her early fiction, specifically in "Melanctha," the longest and most complicated story in *Three Lives.* In "Melanctha" she shows that longstanding habits sometimes reorder themselves when a default reaction is inadequate. By calling on vitalist models of habit, which presuppose change within continuity, Stein presents a new modernist definition of character. She lays the ground for an avant-garde that sees no need to direct hostility at habituated existence. Although critics deem her formal experiments in repetition to run at the expense of psychological development, even to the point of showing indifference to character as a literary value, I suggest instead that Stein recasts how we understand the instruments of change in the first place when they play out in the lives of individuals.[4] She points attention to unpredictable deviations in response that are not necessarily the result of a conscious, deliberative subject.

Stein uses serial narrative techniques in *Three Lives* to explore the day-to-day accidents, behavioral tendencies, and emergent patterns of decision-making that are integrated into habits and that create change in people's lives. But it is not until we get to the portrait experiments of the 1920s that Stein is able to reflect on her own habit of tracking these changes as a writer. The section she devotes to Henry James in *Four in America* allows her to appreciate the evolution of her own writing style by exploring the analogous evolution of a writer, James, who had played an important role in her development. She shows how novel or unconventional alterations in a pattern of writing do not emerge decisively: they reveal their literary value only when their virtual direction takes hold as a more pronounced habit. I return to this piece later in the chapter in order to establish Stein's kinship with the form of literary vitalism that she recognizes in James and also to understand better how nonlinear relations among otherwise discrete events work in concert to shift patterns and create new ones.

Some of the patterns that intrigue Stein concern behaviors that group people into types. As she sees it, such patterns may be perpetuated across populations. In the minds of some critics, Stein's biological interests, as they manifest in "Melanctha," raise a troubling hint of her investment in predestined personalities, especially for characters with racially prescribed traits. In the story, Melanctha is the daughter of a black man and a mixed-race mother; Jeff Campbell, so the narrator tells us, is "a serious, earnest, good young joyous doctor," the issue of a "sweet, little, pale brown, gentle" mother and an intelligent brown-skinned father (*Three Lives*, 77). Daylanne English suggests that Stein's typologies give evidence of her attraction to eugenics, and she, like a crowd of other critics, treats Melanctha as a stock tragic figure in *Three Lives*, a "mulatta" whose conflictual identifications—rooted in biology—are the source of her demise (*Unnatural Selections*, 105). Yet I would argue that Stein, like Darwin, starts from the presumption that tendencies to similarity always coincide with processes of divergent variation. Innovation occurs as a result of small departures from previously assumed behaviors that build over time and are the product, at least in part, of decisions carried out. Also like Darwin, Stein does not presume that typological categories are deterministic, even if they are broadly normative. Despite her provocative and sometimes dubious handling of racial stereotypes, she shows no interest in treating biology as a regulative ceiling that restricts people's fundamental capacity to change.[5] Indeed, it is fair to say that she mounts a challenge to some of the racist orthodoxies of her time.

In the last section of this chapter, I show how Stein's comic impulses create a kind of narrative interference that undercuts the suggestion of tragic determinism underlying Melanctha's character. For Stein, life itself is surprising, and biology is not destiny. As one of three "lives," the narrative raises the question of how life itself enters into narrative structures and departs from them—or, perhaps, how narrative may be rehabilitated as a set of open-ended tendencies and variable units of organization rather than as a predictable diagram. As Brian Massumi phrases it, rather than putting "permutations on an overarching definitional framework," and thus pinpointing "a zero-point of stasis", we need to pay attention to the "field of emergence" (*Parables for the Virtual*, 3, 9) that defines life.[6]

NARRATING HABITS

To clarify how Stein understands the broader place of behavioral change in biological life, we might begin by looking at how habits are treated formally and thematically in "Melanctha." Stein stages an encounter between two lovers with different attitudes toward respectability. She explores their conflictual sympathies and patterns of response, which constitute the edifice of their relationship and in the course of time lead to the relationship's undoing. Melanctha Herbert and Jeff Campbell are constantly confronting or appeasing each other. But their passions, which are wound around their habits and inseparable from them, allow them no easy way of satisfying the qualms they have about each other.[7] Jeff continually asserts the need to be "living good and being regular" (87), dispatching these habitual clackings as accusations against the title character's wandering tendencies, her "subtle movements and denials and vague distrusts" (62). His intensities are of a kind that build up slowly, and so, as he says, "I really certainly don't ever like to get excited," adding that "that kind of loving hard ["real, strong, hot"] does seem always to mean just getting all the time excited" (86). This slow-to-be-seduced lover rejoices in his habits. He continually holds forth on the value of a stable middle-class existence, while Melanctha expresses her desire to wander, revealing a sensibility geared to swiftness and immediacy. Despite the contrast, Stein is not suggesting that Melanctha is any less a creature of habit, even though "she didn't feel the same as he did about being good and regular in life, and not having excitements all the time" (81). Melanctha simply runs at a different speed and has different ways of processing her feelings. For both characters, habits are proclivities and tendencies that help conduct them through an evolving relationship. For Stein, it is not that people can dispense with their habits but that habits reveal themselves in the different ways in which individuals react to change.

Stein is aware that patterns brought about by repetition are not uniform or monolithic. Sometimes two or more different tendencies enter into conflict, one pattern of expression intersecting or interfering with another, causing sequences of repetition to unravel or veer in a new direction. Stein dramatizes the struggle not only between people but also between specific behaviors, habits, and preferences, some of which correlate with vying racial, sexual, and class interests. But the conflicts she depicts between, for example, Melanctha's working-class customs and Jeff's middle-class values merely prove that their respective habits are subject concurrently to social and biological definition.[8] Racial groupings and class pecking orders divide the human species not just into social identities but also into biologically trackable populations—though, as a social or as a biological matter, no one set of interests is intrinsically superior to another. By refusing to validate any set of interests in absolute terms, Stein implies that habits, as an expression of nature, are to some degree open-ended in their effects. Nature, in turn, has different levels at which it works or organizes itself. Broadly, we might say that the interests of individual members of a group may compete with species interests or the priorities of the social group to which they belong, either in regard to biological perpetuation of the gene or any other indirect biological advantage.

Stein follows a long lineage going back to Aristotle when she grants the development and exercise of habit a character-defining function. Yet, unlike Aristotle, she refuses to raise constancy to a moral virtue.[9] She insists on redefining morality by uncoupling it from a system of immemorial standards and showing how things that have been ranked as good are subject to evolutionary alteration. Stein takes advantage of word properties that fail to secure the eternality they seem to promise. Jeff, one of her lover characters, speaks of being "awful *good* and sorry" about giving Melanctha "so much trouble" with his preoccupations, with his "right way of thinking" (112; my italics). A "good" is variously an enduring, stable value and (combined with "and") an emphatic expression, one that ever so slightly alters a fact.[10] Stein's penchant for emphatic words, such as "good," "certain/certainly," and "real/really," focuses on ritualized habits of speech, tics of a sort, that do not mark lasting distinctions but register changes of emphasis. Her language builds on ideals that change as the situation changes in the course of the story.

For Stein, repetitions of thought and behavior have a capacity to disclose or reveal new shades of feeling and new thought processes along with them. To tell the story of the habitual patterns she focuses on is exceptionally difficult. They follow no sequential course, and although they direct characters' responses to each other, they do so by plastic mechanisms that cannot be specified, that are only beheld in the slight pivots that allow people to move from one state to another. As Jeff becomes estranged from Melanctha, he tells her how much he has learned from her about loving (the act, not the state), "like really having everything together, new things, little pieces all different. . . . You see, Melanctha, it's certainly like that *you make me been seeing*" (112; emphasis mine). While overcoming past resistance to this "one good big feeling," he continues to suffer from mistrust that will not go away. The odd grammar of the sentence embeds a slight grammatical irregularity into his statement (the processing of language, incidentally, also entails habits of listening and reading—habits that Stein relies on to pick up deviations). It would seem that Jeff has been seeing something all the while, though only at this moment does his train of ideas coalesce. Jeff does not say that Melanctha makes him see something now or that he has been seeing something from its inception. To put his assertion another way, she makes him see what he has been seeing, or she makes him into someone who has been seeing something about his relationship. For Stein, repetition allows Jeff new angles on what he knows. The perception consolidates a habit-directed process and therefore changes it. But one could also say that habit enables this critical perception to happen in the first place. Only by repeating himself—hearing himself talk the same old talk—is he in a position to feel the changes in his relationship, the alterations of mood and understanding. Events do not definitively happen till they occur multiple times.

Few novelists find drama in depicting habit; they tend to privilege sequences in which people depart from their routines of conduct. Stein, meanwhile, thinks that conventional narrative is unable to capture the inner functioning of an event because it simply reports changes: how A wakes up to a new idea or B falls into despair or C hastens toward drastic action. She proposes in one of her experimental lectures that "narrative concerns itself with what is happening all the time, history concerns itself with what happens from time to time. And that is perhaps what is the matter with history and that is what is perhaps the matter with narrative" (*Narration*, 30). The problem with historical accounts is not that they are more exclusionary in focus than other narratives but rather that they fall back on principles shared with all conventional narratives. By tracing "what is happening," narratives assume a trajectory of events, plotting out the component parts on an abstract grid line. At least in its predictable guises, narrative does not present the real time of happenings that have duration and therefore does not capture the transition that carries one thing into another. Like "history," "narrative" is concerned with logical sequences and ignores how actions emerge from an alteration in a series of repetitive actions. Although Stein thinks that narrative is in a manner inescapable, she insists on "beginning again" and in that way resisting teleological structures.[11] For Stein, consciousness does not spontaneously change. Our lives are not sequential but serial.

I would argue that Stein's descriptions of people do not aim to define their essences. This is because habituation cannot presume to solidify or "realize" an underlying character. Nor does the gravitational direction of the repertoire of behaviors say anything about the preexistence of a substantive personality. Her depictions attempt to diagram what we might refer to as the syntax of a person, the odd contradictions, transitions, and repetitions that make variation possible, alongside a durable stylistic signature compatible with it. She derives from Darwin the idea that the changes that living beings manifest individually and even as a species do not tend toward a specific ideal or outcome. This is basic to Darwin's theory of evolution, and, as she recounts in *Everybody's Autobiography*, when she began as a writer "evolution was still exciting very exciting" (249). Darwin's fundamental claim is that living creatures are adaptable. His ontology prizes what we might call plasticity in the face of changing circumstances.[12] William James clarifies what is at stake in the concept. In *The Principles of Psychology* James defines plasticity as "a structure weak enough to yield to an influence, but strong enough not to yield all at once" (1:106). He insists from the start that a plastic trait involves change and adaptation to change, not repetition in its pure form. Plasticity is the aspect of a thing that confers endurance. It positions anything—a trait, a body, a character, or a person—between the twin dangers of unadaptability (an extreme rigidity that leaves it unfit for new circumstances) and self-dissolution (excessively rapid change). Taking her cue from James and Darwin, Stein insists on the possibility of an endless number of incremental changes taking place within the individual (as well as across populations) in the face of changing conditions.

DARWIN'S SELF-ORGANIZING HABITS

As a sophisticated reader of Darwin, Stein picks up on elements of his work that biologists tend to underrate and that expand biological definition to include more than just patterns of inheritance that reproduce fixed traits.[13] Although in many quarters Darwin is celebrated as an oracle who anticipated key insights of modern genetics, it is worth noting that a number of his treatises take account of innovations in behavior that develop through voluntary action.[14] *The Expression of the Emotions in Man and Animals,* for example, zeroes in on physical reactions that have a somatic component but are not entirely deterministic. At least some of the emotional responses that Darwin calls "expressions" give animals discretion, and they reveal the interface between conscious or intentional activity and unconscious or innate nervous response. These physical reactions, rarely under people's direct control, are nevertheless at the junction of biology and psychology, and they disrupt normal disciplinary alignments.

In *The Expression of the Emotions,* Darwin argues, among other things, that "some actions, which were at first performed consciously, have become through habit and association converted into reflex actions, and are now so firmly fixed and inherited, that they are performed even when not of the least use" (45). Expressions are "serviceable habits" that are reproduced over time and engrained in the nervous system. As Clive Bush suggests, "Darwin had claimed for behaviour the same kind of evolutionary pattern as he had claimed for physical characteristics" (*Halfway to Revolution,* 270). Indeed, the emotional reactions that interest Darwin have their impetus in hardwired response patterns. However, the mechanisms of inheritance he proposes for expressive behavior differ from the physical characteristics that he discusses in *On the Origin of the Species.* Darwin's *Expression of the Emotions* is thought to contradict his own putative refutation of Lamarck's theory of acquired characteristics because his thesis is that expressive actions, once subject to some degree of voluntary control and developed to cope with distinct situations, can be inherited.[15] Emotional responses perceived as irrational are really holdovers—distinct "survivals"—of coping mechanisms that can outlast their causes. The idea has Lamarckian resonance because Darwin presupposes that organisms can incorporate changes over time by means of once deliberate forms of striving. Although these chains of interconnected responses imply a degree of inevitability, Darwin thinks that the resulting behaviors are influenced by complex, intersecting social and psychological urgings. In the first place, such expressions are quite responsive to situational parameters, and, in the second place, they betray a certain amount of unpredictability.

Stein was fascinated with Darwin's ontology, which had profound implications for several fields of study important to her. In a letter to Robert Haas, Stein recounts how she kept up interest in Darwin despite her change of discipline:

> I was at Radcliffe of course and I began specializing in science. I was awfully interested in biology but gradually it turned into philosophy and psychology. I do still think that Darwin is the great man of the period that formed my youth, and I often meditate about his expression of emotions in man and animals, aside from William James, Münsterberg and Santayana I did not work with anybody in particular. (quoted in Bush, *Halfway to Revolution*, 270)

Stein singles out *The Expression of the Emotions* in some measure, I would suggest, because Darwin's topic reminds her of parallel interests in emotional functioning on the part of William James and the other philosophers she mentions. Darwin, like James, understands emotional expressions as ways in which members of a given species react to different kinds of situation. Both appear to treat such expressions as initiatory behaviors that prepare an animal's reaction to a stimulus by allowing it to strike an attitude, itself correlated to a specific bodily posture. To take one of Darwin's examples: dogs stiffen, bare their teeth, raise their head, with hairs bristling, when they are in an attack mode or confronting an enemy, but sink curvaceously and flexuously when they are in a humble and affectionate frame of mind. James follows Darwin by correlating emotions with their physiological accompaniments (*Principles of Psychology*, 449).

Some of the expressions that Darwin discusses develop in offspring at an early age, and he hypothesizes that they are the result of imitative or "sympathetic" instincts. In other words, such behaviors and habits can be quite social as responses. The people and animals that express these behaviors enter into structured relationships with other people and animals, and their habits also respond to and resonate with other habits. For Darwin, expressions organize a body's sympathetic relationship to other bodies. He examines phenomena such as blushes, trembles, and pupil dilations, which are hard to classify either as scripted, biological reactions or as unscripted, cultural ones. He recounts a story told to him of a worthy Victorian lady who, like the rest of her family, suffered from a marked propensity to blushing. At one point, while being examined by a doctor, her blush spread down her neck and onto her chest as she shed individual pieces of clothing. The blush followed the path of the doctor's gaze. Such sympathetic nervous events and others like them are triggered by psychological reactions, and the physiological structures of the body show themselves to be synchronized with, and accountable to, psychological and cultural cues, in this case the response or anticipated response of another person.

Elizabeth Wilson, who sets out to rescue Darwin's biological account from genetic reductionism, insists that his tenacious resistance to cordoning off cultural from biological spheres may not simply be the result of his ignorance of Mendelian genetics. According to her, Darwin insists on "reciprocally configured systems" and a "wide range of mechanisms of inheritance, transmission, and transformation" ("Trembling, Blushing," 69).[16] Wilson refers to Edwin Clarke and L. S. Jacyna, who point out that the term "sympathetic" as pertaining to a nervous system dates back to Galen and refers to forms of "rapport thought to exist between parts of the body, especially the organs, that were not anatomically connected" (Clarke and Jacyna, *Nineteenth-Century Origins of Neuroscientific Concepts*, 102). Originally, "sympathetic nervous response" indicated unexpected lines of causation among distinct organs and among systems that appeared to have strange affinity. Wilson argues that even once the structure of the nervous system was discovered, its actions could not be entirely isolated. She shows how the neurophysiology of the nervous system, which is hardwired and involuntary, has surprising alliances with "psychological proclivities, preferences, and habits, and beyond that . . . other bodies and systems of inheritance and transmission" ("Trembling, Blushing," 74). These sympathetic responses are often unpredictable, though one may detect distinct organization in them once they manifest. She attempts to recuperate for modern biology the implications of an older notion of inventive nervous action. Intricate systems do not act on each other in defined and highly circumscribed ways but through unexpected coordinations or "sympathetic" reactions.

Stein was evidently interested in Darwin's way of coupling discrepant assertions: repetitive emotional responses have a heritable biological signature but one that is also capable of variation. Expressions have a supple, "nervy" character. Habits are not insentient, as Wyndham Lewis would have it. Stein's prose style tracks these habits, which react in small ways to the situation around them and fan out in a constant pattern of variation. The variations Darwin has in mind are not just the arbitrary products of genetic mutation. Nor should they be seen as salutary effects of cultural intervention understood in opposition to nature. For one of the most fundamental and far-reaching consequences of Darwin's thought, distorted subsequently by discourses of social Darwinism, is that cultural systems should be conceptualized in a manner continuous with nature.[17]

"Nurture" is not a disruptive (or as it was often thought in the period, degenerative) force that acts on natural processes.[18] Variations arise, if not quite from willed behavior, than from a singular "liveliness" in the individual organism. This inventive principle emerges at the point where numerous systems intersect, some automatic and others voluntary, some innate and others situational and alterable.

I would propose that, in these respects, Darwinian thought is much closer to Bergsonian vitalism than is often acknowledged, even, arguably, by Bergson himself.[19] Although the vital impetus or *élan vital* that Bergson posited to account for the evolutionary adaptations of living things often strikes modern biologists as a fanciful metaphysical shortcut, an effort to describe a spontaneous and unmotivated adaptation, Bergson's account of evolution as the product of tensions between overlapping systems, each of which has a tendency to self-organization, fits well with at least some of Darwin's ideas.[20]

For Darwin, nervous reflexes—habits acquired and no longer subject to will—are capable of adaptive, one might even say creative, responses. Darwin's famous example is of a decapitated frog, which despite having lost cerebral control of its body is still able to wipe away an irritant, such as a drop of acid on its thigh, with its foot. Astonishingly, if the frog's foot is then amputated, the creature continues to make an effort to complete the act, and, after fruitlessly trying for a short time, it finally uses the other foot to liberate itself of the irritant. Reflex reactions are, as Darwin was well aware, never simple; undirected by cerebral processing, and in the absence of consciousness or intentionality, the frog can still respond to stimuli and modify a sequence of movements. Darwin consistently seeks out neurophysiological events that do not separate discriminating action from biological mechanism. Depicting specific modifications in a train of repetitive responses, Darwin may be said to erode the distinction between an aware, responsive organism and one passively reacting to its situation. Unconscious of what it is doing, the frog can still set in motion a modified sequence of reactions. Nature is dynamically self-directed. As we will see in what follows, Stein adopted Darwin's view that habits are lively, innovative, and unpredictable, and she set out to test the nature and extent of this unpredictability.

AN EXPERIMENTAL EPISODE

Before Stein wrote a word of *Three Lives*, she spent a number of her undergraduate years at Radcliffe conducting experimental research in Harvard's psychology laboratory. William James and Hugo Münsterberg, a young colleague of James's and her supervisor, were important intellectual influences, but they were not the only ones.[21] The psychological models of habit that Stein developed resemble Darwin's as well. Both Stein and Darwin see habit as a creative impetus toward self-organization, one that widens to include synchronies between anatomical organs and even other organisms or people. Also, both consider the crossover between automatic and voluntary movement, behaviors that are partly innate and partly situation-specific.

Stein was drawn to study the intricate role played by impulse in fashioning people's behavior. She created two experimental studies intended to gauge people's reactions by their automatic or unthinking responses to motor suggestion. The published results discounted any hypothesis that relied on a "secondary personality" to explain unconscious volition, targeting implicitly the French school of Pierre Janet and Jean-Martin Charcot, which associated strains of automatism with hysteria and psychological dissociation. Instead of seeing automatism as pathological, as Janet and Charcot did, Stein and her colleague Leon M. Solomons tended to regard it as a normal element of reflexive or involuntary response. In however limited a fashion, the two student researchers set out to disprove that there is an unconscious agency determining behavior behind the scenes and requiring separate explanation. In doing so, they dispensed with models that we tend now to associate with psychoanalysis.[22]

Stein and Solomons employed a planchette, of a type used in Ouija boards, that could be guided by the investigator. Diverting their subjects' attention either by reading or conversing with them, the investigators looked at their subjects' arms and their tendency to movement. In "Normal Motor Automatism" (1896), they relied on each other as experimental subjects, while in Stein's solo study, "Cultivated Motor Automatism" (1898), students from Radcliffe and Harvard were recruited. These students, operating under different levels of fatigue, could be made to learn and maintain certain kinds of movement while in a distracted state. The goal in each case was to devise ways of preventing them from being conscious of their activities, specifically of their motor impulses. The more tired or distracted the students were, the greater their propensity to keep "writing."

In her subject group, Stein carefully isolated their bodies' likely predisposition to movement. As Clive Bush argues, she uncovered a complicated relation between "automatic" writing and "associative" behavior (*Halfway to Revolution*, 279). The mind absenting itself leaves a hand that still picks up movement from surrounding influences and learns to repeat it. The hand, once started, moves on its own and takes on a particular rhythm. The pen it holds has a decided tendency to curve in a certain way and to a particular shape: "the figure eight, a long curve, or an m-figure" (Stein, "Cultivated Motor Automatism," 296). Meanwhile, if the hand fluctuates between movements more natural to it and newly acquired tendencies, then the body can be seen to enact tensions, alternating movements that suggest a struggle as "between two themes in a musical composition" (296). These "sympathetic" nervous responses on the part of her subjects were at once capable of guidance and recalcitrant to it.[23] Though the hand can learn new patterns, it is also subject to errancy. Patterns are transmitted from one person to another through complex coordinations and disengagements, creating a vacillating field of attraction and repulsion.

In the first series of experiments, Stein and Solomons treat the mind as a human motor, capable of action without the interference of reflection or judgment.[24] It would seem, however, that Stein differed from Solomons on the question of whether we can truly tell habit apart from higher-level functioning.[25] Indeed, years later, responding to an article by a young B. F. Skinner in the *Atlantic Monthly*,[26] she objected to his claim that she had ever treated the cases in her experiment as purely automatic writing, as rote, unthinking physical responses to stimuli.[27]

She speculated that a kind of "xtra [sic] consciousness—excess" (quoted in Meyer, "Writing Psychology Over," 141) crept into the display of habits.[28] The mind absenting itself still leaves a remainder, a form of consciousness that crops up in the interstices of distracted attention (Stein and Solomons, "Normal Motor Automatism," 506). At one point in the experiment, Stein and Solomons refer to consciousness as "extra personal," blurring the distinction between the body's own impetus and an influence that comes from without (494).

The continuum Stein insisted on between conscious and unconscious or creative and automatic response betrays telltale vitalist preoccupations. The small-scale innovations within habits—or, as Stein at one point refers to them, "innervations"—coincide with relatively stable patterns.[29] In *The Principles of Psychology* William James considers habit to be an "equilibrium point" in a plastic structure of change.[30] Habits are adaptive nature, forms of autoregulation, orchestrations of undirected dispositions that happen on the level of the body—or between bodies, for in many respects, habits are social assemblages. They emerge through social interactions, and they regulate social life.[31] If habits are incapable of locking the pattern, as I have suggested, they are also incapable of regulating and circumscribing the degree of deviation from it. At the intersection between nature and culture, habits do not exhaustively determine behavior; they shift the biological focus onto matters of inclination, in which an agent can maneuver among an indeterminate number of different directions. Each potential inclination or tendency is equally "natural." Nature may regulate life, but it also deregulates it. Biology does not put a fundamental limit on the capacity for inventiveness, and, as regards habit, it works in combination with choice.

THE HABITUAL UNCONSCIOUS

In *Three Lives*, begun some seven years after the publication of her second experiment, Stein assembled characters defined by their habits. But she seems to understand their habits, dispositions, and other distinguishing forms of personal preference not as indicators of fixity of temperament but as collections of evolving tendencies, sometimes in conflict with each other, hence able to link up in diverse ways. These tendencies are amplified differently in different situations. With a nod to Darwin, she examines how character-defining behavior gets modified on the heels of sympathetic interactions or conflicts with others.

It seems clear that the repetitiousness of the prose in "Melanctha" is meant to mirror the patterns and forms that habits acquire as they develop over time, as they gather duration and move in a progressive direction. Stein's nonstandard use of the present-progressive tense also encourages the sense of ongoing time. Habits are constantly modified in the novel by present circumstances—by the exercise of will in characters or, more remarkably, by an unconscious shift effected in them. It is as if habit itself—the feeling of constraint and orderliness—is manifold and made up of complex parts. These parts incessantly reorganize into new patterns. "Every day now," we are told, "Jeff seemed to be coming nearer, to be really loving."

> Every day now, Melanctha poured it all out to him, with more freedom. . . . More and more every day now they seemed to know more really, what it was each other one was always feeling. More and more now every day Jeff found in himself, he felt more trusting. More and more every day now, he did not think anything in words about what he was always doing. Every day now more and more Melanctha would let out to Jeff her real, strong feeling. ("Melanctha," 109)

Melanctha and Jeff find ways to love each other for a time, though each stands in an anxious and somewhat compromised relation to the other's values. The phrase "more and more" captures the additive nature of events. Jeff Campbell is consistent not because he is identical with his past self but because his changes add to the attitudes and habits of mind that came before. His present self is constantly more than it was before, and the "more" represents the accretions of present time as it becomes past. Nevertheless, character is not simply an aggregation. There is an opposed movement or tendency toward subtraction. Melanctha's ways of "forgetting" what she owes, what she has done, and what she feels are all instances of a character being shaped by subtraction.

The additive and the subtractive movements combine to create a third: the recombinant. Repetitions in Stein are, as I mentioned, never exact replications of the past. Having once commenced, they diverge in numerous directions. The relation between "more and more" and "every day" in the preceding sequence is variable. These phrases are also conjoined with new descriptions of a situation. Repetitions in Stein tend to split apart: individual sequences attach themselves to bits that were once free of them. Certain salient points modulate into other series as the point is prolonged in different directions in relation to to other points. The departures that characters make from their customary repertoire of reactions do not come out of nowhere. They may be unprecedented, but they come into existence as actions from a modification in a series of repetitive actions.

And so in Stein's work attitudes tend to accumulate up to a point and then begin shifting course as people are left to react to their situation. Stein uses frequently contradictory assessments of the characters to underscore not their inconsistency but their plasticity. For instance, the narrator remarks of Melanctha that she "never really lost her sense that it was Jane Harden who had taught her [world wisdom], but Jane did many things that Melanctha now no longer needed. And then, too, Melanctha never could remember right when it came to what she had done and what had happened" ("Melanctha," 74–75). In the next paragraph, the narrator effectively reverses course: "Melanctha began now to feel that she had always had world wisdom. She really knew of course, that it was Jane who had taught her, but all that began to be covered over by the trouble between them, that was now always getting stronger" (75). Why does the narrator use the word "never" if it is so readily contradicted? Stein depicts Melanctha as apt to judge her past by what is immediately going on around her. Yet unconsciously Melanctha still knows her debt of gratitude to Jane Harden. It is registered in her feelings and habits of thought, which, apart from any explicit sense that Melanctha has about herself, keep a running tally of her experience and help direct her choices.

As Henri Bergson understands habit, it is a form of memory created by repetition, one different in kind from the memory that records singular events, which are, as it were, stamped with a date and time. The former is like a lesson learned over a long period: it is "lived and acted, rather than represented" (*Matter and Memory*, 81). In a habit, successive phases melt into each other as the movement or thought process becomes rote. It is still a memory, but one lodged in the body itself rather than recollected in the mind in the form of distinct images. Bergson was in fashion in Paris during the period in which Stein wrote *Three Lives*, and from early on his theories were employed to explain Stein's writing.[32] Stein's friend and fellow émigrée Mabel Dodge wrote a review in 1913 of Stein's experimental writing, describing "perceptions, conditions, and states of being, never before quite consciously experienced" ("Speculations, or Post-Impressionism in Prose," 28) that she associated with Bergson's theory of intuition. These historical links are now out of fashion, but I would suggest that Bergson's work, together with William James's, can still offer an illuminating foundation for understanding Stein's presentation of habits. James sees habit as a groove or mental pathway of sequentially organized responses, and Bergson sees it as a pattern of reaction. Both see it as a registry of movements or potential movements. Although Bergson holds habit in even less esteem than James does, both of their conceptions of psychic life reluctantly depend on it as a key compass point of experience. Stein, however, contests any degree of emphasis that they place on its inertness, thus teasing out the antinomies implicit in their conceptions.

By linking Bergson to William James, I wish to do more than acknowledge the related perspectives and historical ties that bind their legacies together. Most critics, Olson and Schoenbach included, who have examined the connection between Stein and James have done so under the banner of pragmatist philosophy, part of a general trend identified by Steven Meyer (*Irresistible Dictation*, xix). They have not generally viewed her preoccupations (or William James's, for that matter) in the context of vitalism.[33] Meyer, for example, uses James's self-made label as a "radical empiricist" to argue for the independent interest of James's psychology, which he thinks is crucial for understanding Stein's experimental impulses; but for philosophical reasons associated with Meyer's understanding of organic form, he does not associate James's late writings with vitalism (*Irresistible Dictation*, 56). By using a vitalist lens, however, we can begin to see how much Stein's ideas connect to something beyond thematized pragmatist social policy. Stein's well-known interest in repetition and time, along with her early fascination with Darwin, points in the direction of nonmechanistic "life" philosophies and an interest in the nature of psychic change.

For Bergson, habit is a kind of physical or mental disposition to act. It retains the past in the form of an inclination to *do* something. It combines various conscious memories into something that is automatic and that is not necessarily conscious. Stein's writing brings to the foreground certain ambiguities in Bergson's conception of habit. Like Darwin before her, she prefers to underscore the continuity between the unconscious and conscious activity of habit or else to dissolve the distinction. For her, habit is not entirely unconscious or automatic because it is amenable to the purposive exertions of will and can integrate changes within it. And yet habit manages to retain aspects of the past in ways that people in conscious life cannot necessarily grasp or represent to themselves, at least not cognitively.

James calls habit "the enormous fly-wheel of society, its most precious conservative agent" (*Principles of Psychology* 1:120). For Bergson as well, habit is a petrified and lower function of the mind. It has an uncertain status born of its intermediary position between memory and perception. Without habit, perception is not possible. It allows one to digest and absorb the overwhelming data of experience by matching the images one takes in with memories made up of images from the past. But to the degree that our perceptions are overwhelmed by habit, new experiences are assimilated into ready-made responses. Bergson and James imply, then, that in some way habit impoverishes our daily life by treating the present as a mere instance of the past, thereby expressing an arrested development: "Like every habitual bodily exercise, it is stored up in a mechanism which is set in motion as a whole by an initial impulse, in a closed system of automatic movements which succeed each other in the same order and, together, take the same length of time" (*Matter and Memory*, 80). In this view, habit would seem to admit new material rarely, and then only in the impact of the stimuli remaining on its fringes. These are minor shocks of experience left undigested.

But Bergson does not stay wholly within this static view. In his account, habit is capable of reconnecting diverse bodily memories, for instance, guiding one's choice on a more or less contracted plain of mental functioning.[34] Habits are also necessary to higher functioning and to creative activity. If one subtracts from the perception of an object the habit that allows the object to be recognized and therefore positioned in a context, one is left only with fugitive sensations and potentialities that overwhelm the body's capacity to act. Without habit, objects have no way of slotting themselves into place in a form that the body understands.

Habit is thus an assimilative process that makes a sensation—and the potentiality it opens up—meaningful or useful.[35] In the following sense, then, habit is in an "open" circuit with perception: its recognitions continually heighten or extend a person's capacity for thinking and perceiving, and the resulting thoughts and perceptions eventually enter into the habit mill. Habit conserves innovation. As James says, habits "fund and capitalize" our investments in the world (*Principles of Psychology* 1:122). From this metaphor we may conclude that habit produces more than it starts out with. This, I believe, is why it is misleading to imply (as Bergson and James sometimes do) that in initiating regular sequences and pursuing a chain of reactions, habit arrests choice. Rather, it prevents us from straying into the blind alleys of a decision-making process, and it integrates new impulses into our routine actions.

As I have indicated, Stein celebrates the constitutive impurity of habits. For her, they are not straight repetitions, and they do not exist apart from the perceptions that redirect them. To the degree that habit stores elements of the past, the process is for Stein a kind of unconscious routine; the unconscious, however, is not a deep structure that cancels out a character's superficial inconsistency. As Stein recounts in her humorous, offhand way in *The Autobiography of Alice B. Toklas*, William James thought that she, at least, "never had subconscious reactions" (79). Habits exist at the intersection between the past and the present. They may spawn mysterious behaviors, but only because they compress and blend many once distinct tendencies. They are the result of long, multifaceted histories. Habits translate memories into movements and so are a practical engine of the unconscious, but they are not coded messages or indications of repressed desires sent out from the psyche that require hermeneutic analysis. Rather than prompting us to peer into characters, Stein would have us witness the way people go about extending themselves within their situation, how they feel themselves modified by the occasion. To announce an attitude over and over again is to feel it change and accumulate duration.

Despite the small alterations of routine that Stein highlights in "Melanctha"—the lovers' fluid turnings toward and turnings away from each other—the larger story raises questions about the inexorable deterioration of the couple's relationship. Eventually, Jeff comes to be on bad terms with Melanctha. In the process, Stein casts the two in a debate about the nature of their commitment and consistency. Are we to understand the ending of their relationship, the separation, as fated from the start, seeing that the characters stand for ill-matched types? Jeff accuses Melanctha of always failing to remember her love, and Melanctha rejoins that "real feeling every moment when its [sic] needed . . . does seem to me like real remembering" (128). The couple's longstanding dispute about memory is at the heart of their respective conceptions of consistency. Stein, however, does not privilege one above the other. Both have habits of mind, which, as she keeps showing us, maintain a form of memory rooted in disposition and feeling, whether conscious or unconscious. From Jeff's point of view, Melanctha's habitual restiveness leaves no room for anything that is not bound to impulse, to what is immediate, direct, and urgent. He lays claim, however, to the kind of memory that Bergson calls a "memory-image." It is associated with an intellectual removal from the world of everyday responses. Jeff lauds a life lived deliberately, while Melanctha feels no need to square her habits with her representations of herself. Yet his precious memory and the feelings that surround it are, like hers, subject to a degree of automatism. Impulse and the will that drives it intertwine with habit. It may be true that the outcome of his relationship is to a degree predictable once Jeff and Melanctha show themselves to persist along a certain course, but to notice only the large-scale uniformity of disposition over time is, for Stein, to take away all the drama of change—the gradual augmentations and revisions of feeling. She emphasizes continuity over abstract uniformity.

The long aggregating process leaves Jeff wondering how it has come to happen that he must ask Melanctha whether she has time to see him; soon after that, they part ways. Their willful compulsions and quarrels have made their relationship the stuff of slow defeat. As I have suggested, habit is a recording and playing instrument of the unconscious. It is a dynamic force rather than an archive, and one in many ways continuous with conscious life. It is therefore not the frozen, submerged mass of an iceberg that Freud imagined lurking, oblivious to the climate above waters. Though Stein lived to see the increasing dominance of Freud's conceptual enterprise, *Three Lives*, composed well before the influence of psychoanalysis was widespread, was more influenced by vitalist ideas.[36] Vitalism offered a more action-oriented conception of nondeliberate processes than did psychoanalysis (as it came to be known). Psychoanalysis considered the unconscious a repository of irrational beliefs and repressed wishes that needed penetrating interpretation to access. "Vitalism"—often used derisively to label the views of metaphysicians who assume the existence of an extraphysical vital force—might more properly describe the work of Bergson and James whose conceptual models are based on changeable living systems and who give primacy to dwelling within the world and experiencing it in actionable rather than intellectual ways.

Accidental Character

By emphasizing shifting habits Stein is able to present an alternative to two prevailing ways we imagine change brought about in a human life. The active version says that people make deliberative choices that allow them to intervene in their own circumstance. To this, Stein, pursuing a vitalist pattern of thinking, would say that intentional actions belong to the field of unintentional repetitions from which they emerge. The passive version says that unforeseen contingencies or "accidents" play a critical role in shaping the arc and span of a human destiny. One readily associates this view with Darwin, whose *On the Origin of Species* assigns great evolutionary weight to the random, unplanned events that give individuals who can cope with them "the best chance of surviving and of procreating their kind" (51). Conventional narratives tend to treat the resulting changes as decisive events, interruptions within a linear or successive chain of causes that lead people down a forked path. Stein is fascinated by such accidents, but she tends to treat them as nondiscrete events that interact with other gradually unfolding systems with their own patterns or "habits." Every event has its own process of development, and any new directional shift takes place within a field of potentiality. Stein might be said to be borrowing from Darwin in this instance as well. *On the Origin of Species* makes an effort to grasp the crossover of different events in nonlinear relation as a means of understanding the adaptations that organisms develop. These slight "difference[s] of structure or constitution," which we are "apt to consider as of very trifling importance" intermingle by "many unknown laws of correlation of growth" (*Origin of Species*, 54). For Stein and Darwin, definitive alterations of fate are prepared for, however unintentionally and unconsciously, in part by the patterns and physiological habits that people manifest individually or on a species level. Habits are interlaced with accidents, but they also bring them into alignment. They retain within them a history that gives directionality and shape to events.

Although *Three Lives* is not as paratactical as Stein's later novels, such as *The World Is Round* or *Ida*, she does mark the peculiar intimacy between chance events and the character of the individuals who respond to them. For instance, she highlights Melanctha's melancholic habit of wandering, which leaves her particularly receptive to chance as she encounters a number of men in an episodic series. Melanctha's "wandering" stands as an obvious sexual metaphor and, it is implied, a courtship routine paired with a self-protective flight instinct. While "Melanctha liked to wander" (68), we are told, "and to stand by the railroad yard," she "would always make herself escape" (70) when men became too imposing in their approach. But Stein skirts the Darwinian functionalist themes of survival and reproduction. Rather than give too much goal-oriented consistency to this habit of Melanctha's, Stein emphasizes the activity's open-endedness. In this respect, she is closer to Bergson, who uses wandering (in his case, of an amoeba) to illustrate the "liveliness" of an organism's impulse or *élan*, and why it can never be limited to predetermined patterns of behavior (*Creative Evolution*, 15–33). Bergson thinks that living things have an individualizing tendency "that is everywhere opposed by the tendency towards reproduction" (13). Melanctha is a searching figure: her characteristic behavioral patterns and eccentricities make her a natural experimentalist who explores the sexual and emotional boundaries of her metropolitan niche. We might say that Melanctha's wandering habits are also an instance of textual indeterminacy. As Derrida reminds us, the term "wandering" is etymologically related to the term "vague."[37] This vagueness prevents readers from assigning Melanctha or her behaviors too definite a character. Stein puts great store in the lively accidents, random digressions, and wandering style of her narration, which are intended to express the mutability of Melanctha's life and temperament.

Like Henry James, whose work she valued, Stein is alert to the emergent meanings within a pattern of vagueness that build and turn on nearly accidental shifts of thought or action. Indeed, as we will see, Stein learned from James something important about the relationship between habits of mind and the accidents that buffet and alter those characteristic patterns. James's syntax also "wanders," gradually building up in formal patterns that test the limits of language's instrumental communicative function. James shows a preference for situating individuals within a changing field of relations as well, offering Stein a model for how to be receptive to accidental alignments and indeterminate effects.

Although I am suggesting that Stein's early fiction presents characters whose habits form through the integration of such "accidents," I do not wish to ignore the echoes of predictable narratives of enervation that Stein inherits from the naturalist writers who preceded her. In this respect, her formal procedures are in danger of aligning habits with rigid forms of behavior that betray a fatalistic consistency. In the vocabulary of her later writing, one could say that in her early fiction she puts too much faith in "narrative," defined as the presentation of events that follow from each other, rather than find a way to depict the genuine unfolding of movement and accident as it emerges within character, a process she associates with "portraiture."[38] She began experimenting with this form soon after completing *Three Lives*, and she relied on it extensively in later years. Portraiture required her to present character as a novel "happening" without relying on her readers' expectations (derived from their exposure to similar narratives) for anticipating the direction of events that comprise a life.[39] All the same, as a formal practice, narration is not entirely distinct from portraiture. Stein's *Three Lives* incorporates elements of both.

To tease out moments of liveliness within character from the deterministic patterns that critics sometimes attribute to her early work, it may be helpful to look at an instance of "portraiture" that Stein wrote when her formal practice had settled into a more distinctively realized habit. One portrait in particular, written twenty-six years after she completed *Three Lives*, examines the embryonic changes that chance imposes on character formation. It is dedicated to Henry James and examines his career as a writer. Stein had been reading James since her early college days, but the influence he had on her (which she claims to have scarcely felt at first) only made itself evident over time.[40] In *The Autobiography of Alice B. Toklas*, she describes James as "the only nineteenth century writer who being an American felt the method of the twentieth century" (78). In the section devoted to him in *Four in America*, Stein explores the surprises that accrue in portraiture, surprises that James was a master at depicting. She tracks these "accidents" alongside the accidents in James's life, and then she tracks several more that put his life and work in more intimate relation to hers. By doing so, I would argue, she traces a vitalist literary influence that works by indeterminate and indirect means.

The piece on James—which follows formal procedures that are themselves exceptionally oblique or "indirect"—begins not by examining James's life but by parsing the difference between an accident and a coincidence. "An accident," we are told, "is when a thing happens. A coincidence is when a thing is going to happen and does" ("Henry James" in *Writings: 1932–1946*, 149). The coincidences that Stein has in mind are (at least initially) events that cross or overlap in ways that have a minimally detectable (and therefore predictable) pattern, while accidents are events that have no justification for their causes or that depart from expected chains of causation. In the series of alignments that structure the piece, "accidents" are associated with "writing as it is being written"; "coincidences," with "writing as it is going to be written." For example, Shakespeare's plays progress in a manner that is sensitive to the unique, unfolding moment; his sonnets, however, like Stein's own translation of George Hugnet's poetry, have an element of the expected in them: they are written "as if they were going to be written" ("Henry James," 150). In the case of the sonnets it is because Shakespeare relies on established generic codes and emotional patterns; in Stein's case it is because her translation has to adhere to an original that is already a fait accompli.[41] In the course of the piece, however, Stein discovers an element of accident within coincidence and an element of surprise within habits. More suggestive still, she finds that all genuine accidents have potentialities that can be foreseen within them.

Stein's composition would appear to be about personal character, a fact that is made clear by the counterfactual speculation that runs through the piece, which asks: What if Henry James had been a general and not a writer? Thornton Wilder calls this the "parlor game idea" of *Four in America*, a book in which she also treats George Washington as a would-be novelist and speculates about alternative lives for Ulysses S. Grant and Wilbur Wright. She seems to be exploring whether genius is "general" enough (she puns on this word) to make these American originals successful outside their chosen arena. The possibility of James's being a writer by coincidence seems to discount any of his habits of mind, suggesting instead a kind of amenability to circumstance that we ordinarily think is quite implausible. We tend to think that habits are character-defining in ways that are quite resistant to situational contingencies. But Stein does not think that the distinction between cultivated habits of mind and sheer accident is so stark. At the frontier of agency, habits are continually reacting to accidental events in ways that make the one hard to tell apart from the other. As Stein sees it, we change direction not by arbitrarily veering onto some new path but by consolidating or being receptive to forces that are already underway. With a mind akin to a general's, James teaches us to pay attention to the unexpected alignments of an unfolding process. He recovers the surprise within coincidence (otherwise treated in the piece as predictable) and thus recaptures the ordinary meaning of the word "coincidence" itself.

How do coincidences impinge on character? Like a habit, a coincidence might be thought of as a repetition, though a surprising one. Is it a coincidence that James, having begun as a writer, remained one? To revert to *Three Lives* for a moment, is it a coincidence that Melanctha, who "would get very blue" (161), establishes a series of romantically unsatisfying relationships? Stein concedes that the prolongation of a certain direction or course of action is more likely after it has begun: "Once you know that you have written you go on writing. This explains nothing" ("Henry James," 153). A writer like James, however, "came not to begin but to have begun" (167). Stein supposes that the formative process that leads him toward writing has its roots in an invisible incipience that precedes any obvious sign of its commencement. His talent and his temperament are far from accidental or random. Yet his choice of métier cannot be separated from a multitude of other processes, some of which may appear fortuitous: "You make a discovery, it is a coincidence, of course yes a coincidence, not an accent but an access, yes a coincidence which tells you yes" (164).

If we think of an accident as "a thing that happens" in seeming isolation, then a coincidence might be thought of as a *community of accidents.* It is an event that reveals an emergent pattern. Two or more singular events or occurrences synchronize, and they begin to resonate with each other. The meaning that these intersecting events express carries some significance for the person who perceives it, and so they develop in their fortuity a germinal logic. The connection changes the scope of their relations, as when, by putting words next to each other, they have "a different sound and having a different sound they [do] not have a different sense but they [have] a different intensity" (160). Whatever is coincidental is not designed or premeditated. No one has intended it to be thus, and yet the events are surprising in their improbable order. Or rather—this is the delicate balancing act of a coincidence—it appears *as if* ordered. The *American Heritage Dictionary* defines a coincidence as "a sequence of events that although accidental seems to have been planned or arranged." Meanwhile, any evidence that a thing has actually been planned rules out its being called coincidental.

The order that seems to underlie a coincidence is necessarily vague, then. It cannot be preordained. Instead, it opens up a question as to why something happens together with something else. As a chance event, a coincidence cannot be understood in and of itself; rather, it refers, however oddly or obliquely, to the process that has led to it. In this sense, it contains within it an anticipation or expectation of its happening (it is worth recalling that Stein defines a coincidence as "a thing [that] is going to happen and does"). But the event can only be recreated belatedly from the products or outcomes that emerge from it. Thus, "a coincidence," she notes, "is having done so" (160). A bit later, she returns to the thread: "Then it comes over you all of a sudden or very slowly or a little at a time why it is all as it is" (164).[42]

We regard accidents as random and unpredictable, almost by definition. But they do not emerge in temporal isolation, separate from the chain of causes around them, as discrete events or stages. As Stein makes clear, they are the product of accumulated movements and potentials that reach a threshold and are touched off. Certain accidents of people's biography and history, such as James's health and location when the Civil War began, can be seen to spark unpredictable actions and responses. These new actions take serial form not by duplicating earlier actions performed but rather by actualizing the vague halo of possible actions that tend to surround an individual's prospective engagements in the world. The new action is an extension into reality of a virtual or possible action that *was*. Thus, Stein remarks, "Everything that could happen or not happen would have had a preparation" (167). Like Bergson, Stein thinks that events "coincide" with precedents in them that were potential or that were ambiguously active.[43] Coincidences are moments that remind us of particularly scattered, diffuse, and fragile potentialities, which reintersect to create new patterns or probabilistic itineraries.

The coincidences that Stein explores in the piece on James are those that emerge in the act of writing.[44] For example, her own composition takes a certain turn as a result of her having read Shakespeare's sonnets by chance when she was thinking about James. Her response to the one enters into a synchronized relation with her response to the other. The etymological root of coincidence refers to an "agreement" or remarkable concurrence. This agreement is not scripted in advance as a plan. Rather it draws on the potential for order that emerges from accidents. Writing, in turn, that unfolds by means of improvised structures and wandering ("vague") organizations allows coincidental patterns to reveal themselves. Artistic creation remains a powerful analogue for the open-endedness and tendency toward complexity of an evolving life.

Because commonsensically we treat accidents as discrete occurrences without any apparent or deliberate cause, we tend to regard them as events that are external, separate from the activities and behaviors that exemplify a person's character. Like Emerson, however, Stein insists that there is a peculiarly intimate relation between these apparently unmotivated events and the people who flourish despite or even because of them. A person develops certain patterns of response to contingency and thereby becomes personally connected to those contingencies over time. As Emerson puts it, "Nature does not like to be observed. . . . Direct strokes she never gives us power to make; all our blows glance, all our hits are accidents. Our relations to each other are oblique and casual" ("Experience" in *Emerson's Prose and Poetry*, 200). Emerson is suggesting that we are not simply sensitized to fate as to matters foreign to ourselves, but we are the ongoing (hence, casual or ordinary) product of those accidental relations.[45] In this way we are answerable to them. The capacity to accommodate a chancy world that is always changing extends into the corridors of the self. Midway between mindless activity and motivated behavior, habits are places where chance and choice intersect. To appreciate how they intersect, Stein must learn in the piece to "write both ways at once" ("Henry James," 163)—by accident and by coincidence, spontaneously and through recourse to habits of mind—just as James did. She must write "as she is writing" and "as she is going to write."

A genius's supposed lability of character notwithstanding, Stein is self-consciously comical in her affected indifference to the difference between James's literary habits and any potentially military ones he might have cultivated: "If Henry James was a general who perhaps would win an army to win a battle he might not know the difference" (158). She repeatedly mines the farcicality of her suggestions.[46] Yet a general, like a novelist, must survey circumstance and command the available forces with a display of authority and resolve: "If Henry James had been a general which he was what would he have had to do. He would have to do what a general has to do" (169). And later still: "Henry James had no wishes and if he were a general he would have no wishes and he was a general and he had no wishes" (170). Both writer and general must have a preternatural ability to premeditate on the one hand and to sense the opportunities of chance around them without arranging everything in advance on the other, and this leads to the analogy that structures the piece: "Henry James made no one care for plans. Do you see that he is a general" (170). The imagined choice of a martial calling for James is significant. As Catherine Gallagher has pointed out, military history was an early and privileged locus for thinking about counterfactual narrative, insisting on the contingency of events rather than on providential necessity.[47] What distinguishes Stein's portrait from the historical and narrative genres of interest to Gallagher is Stein's presumption that one cannot easily locate decisive turning points in a life marked by habits and long-standing tendencies of mind: all such imagined forking paths are in some manner as absurd and artificial as the conceit she conspicuously and rather risibly pursues. The contingencies that make a "difference" in a life are small, redundant, continuous with the events around them, and so imbricated with habit that they are hard to tell apart. James is intimately responsive to these accidents, and to such a degree that he would not be able to tell the difference were his life to have proceeded otherwise.

In this respect, Stein insists on a kernel of truth within the claim that James is a general. As Gallagher has suggested, counterfactual narratives that invoke multiple possible worlds can only show "the parity of the alternatives" by maintaining that some aspect of the "alternate worlds closely [should] resemble some important aspects of current . . . reality" ("War, Counterfactual History, and Alternate-History Novels," 61). Speaking specifically of alternate-history novels, she suggests that they "posit the ontological parity of the forks of the Y [narrative, which marks a decisive turning point between alternative possibilities] in order to indicate that their alternate worlds actually refer to our social reality" (62). In vitalist terms, the historical tangent is, for Stein, a virtual element of current reality. James's mental habits as a writer contain a general's intellectual aggressiveness and dexterity—not analogically but ontologically.

The forms of accident that Stein associates with a life enable self-alteration, but they are rarely as incurably one-directional as we might suspect. A person's habits may succeed in absorbing these accidents or bringing them into line. And though accidents conventionally imply misfortune, for Stein these erratic occurrences remain vague in their meaning or bearing. These small "happenings" build gradually alongside and through habits, introducing novelty and revealing at once the waywardness and strangeness of a life. In this way, they are difficult to script into regimes of value. Returning to "Melanctha" in the next and final section of this chapter, I show how Stein builds on the relation between novel or accidental events and habits in her early fiction, using comic reversions and nondramatistic changes to undercut fatalistic assumptions about the meaning of her narrative portrait.

THE COMEDY OF LIFE AND THE FATALISTIC NARRATIVE

Stein's casual use of period stereotypes in "Melanctha" seems at first glance to trouble, if not to overwrite, the emphasis on change otherwise manifest throughout her work. The racial typology she relies on comes close to defining African Americans as having rigid and ingrained psychological characteristics. But I would argue that, although Stein relies on racist clichés, her types are fundamentally not unchanging constructs. Like Henry James, who is obsessed with social types and categories as well, she honors emergent changes in character that undercut any suggestion of their fatalistic trajectory. She sees the habits that underwrite them as, in essence, "lively."[48]

Stein explores this liveliness through comic principles of literary form. Although her brand of naturalist fiction veers toward tragic pathos, it evokes an emotional constellation that is something other than lasting grief—or pity and fear. It is true that the trajectory toward death in the "Melanctha" section, as in other sections of the novel (which treat servant characters) draws attention to the deterministic trajectory of the narrative. But Stein's use of subtle comic effects makes possible a disruption or hindrance; these comic bodies cannot simply play out a tragic script, especially one that defines them by an inward "flaw." Stein's characters, beset by certain petrified habits, reveal unexpected forms of autonomy or *esprit* erupting out of an otherwise conditioned life. As Bergson sees it, comedy as a literary form spins off endless repetitive permutations on a rote pattern only to reclaim surprising moments of animation. His theory of comedy is therefore a useful cynosure for thinking about the relation between repetition and novelty.

"Melanctha," as we have seen, is about a black woman of mixed-race heritage whose courtships with various men, both black and white, fail to lead her to the safety and refuge she craves but resists. Her ostensibly tragic nature comes of her resistance to the "good advice and serious kindness" of men distinguished by "intelligence and sympathetic feeling" (69). Early in the story, she wanders among the porters at the train tracks "who often told her exciting things that had happened" to them, but even though she respects them—a "big, serious, melancholy, light brown porter" in particular—"she could never let [his advice] help her or affect her to change the ways that always made her keep herself in trouble" (69).

Stein is toying with a stereotypical and highly schematized ambivalence associated with mulatta characters: identification with people both intelligent and salubrious (linked to their white nature) counteracted by a seed of racial intransigence—or worse, degeneration—that prevents them from thriving. Stein, however, pushes predictable structures to a point of paradox. Melanctha remains airy and evasive as a perpetual strategy for averting her own self-exposure, a fact captured compellingly in the description of her wanderings, in which she "strayed and stood" (67). Her fixity—her repetitive nature—is necessary as an instrument of her self-extension. Although Stein invokes a naturalist narrative structure by letting its eponymous character slope toward moral exhaustion, leading to her demise, she undermines the interpretive protocols that would have us determine the meaning or nature of this fate. Every life must inevitably cease, but this fact does not measure the value of a life or of an individual's attainments or success. Stein declines to see repetition as a sign of a defect that unmasters the self and renders it more vulnerable to external impingements. But neither does she then privilege the alternative narrative trajectory, the teleology mandated by the Bildungsroman, which aims at human enlargement and maturation. The central mulatta figure may be, like others of her kind, a woman who straddles various arenas of social life and is therefore a symbolic instance of "betweenness." But in the first place, she is not a character especially marked by racial ambivalence: Melanctha is no programmatic venturer into illicit sexual territory. (Her principal relationships are with black men.) In the second place, her recalcitrance does not prove her inability to change but exactly the reverse: the fixity of her character, by virtue of its very immobility and its defiance of hygienic logic, exposes Melanctha to new varieties of experience. Despite a number of assumptions, then, about the prevailing style or tendency of one's "race," Stein teaches us to pay attention to small departures of outcome or tendency that modify conventional typologies and that (for her) define all human life.[49]

Stein undercuts the expectation of failure by preventing pathos from being the guiding, sentimental formula of the story. Carole Anne Taylor suggests that Stein exploits "comic indeterminacy" (*The Tragedy and Comedy of Resistance*, 138) that, when it is sustained, allows her heroine to gain "empowerment as a woman in the act of speaking" (159).[50] Despite Stein's repeating that Melanctha is "awful blue" and threading into it her talk about how "she would kill herself" (161), she does not allow her to succumb to suicide. Indeed, the relentless obstinacy and inelasticity of both her character and Jeff's are pushed to the point of exaggeration. Their deportment creates, if anything, a sort of distance from their plight, a peculiar absence of feeling of a kind that Bergson thinks is specific to the comic. "Indifference," he remarks in "Laughter," "is its natural environment, for laughter has no greater foe than emotion" (63). Stein sets the tone of indifference at the beginning of the story when she recounts the death of Rose's baby: "Rose Johnson had liked the baby well enough and perhaps she just forgot it for awhile, anyway the child was dead and Rose and Sam her husband were very sorry but then these things came so often in the negro world in Bridgepoint, that they neither of them thought about it very long" ("Melanchtha," 59). Stein's deficiency of narrative attention to this event mimics Rose's apparent carelessness and comically aligns itself with it. Structurally, Stein reinforces this comic aspect by creating a parallel between the opening of this story and the openings of the other two stories in the volume—one about Anna's disappointment at her dogs Peter and Rags (whom she protests are "guiltless" though it is quickly revealed that she knows one of them has impregnated "a little transient terrier for whom Anna had found a home" ["The Good Anna" in *Three Lives*, 4]), the other, "The Gentle Lena," about the dimwitted Lena's confusion and delightful cluelessness when neighboring girls try to convince her, teasingly, that the paint she has just sucked off her squeaky toy is poison (the truth never to be revealed).

Stein's repetitions can be terrifically boring, but even this has a comic side to it. What passes for dialogue—the tottering syntax, malapropisms, and heaping asseverations—adds equivocal buoyancy to the characterizations. "Rosie grumbled and fussed and howled and made herself to be an abomination and like a simple beast" ("Melanctha," 59), we are told, where the animal likeness recalls the blundering automatism and nonsingularity that Bergson associates with animals. Jeff and Melanctha are typified by their liability to fault and by the relentless script they reproduce. Stein's characterizations use broad brushstrokes, the familiar language of everyday expression, and roundabout descriptions that fit like an oversized costume. In *The Autobiography of Alice B. Toklas*, Stein recalls her delight in "misfit clothes instead of the old classic costume" of the Cirque Médrano, which she visited weekly for a time. These reminded her of Charlie Chaplin's overlarge outfits, and they offer an analogue in physical comedy for the moral "ragging" in "Melanctha." Indeed, Susan McCabe links Chaplin's spasmodic movements (reflex action nervously playing itself out) with Stein's narrative propulsion, relapsing or reverberating in an endless comic circumnavigation ("Delight in Dislocation," 437).[51] The couple may be said to flop around in their dialogue, and their vaudevillian back-and-forth bears some resemblance to a Punch and Judy show. The slapstick quality of their behavior usually goes unnoticed. For example, when Stein describes Jeff contemplating Melanctha's quality of mind, she writes: "He was very friendly with her in his laughing, and then he made his face get serious, and he rubbed his head to help him in his thinking" (84). Then he proceeds with a relentless shtick that anatomizes Melanctha to Melanctha.[52] Her rigid sensibility and the unsociable ends to which it leads her convey a quality that, if not quite droll, feels detached and unserious. There is something almost comical as well in the fact that Jeff

Campbell, a figure who prides himself on his self-possession, unravels so completely while still insisting on the need to be "living regular."

The conversations between Melanctha and Jeff, their constant squabbles and clashes, seem to come from something automatic within them, some reserve of their moral makeup. Stein's approach recalls Bergson, who defined comedy as "a kind of *absentmindedness* on the part of life" ("Laughter," 117), an improper but not very serious distance from life's contingencies. "The laughable element," he remarks, often consists of "a certain *mechanical inelasticity*, just where one would expect to find the wide-awake adaptability and the living pliableness of the human being" (67). Comedy constructs people not as individuals but as ready-made iterations: "Every comic character is a *type*" (156). Meanwhile, character comedy, which conjures up a dangerous automatism within personality, never strays very far from its opposite, an impression of suppleness and dexterity. For Bergson, a funny expression makes us think of "something rigid" in the "wonted mobility of the face," the cause of which is a "habit that has been contracted and maintained" (76).

Bergson goes further, arguing that laughter is an all-too-human way of correcting the outward-seeming display of mechanism within the body. In his conservative account, comedy points at a pathology, an incapacity to adapt, and laughter is a way of healing a threatened inelasticity of character. It inoculates life of its pathogenic susceptibilities: its "function is to convert rigidity into *plasticity*, to readapt the individual to the whole" (174).[53] Bergson goes to some lengths to sever matter from life and to sever the life of the lower animals (shrunken and diminished by habits) from the life of people. He adheres throughout to the formula that comedy is "something mechanical encrusted on the living" (84)—and therefore merely an outward vesture, a façade, behind which may be detected a lithe inward stimulus.

I would argue, however, that Bergson's antinomies are excessively rigid, as Stein's writing helps demonstrate. And if we do not agree with Bergson that repetition is antithetical to life, we might be able to account for comic forms that do not require laughter to have a healing effect. As Wylie Sypher points out, comedy need not always discharge itself in laughter: "Bergson's analysis of laughter is incomplete, which may explain why he thinks comedy works only from 'the outside.' Comedy may, in fact, not bring laughter at all; and certain tragedies may make us laugh hysterically" ("The Meanings of Comedy," 205). The emotional uncertainty of Stein's writing may only occasionally lead to outright laughter. More often it expresses an antisentimental form of humor that lines up with similar examples of deadpan affectivity on the part of other modernists.[54] With this in mind, we can see that Stein's use of the comic is not meant to sever her characters from the world of things (with their repetitive structures) but to bring matter into continuity with life. Even matter's own repetitive structures may have something lively within them. Stein's "Melanctha" is not unfreighted with suffering, but the emphasis of the story is on situations that are not singular and on the interference that material life and its ordinary rhythms place on moral existence. The comic element in the story points to a certain kind of rigidity within Melanctha's character, but it is a rigidity that coexists with and perhaps even underwrites her vivacity.

In "Laughter" (which was a relatively early work), Bergson presents life in its pure form as "evolution in time . . . a being ever growing older; it never goes backwards and never repeats itself" (118). Bergson aligns repetition with mechanism and deems habits to be only a diminishment of life or a flight from it. But as Darwin makes clear, life exists nowhere without habits and repetitions. The living world is full of echoes and duplications, which give stability to living structures. Life would not be possible without some degree of dumb persistency and transposability, which one may associate with repetitive mechanisms. Mechanization and repetition, therefore, do not portend death, do not stall vitality. In fact, the tragic dimension of life would seem to consist in its unremitting, unidirectional flow. Death is not the product of repetition at all; it is the rupture of organization to which living organisms succumb precisely because they cannot reverse the course of certain processes. Rather than rely on a dichotomy between matter and life, it might be better to specify two moments of Bergson's ontology: the first, a relatively diffuse, isolable, and interchangeable relation among systemic elements (roughly correlated with mechanized matter); the second, a highly organized and interconnected one (which he associates with living organisms).[55] Both matter and life may betray unpredictability or "liveliness" to different degrees.[56] Indeed, in his later work, Bergson increasingly comes to appreciate the continuity between the two.[57] For Stein, as for the later Bergson, human beings are caught precariously between a mechanical or formulaic existence and a perpetually mobile life.

We should consider drawing different conclusions from the evidence that Bergson offers in "Laughter." Why, after all, does the body so persistently incline to repetition and error (revisiting its own obstinate and resistant materiality) if such repetition is bad for life? At times, Bergson implies that repetition is a prerequisite for sociality rather than a debased form of it. It is true that he pictures healthy society as a tissue of singular and highly adaptable individuals capable of giving continuous attention to life. But he also indicates that such elasticity cannot sustain itself without repetition. As he exclaims, "You would hardly appreciate the comic if you felt yourself isolated from others. . . . Our laughter is always the laughter of a group" ("Laughter," 64). Bergson aligns sociability with the subterranean wellsprings of habit that fashion us into types and side us with the interchangeable and reversible inclinations of the material world. The unseriousness of comedy gives a glimpse of something very real in life: a capacity to suspend or reverse the fatalistic accession to death. The rigid habits displayed by comic expression do not necessarily display "sickness and infirmity" but rather the playful collision of competing tendencies within life.[58] Indeed, as Michael North argues, in Bergson "the relationship between the mechanical and the living is a circuit and not a simple opposition" (*Machine-Age Comedy*, 16). Human life would seem to be suffused with repetition, sometimes applied in a merely mechanical, disharmonious way and at other times maintaining efficacious routines. As Darwin maintains, "sympathy," a feeling held in common among humans and social animals, is "much strengthened by exercise or habit" (*Descent of Man*, 681). Rather than separate life from matter, the comic, it would seem, resurrects for us, the living, the savor of our thingly origins. Perhaps, then, laughter does not part us from our animal brethren but rather reminds us in a distinctively human way of our animal origins.[59]

Though Melanctha's story has a roughly circular structure in that it concludes by returning to her failed friendship with Rose Herbert, it does not necessarily imply a narrative whose end is contained in its beginnings. Stein deliberately refuses to complete the circle. Melanctha dies, as we are told in a perfunctory telescopic narrative. Though she thinks about suicide and even becomes ill, we are informed mere moments from the end that she "went into the hospital where they took good care of her and cured her" (167). Stein's heedless and comic contempt for novelistic convention reveals itself here. However slight, the comedy prevents the story from being recuperated as earnestness. Like a number of instances of modernist satire that Jonathan Greenberg has analyzed, Stein's story draws attention to its playful stylistic devices, which have a tendency to "under[cut] scenes of high drama" (*Modernism, Satire, and the Novel*, 25). If Stein does not quite achieve the indifference that Greenberg recognizes as "a precondition for laughter" (23), the low affect does reinforce an unsentimental state of mind. This tendentious moment is aimed at disrupting the predictable decline narrative and the supposition behind it that characters must succumb to a fate provided for them by their racial or typological guiding trait. The momentary reversibility of the series reveals a lively interference within the fatalistic progression.

Melanctha's lightning-quick demise only a paragraph later comes close to consigning her to a tragic fate. Yet the incidental nature of her death and the fact that it has no moral relation to her life lends her story a kind of ordinariness: "Melanctha went back to the hospital, and there the Doctor told her she had the consumption, and before long she would surely die. They sent her where she would be taken care of, a home for poor consumptives, and there Melanctha stayed until she died" (167). Stein's narrative seems to confide that life is relentlessly repetitive; it might even take on the brittleness of mechanism. Indeed, the one absolutely knowable aspect of life is that it leads to death; its organic machinery is impermanent. However, the imperturbable matter-of-factness of the narration—its curtness—once again disrupts the tragic implication by curtailing pathos.[60] With it comes the distance peculiar to comedy. Melanctha's death is random (indeed this is the only time consumption is mentioned). Or rather, it is coincidental. It is part of a great pattern that involves all living things, but not one that necessarily offers or insists on great psychological insight. Melanctha's life, like any life, "is written as it is going to be written." Yet her habits do not cause her death; they merely coincide with it in a configuration whose logic is too surprising and vague to be attributed to a grand defect in her. The particular form that grief takes for readers, if they undergo it at all, is thrown wide open because of the undecidability of comic structure.

Stein shows that life has an elusive ontology in which repetition is not inimical to adaptation. It might very well be necessary to it. There is no obvious prescription for what is detrimental to life. The only thing clear is that character as a living substrate offers a delay on the way to self-dissolution, a dilatory moment of homeostasis. Stein momentarily undercuts the conservative impulse to eliminate the character who troubles the dogged separations of social life. She institutes a comic surprise that changes how we might read the ending. We cannot attribute to Melanctha's death the moral certitude of a life gone wrong but only the vagueness of a life marked by restless wandering. Stein traces out one narrative line but leaves several more—those of Jeff, Jem, and Rose—to thread their own repetitive pathways.

Stein may be said to make an original return to Darwin, who thinks that tendencies to variation coexist with niches of stability in the evolutionary line. Although Bergson emphasizes unceasing change, throbs of continual variation thumping through all things, making an enemy of any repetition that does not recrudesce, Darwin's evolutionary conception avoids programmatic judgments about the value or inevitability of self-transformation. He is content to observe intermissions and survivals from previous moments of evolutionary development and recognizes the productive—because sustaining—function of repetition. This is true not only of simple organisms but also of the behaviors and expressions of complex organisms. The dogs that fill the pages of his *Expression of the Emotions in Man and Animals*, with their intelligible caresses, their bristling and barking, their eccentric scratching behavior (behavioral holdovers of their grass-dwelling ancestors) have social rituals in common with our kerfuffles and our yappings. To the degree that human language operates like the variety of animal expressions that Darwin explores, its vocal signs accompany a state of mind and embody it: "Man not only uses inarticulate cries, gestures, and expressions, but has invented articulate language, if, indeed, the word *invented* can be applied to a process, completed by innumerable steps, half-consciously made" (*Expression of the Emotions*, 63). Language, Darwin would seem to suggest, also begins as a habitual process of self-organization, a means of entering into sympathetic response networks.

Darwin gives real vitality to vitalistic concepts and helps us understand the foundations and the distinctiveness of Stein's preoccupation with habits. For Darwin, organisms do not stand in the isolation of a predetermining genetic code. Heredity is not fate. Adaptability in higher organisms involves will, choice, and risk, but also unconscious self-organization. Most readings of Stein assume that her types spring from limitation, that they are a concession to determined lives. I have suggested, however, that they are based in routines and inheritances that are lively. These habits, as we see throughout her writing, are in evidence in characters' simplest reflexes and in their most complex intellectual tendencies. We might say that there is a dumbness—an unconscious repetitive force—in their most lively and vital acts of intelligent adaptation, but also that there is an intelligence (Bergson would call it "élan vital") in their most rote, most confirmed, and most regular of daily actions.

4 INTONING VOICE
T. S. Eliot

All life therefore comes back to the question of our speech, the medium through which we communicate with each other; for all life comes back to the question of our relations with each other. . . . Of the degree in which a society is civilized the vocal form, the vocal tone, the personal, social accent and sound of its intercourse, have always been held to give a direct reflection.

—Henry James, *The Question of Our Speech*

The array of clowns, puppets, fleeting fantasists, apelike dupes, hollow men, seers, and nervous neurasthenics who populate T. S. Eliot's early poetry do not present much in the way of psychological depth. Even the most sustained of these portraits, J. Alfred Prufrock, is, as Hugh Kenner puts it, "a name plus a Voice. He isn't a 'character' cut out of the rest of the universe and equipped with a history and a little necessary context, like the speaker of a Browning monologue" (*T. S. Eliot*, 36). Prufrock, like the rest, is a persona, which as Tim Dean usefully points out, "derives from the Latin phrase *per sonare*, meaning 'to sound through'" ("T. S. Eliot, Famous Clairvoyante," 54), referring in its sources not simply to a mask but to its mouthpiece, a reed inserted into it to amplify the actor's voice. In Dean's account, a persona is less "a means of visual concealment than of vocal channeling"; it represents "a way to inhabit other existences—a way to transform oneself by becoming possessed by others" (54). Eliot sets up identity through such masks, which allow individuals to select, appropriate, and rechannel other people's voices, in the process regulating how they sound to an implied audience. The voice would seem to be not an inalienable part of a person but an imitable element that the individual commandeers for provisional ends. Furthermore, the individual speaker is in a position to cultivate what I. A. Richards calls a "tone," an adjustable property of voice that expresses his relationship to a presumed listener, his awareness of "how he stands towards those he is addressing" (*Practical Criticism*, 182). A speaker's positioning is important, and what I will argue is that, in Eliot's view, it helps to define an individual's identity in a highly contextualized way. No particular identity can install a fixed subject position; rather, a position develops through a person's own or borrowed voice, which allows her or him to project a set of variable relations to an audience within a dramatic or circumstantial context.

We may understand the use of personae as a feature of Eliot's impersonal strategy—in which he dispenses with a language of authenticity, preferring to understand character as an intelligent amalgamator, a habitat, or a "medium" for understanding and integrating various voices. What might seem flat about Eliot's personae is not their inability to express complex structures of feeling but rather their inability to secure cohesiveness and singularity by the normal channels. This is because we tend to look for a coherent, autonomous, predictable personality with an interior organization that is maintained across historical time. But for Eliot, a speaker's character is defined less by personality than by the speaker's relationship to a succession of backdrops and scenarios that change moment by moment. With this understanding, we may find somewhat more recognizable characters in his earlier poetry, but we also gain insight into Eliot's ideas of impersonality in *The Waste Land*, with its cobbled-together voices, unspecified subjectivity, and formal pyrotechnics. Indeed, I will be arguing that Eliot's earlier poetry—both published and unpublished—offers a missing link between his distinctive models of character and his impersonal poetics, clarifying the situational and relational structure of psychic life basic to both.

Generations of critics have assumed that what we might term Eliot's "doctrine of impersonality" forfeits agreed-upon features of selfhood. Indeed, it has often attracted skepticism for that reason. The concept that underlies it would seem, as one commentator puts it, uncomfortably "near in form and meaning to our common 'depersonalize' and 'depersonalization' with their discomfiting adjunct 'dehumanize'" (Lee, *Theory and Personality*, 10). Dean, one of Eliot's most persuasive defenders, accepts the underlying premise and depicts Eliot's strategy as a gainful form of self-dissolution—figured in *The Waste Land* as a "specifically sexual experience, a violation of bodily integrity" ("T. S. Eliot, Famous Clairvoyante," 55)—that gives "access to regions of voice beyond the self's" (54). But I would argue that Dean's assumption that ethical entrée to or contact with others requires passivity, dispossession, or self-divestment is not an assumption that squares easily with the essentially self-affirming and creative impulse behind Eliot's doctrine. Dean, of course, is simply picking up on Eliot's rhetoric of "escape" and "extinction" in "Tradition and the Individual Talent." And yet, tempting as this reading may be, it does not appreciate fully the rhetorical and philosophical underpinnings of Eliot's insights into character. Eliot makes us aware that each voice represents an assumed part, and assuming or espousing it as a perspective does not require absenting one's own self. The level of sensitivity or honesty with which individuals accept responsibility for their voice—and specifically their tone, even when it is precarious, hard to control, or unsettling to their self-command—is an ethically defining index of their character.

As we will see, Eliot's intensive several year engagement with Bergsonian vitalism and later with F. H. Bradley's idealism led him to an account of self and a conception of voice that are theatrical in this sense: they require individuals to take self-conscious grasp of perspectives outside their own. I propose that such self-consciousness helps to establish—in fact, to reinvent—the affective and intellectual relationships that define a person's encounters with others. Indeed, I am tempted to reverse the customary formula and assert that the interpretive frameworks that posit a personality are, in fact, profoundly depersonalizing. Frameworks that attempt to discover a predictable matrix of behaviors, dispositions, and interpretive inclinations within us, as though within an inviolate interior, conspire to deny the self its situational variability and outwardness.

I take a cue from recent critics who find in impersonality a way to allow expressions of emotional intricacy in our intellectual and affective adjustments to others, a way to allow "us to hear 'what matters to other people'" as Rochelle Rives puts it, quoting Charles Altieri, "without positing the individual as the repository of feeling and identity" ("Things That Lie on the Surface," n.p.) Like Rives, I see impersonality as a "reparative vision of collective empathy" that requires us to theorize emotional engagement in ways that disable "the boundaries of the self-contained individual" (n.p.). At the same time I do not believe, as she does, that Eliot's representations forsake selfhood. Instead, I see Eliot insisting that to define a self as something that exists apart from its context—dramatically and socially conceived—distorts and sometimes impoverishes the self that is represented in this way. In this chapter, I will argue that tone and voice, terms traditionally reserved for formal strategies of poetry, function richly as character-defining features of self. Indeed, they reveal an adaptable, open-ended, highly contextualized form of character. Speaking individuals define themselves by relating to a real or potential audience, not by focusing on any consistent, inward qualities of their own. As I probe the expressive features of tone and voice, locating their basis in feeling, I also trace Eliot's technical understanding of these concepts. Their continuous presence for him as theoretical as well as practical-poetic preoccupations allows us to follow the development that brought Eliot from his early poetic experiments to his occupation with vitalist and idealist strains of philosophy as a young man, and then to the poetic commitment to impersonality that made him the most celebrated Anglo-American writer of his time.

TONE, VOICE, FEELING

Because Eliot so valued tone and voice and did so much to launch them as critical expressions of common use, it is worth unpacking these concepts to see how he used them. I start by examining what tone and voice reveal about language as a relational endeavor, one that establishes a speaker and an addressee in an overlapping set of contexts. For Eliot, poetry is a medium or form that engages feeling and, in so doing, offers access to these contexts, which are implicit as well as explicit. But as we will see, if voice is context-dependent, then it follows that the agent who is voicing a thought in a poem is also profoundly context-dependent. Thus, character is made legible only through a specific quality or tone of voice that helps to clarify the speaker's relations to others.

Eliot endeavors to prove in the first part of his essay "The Three Voices of Poetry" that the poet—whether he is talking to himself, addressing readers or listeners, or creating dramatic characters who are responding to each other in situationally defined settings—is always presenting a voice that offers itself up to different kinds of contextualization. Robert and Elizabeth Barrett Browning, for example, may have written love poems to each other, but "a good love poem, though it may be addressed to one person, is always meant to be overheard by other people" (*On Poetry and Poets*, 97). John Stuart Mill is the unacknowledged source for this claim, having famously asserted that "eloquence is *heard*, poetry is *over*-heard" ("What Is Poetry," 188). But whereas Mill insists that "the peculiarity of poetry appears to us to lie in the poet's utter unconsciousness of a listener" (188), Eliot thinks that the act of making poetry elicits self-consciousness. This is not to say that the speaker is simply playing for effect, less than fully absorbed in the scene that she or he is conjuring. Rather, poetic voice constructs several different, but overlapping, relations of address. Some of these relations are exhibited *in* the circumstantial, dramatic, or fictive context set up by the poem. Others appeal to perspectives *outside* these contexts. The poet speaks to readers who can occupy the role of eavesdropper as well as addressee. They may hear or overhear other relations, other voices within voices. They displace or overlay the original context of the address by considering it within a more expansive whole. For example, they might view the poem as a species of love poetry—one that borrows from a tradition of ways of expressing affection—or as an adaptation of an intertextual reference.

Following Bergson, one might call this the "virtuality" of texts. As he observed, one can analyze language by associating it with various strata of memories or virtual relations.[1] Bergson refers to the hearer's finding an appropriate recollection and placing "himself at once in the midst of the corresponding ideas" (*Matter and Memory*, 116). In his dissertation, Eliot makes a similar point, though he is more apt to speak of "passing from one point of view to another or . . . occupying more than one point of view at the same time" (*Knowledge and Experience*, 147). Gaining a broader perspective allows us to discover more of the relations and contexts that are implicit in a text.[2] Some of the relations that a text exhibits are consciously intended, while others are inadvertent, byproducts of the linguistic history that a poet mobilizes or the state of mind that her or his chosen voice expresses. Although any voice presents a perspective, a way of regarding a situation, it is implicitly staked out and infiltrated by other possible perspectives, which it captures or summons up as a fugitive reminder. The linkages to the past that a text maintains require a possible reader to discover them. In a sense, texts project these virtual readers, who are in the best position to unveil or discover their virtual past for them.

So far, I have argued as if a text has a "voice" roughly equivalent to auditory speech, but this is not exactly the case. When conveying words through articulated sound, a speaker is usually addressing an audience in a way that is explicitly context-dependent. A written text's relation to an audience, however, is more indeterminate. Written speech deposes the auditory community that gathers around a verbal act. As Jacques Derrida is fond of pointing out, texts are disseminated in ways that allow for a great deal of unpredictability in their reception.[3] Still, when we invoke the term "voice" metaphorically to describe the construction in a text of a point of view, attitude, or opinion, we still find a degree of sensitivity to context. A text, like a spoken statement, lays the ground for its own reception, which lends it specificity. This ensures that each occasion on which a text or vocal speech act meets a receiver is distinctive and unrepeatable, even if what is expressed is never entirely original. The very material of which speakers avail themselves—words, phrases, linguistic formulas and set pieces, as well as the constituent ideas expressed in them—is adapted and reassembled from the fossilized remnants of once existing voices, which they make use of in analogous contexts.[4] It may not be necessary to know the history and usage of a word—or the allusions, intertextual references, or borrowed forms—to construe the denotation of an utterance, but it is indispensable for discovering the rich tonal relations, verbal texture, and emotional force within a pattern of statements. Such knowledge allows us to consider the larger context and history in which any combination of utterances takes place, which adds significance to the expressions at issue and therefore to the character who conveys them.

In Eliot's account, language depends on a receiver, real or potential. Any perspective voiced by a speaker is dependent on constituent interpretive standpoints outside the self. Many of the *March Hare* poems, which Eliot originally intended as a discrete volume, go out of their way to demonstrate this point, refusing to grant characters the immunity they desire from relationality. In the process, Eliot erects a novel theory of character. He offers up Prufrock, the unnamed young man in "Portrait of a Lady," and others—individuals who attempt to withdraw inward into fantasies of self-containment through ironic distance, hysterical compulsion, or jaded wisdom to protect themselves from the disturbing knowledge that who they are is not up to them. Once nestled in their purported personalities, they seek to recover orderly, predictable lives, however pained by their isolation. Prufrock, for instance, lays claim to the eminence not of Prince Hamlet but of "an attendant lord" who is "Deferential, glad to be of use, / Politic, cautious, and meticulous" ("The Love Song of J. Alfred Prufrock" in *Complete Poems and Plays*, 7). His modest ambition becomes yet another sham effort to recover some blueprint, substance, or unassailable core of judgment within himself. He imagines "a magic lantern" that might have thrown his "nerves in patterns on a screen," which would not clarify the soundness of his character but would prove to him, "It is impossible to say just what I mean!" (6). Like Eliot's other dramatis personae, he is far too aware of his own variability to suppose that the impulse to fix his form is anything but a self-mystifying fantasy. Prufrock understands that others can frame him in ways that he cannot control; hence, his jittery need to preempt any comparison with Hamlet and Michelangelo, a comparison that casts him in a trivial light.

Prufrock's dream of immovability cannot stop reality from encroaching on his life in unpredictable, difficult-to-control ways. Eliot's characters have no means of shielding themselves from the depredations of time and its mutable effect on character or from the vulnerable consequences of their relational being. They can only welcome more relationality and stay open to the minute modifications of perspective and indeterminate transmissions of feeling that give them a handle on themselves. Whether they like it or not, the conception they hold of themselves requires them to be responsive to other people's attitudes toward them because it is these relationships, not internally construed traits, that construct their identity.

Eliot's strategy of impersonality presents feeling and its exterior vocal manifestation, tone, as levers of social experience. They offer ways of registering the relations, often implicit, that define people's stances or demeanor to each other. Yet his early lyrics begin not necessarily with the social function of feeling and tone but with their orientational function. The relations that define a self are not exclusively intersubjective or, for that matter, even linguistic. At the same time, Eliot is concerned with how to translate these elemental feelings into a shared experience, one that crystallizes through an act of poetic reflection. If character is the sum of the relations that define it, then feeling refers to the intuitive state of awareness of these relations as they compose a scene or unveil a situation, and tone describes their cumulative effect as they reveal themselves within a vocal performance or a literary work.

Eliot makes both concepts central to his poetry. He mobilizes the term "feeling" very early, first in his unpublished philosophical writings on Bergson, subsequently in his dissertation on F. H. Bradley, and, most famously, in "Tradition and the Individual Talent." The genealogy itself is telling. For Bergson and Bradley, who figured prominently in Eliot's early philosophical education, feeling as a concept includes an awareness of how one is embedded as an agent or an object in any scene one witnesses or participates in. We use the term "feeling" not only to pinpoint our sense of what is going on but also our attitude toward it—and our attitudes are not static but are liable to shift as our involvement in the situation shifts. At this point, Eliot writes, the feeling can become an object of consciousness, expanding "because . . . it has developed relations which lead it beyond itself" (*Knowledge and Experience*, 23). Feeling, for him, is constantly inputting more facets and components that contextualize an experience at the same time that it privileges the participant as a central—but changing—organizing relation.

A number of Eliot's early lyrics—his "Preludes" and the series of "Caprices"—record the alterations in people's intentional states, the modifications of feeling that a slight detail may create when it alters their point of view. Consider Eliot's attempt to document a "turn [in] the corner of the street" ("Fourth Caprice in Montparnasse," *Inventions*, line 1) or the "charm of vacant lots" that "Entreat the eye and rack the mind" ("Second Caprice in North Cambridge" lines 1, 4) or the stark observation that "The morning comes to consciousness / Of faint stale smells of beer" ("Preludes" in *Complete Poems and Plays*, 12). These details gather psychological significance as individuals define themselves by submitting to or reacting against the scenes that their minds are processing. Emotionally fraught, they implicate the speakers who participate in the scenes, however detached or removed they may be.

The innovative nature of the subject matter in Eliot's lyrics springs from a number of striking insights into character. Eliot presents the hard-to-digest but remarkable idea that there is no context-independent self. Even if it is possible to treat certain elements of character as common enough and discrete enough to be considered properties, they are, as isolated facts, relatively insignificant, and we still have to grapple with the social contexts and relational frameworks that situate these properties within the world.

For Eliot, the most expedient way to do this situating is to show how the self is a subject of judgment and intentionality as well as an object for interpretation. In his poetry, he insists on letting feeling extend itself, as the speaker comes closer to a social reckoning. Both "Preludes" and the "Caprices" are patterned so as to lead the speaker by continuous steps to a synthetic moment of sharpened reflection. In them, feeling and tone register experience as a holistic effect, which undergoes a process of revision, widening or focusing over time, as each speaker develops a sense of how his point of view might impinge on or qualify other people's points of view. In other words, as feeling and tone resonate and permeate, the speaker must notice not only his or her own attitude but also the potential or actual reaction of an implied listener, which in turn modifies that attitude. Tone is, as Sianne Ngai describes it, a set of social relays, a "reflexive circuit between subject and object, or 'transmitter' and 'receiver'" (*Ugly Feelings*, 82). For Eliot, the speaker's tone is at its most complex when the speaker becomes aware of his or her voice as a performance or experience *for* others. Thus, tone as a feature of speech sheds light on the ethical value of achieving impersonality. When speakers are made accountable to other people's perspectives, they become more intelligible to themselves. When this receptiveness does not occur, the result is impoverished judgment and also, it would seem, a form of insensibility that makes one resistant to change.

The impersonality that Eliot seeks, if it is to absorb differences of interpretation or create genuinely new perspectives, must make allowances for what is vague and unpredictable in ordinary social encounters. He calls attention to tone as a particularly subtle instrument of social adjustment. Tone as a metaphorical property of voice highlights what is implicit in a person's communications rather than what is explicit. As Ngai points out, it has a specifically emotional valence, akin to a mood, that while hard to describe is conveyed in the non-discursive shadings of words (*Ugly Feelings*, 42). People use these vague, self-adjusting qualities to "fine-tune" their relation to each other, whence comes the metaphor of tone in the first place. It refers to an element of voice that conveys emotion indirectly, by analogy with music—through cadence, word choice and arrangement, pacing, or vocal intensity—but is often deployed when describing adjustments in manner or attitude, such as when one "tones down" a statement.

Of course, unlike musical adjustments to a reference pitch, anchored in a scale of fixed frequencies, matters of literary tone are gauged or assessed relationally, by the presumed impression that one's words make on an audience. These adjustments (like all efforts to enlarge one's horizon by taking account of how other people do or might hear the same thing) are an "extension" (*Knowledge and Experience in F. H. Bradley*, 39) of reality, as Eliot's dissertation puts it. They allow one to gain greater coherence, or what is the same, greater impersonality by creating receptiveness and training the mind to recognize how one's own perspective stands in relation to the perspectives of others. The same impersonality obtains for poets. They find ways of digesting and transmuting the cultural frameworks—the judgments, sensations, and attitudes—that make the voices they project legible, an activity that is as much emotional as intellectual. But if, as Eliot suggests, the poet's mind is a mere "medium," then the voices she or he appropriates—and, with them, the writer's perspectives—are not unassailably her or his own. Folded into Eliot's view of the self is the assumption that we can intuit another person's point of view under the right circumstances and with the right sympathies. Yet what is there to guarantee that, under such circumstances, anything of our own self remains? We are prone to assuming or, to use an inexact term, "internalizing" other people's points of view. The following section examines whether or how one's feeling renders one susceptible to adopting the perspectives or emotional state of others. I will consider the general models of character to which Eliot adheres, an understanding of which will help underscore the importance of vocal performance in his poetry.

THE POLITICS OF PERSONALITY

Critics have not paid much attention to the wholesale redefinition of self that accompanies modernist impersonality. With a few exceptions, they have shown more interest in the political anxieties expressed in the doctrine because the self's constitutive relationality renders it vulnerable to being overtaken by others. Ella Zohar Ophir has argued that in the hands of Eliot's arch-conservative friend, Wyndham Lewis, impersonal strategies of abstraction—with their corresponding flattening of character—are a means of stalling empathic response to other selves, thus averting the hazardous loss of control that feeds crowd psychology, the blurring of boundaries between individuals who, "once massed together, relinquish their psychological autonomy" ("Toward a Pitiless Fiction," 96). Many recent critics have thought that Eliot too betrays fear that his personae's inward vitality may be overtaken by the "slither"—Lewis's term—of a feminized society that fails to maintain boundaries between individuals. The thinking is that impersonality is a method of curtailing relationality, that Lewis and Eliot present character as empty of content and co-opted by mass-cultural ideology, because they sensed that its underlying authenticity is threatened by public perspectives from which they are obliged to extricate it.

M. A. R. Habib points to the constitutive paradox of this way of thinking, that for Eliot the self is entangled with social perspectives it would like to reject.[5] Nonetheless, she adheres to a version of the claim in her reading of "The Love Song of J. Alfred Prufrock," in which the titular character blames a congregation of ladies for fixing him "in a formulated phrase," "pinned and wriggling on the wall" (*Complete Poems and Plays*, 5). In her view, the mock-comic poem presents the ironic mismatch between Prufrock's unique, particularized self and the women's—and society's—reduction of him "to an instrument or automaton, 'an easy tool' of the social mechanism" (*The Early T. S. Eliot and Western Philosophy*, 82). Other people's voices wake him from his dream, drowning his "authentic identity" or "repressed depth," which lies "beneath his social identity" (86).

I would argue, however, that Eliot treats the notion of authenticity with a great deal of skepticism. It is worth remembering that in "Tradition and the Individual Talent," Eliot examines the celebratory concept of "personality"—the liberal-humanist catchword for a vital or essential self—and intimates that its conception of character as an unassailable, if buried, property renders it a static, neurotic shell. The recalcitrant material that defines personality prevents people from having a more robustly adaptive or heteropathic response, causing them to be estranged from others. Eliot argues that the poet cannot work backward, cannot dig into the regressive and least socialized dimensions of self, to discover clues to an individual's character. She or he must move forward, multiplying the social contexts and frameworks—the relations, proportions, values" ("Tradition and the Individual Talent" in *Selected Essays*, 5)—that make people's vocal expressions intelligible to one another. And the poet must grant that individuals, in principle, have the sensitivity or intelligence to broker such understanding. Eliot develops his notorious concept of impersonality not solely as an aesthetic program but also as an imaginative ideal for restructuring social interactions.

For Eliot, the interpretation of the self as a predictable mass of qualities is not "natural" or inevitable. It is first and foremost an observer's error: people fall into such simplifications when they fail to view another person's character with proper sympathy, treating the person as an object among other objects—thus, as a thing whose behaviors are contained and expected. Bergson, the earliest of Eliot's significant philosophical influences, identified the pragmatic nature of such distortions. He suggested that, because our perceptions are tied to the practical need to anticipate outcomes, we tend to sever the particular qualities of a person's character from the context in which they are embedded so that we can make predictions about them. But these predictions, although they serve as mental conveniences, tend to break people down into atomistic parts, ignoring the adaptable dispositions that define them as well as the unified ensemble from which these dispositions emerge. Many of our analytic practices have their origin in these cognitive simplifications. Bergson holds up for particular censure the modern psychologist who insists on taking a "snapshot of the mobility of the inner life" (*Introduction to Metaphysics*, 32). The psychologist's "artificial reconstruction," which treats the psyche as an invariant ego, isolates facts and seeks a false unity so as to connect a series of putatively separate states.

In this sense, Eliot would probably agree with Lewis, who heaps scorn on the mass of people who acquiesce to these mischaracterizations of themselves. Those who think that they are "'expressing' their 'personality,'" Lewis writes, merely reveal "somebody else's personality they were expressing" (*The Art of Being Ruled*, 164). Such people get the framework for defining their own selfhood at second hand and deserve to be called empty. If we think of character as social by definition, this should not be alarming perhaps. But I would like to suggest that personality for Eliot as for Lewis is a relational fact that obscures its relational character.

And both writers are exceptionally conscious of the individualist ideologies that reinforce a conception of the self as a self-contained unit.

Lewis's attack on personality is based on a more explicit critique of democratic individualism than Eliot's.[6] But the two collaborators and friends share a similar polemical scorn for what Justus Nieland calls the "mass-mediated romanticism" (*Feeling Modern*, 64) that suffuses personality's claims to authenticity.[7] They also share an important metaphor. Lewis declares that most people desire to be puppets, "to be looked after, disciplined into insensitiveness, spared from suffering by insensibility and blind dependence on a will superior to their own" (136).[8] As we will see in the next section, Eliot plays on the metaphor of the puppet or marionette in one of his earliest poems, "Convictions (Curtain Raiser)."

THE MARIONETTE AS VOCAL MEDIUM

Eliot commenced his writing career with the proposition that character varies tremendously depending on the context that we bring to bear to understand it. Defined relationally, identity is inevitably provisional. We depend on others because we borrow our voices from others and adapt them for the occasion. Whatever meaning we convey through voice depends on the way we project an awareness of others. It is worth noting, for example, that "Convictions (Curtain Raiser)" does not stipulate which performance contexts and philosophical and literary frameworks will help readers make sense of its characters. If anything, it leaves those contexts suspended, implicit in the tone of the piece. Eliot thinks that poetic attention to tone of voice recovers the relational basis of self because it draws connections that the author is only partly aware of, increasing the range of registers in which that self is defined.

In "Convictions (Curtain Raiser)," Eliot dramatizes a set of individual characters, played by marionettes, who express humdrum enthusiasms that they inherit from a familiar and rather derisory collection of romantic plots. These characters, of course, stand in for real people slipping back into the rank of marionettes.[9] The poem is told from the perspective of the puppet master who sees the marionettes as a symbol of his own lack of autonomy because he, like them, achieves animation as a desiring subject only through an audience whose expectations he anticipates and fulfills:

> Among my marionettes I find
> The enthusiasm is intense!
> They see the outlines of their stage

Conceived upon a scale immense
And even in this later age
Await an audience open-mouthed
At climax and suspense.

(*Inventions of the March Hare* 1–7)

The speaker might be likened to Geppetto, the carver of the wooden puppet Pinocchio, who in Tzachi Zamir's account feels "an experience of dispossession" (390), a waning of his self-determination, as he is startled by the surprising liveliness of his creation. Pinocchio, we recall, dreams of being a real boy and begins to kick and agitate as he is created. For Zamir, puppetry dramatizes a theatrical dimension of subjectivity. We, like puppets, have a brute "thinghood," and our disorganized being emerges from it by taking on a performative role as a subject set against objects.[10] Geppetto, like the speaker in "Convictions," is not merely the maker, the father of his creations; he is "reciprocally made" (390).

The puppeteer in the poem situates himself in the background, moving in and out of theatrical space. Zamir describes the powerful fantasy to which such stage-managing gives rise as a "detheatricalized reality" in which puppeteers occupy an existence apart from the fitful roles of their characters, even if the "noninteracting puppeteer. . . ironically . . . is itself part of theater" (406–407). Yet Eliot does not harbor quite the same wistfulness about the state prior to subjectivity or theatricality. People, he thinks, cannot escape from a theatrical relation or at least a context that establishes them.

Eliot implies that the real people who crave being marionettes in "Convictions (Curtain Raiser)" are ignorant that they are pretending to be marionettes. They take on a voice that belongs not to themselves but to their puppet master. They are mouthpieces uttering clichés. Eliot's complicated metaphor presents the self as marionette-like and therefore an empty vessel, but this is meant as a jibe and a rhetorical exaggeration, not an exacting description of the self, and it would be a mistake to see it otherwise. For, as Eliot would have it, the self is not a container at all: it is a privileged organizing hub for the relations that it acts on and that act on it.[11] His metaphor is meant to convey passivity and a greater susceptibility to mimicking others. Meanwhile, if Eliot's idea of character begins from the premise that people take on other people's voices and perspectives, then the impoverishment of the marionettes' existence consists not in their being puppets per se but in the diminished range of voices or points of view available for them to build on or recognize. They default to the narrowest and most generic attitudes, thus willing their own passivity before already established perspectives. For instance, "A lady with a fan"

> Cries to her waiting-maid discreet
> "Where shall I ever find the man!
> One who appreciates my soul;
> I'd throw my heart beneath his feet.
> I'd give my life to his control."
>
> ("Convictions [Curtain Raiser]," lines 21–26)

This character's readiness to renounce control is not tantamount to surrendering an authentic point of view. But the flatness of her sentiment reveals her abdication of any effort to rearticulate the meaning of her relations to others. Yet Eliot's ironic handling of the woman's desire is not as absolute as it would seem. She may wish to give up control, which is itself a cliché that suggests that she has already given up control. And yet the gesture of such self-renunciation, like the "awful daring of a moment's surrender" (*Complete Poems and Plays*, 404) in *The Waste Land*, reveals a self whose authority always—and necessarily—lies outside itself. The lady may simply be aligning her will with metaphysical or at least characterological necessity.

The characters in Eliot's poem deceive themselves because they assume that they have an authentic identity that preexists their performance. In this respect, they capitulate to an impoverished personality schema that presents their internal consistency as a set of anterior laws. Eliot intimates that society controls them through such attachment to a fixed personality. For mouthing this reified interpretation of themselves, they will their own depersonalizing submission to society:

> And over there my Paladins
> Are talking of effect and cause,
> With "learn to live by nature's laws!"
> And strive for social happiness
> And contact with your fellow-men
> In Reason: nothing to excess!"
>
> ("Convictions [Curtain Raiser]," lines 14–19)

In the poem, the concept of personality can be seen as granting them substance, but only by ignoring the context in which they are asked to profess it.

Meanwhile, the points of view or "convictions" that the puppets yearn to express are so canned and so indifferent to context as to lack specificity, thus losing any claim to singularity. But we might note that Eliot does not celebrate novelty or "eccentricity" in the first place, at least for its own sake. In "Tradition and the Individual Talent," he prefers to claim poetic tradition as a site for the stabilizing rearticulation of the self and its forms of expression. Some critics have contended that his authoritarian politics taints his doctrine of impersonality, which they see as promoting the abandonment of the self before the altar of higher authority.[12] But we should remember that the tradition in question is not a fixed anchor, averse to novelty, nor does it sacrifice the self. In fact, as a poetic storehouse, it is effectively a record of novelty, offering values, emotional compounds, techniques, and perspectives that give people's characters a greater range of expression. It does so by multiplying and strengthening the relations between a given point of view and its antecedents. For Eliot, the very language of the self's interior inevitably relies on a voice that is composed of social language to embody it. Therefore, the form of authority that Eliot has in mind validates itself by expanding the repertoire of ideas and relations that situate a point of view, allowing people to get out of their predictable forms of self-representation.

"Convictions (Curtain Raiser)," one of Eliot's earliest poetic efforts to explore the psychological determinants of character, uses interlocking perspectives to rearticulate the relations between selves. The puppeteer presides over his puppets as artist-impresario and creator of their thrown voice. But he is also positioned as a spectator observing facets of his creation. Every change of aspect that allows the puppeteer to be either voice for or audience to his marionettes requires a corresponding adjustment of point of view.

As Steven Connor remarks, ventriloquism, considered from a cultural-historical point of view, offers a means to explore the power and meaning of the voice itself. The practice reminds us that voice is an identifying attribute over which a person does not have a proprietary relation: my voice involves a "passage of articulate sound from me to the world" (*Dumbstruck*, 4), even though it "belongs to me in the way in which it issues from me" (5). To speak, we need to learn to hear ourselves speaking, which is to say, learn to hear how we are heard: "my voice is the advancement of a part of me, an uncovering by which I am exposed, exposed to the possibility of exposure" (5). At the same time that Eliot's puppeteer regards his puppets' "convictions" and sentimental beliefs with what can only be described as irony, he also cannot help but sympathize with the characters' vulnerabilities before an audience. The marionettes' triviality is very close to ordinariness. They play a part in the theatrical genre of the curtain-raiser—the world of minor vignettes at the margins of heroic life. Yet through such figures Eliot may be able to reclaim the poignancy and significance of insignificant lives. To take on the voice of such personae, as the puppet master (who is himself a stand-in for Eliot) does, suggests a willingness to recognize analogies between one form of unlikeable vulnerability and another. Even as the puppet master takes his distance from his characters, he also sympathizes. Like so many poems Eliot goes on to write, "Convictions" traces the ethically ambiguous position between identifying and being repelled.

While the characters' words and pantomimes remain conventional and one-dimensional, their tone registers an almost imperceptible theatrical consciousness that allows something tentative and surprising to emerge from their attitudes. In terms of semantic content, their words matter less than the affective relations that shadow them. Even if, as the poem indicates, the puppets' emotions are automatic and their expressions a "monotone / Of promises and compliments" ("Convictions," lines 11–12), the thinned-out emotions are capable of thickening as they are lived vicariously or at least experienced from the outside. The supposed monotone of the marionettes' playacting is engulfed by the larger tonality of the poem, which helps to define their relations to an audience even when those relations are indeterminate.

For Ngai, the predominant feature of tone is the ambiguity of its boundaries. Like paranoia and other "ugly feelings" (her phrase), tone replicates "the subjective/objective oscillation in its basic structure: Is the enemy *out there* or *in me*? Confusion about the feelings' objective or subjective status becomes *inherent* to the feeling" (*Ugly Feelings*, 19). The uncertainty of tone follows from its being merely inferred. Although it expresses an attitude toward an audience, that attitude is not limited to what the speaker intends to communicate. Rather, tone anticipates an imprecise range of *potential* reactions, which the interpreter treats as if immanent within the vocal utterance. These responses are virtual in Bergson's sense: a repertoire of not yet actualized experiences (in this case, of language) that reverberate beyond the words themselves. These potential reactions, properly anticipated or felt, show the way to how such vocal expressions might act on auditors. Tone is in some sense impersonal because we do not treat it as a manifestation of a speaker's attitude or an audience's interpretation alone. It spreads out to encompass relationships that go in both directions, a constellation of feeling-based reactions that one experiences "all at once." Thus, Eliot can speak of the "emotional unity" of poetic drama, which "must have . . . a dominant tone; and if this be strong enough, the most heterogeneous emotions may be made to reinforce it" ("Philip Massinger" in *Selected Essays*, 190). Tone is "in" the work or the voice because these organize and coordinate potentially sharable feelings, at least for an audience perceptive or susceptible enough not only to register their own personal reaction but to allow for how other people might react.

As a rhetorical feature of language, tone is inherently contextual: it presents problems of interpretation that require one to decipher the speaker's relation to a more or less situated audience. The related concept of intonation—the rise and fall of voice—treats tone's contextual relations as a theatrical matter, as it involves modulating pitch for declamatory effect, thereby revealing an awareness of audience, even if only a nascent awareness. I would like to suggest that the puppets' theatricality exemplifies a complex kind of cognizance, which I will call "double consciousness." I am not invoking the fraught and divided self-consciousness to which W. E. B. Du Bois referred when he coined or adapted the term. Du Bois—who, like Eliot, studied philosophy at Harvard (Ph.D. 1895) though under the tutelage of William James who had retired by Eliot's time—uses "double consciousness" to describe a form of self-consciousness that is typical of the racialized experience of Black Americans: a "sense of always looking at one's self through the eyes of others" (*The Souls of Black Folk*, 215). For Eliot, double consciousness presents something related: a capacity to register a minimum of distance from one's own situatedness. Yet in contrast to Du Bois (who is dealing with the specific social and visual character of racial experience), Eliot's presentation of double consciousness does not lead characters to seek out recognition from those who claim to wield a stable, socially valorized, and putatively normative perspective within society.[13] The unfinished feelings of Eliot's characters ramify as their consciousness spreads out to encompass new relations and potential sites of value, which themselves remain indeterminate rather than fixed by norms. The phenomenon I have in mind has more in common with the "oddity of a double consciousness" (*The Ambassadors*, 56) attributed to James's hero Strether, whose impressions, born of detachment, seek out connections, further and further, to anchor his rickety and ever ramifying sense of values.

Double consciousness intensifies one central feature of the social world as Eliot understands it: people become audiences to themselves as they are socialized. They are placed in a situation in which everything *means*, and with such overwhelming force that no attitude of theirs can escape being locked into a position or identity. Much more than Henry James's or Gertrude Stein's characters, Eliot's personae anticipate the perspective of others; indeed, they count on there being an established point of view. At the same time, his poems explore the predicament that any social perspective is merely one in a network of imbricated perspectives, every affect reiterated but also prone to dislocation by another angle of vision. The mobility that Eliot presents is hardly limitless or free-floating, but he does think that people extricate themselves from the position of excessive legibility in which they find themselves by tapping into feelings that make possible less obvious judgments and attitudes. A person is at once a dense point within a system of intellectual mappings that can be painfully intimate and a thing that is capable of exceeding or resisting that position. As Emerson puts it, double consciousness mines a felt difference between a man's "private and his public nature" ("Fate" in *Emerson's Prose and Poetry*, 278).

In "Convictions," the marionettes feel something like wonder at the spectators of their divertissement, and their audience would seem to reciprocate that feeling. Indeed, the poem leaves ambiguous who is "open-mouthed / At climax and suspense." The puppet master, Eliot's artist-persona, nonetheless directs his contempt at these spectators, who are excited by banal plot-driven emotional repertoires. In "Convictions" as in other poems, their dumbstruck response is not so simple or easy to dismiss as it would appear. Their double consciousness can always lurch in unforeseeable directions. Eliot's stagey poem is not rejecting theatricality, as if there were any way to recover a nontheatrical or at least noncontextual form of selfhood. The identity of the puppet characters, like all identities, cannot be disengaged from their extension or continuation within a dramatic context. The poem merely shows that the theatrical relation does not have to limit itself to anticipations of predictable or determinate audience responses.[14]

As the puppeteer trots out his marionettes, they present various fragments of him: "As one leaves off the next begins" ("Convictions," line 20). Although the multiplicity of puppet voices implies endless seriality, the speaker draws his performance to a close by attempting to encapsulate his experience in a new stable overview: "My marionettes (or so they say) / Have these keen moments every day" (lines 28–29). Yet the concluding lines end up being scored by indeterminacy. What attitude does Eliot wish to realize here? Is the speaker ironic, amused, uneasy? We do not know whether the puppet master is expressing the propriety of his austere discretion, the pathos of his emotional truncation, or the feeling of being blunted by meaningless replication. The poem leaves the reader with an ambiguous tone, pregnant but unidentifiable. The grasp of tone that Eliot demands relies on something akin to aesthetic judgment, not only because tone divulges a qualitative dimension of words (their palpable "coloring") or because the feeling is hard to translate or paraphrase apart from the sensuous details, arrangement, and minutiae of the language, but also because we are forced to draw connections between these different details and the underlying perspectives that make sense of them. At least as Kant endeavored to theorize it, there is no finality to aesthetic judgment; it is necessarily "indeterminate." The judgment appeals to a *sensus communis*, a community that might be presumed to share in the response. But the perspectives of this community cannot be limited to an extant range of findings, just as the community itself is always felt to be open to the membership of a not-yet-created public. As Kant puts it, any effort to correlate a specific individual's response with the "position of everyone else" must follow "not so much [from their] actual as [from] the merely possible judgments of others" (*Critique of Judgment* 1.40.294).

Despite this sense of open-endedness, however, Eliot's conclusion does seek analytic distance and finality. He captures his marionettes' layered attitude in a contained moment of generalization that threatens to damp down the resonance—the tonal alternations—of the poem. One senses that Eliot wants to resolve, finally, the various possibilities of reading in a surrender to world-weary lucidity over the puppets' plight, their life in a world of bourgeois constraint. For this reason, critics have sometimes regarded the attitude of superior irony on the part of speakers of his early poems—and, in the case of "Convictions," the quietistic inevitability of his marionettes—as juvenile.[15] Indeed, "Convictions" tends to pigeonhole the feelings of the characters by securing dramatistic distance over them. This would not satisfy Eliot for long. Soon after, he would seek other means of taming unruly affects by asserting cultural authority over them. He turned to philosophy partly because it could lend its considerable intellectual prestige to the task of finding a ground for social life—a way of grasping some reality beyond the confusions and ambivalences of immediate experience.

THE FRINGE OF CONSCIOUSNESS

The magnetic orbit of Bergson attracted Eliot, and his lectures at the Collège de France lured Eliot to Paris some months after he composed "Convictions" in 1910. It could be said that "Convictions" anticipates the period of Eliot's full immersion in Bergsonism, although at the time of its composition he was already reading the philosopher in his courses at Harvard with Irving Babbitt (Jain, "Eliot, Babbitt, and Paris," 44–51). It is significant that in his various encounters with philosophy, Eliot gravitated toward the style of philosophizing closest in procedures and methods to the poet's. For example, Bergson laid emphasis on the creative nature of any philosophical advance[16] and, like William James, he did not make a strong distinction between feeling and thinking.[17] Feeling lets individuals make new connections between their ideas, and these solidify into intellectual modes of thought as they are arranged in more formal patterns. In short, Bergson allowed Eliot to refine his existing intuitions about character as a relationally defined complex, and he did much more to help him develop his doctrine of impersonality than critics have generally grasped. At the same time, Bergson disparaged the intellect as an instrument of analysis, one that is unable to capture the mobility of changing experience—although, of course, vitalism, like all philosophies, relies on discursive procedures of the intellect to convey its particular claims to truth. Bergson thus rejected the one thing that could secure philosophy's superiority to poetry.

For this reason, Eliot would eventually turn his back on vitalism, but before he did so he derived from Bergson a relational account of feeling that enabled him to reconceive the very nature of psychic life. He then adapted that account for use in his poetic theory and practice before turning to Bradley's idealism for a more rock-solid philosophical ground for experience. In the end, he abandoned philosophy altogether in favor of the more limited authority that poetry and the poetic tradition could bring to the examination and safeguarding of character (even as he reinvented poetry as a legitimate foundation of identity). At present, I am concerned with the theoretical underpinnings of Bergsonian intuition, which, as Eliot understood it, is the faculty charged with sensing or "feeling" the relations between elements of psychic experience. I would like to link the forms of consciousness associated with intuition to a tonal sensitivity or discernment. Later, I proceed to examine the characterological models that Eliot derives from his account of feeling. I will also show how he imports these theories into such poems as "Prufrock" and "Portrait of a Lady," even as he seeks out a stabler intellectual reality for grounding the intuition of relatedness.

It is not hard to find evidence of Bergson's influence on Eliot as a philosopher in training and as a poet embarked on an early career.[18] Bergson helped him find a role for lyric, whose cultural authority was in the process of shrinking as the genre became increasingly obscure and specialized, purged of the narrative elements and engaged social commitments that might have attracted a broader audience.[19] What significant task could it find for itself if not as the purveyor of belief or the teller of stories? Eliot proposed that lyric concern itself with a generalized state of feeling like the one that Bergson had theorized. In effect, feeling arouses a primordial sympathy with things whose virtual but unrealized connections create an environment in which everything is definitionally interdependent, at least at the deepest level. Speakers have a capacity to broker understanding with others by developing personas, which in turn force them to engage emotionally in ways that do not seal themselves off from potentially repellent perspectives. Lyric thus invests in nonbiographical, nonnarrative ways of defining character.[20] It allows poets to explore analogues between themselves and others, inhibiting the pathologizing gaze. And it presents experience in a form that is suspended from the world of practical judgment and action. At its best, then, lyric frees up readers' thought processes, transforming their experience and, in some manner, transforming them too.

Bergson, unlike Eliot's most significant later philosophical influence, F. H. Bradley, was a realist and did not believe that "what I experience will depend . . . on the point of view I may take up in regard to the object" (*Introduction to Metaphysics*, 21). Eliot had his doubts about Bergson's formulation: it does not clarify how "qualities can exist without a consciousness to perceive them" (Eliot, "Draft of a Paper on Bergson," 22). Nonetheless, he recognized that Bergson was not discounting subjectivity but simply equating a point of view with a symbolic representation that proceeds by analysis, distorting the unity of experience by breaking apart the object into successive fragments. Beneath the "sharply cut crystals" and "frozen surface" of one's self, Bergson thinks that there is "a continual flux," a "succession of states, each of which announces that which follows and contains that which precedes it" (*Introduction to Metaphysics*, 25). For Bergson, these states are "so profoundly animated with a common life, that I could not have said where any one of them finished or where another commenced. In reality no one of them begins or ends, but all extend into each other" (25).[21]

Eliot later broke with Bergson and his venerated intuition because his formulation granted analytic thought and the precedents of a cultural tradition too perfunctory a role in experience. He came to prefer F. H. Bradley's philosophy, which he thought could stabilize the reality of identity by advocating an increasingly ample, historically defined point of view. He complained that Bergson's self "has none of the marks of a final reality" ("Draft of a Paper on Bergson," 10). Significantly, however, as William James made a point of noticing, both Bergson and Bradley commence their metaphysical peregrinations by positing a plane of experience dominated by feeling, and both figures "run parallel for such a distance" in how they understand this state before they ultimately diverge: "In his 'Logic' as well as in his 'Appearance' [Bradley] insisted that in the flux of feeling we directly encounter reality, and that its form, as thus encountered, is the continuity and wholeness of a transparent much-at-oneness. This is identically Bergson's doctrine" (James, "Bergson or Bradley," 29). Bergson insists on a "theory of life" that does not hypostatize and isolate systems, as we are apt to do when we perceive the world in purely intellectual terms. There is no way we can artificially isolate a person, object, or situation to contemplate it. Thus, intuition proceeds by a feeling of "*intellectual sympathy*" ("Introduction to Metaphysics," 23); it is an effort of imagination that enables us to experience things as a unity, even if it is one that does not presume an already established world of relations. The character of metaphysical intuition is, Bergson remarks, "essentially active, I might almost say violent" (45).

Intuition has many guises in Bergson's work, but it would be a mistake to view it, as many of Bergson's early critics did, as a purely primitive state of awareness, called on only when the intellect is unseated. Bergson is not the arbiter of the raw and instinctive that Bertrand Russell, Eliot's Cambridge friend and future financial sponsor, alleged in a 1912 critique. "We are condemned, in action," Russell declared of Bergson's system, "to be the blind slaves of instinct" pushed on from behind by a life-force that is alleged to toil "restlessly and unceasingly" (*The Philosophy of Bergson*, 25). But Russell's understanding of the Bergsonian opposition between intuition and intellect is excessively rigid, seeing conflict and antagonism where Bergson instead stresses a complementary relationship. The intellect, according to Bergson, "dislikes what is fluid, and solidifies everything it touches," and therefore intuition "rejoin[s] to the intellect proper" the movement that it would otherwise discount (*Creative Evolution*, 49). Intuition allows one to look beyond a fixed frame of reference to the relations that extend beyond them.

As a practical matter, Bergson concedes that we tend to see objects as fixed and separate because it is thus that they offer points of orientation. But surrounding "our distinct—that is, intellectual—representation" is a "fringe of vague intuition" (*Creative Evolution*, 49) that allows us to see the continuity between objects. Bergson was decried as an irrational "spiritualist" from the moment he entered onto the philosophical stage;[22] in fact, he does not disown the intellectual mappings we have of the world but tries by an intuitive method to assess the workings of associative connections that thread objects and ideas together in ways that we experience but are not used to recognizing.

Lyric, because it affirms the "useless" or noninstrumental operations of language, is well positioned to draw out resonances among states and attitudes usually thought of as incompatible. Bergson implicitly aligns the higher-order efforts of intuition with aesthetic leanings. Instinct, he notes, requires a relation of sympathy with its object, and intuition is a special or higher form of instinct: "it is to the very inwardness of life that *intuition* leads us—by intuition I mean instinct that has become disinterested, self-conscious, capable of reflecting upon its object and of enlarging it indefinitely" (*Creative Evolution*, 176). The intellect identifies things and puts them in an already established frame of reference. As such, it makes identification into a practice of assimilation, which he contrasts with intuition. Lyric, which relies more on intuition, offers readers a great deal of imaginative latitude in how they understand or approach the objects, characters, and situations that poems present for contemplation.

Eliot's engagement with Bergsonism is well documented, and several books detail the complexity of his affiliation.[23] After he returned from his stint in Paris, either at Harvard or in his time at Oxford he wrote a paper that entered into the technical details of Bergson's philosophy, and in other papers he used him as a strong point of reference. Given that in 1910 Bergson's philosophy was "current," was attracting all the right people, and was discussed in important intellectual and artistic circles, we might expect that a number of social and political considerations intervened between the philosophy and its reception. In a manner, they did. Eliot expressed his sense of the scene in 1913 when he wrote: "The landscape is decorated with Bergsonians in various degrees of recovery from intellect" ("The Relation between Politics and Metaphysics," 2). The cabal of Bergsonists included older notables, such as William James and the anarchist Georges Sorel (Eliot's review of Sorel's *Reflections on Violence* appeared in 1917), and younger figures, such as poet-critic T. E. Hulme, then a member of Action Française.[24] It is important to note that Eliot had ambitions to become a professional philosopher when he first attended Bergson's lectures and when he returned to Harvard as a doctoral student in philosophy. And the relationship between Eliot's work and Bergson's is more intimate and more revealing than one might expect of a lay reader. Therefore, I would argue that Eliot's initial reception of Bergson's thinking (and his later dismissal of it) require a more intricate account than is ordinarily offered by critics.[25] His sympathies toward vitalism as well as his points of resistance, which he maintained throughout his life, defy most of the philosophical labels that critics generally want to apply. Eliot was attracted to the idea that philosophical truth is made, not found, and he had no problem mixing a range of metaphysical, pragmatist, and vitalist concepts to bring home the point.[26] Ultimately, though, he wanted to harness the creative power of feeling for more secure and lasting cultural ends.

Remember, Bergson relied on the metaphor of a "fringe" to describe the nimbus of intuition that expands the "intellectual form of our thought" (49). His usage recalls a slightly earlier mention of the same metaphor by William James. In *The Principles of Psychology*, James uses the image of a "*psychic overtone, suffusion*, or *fringe*, to designate the influence of a faint-process upon our thought, as it makes it aware of relations and objects but dimly perceived" (1:258). He is more concerned than Bergson with the psychological forms of continuity that our thoughts preserve with each other, using the metaphor of an "overtone" to describe them. He likens the concord that enables thoughts to cohere into a personal identity to the "upper harmonics" of musical notes when instruments play in the same key, though "in a different voice"—each blending into the other and altering the psychic effect. The interrelation among thoughts composes a stream of consciousness, which is not self-enclosed but extends out into the world and is organized by a certain bearing or attitude toward it.[27] Meanwhile, the fringe of relationships allows our thoughts to extend beyond us.

I would argue that James's idea of an overtone provides a useful way of thinking about the psychic effect of the disparate vocal elements in Eliot's poetry and the way that they create a sense of subjectivity or at least a shared climate in which voices can sound out. James allies this overtone or fringe of thought-relations with the dynamic reserve of associations or contexts that dilate the meaning of our words and broaden them beyond their denotative content.[28] The overtone that James describes and that Eliot creates does not have to be exclusively personal; in fact, it is better understood as a vibrational pattern of virtual effects, a relay of interrelationships that extends beyond a speaker to create a common mood. This overtone relies on common familiarity with how words are generally "supposed" to sound. It depends not only on their semantic properties but on their material and formal characteristics (sonority, repetition, metrical rhythm, assonance, and dissonance) to convey relationships of meaning. The indeterminate nature of such effects—the fact that they cannot be looked up in a dictionary—does not stop them from playing an important expressive function. Their vagueness, as Eliot notes in his essay "The Music of Poetry," comes of conveying an idea at the "frontiers of consciousness beyond which words fail." They create ambiguities of meaning in which "the reader's interpretation may differ from the author's" because there is "much more in a poem than the author was aware of" (*On Poetry and Poets*, 23).[29]

For Eliot, the ordinary rhythms of speech on which the poet relies for conveying musical effect must be sensitive to "developments in vocabulary, in syntax, pronunciation and intonation" that contribute to "the capacity of the language to express a wide range, and subtle gradation, of feeling and emotion" (*On Poetry and Poets*, 31). His attention to feeling is significant, indicating a state in which, as Rochelle Rives puts it, "both subject and object . . . escape their respective boundaries" (n.p.). Feelings are nestled reactions, person-situation interactive complexes of an unpredictable order. When they cast moods or delineate overtones, they work, in part, by intensifying connections between thoughts or sensations, recalling, for instance, an experience of suddenness or fluency or, to quote Eliot quoting William James, "of space, of intensity, of flatness, brownness, heaviness, or what not" (James, *Essays in Radical Empiricism*, 28; quoted in *Knowledge and Experience*, 19).

These feelings create associations. Eliot's studies in literary character rely on his own general account of emotional functioning, with its roots in vitalistic images of currents, relays, and streams, as well as idealistic conceptions of ramifying self-consciousness. As a temporal occurrence, a feeling builds or feeds on itself as a reaction to a reaction, each subsequent response passing on and altering the feeling of what came before. In his dissertation, Eliot describes feeling as a state of "confusion . . . out of which subject and object emerge" (*Knowledge and Experience*, 20). Bradley characterizes this state as "immediate experience," which he defines as the nonrelational background of relations. It is for both Bergson and Bradley a condition in which the connections between person and world are profuse but undefined. Both think that our need for practical orientation in the world eventually leads us to make order of our experience, analyze it, find causes, and discount all the other connections, mental and otherwise, that are of no use to us. Yet even then, we still access the unity of experience *as a feeling.*

We are accustomed to attributing feelings to subjects and even on occasion to saying that they are an event that happens *within* a subject. In his dissertation and subsequent critical writings, however, Eliot goes to great lengths to dispel this conception of feeling:

> It is hard to disabuse ourselves of the prejudice that feeling is something subjective and private, and that it affects only what feels, not what is felt. The reason for this is not far to seek. Feeling itself is properly speaking neither subjective nor objective, but its development into an articulate whole of terms and relations seems to affect the conscious subject, but not the objects of which the subject is conscious. (*Knowledge and Experience*, 21)

In basic terms, we commit this error because we think that we are the entities doing the interpreting, recalling, or responding necessary to have feelings at all. But if we take a less human-centric point of view, objects may also be said to act, even if they are not conscious agents, because they affect us as much as we affect them. As qualities, feelings are action-reaction circuits that apply to objects as well as to subjects. Indeed, in certain moods or atmospheres, objects "pick up" features and elements from their surroundings when they make visible their relations to those surroundings. The feelings they convey are not strictly "in" us, but the privilege that our perception confers is "for" us (that is, the relations they communicate are of intellectual or practical concern only from our point of view).[30] Nonetheless, as Eliot sees it, feelings manage to decenter us; they interfere with the sorts of attributions or distinctions we make. We see this above all in the case of tone, which breaks down points of view and gives objects a "feel" that we are accustomed to attributing to subjects.

The unswerving attention that Eliot gives to feeling and emotion may surprise those who think that impersonality resists or forsakes outpourings of emotion. But even his manifesto on impersonality, "Tradition and the Individual Talent"—which likens the mind of a poet to the "inert, neutral, and unchanged" behavior of a filamented platinum catalyst (*Selected Essays*, 5) and equates poetry with an "escape from emotion" rather than "a turning loose of emotion" (10)—mines an extremely refined set of distinctions regarding the various affects. Effectively, Eliot privileges feelings over emotions. Feelings create responsiveness to a situation, drawing novel connections among particulars, licensing the leaps of interest that allow people to attune themselves to their environment or axis of attention. Emotions (for example, love, hate, jealousy), however, tend in his view to constrain people's responses. They imperiously dictate attitudes by enforcing people's long-term behavioral patterns and personal histories.[31] For Eliot emotions are associated with expressive models of character that assume a stolid, subterranean affective life, waiting to be uncovered. Eliot seems especially hostile to emotions aroused by a work's narrative sequence, whereby each step in the plot predicts and structures what follows. Yet he does use the term "emotion" with some degree of freedom and grants that it coexists with feelings in surprising constellations.[32]

Meanwhile, Eliot prizes poetic effects that unfold unexpectedly when feelings, hovering in a *suspended* state, enter into combinations that are not prestructured by a typologically defined and discursively constructed affect (emotion).[33] His examples, drawn from Dante and from Thomas Middleton's *Revenger's Tragedy*, focus on moments of idiosyncratic response that do not have an immediate connection to the narrative tensions that define the dramatic situation. For Eliot, tone offers a means of access to such moments: "The whole effect, *the dominant tone*, is due to the fact that a number of floating feelings, having an affinity to this emotion by no means superficially evident, have combined with it to give us a new art emotion" ("Tradition and the Individual Talent" in *Selected Essays*, 10; emphasis mine). The classic critical view has been that Eliot is distinguishing between art and life, protecting himself from personal suffering by taking refuge in aesthetic affect, which offers immunity from such suffering.[34] Although critics point to Eliot's declaration that the difference "between art and the event is absolute" (9), I do not see Eliot making a claim for wholly separate classes or objects of experience. Such a facile position cannot be attributed to Eliot, who suggests in 1930 that art for art's sake was a doctrine that applied to no one, least of all to Pater, "who spent many years . . . expounding it as a *theory of life*" ("Baudelaire" in *Selected Essays*, 372). Eliot simply favors states of intensity that emerge freely, as it were, by the spontaneous alignments and connections that set up the tone of a work, rather than under the constraint of the narrative or dramatic context, dictated by the causal sequence of events.

Eliot, however, wants to discern something more than a world of interconnected feelings and fluid adjustments of perspective. Even in his earliest writings, his interest is always in the particular forms of reality that such perspectives create as they solidify and effect changes in a field of experience. Understood in this way, delusions or resistances to reality are, in some manner, part of reality. Therefore, it is not surprising that Eliot eventually migrated from Bergson's conceptual framework to Bradley's. After all, Bradley offered a theoretical account of how we acquire increasingly robust and forceful points of view and insisted that we consider a thing's reality not as a lump sum but as a series of degrees. "The reality of the object," Eliot remarks in his dissertation, "does not lie in the object itself, but in the extent of the relations which the object possesses without significant falsification of itself." As we take in more and more of the sensations, decisions, movements, classifications, and expectations that lead to "different points of view upon the object," we fit them into increasingly elaborate wholes and include ourselves as part of those wholes. In the process, "the object itself is altered" (*Knowledge and Experience*, 91). (Bergson, however, tended to avoid talk of "wholes," except provisional ones, because everything in his system is in transit.) More than Bergson, Bradley granted determinative force to mental processes and acts, which combine to form a point of view.

Eliot found in Bradley a foundation for his theory of impersonality, one that established ways of giving greater clarity and intellectual heft to an individual's perspectives by grounding it in wider knowledge and experience. It seemed to Eliot that the more "impersonal" anyone's perspective is, the more it breaks away from the self as a sole reference point. In the course of his dissertation, Eliot shifted from Bradley's discussion of feeling to his anatomy of knowledge. He thought that knowledge is given to us when we succeed in enlarging our perspective, which does not preclude or override feeling: "A toothache, or a violent passion, is not necessarily diminished by our knowledge of its causes, its character, its importance or insignificance" (*Knowledge and Experience*, 23). Indeed, feeling expands or supplements knowledge by giving access to wider-ranging and more unpredictable connections through leaps of thought that integrate the plot-points of our understanding, suggesting to us how they are interrelated.[35] In this respect, impersonality builds on feeling, challenging the integrity and internal consistency of the self and rendering boundaries between self and other permeable. Even in our ordinary understanding of what is entailed in a "perspective," it consists not only of an observation from a specific vantage point but also an awareness of how such an observation stands in implicit relationship to the constituent points of view of other selves. In the Bradleyan ontology that undergirds Eliot's theory, points of view are not piecemeal fragments, nor are they simply additive. Like radiating concentric circles, each broadened point of view overtakes previous points of view: "We vary by passing from one point of view to another or as I have tried to suggest, by occupying more than one point of view at the same time" (*Knowledge and Experience*, 147). In other words, according to this model we develop a perspective by integrating a number of immediate observations into a greater picture that includes the set of ways other people do or might see the same thing.

Even before Eliot began engaging Bradley's philosophy in earnest—and then throughout the period in which he was formulating his reading of this melancholy man's thought—he wrote poems that sought to ground identity in a greater reality, presenting speakers who rise above themselves as distinct centers to perceive the evolving ramifications of other people's consciousnesses. Yet as much as Eliot was drawn to the stability promised by point of view, he never quite abandoned his concern with feeling, whose alternating swings and unpredictable feints of mind prevent one from claiming global mastery over a situation.[36] Voices in particular—one's own as well as others'—resonate in ways that are vague and unstable. For this reason, the character attached to a voice is also inherently incomplete, subject to ongoing redefinition in a reality that is in part virtual. Even as Eliot pursued a more modest version of Bradley's effort to obtain a reliable foundation for identity, he wrote poems that revealed the impossibility of insulating oneself from error and conflict or from the emotional upheavals brought about by others.

DEGREES OF REALITY

It does not much matter that Eliot had not read Bradley, as Hugh Kenner points out, when he was composing "Prufrock" (*The Invisible Poet*, 43–45). His reading of Bradley simply allowed him to formulate certain ideas to which he was already committed: ideas about the reality-transforming nature of mental activity and thought. Returning for a moment to this and other early poems, we see that they testify to thought's being a constituent of reality, however contingent and circumscribed it might be. The threat or implication that Eliot wishes to frustrate in these poems is that his speakers will remain entirely in their own self-enclosed world. Relying on the dramatic monologue form, "The Love Song of J. Alfred Prufrock" depicts a state of painful self-consciousness that leaves the title character so overwrought that he is prone to overstressing and distorting the judgments of others. First, for example, Prufrock establishes the gaze of the chattering women within his social niche (he has "known the eyes already, known them all" [*Complete Poems and Plays*, 5]); then he becomes the predicted object of that gaze, an ineffectual creature who cannot act. "So how should I presume?" he bleats, his question merely trapping him in a self-perpetuating pattern of response. He thinks these women define him by a set of essential properties or features (his balding, his infirmity, his dithering), thus confirming for him the botched substance of his character. Within the poem, the grounds for this chain of inferences are not evident, but Prufrock's expectation that the women are stereotypical or predictable prevents him from expecting anything but a stereotypical response.

Eliot calls attention to the symmetry between how Prufrock sees society and how (he thinks) they see him: "[They will say: 'How his hair is growing thin!'] / . . . [They will say: 'But how his arms and legs are thin!']" (4). Accepting their supposed imputation that he is all too consistent, Prufrock diminishes his capacity for risking more intricate, satisfying, and open-ended connections with them (or with anyone else). Thus, Prufrock reveals that his character is not antecedent to the idea he has accepted of himself. At the same time, ideas have social reality, and Eliot emphasizes this. With "Prufrock," he reacts against the perspectivism of the Victorian dramatic monologue.[37] Prufrock's fretting emerges as a response to a social milieu that he understands all too well, though he appears to distort its character out of too great a sensitivity to it rather than out of ignorance of it. Prufrock may be stuck in a state that Jacques Lacan calls the "Imaginary," in which he projects onto his counterparts a view he has of himself.[38] In the familiar version of this account, the subject (in this case, Prufrock) sabotages the possibilities of achieving a genuinely intersubjective relationship by adhering to the displaced but idealized image of himself, while also casting others in the role of corroborators who bear out or affirm this ideal. Prufrock's defensiveness would thus emerge from the inherent vulnerability of his need to be substantiated in his attitude. Yet Eliot does not present Prufrock's logic as false or delusional, as mere narcissistic anxieties that he projects onto a number of bloviating ladies, whom he, in turn, reproaches. The problem seems to be that Prufrock tends to generalize too much and thus restricts himself to a diminished set of perspectives.

Viewed through a Bradleyan understanding of the Imaginary, Prufrock's failure appears to stem from his propensity to discount or *subtract* a great many images and relations that, if included, would round out his perspective; his failure is not that he imposes a private fantasy of his own through a process of mental *addition*. Because he integrates too few external perspectives, he fails to intuit the points of contact with other people's experience. Bradley would see Prufrock's problem as one of degree and his only antidote would be more relationality—or, what is the same, more reality.

Meanwhile, Eliot progressively undermines Prufrock's romantic notions of singularity. Prufrock seems to think that he has a personality schema that exists apart from his mutable relations to others. In this way, he is prevented at the outset from recognizing how his point of view gains its coherence from its ongoing entanglement in other points of view. The poem ends with his "drowning" in the one kernel of reality to be found in his fantasy: the ghostly voices of other people that intrude into his nervous monologue. Eliot, not by accident, associates voice with a "reality principle," an unavoidable reminder of human interconnectedness:

> We have lingered in the changes of the sea
> By sea-girls wreathed with seaweed red and brown
> Till human voices wake us, and we drown.
>
> (*Complete Poems and Plays*, 7)

While Prufrock does not discern an articulated discourse (confirmable perspectives other than his own), the very fact that the voices exist reminds him that his own monologue has a potential audience. And the potentiality of an audience enables Prufrock to hear himself afresh, offering him an equivocal form of contact with others that brings home to him an unsavory truth.

Eliot suggests that Prufrock's fate is determined by his own misguided ideas about his character and his failures of will. His fantasy life has real effects within the world. Resistances to reality, combined, create a new reality. Prufrock's life ends up being determined by his own suspended decision-making. He drowns precisely at the point at which, waking up to his predicament, the voices that haunt him do not so much confirm as create the circumstance that he fears.

Eliot followed the writing of "Prufrock" with another poem in the *March Hare* sequence that he elected not to publish, "Entretien dans un parc," which makes it clear that the Imaginary order is not a single state but a continuum of states presenting various degrees of reality. It depicts a Prufrock-like speaker breaking through his inaction to finally offer a romantic sign to the woman of his interest:

> We walked along, under the April trees,
> With their uncertainties
> Struggling intention that becomes intense.
> I wonder if it is too late or soon
> For the resolution that our lives demand.

With a sudden vision of incompetence
I seize her hand
In silence and we walk on as before.

(*Inventions of the March Hare*, lines 3–10)

Wishing to submit to an impulse to give himself "the slip" (line 28), he finds his isolation unbroken. His companion, meanwhile, is "surprised to see / So little her composure disarranged" (lines 13–14). The speaker and his lover fall back almost by default on a kind of timidity or self-composure that limits their capacity to react. Rather than use his gesture as an occasion for greater intimacy, they remain unchanged by it . . . almost. The speaker's irritation mounts as he registers that he has not broken out of what I have called his Imaginary: the saga continues as he might have predicted before he attempted contact. His exasperation registers a permeable transition between his fantasy and the reality with which it is continuous.

"Entretien" is an alternate version of the circumstance depicted in "Prufrock." Indeed, one could imagine Prufrock placing himself in the role of the speaker of "Entretien" and, anticipating the result, deciding not to take a romantic gesture into his hands. In this sense, "Prufrock" depicts an experience different not in kind from that of "Entretien" but in the degree to which the reality of the speaker is attenuated. Both poems offer a critique of a form of aesthetic disengagement that slips too far into the world of ideality to arrange and assemble the pieces of other people's perspectives—even as "Entretien" proves that the resulting viewpoints and predictions are not necessarily wrong.

Eliot, like Bradley, does not collapse reality into fantasy, but neither does he turn fantasy into reality. All is predicated on the sorts of relation or contact between the two. Bradley, according to Eliot, thinks that people are constantly anticipating some aspect of the world they have yet to confront; this, however, is not the same as saying that they are projecting a false account: "An anticipated idea, then, cannot be wholly imaginary, and on the other hand it cannot essentially refer to an event which becomes actual" (*Knowledge and Experience*, 53). In the very act of prediction, an individual alters the world, even if modestly. For Bradley, but not for Bergson, that individual creates a minimal but more than nominal difference in reality simply by regarding his or her situation in a different way. Thus, fantasy can never be contrasted with reality, only folded into it in complicated ways. As Eliot declares, "some of our sharpest agonies are those in which the object of desire is regarded as both possible and imaginary" (54).

The possible—the moment it is conceived as possible—already adds lines of determination that place it, however distantly, within the orbit of the real. Realities, in turn, have different contexts or different aspects in which they are taken as real. Bradley grants human agonies of misdirected calculation a place in the order of reality. The affective logic of "Prufrock" and "Entretien" presents minute dislocations of point of view and adjustments of tone, and gauges character by those things rather than by their determined behavioral patterns, which are susceptible to change. Tone, which defines the character of a specific voice, is always dependent on the contours of the situation in which a voice resounds (indeed, "Entretien" was originally titled "Situation"). Situations can be quite indeterminate, as the endings of both poems prove, even as Eliot also shows the psychologically defining effects of such indeterminacy.

Monologue proves itself a mode capable of allowing alternative perspectives to slip in. All the same, it has its limitations. Eliot moved on from monologue to poetic forms that presented multiple voices because he wanted new ways of testing the putatively self-contained point of view of a central speaker. In "Portrait of a Lady," for example, written right after "Entretien," he pits a society matron against a speaker who is ill-disposed to her solicitations of friendship. In marked fashion, tone takes over as the governing conceit of the poem, becoming the register in which all psychic exchanges happen. The parlor scene arranges itself, "as it will seem to do," around snippets of mannered conversation and deliberate detail. Yet Eliot does not content himself with an atmosphere of unstated reactions and overworked statements. He wishes to show how the speaker's character and point of view are implicated by his reaction to the woman's tone, which is the embodiment of her manner to him:

> We have been, let us say, to hear the latest Pole
> Transmit the Preludes, through his hair and fingertips.
> "So intimate, this Chopin, that I think his soul
> Should be resurrected only among friends
> Some two or three, who will not touch the bloom
> That is rubbed and questioned in the concert room."
> —And so the conversation slips
> Among velleities and carefully caught regrets
> Through attenuated tones of violins
> Mingled with remote cornets . . .
>
> (*The Complete Poems and Plays*, 8)

Music enters as a metaphor for the orchestrations of feeling between the two parties, a form of counterpoint whose resulting tone registers the unspoken sexual implications of the woman's conversation. Yet precisely because music is not discursive, it allows for a degree of ambiguity, diffusing her intention.

The speaker is installed in the *rôle d'honneur* in the woman's scripted intimacy:

> I am always sure that you understand
> My feelings, always sure that you feel,
> Sure that across the gulf you reach your hand.
> You are invulnerable, you have no Achilles' heel.
>
> (9–10)

Although the lady in question is surpassingly adept in the language of feeling, anticipating his reservations, her supercharged flirtations merely secure an ever more constricted position for him. She appears to talk around him to frustrate his attempt to maneuver within the conversation or even to sound his unpredictable voice. His resulting silence succeeds, nonetheless, in communicating his potential defiance of her perspective, provoking an even more desperate effort on her part to establish like-mindedness in their attitudes.

Even as the woman presumes that he is in lockstep with her—that he expresses her outlook and sentiment exactly—the tone of her discourse betrays a structuring awareness of the young man's conceivable difference of perspective. In his mind, the speaker orchestrates a counter-movement, which combines with her tune to produce a sour note:

> Among the windings of the violins
> And the ariettes
> Of cracked cornets
> Inside my brain a dull tom-tom begins
> Absurdly hammering a prelude of its own,
> Capricious monotone
> That is at least one definite "false note."
>
> (9)

This moment corresponds to the feedback effect that Ngai attributes to tone when signals that pass back and forth amplify each other, emitting a noisy distortion that short-circuits the affective exchange (*Ugly Feelings*, 83–86). As the speaker reacts to her reaction to him, her innuendo develops into unpleasant sharpness. The equation that the woman draws, Tom = friend, is disrupted by the enveloping monotone beat of the tom-tom (his insistence that Tom = Tom only). This insistent yet dampened tone cannot drown out her voice through clamorous volume, but its rise in intensity creates redundancy, amplifying feedback. Far from allowing him to escape (by fortifying him against her), feedback intensifies the manic agitation of his response. As he becomes aware that he is implicated by her response, his "self-possession flares up for a second," then it "gutters" (*Complete Poems and Plays*, 11).

Initially, the woman does everything to secure in him a false sense of solidity or substantiality of character. "You have no Achilles heel" (9), she tells him, implying that he is impervious to her. This enables her to spin his upsetting distance from her in a way that is less threatening and potentially grants him some relief from her disturbing effect on him. Nonetheless, the weirdness of their interaction succeeds in obliterating any sense of detachment he might wish for. Although the image of the speaker's smile, which recurs throughout the poem, is a "metaphysical mask," in Habib's suggestive phrase (*The Early T. S. Eliot and Western Philosophy*, 92), a concoction of politeness, embarrassment, self-screening aloofness, and irony, it does not offer him a stable form of distance.[39] In some respects, as Habib points out, "his viewpoint exceed[s] hers" (89) because he, no doubt, registers the socially impermissible longings in her talk and has some inkling of how he is cast in her seduction fantasy. But he can no more clarify her point of view, except as a reaction to his own, than he can understand himself apart from her. His attempt to fashion a stable, authoritative external perspective implicates his self-consciousness in its own act of separation or detachment. His smile, then, does not allow him to maintain his ironic distance except as a preliminary form of deflection. The tentativeness of the smile signals his fundamental discomfort with himself. The speaker ends the poem asking whether he has the right to smile. His question, like the expression that the smile conveys, only confirms his tentativeness as he considers other people's perspectives and the reality they might carry. Such reality is itself indeterminate. It depends on a future that neither party can script for him- or herself. The two in this parlor drama remain vulnerable to each other, even as they make efforts to escape from their vulnerability, and in due course they are both altered by the inconclusiveness of their mutual interaction.

Eliot, like Bergson, believed that reality must encompass not only actual objects and proceedings but also what Bergson calls "virtual" relations. These are potential contact points and interference patterns that cause events to veer in new, unpredictable directions. "Portrait of a Lady" points to its own immersion in Bergsonian ideas by depicting two vocalized points of view interacting unpredictably. Bergson was not any likelier than Bradley to assume that a world of truth existed prior to the thought-relations that impose decisive transformations within experience. Yet within a matter of months, Maud Ellmann tells us, "Eliot had rejected Bergson's 'meretricious captivation' for the 'melancholy grace' of Bradley" (*The Poetics of Impersonality*, 23; quoted phrases are Eliot's). She explains the split by linking it to Eliot's nascent "doctrine of impersonality [which] was launched specifically as an attack on Bergsonism" (12). As Ellmann understands the history, Bergson endorsed a form of individualism that trumpeted one-off novelties—a self that is altered moment by moment in ways that evade any conscious efforts to grasp it. In her view, Bergson's time philosophy left Eliot a target as dangerous as it was seductive, defining "personality as the resistance to our attempts to know it" (28). Her case draws on Eliot's unpublished papers, which nibble at the edges of Bergson's doctrine by, for instance, criticizing his contradictory use of spatial language to overturn spatial thinking.[40] Nevertheless, as I have been suggesting, Eliot's principle of impersonality and the relational account of character that underlies it remain unquestionably in Bergson's debt. It is certainly true that Bergson insisted on the deficiencies of conscious efforts to grasp the self by symbolic means, but Ellmann, like Russell and other early critics of Bergson, exaggerates his critique of the intellect.

I would propose a slightly different emphasis. Bergson, though he had an immensely sophisticated framework for an ontology of events, could not—so Eliot came to think—do justice to the objective reality of a social position or perspective. He was so attuned to the relational organization of all positions that he was not able to describe how any one ensemble of relations in and of itself comprised a greater reality or a new kind of whole. Though Bergson focused on the intellect as a distinctive practical force, he tended at various points to discount its reality and brush it off as a distortion of the truth (*Creative Evolution*, 274). He argues that the intellect secures a picture of the world only if it can immobilize it: "Preoccupied before everything with the necessities of action, the intellect, like the senses, is limited to taking, at intervals, views that are instantaneous and by that very fact immobile of the becoming of matter" (*Creative Evolution*, 273). But just what this immobilization amounts to as a set of lived effects, and how it reintrudes into reality, Bergson would not say.[41] As Eliot saw it, the intellect would need augmentation and refinement, not sacking.

Bergson simply could not demonstrate why a certain accumulation of perspectives in and of itself has social value. In a paper written in 1913, about three years after "Prufrock," Eliot writes:

> Bergson, on the one hand, emphasizes the reality of a fluid psychological world of aspect and nuance, where purposes and intentions are replaced by pure feeling. By the seduction of his style we come to believe that the Bergsonian world is the only world, and that we have been living among shadows. It is not so. Bergson is the sweet Siren of adventurous philosophers and our world of social values is at least as real as his. (quoted in *Inventions of the March Hare*, 409)

Eliot wished to ascribe a normative function to value by grounding it in a "tradition"—his word for the accumulation of historical and cultural perspectives that grant much of the significance to human judgments. Eliot was no more interested in fitting the world into a fixed social grid than Bergson was, but Bergson, he thought, denied social perspectives any jurisdiction or prerogative over individual souls.[42]

Eliot turned to Bradley in part because Bradley's sensibility, his saturnine dignity, was a better, more alert fit for the spectacle of modern life, as Eliot saw it. He felt that Bradley could account, in a way that Bergson could not, for the contexts in which social value has determinate force—contexts that can produce a perspective that is greater than the sum of its parts.[43] As Paul Douglass observes, Eliot did not reject Bergson wholesale; he accommodated him to Bradley (*Bergson, Eliot, and American Literature*, 49–53). Those features of Bergson's metaphysics that could not be supported by Bradley's framework, Eliot simply wrote off. But it should not be overlooked that the two overlapped significantly.

CHARACTER WITHOUT CONTENT

To summarize: Eliot inherited from Bergson and Bradley a context-sensitive account of character, which grants that the self has some fixed properties, at least notionally, but which dismantles claims for their independent significance. Dispossessed of intrinsic substance, the self finds its identity by projecting a voice that establishes pragmatic, intellectual, and emotional relations with the world of which it is a part. Encounters with others are potentially "reality extending." Amid all else, they allow us to overhear ourselves—to test our voiced perspective against those of others. But the theatrical distance that individuals have on themselves is not limited to the explicit points of view of specific individuals before them, for those points of view are fringed by other points of reference in vague, open-ended frameworks. The province of the poet is to jog these frameworks into motion. The richer and more fertile the analogues and vantage points employed, the more the person is able to transcend her or his immediate, pragmatic orientation. Particularly in poetry, where the practical motivations of the vocal act are not primary, the imagination is free to make connections that thread perspectives together. For this reason, Eliot insists that the imagination is an important barometer of reality. The mind of the poet, he avers in "Tradition and the Individual Talent," is in a position to "digest and transmute" the contexts it confronts or inherits; it is "empty," merely a "medium in which special, or very varied, feelings are at liberty to enter into new combinations" (7).

Eliot's "impersonal" understanding of character emerges from the ashes of Bradley's contentions. The danger of Bradley's philosophy is that it tends to encourage a conception of the world as a grandiose vista or increasingly integrated totality.[44] As we consolidate other people's perspectives into a larger point of view, we gradually rely on our powers of anticipation to characterize and identify the social world and to stabilize our identity as speakers. Therefore, the precedents of the past—including a historically defined tradition—increasingly overtake the present as they define the parameters through which we interpret any instance of voice. As we have seen, quite a number of Eliot's early poems present diffident characters who, like Prufrock, escape the present by compulsively anticipating how others react to them. In Prufrock's case, those others are a society of ladies. He claims to "know them all already, known them all" (*Complete Poems and Plays*, 5), an attitude that prevents him from engaging with them in meaningful ways. Yet far from endorsing such attitudes, Eliot depicts the bungled relationships and social failures that result. He insists that the present ultimately overrides whatever his characters are capable of foreseeing or awaiting. Although they wish to escape the situations that render them vulnerable to others, Eliot's personae necessarily come back to the unpredictable context in which they exist as embodied agents. Poetry, because it allows for fresh means of connecting the present to the past, expounds an identity that is open to redefinition. Eliot acknowledges that voice indexes and creates degrees of reality, but one cannot secure any absolute truth or knowledge from it (and he rebuffs any effort, philosophical or otherwise, to claim the contrary). For experience is, in essence, evolving, unpredictable, and self-ramifying. In a crucial realization that affected his intended vocation, Eliot eventually concluded that poetry, not philosophy, is the better aid in presenting and encapsulating such experience.

Even in his dissertation, Eliot remains skeptical that an imaginative form of involvement can ever reach more than a provisional state of fullness or finality. He pointedly refuses to endorse Bradley's concept of the Absolute. He observes that "the ideal can never be set over against the real absolutely, but tends to run, either forward or back, into the real which it intends, or the real out of which it may be said to be made" (*Knowledge and Experience*, 57). Still later, he insists: "the absolutely objective is nowhere found" (68). Tim Dean, noting the ambivalences and anxieties built into Eliot's impersonalist creed, refers to its counterintuitively antiauthoritarian undercurrent, which "undermines, first and foremost, the authority of the self" (50). Eliot understood better than many the inherently contingent nature of any ultimate claim to mastery. Even poetry, he thought, was best when it incorporates into its representations a firm sense of the limits of understanding as part of its claim to understanding. Bound to the example and authority of the literary tradition, poetry is an elevated instrument of imagination, but it can do no more than foster degrees of sympathetic awareness. It was as a psychologist that Bradley interested Eliot, not as an obscure metaphysician.

Eliot writes an intriguing little poem called "Suppressed Complex" in 1914, in the midst of his period of reflection on Bradley. It takes up a depth model of character only to upend it by insisting on the relational terms that define personality, and I end with it because it helps to flesh out how the psyche derives its character from the imaginative work of other psyches. The poem features a lover who hovers in the corner of a girl's bedchamber, gazing luridly at his vulnerable object.

> She lay very still with stubborn eyes
> Holding her breath lest she begin to think
> I was a shadow upright in the corner
> Dancing joyously in the firelight.
>
> (*Inventions of the March Hare*, lines 1–4)

According to Lyndall Gordon, "Eliot's lover has no sense of the sleeping girl, who is merely a prop to arousal, and the result is an immature bore boasting an imaginary escapade" (*T. S. Eliot*, 101). It is not clear in this assignation fantasy, however, whether the sexual agitation is the lover's, who delights in access to a girl's suppressed feelings, or the girl's, who is dreaming of her inamorato.

The very title is ambiguous. It invokes a "complex," which, Gordon supposes, "is used in the technical sense of the new psychologists to mean obsessions arising from repressed drives" (101). But one might view the same word "complex" as a play on Ezra Pound's definition of the image in his famous Imagist manifesto: "an intellectual and emotional complex in an instant of time" whose presentation gives "that sense of sudden liberation . . . which we experience in the presence of the greatest works of art" ("A Retrospect," 4). Like another of Eliot's poems from a slightly later period, "Hysteria," "Suppressed Complex" mixes metaphors of depth, concealment, and psychic incorporation with a rather different set of logical associations that are bound to the surface image, allowing the mind to yoke together multiple registers of experience through an act of imaginative compression.

The two figures appear to set each other's imagination to work, entering into an indefinite relay. The lover's thoughts cause the woman to stir "in her sleep" and clutch "the blanket with her fingers" (*Complete Poems and Plays*, 5), and he, in turn, takes joy in her state of arousal. The self unfolds as an interactive complex in which consciousness registers not only the things set before it but also how it is implicated or addressed by them. The young man is aroused by the thoughts that the woman has of him, and she in turn is aroused. In his dissertation, Eliot would insist that no psychological event stands alone as a mental content: "There is, in this sense, nothing mental, and there is certainly no such thing as a consciousness if consciousness is to be an object of something independent of the objects which it has" (*Knowledge and Experience*, 83).[45] As an isolated datum, a self has no mind-stuff; its thoughts are not private events. The only thing it offers is a point of view—a set of relations that it organizes and a provisional context in which its perspective is employed.[46] By extension, in this poem each of the lovers is not a world unto itself. The suppressed acknowledgment in the poem, if anything, appears to be the proposition that each lover depends in some respect on his or her counterpart for the complex of passions, hot terrors, and dreamed-of prospects that each variously experiences as his or her own.

The poem ratifies another line of reasoning that Eliot weaves into his dissertation: an individual, who is never a contained object, is only treated as such through the validation of an outsider's perspective. According to Richard Wollheim, Eliot insists on an asymmetry or discrepancy between how a subject understands her own thoughts and how an observer does: "From the point of view of the subject, an 'idea' or 'psychological event' (to talk generally) is something that is . . . objective: it belongs to the external world. From the point of view of the observer, however, a psychological event belongs to the history of the subject who experiences it: it is something personal" ("Eliot and F. H. Bradley," 177). The boy-lover, gazing at his object in "Suppressed Complex," may treat her as an independent entity, even if her thoughts refer to him or to the external world of which he is a part. This is his prerogative as an observer: he is not especially interested in the context in which her point of view rests; to him, her thoughts say something about her, her finite experience and history. The dreaming girl, in turn, may be less interested in herself as a first-person ideational complex (or "psychological event") than in the objects of her experience and their train of connectedness. Each object refers to a world of things outside her; each is connected in absorbing ways to the others. Her point of focus is not herself as an identity apart from others. In other words, people focus on the subject side or object side of the same psychological event alternately depending on their vantage point or interested relation to it.

Eliot confers the label "personality" on any interpretation of the self that considers it an abiding content or emotional interiority. Personality is a perspectival illusion that occurs when we treat individuals as coextensive with the objectifying gaze of an outsider's perspective while remaining blind to the context or situation in which that perspective is made possible. The observer thinks: *She is a thing I see; how I see her, in some form that must be what she is.* Under observation, the person suddenly appears to exist independently of the context in which the judgment is made. She is no longer the product of ongoing and negotiated relationships with the world; she is driven and thinglike, an alloy of predictable attributes sustained across her history. In Eliot's view, to contend that someone is defined by her personality would be to mistake the normative, external perspective on the self for substantive immediacy.

Because we rely on people within a shared community (on their judgments and ideas, on the forms of rapport they establish) for our self-conception, we can never confirm the self-sufficiency and integrity of our image without distorting the social character of the self. Although the "suppressed complex" of the title refers in one sense to the enclosed interiority of the sleeping girl, that interiority, the poem urges, calls for the dreaming presence of another figure "in the corner" to construe it as such. Yet by that fact, the poem would seem to confirm a notion on which Deleuze and Félix Guattari insist, to the effect that "fantasy is never individual: it is *group fantasy*" (*Anti-Oedipus*, 30). The interior life is already constituted by social perspectives that implicitly or explicitly enter into the frame of any fantasy.

Abstractly considered, what is the alternative to submitting to the logic that would identify one as a personality? We have to acknowledge that others see us in ways that we do not see ourselves—and necessarily so. In other words, we have to measure the differences between our own and other people's perspectives by recognizing their emergence as context-specific judgments. We have to pool together a variety of frameworks and perspectives on ourselves. In Eliot's language, "the life of a soul does not consist in the contemplation of one consistent world but in the painful task of unifying (to a greater or less extent) jarring and incompatible ones, and passing, when possible, from two or more discordant viewpoints to a higher which shall somehow include and transmute them" (*Knowledge and Experience*, 147–148). We are not in a position to internalize someone else's point of view because our relation to it is different. Eliot uses the word "inference" to describe what he extols as the empathic assessment of another's mind, though the term may be more misleading than useful. For we are not extrapolating others' experiences on the basis of our own: "When we qualify our world by the recognition of another's it is not his world as it is in reality, but his world as it affects us that enters into our world" (147). We simply learn how we are implicated by other perspectives. Yet individuals "intend" upon the *same* world; therefore their separate standpoints are often not entirely distinct. They dissolve or bleed into each other in a zone of shared implication or feeling.

Each of the figures in "Suppressed Complex" exists not only as an object of desire but also as a virtual perspective on the other. The poet-persona who speaks in the poem helps to resituate the dreaming girl's desires, and she, his. Their emotions, which appear to resonate with each other, make them intimates, and so their mutual points of view—whether seductive or off-putting, accurate or inaccurate—impinge on their counterparts in ways that alter both sides. To the degree that they are implicated in each other's lives, they must assume some responsibility for each other's perspective, even if individually they are not in full control of the impression they make. And as I have suggested, this is because they are the unremitting product of these relations and others like them.

It is worth noting that in their intertwined Imaginary, Eliot's characters seem to resist such recognitions. One of several variants of the poem (which Eliot sent off first to Pound, then to Conrad Aiken) has a period after "think" (Smith, "T. S. Eliot and the Fragmented Selves," 417): the girl lies still "Holding her breath lest she begin to think. / I was a shadow upright in the corner." The insertion plays on two levels: (1) as an acknowledgment on the girl's part of the phantom in her room, and (2) as the male speaker's fantasy of concealed access. Perhaps the sleeping ingénue refuses to acknowledge the social character of the self—more specifically, of herself—but just as likely she does not welcome rendering herself open to *this* particular figure before her. In this poem, only one voice is speaking—and therefore the relations are not symmetrical. He appears to be an intruder and clearly disturbs her dreams. We are told: "She was very pale and breathed hard" (*Complete Poems and Plays*, 6). Even if he infringes on her privacy, however, the speaker is not peering into a strictly hermetic interior because, in Eliot's conception of character, there is no such space. The relation between the counterparts is too psychologized for Grover Smith to be quite right in claiming that "the crisis in [her] emotion [is] foreign to the shadow's equally solitary spasm of delight" ("T. S. Eliot and the Fragmented Selves," 420). If, as he suggests, the poem portrays a state of dissociation, it is first premised on a condition of mutually implicated perspectives. Yet the speaker wishes to immure her in his masculinist fantasy, which requires the privileging of his perspective and the sounding of his voice.

In this aestheticist dreamscape, the male figure's puerile fantasies of control—if that is what he displays—are nevertheless no more impervious to other vantage points than the girl's are. For the figure is a persona, a voice, a theatrical part dependent on another audience—invisible in the scene but profoundly implicit within it—whose range of possible responses (including judgments as to his state of exuberance or puerility), exposes the prison house of his own Imaginary as an illusion. Tone, as a set of virtual responses or implicit feeling-based relations, I have suggested, is the regulating instrument of such attunement to an audience. Lyric encourages levels of awareness of a speaker's tone that may be at odds with a speaker's sense of himself. Sometimes we attribute such implications to the author, but even so, it is still the author speaking provisionally through his characters, like the puppeteer in Eliot's "Convictions (Curtain Raiser)," and, like their oblique "sentiments," open to unpredictable forms of interpretation.

In "Suppressed Complex," the tonal complexity has to do with, among other things, the assessment of the speaker's dreamy, wistful lyricism and the competing conceptions of vagueness that it points to in the poem. We can see, perhaps, why Eliot chose not to publish the piece. The poem is in danger of celebrating the girl's vagueness as a blank, an absence of content ready to be filled by the speaker, rather than—as I have been suggesting—a means of contesting the models that imply that character can be filled in in the first place. Eliot risks the reader's conflating the imagination with the Imaginary. Yet without actually endorsing the speaker's perspective, the poem implies that vagueness is a constitutive aspect of reality—an indication of the open-endedness of character itself and a generative condition of meaning-making. The girl is not simply a projection or fabrication of the speaker's. The pair weave together a reality whose degree of validity rests on their mutually entangled, but nonetheless vague, sense of one another. The boy-lover abandons any pretense of finally knowing the object of his desire by escaping in the morning—passing "joyously out through the window" (*Complete Poems and Plays*, 8).

Eliot's persona-hero wafting out of the room and away is like Eliot himself—who leaves the parlors and bedchambers of his earlier work for the less contained geographical and emotional spaces of *The Waste Land*. It seems clear that Eliot wanted to make good on the promise of tonal complexity while ridding his poems of any suggestion that one central perspective or persona-speaker has any imaginative license or special prerogative over another. And so, nearly a decade after poems such as "Suppressed Complex," he found new ways of testing voices against each other, moving or skittering among vocal positions, combining points of view in more expansive frameworks that targeted myth, history, and literary traditions, as well as popular song and vernacular conversation—all to heighten tone as these voices integrate at a certain tonal frequency. It may be hard to recognize *The Waste Land*'s voices as that of distinct characters, but that is Eliot's point: they are not.[47] Eliot's most famous poem thus presents a turning point. He makes explicit what is only implicit in his dramatic monologues and earlier lyrics: what makes character animated is not the voice per se and certainly not the voice as a marker of an enclosed identity, let alone a superior one. Voices are materials—remnants of the near and distant past—that can be recontextualized and thus given a new life. The points of view represented by these voices may be other to oneself; they may be profoundly foreign. But to understand them, to hear them, is to recognize the constituents of one's own points of view, real as well as potential. In other words, "to draw a circle of consciousness around fragmentation," as Michael Levenson describes the task of the poem (*Genealogy of Modernism*, 176), is to discover external points of view that are basic to who one is or could be. The dead past has life in it, and life is erected on the materials of the dead. For human beings, the past includes not only the molecules and physical constituents that bodies take up and recycle but also the voices and intellectual fragments of our history that we reorganize. Their vital role is to strengthen our ability to engage with each other and with a world that peers in from just beyond the realm of the intimate and the familiar.

Tiresias, says Eliot in a famous footnote to *The Waste Land*, "although a mere spectator and not indeed a 'character,' is yet the most important personage, uniting all the rest. . . . What Tiresias *sees*, in fact, is the substance of the poem" (*Complete Poems and Plays*, 52). The poem's witness (which could be Tiresias but could be, provisionally, ourselves) weaves among the fragments of these foreign voices that haunt him to find a logic among unpredictable associative patterns. The proliferating and dissolving metaphorical frameworks allow us to extemporize a unity for the poem, though one that is promissory and provisional. Rather than a discrete speaker or discrete characters, we have what we could understand as a ventriloquized style of speech integrated into the structure of the poem—a way of creating a new identity out of the crossing of voices. Eliot's achievement is to play with the alignments or collapsing differences between us and these speaking positions. Yet as extraordinary a breakthrough as it is, *The Waste Land*, Eliot's first masterwork relies on the impersonal psychology that he develops in his early verse. Like those poems, it rejects as ethically damaging models of character that stake identity or self-definition on fixed properties impervious to the welter of other people's vocalized perspectives.

Literature teaches us how to recognize tonal complexity and in so doing unveils the social character of personhood itself, its constructedness and its dependency on relations and angles of interpretation outside the self. Paradoxically, modern lyric, which—no longer sung—has to forego many of the more directly aural and acoustic properties of voice, becomes for Eliot the best available instrument for gauging tone or for training a reader in its niceties.[48] In this context, tone has to do with manner of speech as much as with matter or signification—that is, with indicators that indirectly express people's sentiments or reveal their character by establishing relations with an audience. Eliot did as much as the New Critics who followed in his footsteps to introduce this particular employment of "tone" into the lexicon of modern literary criticism. That he thought to do so in relation to lyric, I argue, has to do with the orchestration of complex registers of speech, the performative and expressive dimensions of voicing, and the nonstraightforwardness of the intentions behind the work—all recognized though highly contentious features of lyric address because, to the dismay of some philosophers and critics, they privilege affective and associative rather than strictly semantic modalities of language use. Such voice finally destabilizes the self-coherence and consistency of the individual. The band of voices that Eliot borrowed, adapted, and refashioned in his early verse surrenders to self-alteration as their perspective becomes mediated through others. In so doing, Eliot fundamentally redefines the nature of character itself, privileging emotional receptivity, open-endedness, and a capacity for attunement; these, he insists—rather than any supposed "personality"—give fullness and dynamic reality to the lives of human beings.

AFTERWORD
Vital Signs

This book has argued that life is open-ended, unpredictable, filled with accidents, uncertainty, risk, impermanence. As a consequence, ethics, which is about what is good for human life, must take into account attitudes and dispositions that allow individuals to change in accord with their circumstances, to adapt and self-regulate in the face of the unexpected. The impulse to draw conclusions about how to live on the basis of what life is like is basic to nineteenth- and twentieth-century vitalism as an intellectual inquiry. Yet Bergson, William James, Nietzsche, and Darwin (considered, as he is here, among the vitalists) do not impose hard-and-fast principles for defining life or its parameters and conditions of possibility. Life produces innumerable creatures with differential forms of development, subject to competing polarities and divergent modes of existence. Because there is no fixed basis for assessing the value of an ethical system, vitalists push us to ask instead: What approaches to existence can best strengthen the forms that human life takes at any given moment (understood in situationally specific terms), and what other more robust, forceful, or exuberant forms of life are possible?

I have suggested that the modernist writers in the Anglo-American tradition who were most influenced by a vitalist style of thought explored, indirectly, questions about how to live, through their literary depictions of people. They created characters who are minutely responsive to their environment, who are capable of altering their desires, attitudes, habits, interests, and ultimately the very contours of their own selves to adjust to the changes occurring around them. The writers who devised new formal methods of depicting these changes exalted their characters' power to improvise, which allowed them to triumph over the historical patterns of thought and action that would otherwise dictate their future to them. Concentrating on Henry James, Stein, and Eliot, we have seen how profoundly occupied they are with the mind as an organ for gauging and effecting changes in an individual's psychic blueprint and schemes of action. Figures such as Bergson and William James serve to clarify how such changes swell up as a result of lively temporal processes, which are accelerated by the mind in its stream of unpredictable thought.

The wonder really is that vitalism has until the last decade received so little attention as an intellectual framework for understanding the climate in which literary modernism developed, with the exception of sporadic monographs focused mostly on Eliot. The reasons are manifold. For one, modernists regularly subjected their vitalist impulses to skeptical treatment. I do not refer only to Eliot, who, as we have seen, had qualms about Bergsonism and who speaks of "the fallacy of progress, which is the Bergsonian fallacy" (Sanford Schwartz, *Crisis in Modernism*, 297). At times, James parodied his vitalist impulses, haunted as he was by a vision of the past that threatens to overtake the present. He wrote such cautionary stories as "The Beast in the Jungle," about a man who thinks his future is set for him because of a premonition he has felt since his earliest days. James's unfinished novel "The Sense of the Past" also expresses his protagonist's unseemly attachment to the past. In these fictions, James's vitalist commitments are still in evidence, but so too are his worries about the limits of the human capacity to act on the future. The compulsive need to repeat, expressed in different ways in James's and Stein's writing, suggests—at least superficially—a limit on their characters' capacity for self-alteration. A useful step for any forthcoming account of modernism would be to clarify the precise character of modernism's own misgivings and worries, less about vitalism or vital experience than about forms of recalcitrance that people evince in the face of it.

The relationships and intellectual affinities that developed between modernist writers and vitalist theorists were burdened with a number of tensions. Though Henry James was capable of reporting to his brother William that he read his works "with rapture," begging him to send more of his "recent papers & discourses" (*William and Henry James: Selected Letters*, November 23, 1905), the two repeatedly clashed over the "interminable elaboration of suggestive reference" in Henry's last novels and the "twilight or mustiness" that William ascribed to Henry's plot constructions and niceties of style (*Selected Letters*, October 22, 1905).[1] For Eliot, Bergson and vitalism came to be associated with a species of romanticism, but we can consider this as much a reaction against the philosopher's appeal to political leftism as it is a philosophical claim.[2] However that may be, there are sides of Bergson that manifestly speak to Eliot's notion of impersonality, as I have argued. There are writers of the period, such as Hulme, who make that connection evident.[3] Vorticist writer-painter Wyndham Lewis expended bile in *Time and Western Man* on Bergson's "time cult," whose ranks, he alleged, included D. H. Lawrence, James Joyce, and Gertrude Stein. Lewis's hard-edged aesthetic brooked no blurring of the lines, preferring the frozen morphology of the wasp as a model for character—with its rigid exoskeleton and segmented parts—over the ecstatic, organic gush that gave vitalism a hold on the sympathetic organization of public life.[4] Lewis repudiates his own early flirtation with vitalism and responds by forging a "cold modernism" (in Jessica Burstein's phrase), renouncing feeling and embracing a line of evolution approximating the insect's that indicates "the inertia of the élan vital."[5]

As a target for Lewis, D. H. Lawrence was a natural choice. Lawrence's screed against psychoanalysis, *Fantasia of the Unconscious*, reveals its vitalist commitments on its sleeve, particularly Lawrence's celebration of "pre-mental" or "nonmental" consciousness, which he understood to be embedded in the body's nervous functions. But his kooky talk of the solar plexus as the regulating center of emotional life reads more like a mash-up of different lay mysticisms than a respectable physiological explanation. It had the cursory trappings of scientistic gibberish to which vitalism was always prone, though Lawrence had drawn on the work of a number of now largely forgotten figures in late nineteenth-century physiological psychology, such as William Benjamin Carpenter, Thomas Laycock, and George Henry Lewes, who emphasized unconscious or nondeliberative action.[6] As Lawrence predicted, his essay received uncomprehending responses from critics, and his fixation on sex-consciousness in fiction and criticism summoned up evocations of Freud's theories, notwithstanding his protestations.

More broadly, vitalism, as a richly psychological discourse, lost currency as it was displaced by psychoanalysis. Vitalism did not seem to outlast the historically contingent conditions of its emergence. One way to understand the relative success of Freudian discourse is to note that, unlike his vitalist contemporaries, Freud could claim for himself a disciplinary niche within larger medical and therapeutic institutions. Although psychoanalysis was not less likely to run afoul of an empirically inclined culture in search of causes, at least it did not have to defend itself first and foremost in the philosophical arena, where hostility to speculative and antirationalist methodologies was pronounced. Unlike Freud, Bergson preferred not to engage his critics directly and remained silent in the face of mounting hostility to his work in the 1910s and 1920s by figures as varied as the French philosopher Julien Benda and the far-right monarchist and political theorist Charles Maurras not to mention the Catholic Church itself, which put his works on the Index in 1914. Bergson's ill-fated but misunderstood debate with Albert Einstein did not help vitalism's reputation either.[7]

A skeptic might say that vitalism did not succeed in entrenching itself as a psychology woven into the very fabric of daily life and its modes of reflection, as psychoanalysis did for artists and writers of the 1930s, 1940s, and 1950s. Psychoanalysis somehow managed to get absorbed into the psychic back-and-forth of daily experience, not as a theory necessarily, but as a pattern of consequences, probabilities, pragmatic aims and functions, stresses played up, ways of remarking on things. Psychoanalysis had a way of bookmarking psychic experience for those who cared about it—bookmarking it, of course, partially in terms of wild, outrageous mythic structures. But that was and still is part of its appeal. As Wittgenstein said of Freud, his theories cannot be measured in terms of a set of discoveries made so much as by their persuasive power, which on some level creates effects and solves problems.[8]

To a greater degree than vitalism, psychoanalysis seems to have had a way of claiming and giving dividends on all that was groundbreaking and searching about psychology. Psychoanalysis put on the map such psychic phenomena as wishes and fantasy, and it arrayed them against the background of Freud's famous mechanisms of defense. Psychoanalysis, that is, spoke about desire, and it immersed it in a richly theatrical medium. But its emphasis on unconscious mental processes insisted on a person's conformity to a prior self. It sought antecedents in infantile complexes and attempted to clarify behavior in sources detached from a situation or constellation of circumstances. Yet this meting out of reasons for behavior leaves little room for reckoning with situations that are incomplete: when information is unavailable, when inputs are too fast or too indeterminate for one to gain any kind of cognitive handhold on the situation, when the will must act without reckoning its consequences. Vitalist psychology does not strive first and foremost to *explain* behavior, to trace its antecedent causes, because something qualitatively new is presumed to intrude on any impulse. And the writers we are concerned with, James, Stein, and Eliot, responded to something in that vision. They created characters who refuse the interpretive instruments that account for or justify the progress of their behavior to others, especially by ferreting out symptoms and diagnosing illnesses.

As I have attempted to document in this book, modernists' point of access to vitalism was through the mind as an embedded organ within a larger physiological complex or "sensori-motor schema," in Bergson's phrase. More generally, Bergson frames for us the place of the psyche within a materialist ontology. He insists that the psychological experience of time exposes the way change happens on a larger impersonal scale, revealing a "continuous progress" in which each "upspringing" of novelty is "incommensurable with its antecedents" (*Creative Evolution*, 27). The mind does not treat any moment as an isolated point in time; it remembers past moments that have led up to it, which preside over any instant, giving it directionality. This agglomeration of the past, available to the mind in the form of memories and habits, serves as a virtual resource in a person's bid to react helpfully to unfolding events. It is not much of a leap for Bergson to suggest that "organic evolution resembles the evolution of consciousness" (*Creative Evolution*, 27). Paul-Antoine Miquel asks why we should not conclude that this analogy is "a pure anthropomorphism" ("Evolution of Consciousness and Evolution of Life," 1156). I would suggest that, for Bergson, the mind functions as a central model for understanding material systems because it intensifies the self-ramifying force of time itself: it acts in a dynamic relationship to the *whole* of the past, to an accumulation of causes, some quite remote, that are multiple and unpredictable in their effects. The analogy between consciousness and organic evolution is undergirt by ontology. Indeed, consciousness is the product of the creative force of duration itself. Bergsonian metaphysics begins as a psychology not because it limits itself to an account of human experience but because that experience exemplifies a living material process at its most complex.

The recent reemergence of vitalism as a significant critical discourse has coincided with a focus on the organization of material systems that displaces the centrality of the subject and subjectivity as a means of conceptualizing vital experience. As Deleuze puts it, "We believe in a world in which individuations are impersonal, and singularities are pre-individual [making] apparent . . . the advent of a coherence which is no more our own, that of mankind, than that of God or the world" (*Difference and Repetition*, xxi). Suzanne Guerlac contends that Deleuze's articulation of Bergsonism "is sensitive to the discursive context of an emerging poststructuralism. His acquired hostility to subjectivity causes him to separate the anonymous forces of "duration from psychological experience and subjectivity as much as possible" (*Thinking in Time*, 180). Deleuze underemphasizes consciousness because the idea of a mind reacting to itself—to its own thoughts, ideas, or memories—is too close to idealist frameworks popular in the 1950s and 1960s, inspired by Hegel and his dialectical inheritors, against whom Deleuze established his most sustained critique. Instead, he focuses on human-nonhuman assemblages. His resulting intervention has given renewed relevance to vitalism in the realm of cybernetics, where it assists in a critique of artificial intelligence, environmental science, neuroscience, and new media studies, all of which owe a debt to Deleuze's translation of Bergsonian vitalism.

The vitalist mantle is carried to the present day in the work of affect theorists such as Brian Massumi, and new materialists such as Jane Bennett. Massumi uses affect to explore interactions between bodies and objects that resist being named or identified sociolinguistically. He is attentive to the incipient nature of experiences that disrupt the coherence of fixed identities because they are still ongoing and because their surprising effects introduce contingency into everyday events. He seeks to understand affect by engaging with neuroscience and other related disciplines. Although his disciplinary resources may be different from those of modernists, he shares with them what I take to be a noncognitivist orientation: he is interested in how people register changes when they are not yet cognitively grasped (*Parables for the Virtual*, 30). Bennett sets out to displace the privilege of human experience and agency in political theory, allowing us to think of a world of things—from food to infrastructure (electricity grids, landfills) to metal, stem cells, and worms—as having vital power. To my mind, the erosion of the radical divide between life and nonlife and the effort to displace the hubristic centrality of human perspective teach us profound things about our late emergence and smallness in the order of things and our likeness to many creatures and processes in the world superficially different from ourselves.

Despite such salutary correctives, current vitalisms have lost a great deal that was important not only to Bergson but to the writers of a nascent modernism who were contributing in their way to vitalist reflection. They have for the most part passed over how much our ways of understanding ourselves—our agency and our character—may be transformed by models that treat mind or consciousness as exemplifying the unpredictable effects of novelty. Because minds interpret the world as well as act on it, the particular way they draw connections and discover or amplify the virtual implications of situations, as well as how they stage the practical or deliberative relation to their own mental life, deserves special scrutiny. These mental processes are not always best understood according to a strictly somatic and materialist language of brain response, sensory or perceptual thresholds, reflexive reactions, biofeedback systems, and the like, but rather—as I have observed throughout—in more culturally and semantically embedded terms.

Emphasis on minds does not mean that modernist writers are inattentive to the scenes and material environments that activate personal agency and generate potent affective responses. Indeed, as I have argued, modernist character is prevailingly situational. James, Stein, and Eliot understand the self as an exquisitely attuned system or assemblage, a mind that is not contained within a bodily envelope but that spills over into the environment with which the individual is in interactive relation. Yet the relays between self and world are most engaging and self-transforming, they thought, when they concern relations between selves. Perhaps surprisingly, this book has lingered longest on moments of interpersonal intimacy as a site for vitalizing exchange. However much our interface with the world changes as a result of material, technological, and ecological alteration, some of our most powerful attachments and responses as human beings remain with other human beings, even as what it means to be human in such cases changes as our world changes. That said, the lessons of vitalist modernism do not end in the intimate sphere, and so it continues to remain an open question how people's vital commitments to each other impinge on the more aleatory and improvisational elements of public and political life.

The idea that human beings are imbricated with their environment has become a central tenet of recent media theory, which proposes that our extension into new media ecologies constitutes a central mode of our social and experiential evolution. This has coincided with a general move to consider modernist textual production, as Julian Murphet puts it, "in [its] extended media contexts" (*Multimedia Modernism*, 9). Texts such as Eliot's *Waste Land* incorporate other media idioms, such as pop music, and framing devices, such as those adopted by cinema, and become subject to remediation in turn, thus creating a system in which "lived experience" becomes legible or knowable through the convergences of various media's "means of representation and inscription" (17). The founding premise of current media theory is that there is no authentic state of presence or "unmediated" experience to be had that allows us to encounter our natural state. To put it in other terms, there is no way to pare down human existence to our biologically constituted grounds because we are inevitably immersed in a media environment that is in part composed or manufactured. I am drawing on Robert Mitchell's reminder that a medium may be thought of in the biological sense as the features of an environment that facilitate the growth and development of living entities (*Bioart and the Vitality of Media*, 11). One implication is that if media are a prosthesis or, better put, a human-nonhuman assemblage, then nature itself is always in some sense made, not given, is already vitally mediated.

On this basis, it might be said that we are dependent in a range of far-reaching but imprecise ways on these media for our existence and, as I would argue, even for our sense of self; human character changes along with media environments. Without veering into a much broader discussion that takes us from the increasingly mass-mediated context of modern life in the early twentieth century to the digital landscape of the present, I simply note how much our social relations as well as the baggage of our cultural past depend on media whose modes of presentation and circulation are constantly altering along with technology. The question for vitalist-inspired media theorists is how to keep up not simply with reality but with what is potential in the media systems of today. Vitalism can thus play its part in chipping away at what Murphet calls the "critical myth of 'technological determinism'" (*Multimedia Modernism*, 1), the belief that the technological properties of the medium determine how social relationships and, therefore, in some broader way, human experience, are structured.

Following Deleuze's Bergsonian reading of cinematic potentiality,[9] Mark Hansen has offered a fresh account of digital media. In it, he puts the body at the center of a dynamic of coevolution between human beings and media technologies. Hansen has turned back to Bergson to understand the role of the body as a framer of information and hence as an active agency helping to organize and draw out the sensory and affective potential of the media world it confronts.[10] Although he focuses on the human-media interface as an embodied relationship, Hansen nevertheless tends to ground the potential at work in the encounter with media on the basis of the abstract or theoretical capacity of the medium itself to distort and reassemble the image world without any fidelity or necessary relation to an indexical reality. "Following its digitization," Hansen remarks, "the image can no longer be understood as a fixed and objective viewpoint on 'reality' . . . since it is now defined precisely through its almost complete flexibility and addressability, . . . its constitutive 'virtuality'" (*New Philosophy for New Media*, 8). Instead of thinking about how media mediate social relations or remediate and recompose the voices, texts, images, and sounds of the present and past, he sticks to a largely corporeal (proprioceptive, interoceptive, haptic) account of digital media's effect on its receivers. He thus reproduces some of the narrow somatic concerns that dominate the new vitalisms. He is in danger of reinforcing complaints originally directed at Bergson to the effect that all he cared about was the solitary sensory flux of an interior life.

Whatever we may think of Hansen's Bergsonism, Bergson's own theories, as I have argued, offer something more: a view of the self as sensitive to historical alteration and fiercely social. Yet some critics remain unconvinced. Bergson has not quite shaken the old complaints about his solipsism. Exploring possible grounds for enmity toward Bergsonism, Donna Jones points to his determination to treat profound aspects of individuality as incommunicable, which burdens the self with radical inwardness: "It is not clear why we [should] find the deeper truth or reality in what is incommunicable rather than in what is shared and mutually understood. We are told that deeper truth is grasped by withdrawing from action and intuiting our own inner duration. But why should we understand ineffable subjective experience as reality?" ("The Eleatic Bergson," 25). Her point is well taken. Bergson undoubtedly relied too much on what sounds like a humanistic language of authenticity for grounding his models of subjectivity. But I have argued that his models are more conducive to understanding the indeterminacy of selves than their inexpressibility. As it turns out, modernist writers found ways of expressing this indeterminacy by depicting people negotiating their future in the moment of real or imaged social interchange. As Lisa Blackman argues, vitalist figures (she names William James in particular) measure personality by the criterion of "aliveness" not organized "through a contrast between the authentic and false self" ("Affect, Relationality and the 'Problem of Personality,'" 30).

William James and Bergson do not promise any surefire techniques for personal or collective self-renovation in the face of an increasingly socially fragmented and alienated public sphere. They simply urge creativity itself as a means of combat against the problems of modern life. The modernists explored in these pages understood that such creativity must be directed at material institutions; it is not a self-willed product of mind alone. Bergson might have appealed to those who sought consolation in an ahistorical spiritual impulse, but we do not have to view Bergson's conception of *durée* as "abstracted from 'real' time" (Horkheimer, "On Bergson's Metaphysics of Time," 14) or as an evasion of the material dimensions of life, something that Max Horkheimer accuses Bergson of (and which has been echoed by Fredric Jameson[11]). Rather, to my way of thinking, *durée* records and activates the historical past and brings its presence into view within the material structures of everyday life. Bergson's work may not have had expressly political ambitions; he was content to sketch out broad tendencies that invigorate social systems rather than work toward shaping "new forms of life of society" (18), but he was no quietist whose "philosophical attitude to the world is contemplative" (11); he spoke of the priority of doing over thinking. And as Deleuze demonstrates, Bergson's thought can be recruited for political goals.

Although the left has accused Bergsonism of being apolitical, Jones also raises the specter of a covert Bergsonian politics or biopolitics. "One cannot understand twentieth-century vitalism," she exclaims, "separately from its implication in racial and anti-Semitic discourses and . . . we cannot understand some of the dominant models of emancipation within black thought except through recourse to a vitalist tradition" (*Racial Discourses of Life Philosophy*, 5). If vitalism aims to differentiate the animate from the inanimate, less vital, or "mechanical," then it would seem to participate in the broad range of disciplinary institutions that enforce what Michel Foucault calls "biopower": it provides the groundwork for regulating what kind of people (understood racially, for instance) count as proper life and therefore deserve to be accorded special social rights and privileges, and what kind of people ought to be ranked as nonlife or lesser life. Although Jones concedes that "vitalism has represented the refusal to reduce life to physiochemical reactions," she also argues that racial thinking "depends on thinking of and reducing human group diversity to sadistically imagined physiochemical group differences" (6) and suggests that vitalism has a stake in preserving such group differences in its speculative thought. It does so by preserving the boundaries between the more and less vital as a form of racial hygiene, in effect, as immunotherapy (15). As we saw in Chapter 3, Bergson cannot be absolved from making such noxious metaphysical distinctions. Nevertheless, taken as a whole, Bergson's philosophy disputes the founding premises on which biopower is exercised because, as I have argued, it erodes the boundaries between life and nonlife and grants vitality to the entire spectrum of the universe, from people to subatomic particles. Just as important, vitalism resists the kind of determinisms that make "vital" and "less vital" meaningful predictive categories in which to place people. It does matter, in other words, that vitalism is antideterministic in its historical and scientific orientation.

In the humanities and social sciences, vitalist criticism has joined the chorus of complaints against gene-centric accounts of evolution, with their pervasive bias toward mechanistic or deterministic presentation of causal change. It also works against the bias in favor of a reductive genetic explanation for evolution, which still has a pronounced, if dwindling, currency. Recent vitalisms follow Bergson in pushing natural science into the position of chief intellectual starting point for critical conversation, even if vitalists do not regard science as a supervening authority. Bergson thought of science as an allied discipline and dreamed of a state of collaboration between scientists and philosophers, so that each would get from the other valuable tools: for the scientist, a way of breaking out of a priori assumptions, and for the philosopher, experimental data about life (*Creative Evolution*, 78). Proponents of science have not generally welcomed the talk of such alliances, and vitalism remains anathema in many scientific circles—dismissed without much ado by the likes of Richard Dawkins in *The Ancestor's Tale* (552) or Daniel Dennett as belonging to the "trash heap of history" for its "view that living things contain some special physical but equally mysterious stuff—*élan vital*" (Dennett, *Kinds of Minds*, 23). And yet vitalism remains persistent. As Jane Bennett observes, "Vitalism has repeatedly risen from the ashes of scientific critiques of it" (*Vibrant Matter*, 90).

As we have seen, a vitalist orientation toward scientific thought percolated into the work of Gertrude Stein, and similarly, I would add, into that of Virginia Woolf, Marianne Moore, and D. H. Lawrence, among other experimental writers of the period. All are aware of the profound analogies (morphological, behavioral, and otherwise) that link human beings to other animals. All model what we might term their "bio-fictions" on nature's experimental processes. The turn of the century and the turn of the millennium share in common a resurgent investment in science as an unsurpassed body of work for provoking questions and shaping answers about the primitive origins of human life, our relatedness to other beings in our midst, and our own continual evolution as a species. Yet because the prevalence of vitalist thought was, arguably, more pronounced for modernists, they asked somewhat different questions of science than the current generation of scientifically informed writers, such as Ian McEwan (a capable novelist of psychological fiction in his own right). Modernist writers put pressure on some of the adaptationist assumptions that ground many forms of biological discourse and wished to consider Darwinian accounts of natural selection among other kinds of evolutionary force, not all of which have survival as their sole purpose. Because these writers were so invested in art and aesthetics, seemingly "pointless" forms of human endeavor (nonfunctional, excessive from the perspective of survival), they were in a position to appreciate biological embellishments that demonstrate evolutionary complexity but which are sidelined within biological discourse. These writers can still teach us much of importance about how to approach the profusion of scientific ideas and "think with" science as a system that is avowedly fallibilistic, valuing experimentation and hypothesis testing. Bergson offered the modernists (as well as us) an extremely persuasive model for investment in scientific research. For he was certainly as well informed as any humanist of his period about scientific developments.

Yet Bergson was also in dialogue with other intellectual currents of his moment that appear retrograde from the perspective of postmodern vitalisms. For instance, he had a roundabout way of prosecuting arguments that engaged in prevailing theological debates and even gave ammunition to those who saw in his work a commitment to something like an immortal soul. This is because he regarded memory as a feature of the past that is retained in the present only as an idea. In its virtual or "pure" state, it exists with no active function and cannot be reduced to material causes. Bergson argues that memory is not stored in the brain; rather, it is "a power absolutely independent of matter" (*Matter and Memory*, 73) with its own reality, which is latent and inactive, giving rise to "a psychical state which is unconscious" (141). A body simply takes from this reservoir of the past what it needs to act on the present: memory becomes actual "by borrowing the body of some perception into which it slips" (67). At that point, the brain becomes "an instrument of action" (74). Pure memory is different in kind from this active or embodied form of memory. It follows that "spirit is a reality" and that "it is here, in the phenomenon of memory, that we may come into touch with it experimentally" (73). Bergson's resolve to make proper distinctions between the metaphysical reality of memory and the psychological existence that mobilizes it for consciousness seems to crumple when he treats pure memory as a specifically "psychical state" (however unconscious) rather than as a transpsychic plane of existence. He thus leaves open the possibility that this *esprit* (which might be translated as "mind" rather than "spirit") is personal. For some critics, this established the grounds for belief in an afterlife. Others, like Horkheimer, objected to Bergson's vague talk of "ourselves as eternal," retorting that the "metaphysician Bergson suppresses death" ("On Bergson's Metaphysics of Time," 14). Bergson was deemed a spiritualist or "romantic" harboring old-fashioned metaphysical commitments, and the reputation he acquired turned off a generation of secular-minded critics in the postwar years.[12]

In my framing of vitalism, I have largely avoided discussion of Bergson's account of memory as an autonomous block of time, even though it occupies a significant place in the elaboration of his thought, for the simple reason that, on its own, the account might lead one to confuse the state of virtuality with latency (the view that the past expresses a delayed state of what is to come). For Bergson, the past only yields new possibilities when agents enter into practical relation with the present or the future. In this respect, I give central emphasis to Bergson as a pragmatic psychologist rather than as a rarified metaphysician. I take up those moments when virtual time is actualized through an individual's perceptive powers, presenting the mind in a state of productive tension in which people are capable of seizing on qualitatively new relations to the object world. In other words, instead of regarding the virtual as a force that has real ontological standing of its own outside a given agent's relation to the present, I have emphasized the constitutive relation between the virtual and its actualization, without which virtuality remains inert and empty. Arguably, Bergson should have defined what is a singular, irreproducible moment on the basis of the dynamic present or interval of becoming rather than in its relation to the finished past. His failure to do so has left his adherents, Deleuze included, to give too much weight to the virtual as an autonomous sphere, hovering in a pure state that delivers near-unimaginable potential.[13] I have chosen to dwell on an "impure" experiential time over any investment in "pure" potentiality suspended from all possibility of realization. Any such emphasis on "purity" discounts our experience as embodied agents. From a Bergsonian point of view, we are contingent assemblages of matter and *esprit* whose finitude is central to our being. Likely, even Bergson would grant that we can at best expect to enter into some new, unforeseeable, and likely impersonal form on the dissolution of our body.

For a study that has insisted on the centrality of a vitalist intellectual history to modernism, this book has curiously (and surely for some readers, tendentiously) left out what might seem to be crucial preoccupations of vitalist thinking. I have not made common cause with its occult side or with the prevailing mysticisms of the period. Both William James and Bergson were engaged members and eventual presidents of the London Society for Psychical Research, and their healthy, open-minded fascination with the paranormal expresses their resistance to the prevailing positivist climate of the period. Bergson wrote important essays devoted to telepathy and déjà vu as psychical experiences.[14] James documented his interviews and séances with a Boston spirit medium named Leonora Piper and devoted substantial research time to her claims to being able to channel the voice of James's dead friend Richard Hodgson, who vowed before he died to return and placate William's skepticism about paranormal phenomena. James sought out but failed to obtain veridical information to which Leonora Piper would not otherwise have had access. Even so, he did not discount other affective dimensions of his grappling with the spirit and memory of his friend through Leonora Piper as medium or "control." His brother, Henry, was even commissioned to deliver one of William's reports on her for a London lecture to the Society for Psychical Research.[15] For my part, I have not explored these sometimes fascinating excursions into paranormal research, not because I wish to discount them, but because their significance is ancillary to the ambitious conceptual claims that William James and Bergson dedicated themselves to regarding time, intuition, and the psychic experience of virtuality. The detractors of vitalism have always been willing to conflate such things as Bergsonian intuition with extrasensory perception, telepathy, mediumship, and other supernatural phenomena. James and Bergson made claims that were substantiated on naturalistic foundations, and they were, themselves, skeptical examiners of such touted wonders. Like the modernists I have chosen to focus on, Henry James, Stein, and Eliot, I have deemed the secular ramifications of vitalism a more vital and weighty matter.

Although W. B. Yeats and other distinguished modernist writers were sympathetic to the occult, Henry James, Stein, and Eliot were too grounded in empirical culture to take much stock in the possibility of communication with ghosts and revenants as well as other paranormal portents.[16] If we can judge by the series of ghost stories James wrote later in his career—the most famous being *The Turn of the Screw*—he was much more fascinated with the psychic desires that give rise to beliefs in the paranormal. He used the figure of the ghost as a way of spoofing his own vitalist commitments to near telepathic but decidedly more commonplace mental communications between people, and his likening of intuition to occult phenomena in such stories as "The Private Life" and in his unfinished novel "The Sense of the Past" was intended, I would argue, as self-parody. In later life, James penned a searching essay, "Is There a Life after Death?" which plaintively shelved any hope for a remedy against finitude by recourse to belief in a spirit world. The only encouragement toward belief he cited was the belief in the endurance of a personal legacy after death—the afterlife of one's thoughts and their spirit-presence (220–222).

Although James and Eliot eschew necromantic forms of animism, both return in various ways to a world alive with possibility and suggestive of alternate trajectories of reality—or, as Eliot puts it in "Burnt Norton," the infolded time of "perpetual possibility" that leads to "Footfalls [which] echo in the memory / Down the passage which we did not take / Toward the door we never opened" (*Complete Poems and Plays*, 117). This virtual world, with its alternate currents of time, animates the present or existing world, requiring only affective attunement to it. James's story "The Jolly Corner" is similarly obsessed with the immaterial remainders of a life that might have been lived otherwise. These are episodes in modernism's animistic experience of the present, and the themes and preoccupations they convey are more legible, I would suggest, in the context of modernists' deep, sustained and remarkable prescient efforts to grapple with vitalist thought.

Whether, to borrow Eliot's metaphor, we can open the door to vitalism and reveal the passages of thought that are potential in it remains a rousing but still spectral prospect. I have tried to articulate reasons why we might wish to do so. In this, I am encouraged by the resurgent vogue of vitalist ideas. Vitalism's place as a discourse about psychic life remains less assured. But I would suggest that the stunning and strange insights into character that James, Stein, and Eliot have succeeded in striking offer a potent starting point.

NOTES

NOTES TO INTRODUCTION

1. It is not arbitrary that, historically, literary character has often tended to reinforce models of consistency. Aristotelian literary criticism gives at least one indication why. Aristotle regards the poet's function as describing "not the thing that has happened, but a kind of thing that might happen, i.e. what is possible as being probable or necessary" (*Poetics* 1451a–b). Reproducing or imitating character within poetry requires the projection of a probability that a specific type of person would react in a certain way. Aristotle's approach has doubtless tended to promote definitions of literary character as themselves probabilistic and highly regimented along predictably defined narrative lines. One has "to make [characters] consistent and the same throughout; even if inconsistency be part of the man before one for imitation as presenting that form of character, he should still be consistently inconsistent" (*Poetics* 1454a). As agents of probable moral behavior, characters in poetry are defined by their capacity to model forms of psychological reliability. This account intersects indirectly with Aristotle's ethics, which lauds habits of consistency.

2. Blakey Vermeule speculates that the novel originated at a moment in British culture when changes in the ruling powers required new training in mind-reading skills, which the novel provided. The rapid proliferation of narrative prose fiction in the seventeenth and eighteenth centuries coincided with a period of political instability when status no longer guaranteed power and contract became increasingly important. Thus, makers of fiction trained individuals in how to deal with anxieties about distrust. In Aphra Behn's *Oroonoko*, "so-called moral life centers on trading, credit, promises, and contracts, most of which end up broken" (Vermeule, *Why Do We Care About Literary Characters?*, 59). But this also indirectly strengthens the correlation between the novel's depiction of characters and a moral investment in consistency.

3. For antipsychological accounts of modernism, see Jay, "Modernism and the Specter of Psychologism." See also Matz, "T. E. Hulme, Henri Bergson, and the Cultural Politics of Psychologism."

4. The precise contours of vitalism as a self-conscious movement are not well established. Clearly, as Scott Lash and Monica Greco argue, vitalism bleeds into a variety of intellectual traditions. Lash describes its genealogical connection to *Lebensphilosophie*, Situationism, Heideggerian phenomenology, and Derridean deconstruction (2). For Greco, "The term 'vitalism' is most readily associated with a series of debates among 18th- and 19th-century biologists, and broadly with the claim that the explanation of living phenomena is not compatible with, or is not exhausted by, the principles of basic sciences like physics and chemistry. . . . However, scientists and philosophers have continued to address vitalism—if mostly in order to reject it—well into the second half of the 20th century, in connection

with classic concepts such as mechanism and reductionism, but also in connection with the concepts of emergence, complexity, artificial intelligence, and with approaches such as information theory and cybernetics." ("On the Vitality of Vitalism," 16–17)

Greco suggests that the inability to shed or permanently reject vitalistic concerns indicates a pattern of unsettling thought intrinsic to biological discourse.

5. Eugene Thacker, for example, refers to traditional vitalism as "the idea that living organisms are alive due to a 'vital force' that courses through them, but which cannot be reduced to their material components or to the mechanism of their physiological processes" ("Thought Creatures," 314). Vitalism's antagonism to mechanistic science has often put it at odds with the research agendas of formalized science. For Garland Allen, vitalism "claimed that living organisms defy description in purely physico-chemical terms, because organisms possess some non-material, non-measurable forces or directive agents that account for their complexity. Vitalism was regarded by early twentieth-century mechanistic materialists such as Jacques Loeb, T. H. Morgan or Wilhelm Roux as fuzzy-minded and subjective nonsense that offered no concrete research agendas, and provide no real guidelines for practical investigation" ("Mechanism, Vitalism and Organicism in Late Nineteenth and Twentieth-Century Biology," 266–267).

6. For an account that juxtaposes Darwin, Nietzsche, and Bergson, see Grosz, *The Nick of Time.*

7. For an extended account of George Eliot's influence on Stein, see Meyer, *Irresistible Dictation*, 62–73.

8. For Hertz, the trace that remains of certain marginal characters—and their disturbing presence in the narrative—offers an allegory of the equivocal nature of signification itself, "the open and indeterminate self-dispersion associated with a plurality of signs or with the plurality of interpretations that writing can provoke" (*George Eliot's Pulse*, 30–31).

9. The affinity between James and Conrad features centrally in Levenson's account of early modernism: *The Ambassadors* and *Heart of Darkness* share, "most notably, the confrontation between cultures, the 'sharp rupture of an identity,' and the transvaluation of values" (*Modernism and the Fate of Individuality*, 3). "Both Marlow and Strether," Levenson notes, "take exceptional pains to preserve their integrity within morally suspect contexts" (3). Even so, James was aware of his difference from Conrad. In a review essay originally published in the *Times Literary Supplement* that is said to have hurt Conrad's feelings (*Critical Muse*, 595), James reacted negatively to Conrad's "obscuration" of character, his way of sharpening suspense by invoking "a mystic impulse from within" (*Critical Muse*, 610).

10. See Miller's *Poets of Reality* and his later statement, "Heart of Darkness Revisited." See also Meisel, "Decentering *Heart of Darkness*," and Krupat, "Antonymy, Language, and Value in Conrad's *Heart of Darkness*."

11. "The thought that moral life is not superimposed on experience, that the authority of the moral beyond already lies securely within the domain of fact, and that in order to pursue value we need only perceive with acuity—this thought is central to the workings of [*Heart of Darkness*]" (Levenson, *Modernism and the Fate of Individuality*, 56).

12. It is a virtual certainty that James had not read *The Confidence-Man.* Melville, observes Andrew Delbanco, "had become so thoroughly obscure that Henry James, despite the immense scope of his literary awareness, mentions him only once in all his critical

writing, as part of the 'Putnam's group'" (*Melville: His World and Work*, 294). In this reference, James displays little direct familiarity with Melville's range of work.

13. D. H. Lawrence remarks in his study of *Moby-Dick*, which did much to spark American interest in the novel, that the narrator, Ishmael, sets out in a "voyage of the soul" (*Studies in Classical American Literature*, 148) to penetrate the secret intensities within those whom he comes in contact with, wanting, as it happens in the case of his exotic shipmate Queequeg, "to get the 'clue' to [his large, deep eyes]. That was all" (148). As Samuel Otter has argued, however, Melville's anatomies of character present contrasting ways of "knowing other bodies" (*Melville's Anatomies*, 159). Melville toys with the anatomist's ocular penetration into lifeless interiors: he hungers for "a self-illuminating body displaying its mental faculties on its interior walls" (153). But Melville also promotes touch as an alternative to the fantasy of plumbing the body's depths. As with the famous section in which Ishmael loses himself in the community-building activity of squeezing whale spermaceti, Melville's characters are led to celebrate the surface variability of bodies and their strictly transitory nature. Such moments reveal an alternative language of sociability that interrupts or delays the impulse to chase after secret interiors but that is resolutely anchored to the present moment. As I argue, Melville celebrates the surface character of things and people, but such surfaces deny any need to extrapolate about their various possible futures.

14. Ahab clearly has an urge to vest both whale and man with a stubborn, buried meaning—"the unknown but still reasoning thing . . . behind the unreasoning mask" (Melville, *Moby-Dick*, 167). And Melville's *Moby-Dick* sets out to investigate the interpretive logic as well as the personal projections that inspire his ambition. Scholars argue over the degree to which we are obliged to align Melville with his protagonist Ahab. According to Elizabeth Renker, Melville is "a frustrated idealist" who "wanted to pierce the material world to reach the ultimate and enduring Truth it masked" ("'A______!': Unreadability in *The Confidence-Man*," 116) Yet Melville's need to interrogate Ahab's interpretive logic leaves ambiguous how much of Ahab's truth-seeking impulse and consuming desire for clarity he shares.

15. For Deleuze, Bartleby is a diagnostician of culture, an American original who in his terms "abolishes any paternal function" ("Bartleby; or, the Formula," 77). In other words, by refusing pity and charity, his act of disobedience offers the possibility—however unachieved or unfinished—of less hierarchical and more experimental lines of filiation.

16. *The Confidence-Man*, argues Sianne Ngai, "might be described as an exploration of the new emotional economy produced by the general migration of 'trust' from personal relationships to abstract systems—a key theme in the twentieth-century sociology of modernity" (*Ugly Feelings*, 40).

17. As indication of the eroticized nature of the encounters among strangers, Charlie Noble's countenance falls when his new fast friend Frank, an ostensible confidence man he has just met, mentions his prior engagement with friends. The narrator describes his reaction as that of "a jealous lover's . . . at hearing from his sweetheart of former ones" (*The Confidence-Man*, 164).

18. Thus, for example, the con man who brokers hired hands (and refers to himself as a Philosophical Intelligence Officer) finally convinces the Missourian to acquire a boy as a man-servant, despite the Missourian's initial repugnance at the spectacle of groveling

servitude and fecklessness ("won't have 'em!"). The broker points to the prospective disposition of boys, their unfinished character, as an argument for their suitability. They are "an incipient creation; loose sort of sketchy thing" (*The Confidence-Man*, 126), open to being remolded at a stroke for a known commercial ideal without the burden of the past to weigh them down.

19. Hereafter emphasis in quotations appears in the original unless otherwise indicated.

20. Nietzsche's meditation on Descartes's *cogito* leads him to consider "it thinks" as a more apt grammatical summation of will but qualifies his statement in the following way: "one has even gone too far with this 'it thinks'—even the 'it' contains an *interpretation* of the process, and does not belong to the process itself" (*Beyond Good and Evil*, 24).

21. For a declaration of Eliot's "temporary conversion to Bergsonism," see Ackroyd, *T. S. Eliot*. For an account of Eliot's reaction to Bergson's thought, see Habib, *The Early T. S. Eliot and Western Philosophy*, 39–60.

22. On some of Eliot's off-hand allusions and references to Bergson, see Schwartz, "Bergson and the Politics of Vitalism," 297.

23. In *Bergson and American Culture* Tom Quirk argues for the importance of Bergson to Willa Cather and Wallace Stevens. For Bergson's influence on Joyce, see Kumar, *Bergson and the Stream of Consciousness Novel*. For the Bergsonian and Nietzschean influence on the visual arts—specifically on the cubist avant garde—in early twentieth-century Paris, see Antliff, *Inventing Bergson*. Wyndham Lewis alludes to his own early vitalism in his autobiography, *Rude Assignment*, 58–59. For an account of Lewis's decisive turn away from vitalism, see Nieland, *Feeling Modern*, 52–58.

D. H. Lawrence's characteristic celebrations of atavistic consciousness, intuition, and dynamic structures of feeling present many of the hallmarks of vitalism. For the political context of Lawrence's vitalism, see Wientzen, "Automatic Modernism."

24. See Hulme's chapter "Bergson's Theory of Art" in *Speculations*. Hulme was also the first to translate Bergson's "Introduction to Metaphysics."

25. For an elaboration of William Faulkner's affiliation to Bergsonism, see his "1952 Interview with Loïc Bouvard." For an account of the affiliation, see Gidley, "The Later Faulkner, Bergson, and God."

26. On Virginia Woolf's allusions to Bergsonian flux, see Gillies, "Virginia Woolf: Bergsonian Experiments in Representation and Consciousness." On the importance of Darwin to her work, see See, "The Comedy of Nature."

27. On Bergson's family ties to Marcel Proust, see Guerlac, *Thinking in Time*, 9. For further elaboration of the the intellectual ties between the two men, see Church, "Bergson and Proust," and Pilkington, "Proust."

28. Thus Jane Bennett, for instance, aims to "bracket the question of the human" to "explore a fuller range of the nonhuman powers circulating around and within human bodies" (*Vibrant Matter*, ix).

29. Deleuze, the figure most responsible for the recent emergence of vitalism, has consistently staked ethical claims on life itself. He tells us that what is good and bad does not "have a primary, objective meaning, but one that is relative and partial: that which agrees with our nature or does not agree with it" (*Spinoza*, 22). For him, ethics is just the means by which we question the "modes of existence" of different beings (23).

Because there are many modes and they change over time, an ethics is always contingent on the real or virtual forms that life takes at any moment. Deleuze insists that there is no teleology to life.

30. I do not mean to minimize the differences between new materialisms and Marxist materialist orientations, for instance. Debates are ongoing about what is gained or lost by shifting conceptual paradigms, and obviously I have my own stake in these debates. For a justification of a new materialist conception of agency, see Krause, "Bodies in Action." For a defense of the "old" materialist methodologies, see Warshick and Wingrove, "Politics That Matter."

31. See Nietzsche:

[The man of revenge] has *deprived existence* in general *of its innocence*; namely, by tracing back every state of being thus and thus to a will, an intention, a responsible act. The entire doctrine of the will, this most fateful *falsification* in psychology hitherto, was essentially invented for the sake of punishment. . . .We others, who desire to restore innocence to becoming, would like to be the missionaries of a cleaner idea: that no one has given man his qualities, neither God, nor society, nor his parents and ancestors, nor he himself—that no one is to *blame* for him." (*The Will to Power*, 401–402).

Nietzsche insists that risk-taking behavior is experimental and resists being evaluated because it is future-oriented, and one does not have at one's disposal a sense of all the forces, outcomes, and affinities that actions display. Prevailing normative judgments are thus profoundly inadequate measuring sticks. Furthermore, Nietzsche insists on rethinking the nature of will itself, refusing to interpret it as a voluntarist fiat that proceeds on the basis of a predetermined intention—thus targeting the accounts that provide the rationale for moral blame.

For an account of his criticism of morality, which yokes together an action and a target ("the person who did the action and who goes from the action to meet the blame") to preserve a connection to a psychology of blame in its pure or Christian form, see Williams, "Nietzsche's Minimalist Moral Psychology," 10–11. One of the most distinct features of this psychology, Williams suggests, is the particular kind of fantasy it encourages in a victim: "As victim, I have a fantasy of inserting into the agent an acknowledgement of me, to take the place of exactly the act that harmed me. I want to think that he might have acknowledged me, that he might have been prevented from harming me. . . . The idea has to be . . . that I, now, might change the agent from one who did not acknowledge me to one who did" (11).

32. As testimony to James's importance to Ezra Pound, see his essay "Henry James." For an account of T. S. Eliot's relation to James, see Holder, "T. S. Eliot on Henry James." Jonathan Freedman claims in *Professions of Taste* that James invents the ethos of high modernism.

33. In all of James's novels, early and late, he binds his protagonists' unfolding character to their contingent circumstances. In the later novels, especially from *What Maisie Knew* onward, he devises distinctive formal techniques for showing how the mind responds to its own responses and therefore becomes a significant feature in itself of the circumstances in which it takes part. Thus, James claims to treat Maisie as the novel's main "register of impressions" (preface to *What Maisie Knew*, 3). For this to happen, James has to desert the more conventional narrative structures of novels such

as *Washington Square*, instead defining events through a series of branching connections in the protagonist's mind.

34. It remains an open question whether, or to what extent, psychoanalysis programmatically validates only the most socially respectable of pleasures associated with normative sexuality. For an argument that attempts to make room in psychoanalysis for "free flowing" or ecstatic forms of desire at odds with a prescribed normative order, see Bersani's *Freudian Body*.

35. I am thinking in particular of readings of James inspired by Bersani, who argues: "Complexity [in James's late novels] consists not in mutually subversive motives but rather in the expanding surface itself which, when most successful, finds a place in its intricate design for all the motives imaginable" (*A Future for Astyanax*, 131). See my account of Bersani in the section entitled "Relational Being" in Chapter 2.

NOTES TO CHAPTER 1

1. On the pains various modernists took to acquire institutional authority, see Levenson, *A Genealogy of Modernism*.

2. For a history of the debate, see Lobb, *T. S. Eliot and the Romantic Critical Tradition*.

3. Maud Ellmann argues, for instance that Eliot's claims about impersonality in "Tradition and the Individual Talent" deconstruct themselves: "Eliot . . . insists that poets should suppress their egoism, and keep their poetry and personalities distinct. But his arguments recoil against themselves. The very terms that frame his doctrine of self-abnegation—time and space—are steeped in the antitheses that they repress" (*The Poetics of Impersonality*, 197). Although I have no wish to deny the contradictory elements of Eliot's text itself, I do think that the internal coherence of his argument bears closer scrutiny. For an account that reads Eliot's pronouncements on impersonality as coherent, presenting "the co-existence and dialectical play of opposites," see Brooker, "Writing the Self," 42). Ultimately, I share Tim Dean's skepticism about the utility of "demystify[ing] impersonality" ("T. S. Eliot, Famous Clairvoyante," 46).

4. The understanding of impersonality as an aesthetic strategy may be traced to T. E. Hulme's distinction between "romantic" and "classical" sensibility (*Speculations*, 111–140), in which the former is associated with excessively emotional, ecstatic, individualistic expression and the latter with orderly, constant, depersonalized art.

5. One can disagree with Eliot about whether Hamlet's baffled ethical response counts as an fascinating subject for art or even whether on a second-order level Shakespeare's play doesn't make an interesting situation out of its melancholy hero's compulsive self-interrogations. Still, Hamlet's struggle to find the motives that would make sense of his delayed revenge reveals him only indirectly and, it would seem, negatively. Eliot's point is that Hamlet is dominated by an intense emotion that solicits forms of interpretation that can only remain an "insoluble puzzle" for the interpreter. "We should have, finally, to know something which is by hypothesis unknowable" ("Hamlet and His Problems" in *Selected Essays*, 126) because Shakespeare, the play's creator, did not have access to it. Eliot's assumptions about the dead-end of analysis are not proof against other interpretive modalities, most obviously those propelling psychoanalysis. One could employ biographical criticism or simply turn to a penetrating analysis of the text for evidence of Hamlet's psychological problem (as Freud and Ernest Jones both do; see Freud, *Inter-*

pretation of Dreams, 298–300, and Jones, *Hamlet and Oedipus*). For Eliot, however, the kind of interpretation it provokes can only be a "study for pathologists" ("Hamlet and His Problems" in *Selected Essays*, 126).

6. "The normal man," Jung argues, "is, by definition, influenced as much from within as from without. He constitutes the extensive middle group, on one side of which are those whose motivations are determined mainly by the external object, and, on the other, those whose motivations are determined from within. I call the first group *extraverted*, and the second group *introverted*" (*Psychological Types*, 516). Significantly, Jung thinks that the degree of the individual's susceptibility to an outside environment is itself referable to, if not regulated by, the individual's personality type. Allport, however, is much more skeptical about the objective validity of personality types and more attentive to the variable context in which such typological distinctions emerge: "*Personality is the dynamic organization within the individual of those psychophysical systems that determine his unique adjustments to his environment*" (*Personality*, 48). His emphasis on the dynamic integrity of personality compels him to treat typological distinctions as provisional. Nonetheless, he too thinks that personality reproduces traits and typological attributes: "Typologies that are independent of one another cannot be all-embracing. Every typological doctrine tends toward extravagance. In reality types are only valid for a limited characteristic; they embrace a segment of individuality, but never the total individual" (15).

7. I do not mean to argue that all therapy deserves to be lumped into the same category. Jacques Lacan may be deemed the other pertinent theorist of "personality." He sees a merely empirical ego as "imaginary"—the goal of therapy being to reveal to the subject its own structuring activity and then to show ego formation as itself a symbolic fiction. Take Slavoj Žižek as a representative of this position: "*the subject has to relate to itself, to conceive of itself, as (to) an empty 'bearer', and to perceive his empirical features which constitute the positive content of his particular 'person' as a contingent variable.* This shift is again the very shift from S to $, from the fullness of the 'pathological' subject to *cogito* qua empty self relating which experiences its own positive, empirical content as something 'posited', i.e., contingent and ultimately indifferent" (*Tarrying with the Negative*, 29). Žižek has his limits in the present case, however; he makes available a very limited psychology outside the quasi-transcendental dynamic of sublimity that this passage suggests, which denigrates all subjective particularity whatsoever.

Lacan is less susceptible to this criticism, though to my thinking, he is not able to account for the ways agents go about fashioning or ordering their experience through intelligent confrontations with their circumstances. The Lacanian individual as a rule is given to reacting to the structure of his or her own being rather than to a social situation that demands an adjustment in his or her mode of comportment. Obviously, such remarks do not suffice of their own as critical commentary, but perhaps they can serve to designate a direction of interest that Lacan's work does not capture or is not of particular concern to him, but which I will take it as central to the purposes of this book.

8. Accounts of personal development bind emotional functioning to agent-centric narratives of self-fashioning. One can understand ego growth as a process of "stepping back" and regarding one's compulsive behaviors as alien empirical elements lodged within one. We can see these elements as impulses with an unconscious source or simply as "reason-

responsive" dispositions that one can no longer approve of from the new vantage point one has adopted. For this process of "stepping back," see Moran's "Sartre, Self-Consciousness, and the Limits of the Empirical," 77–83, and "Reflection and the Demands of Authority: Apprehension, Arrest, and Conviction," 138–148, in *Authority and Estrangement.*

9. As Goldie points out, not all psychic dispositions are the same. He privileges those that are "reason-responsive," for example, traits such as kindness or vanity, as opposed to other preferences and temperamental tendencies that are not. He clarifies that these character traits involve "a disposition reliably to respond to certain kinds of reasons—unlike mere action-tendency, behavioural habit or temperament, like being charming, or being fidgety or being gloomy" (*On Personality*, 13).

10. Cf. Michel Foucault: "Couldn't everyone's life become a work of art? Why should the lamp or the house be an art object, but not our life?" ("On the Genealogy of Ethics," 236).

11. Skinner argues that the first step in turning behavior into a scientific subject is to transform a single event into a "uniformity" (*Science and Human Behavior*, 15) grounded in a general rule. He describes the environment as capable of being broken down into "independent variables" (31), which one can manipulate to predict behavior. See his chapter, "The Controlling Environment" in *Science and Human Behavior*, 129–140.

12. T. S. Eliot, for instance, refers to behaviorism as one of "those unbalanced philosophies . . . of which we hear a great deal. A purely 'scientific' philosophy ends by" rejecting common sense and "denying what we know to be true" ("Francis Herbert Bradley" in *Selected Essays*, 403).

13. See Milgram, "Behavioral Study of Obedience." See also his *Obedience to Authority.*

14. See Isen and Levin, "Effect of Feeling Good on Helping."

15. See Haney, Banks, and Zimbardo, "Impersonal Dynamics in a Simulated Prison."

16. See Batson and Darley, "From Jerusalem to Jericho."

17. None of the experiments, it is worth noting, present protracted temporal intervals for studying people, leaving their subjects little possibility for developing alternative responses or widening the scope of ethical reflection over time. Human beings, among other things, establish and modify situations, something that the short duration of the experiments does not allow for. The Milgram authority study and the Stanford prison experiment elicit behavior that is decontextualized from the ordinary lives of the subject groups. Nevertheless, the prison study did try to mimic ordinary prison routine both for the guards, who needed to "report for their 8-hour work shifts promptly and regularly" (Zimbardo, "Prison Life Study: General Information," 1) and for the incarcerated prisoners, who were unable to leave during the course of the experiment.

18. Bergson, for example, suggests that "our freedom, in the very movements by which it is affirmed, creates the growing habits that will stifle it if it fails to renew itself by a constant effort: it is dogged by automatism" (*Creative Evolution*, 127). Cf. Nietzsche: "punishment, as requital, evolved quite independently of any presupposition concerning freedom or non-freedom of the will . . . —to such an extent, indeed, that a *high* degree of humanity had to be attained before the animal 'man' began even to make the much more primitive distinctions between 'intentional,' negligent,' 'accidental,' 'accountable,' and their opposites and to take them into account when determining punishments" (*On the Genealogy of Morals*, 63).

19. Doris suggests that "consistency alone does not a virtue make" and that integrity

"can figure in a life that is morally suspect or even morally reprehensible; the Nazi who cannot be bribed to spare Jews very arguably displays integrity" (*Lack of Character*, 18).

20. For a discussion of ethical and nonethical predicates, see Williams, *Ethics and the Limits of Philosophy*, 122–24, 140–155.

21. Conceptions of a good life from within an internalist framework presuppose a sociology, a set of axiological commitments on the part of any specific society that leave little means of criticizing the totality of a culture's values from any neutral position apart from it (MacIntyre, *After Virtue*, 22). Kant's moral centralism, according to J. M. Bernstein, is inattentive to the pragmatic, affective motivations of individuals, though it is capable of specifying culture-independent moral criteria, while internalists' reliance on the extant values of a community have no means of accounting for new valuations in their ideals of a good life or pronouncing negative judgment on the increasing impoverishment and relativism of norms that are, in Bernstein's terms, "in their scope, meaning, and possibility . . . socio-historically determined" (*Adorno*, 63). Both views, I would suggest, are therefore by themselves inadequate ways of staging people's ethical deliberations.

22. For Bernard Williams's understanding of the self-transforming nature of ethical reflection, consider Martin Hollis: "Williams' kind of meaningful life *creates* the individual whose life it is" ("The Shape of a Life," 181).

23. For complaints that literary historicism does not have an explicit theory of history and therefore does not make itself available for critical reflection, see Dunn and Haddox, introduction to *The Limits of Literary Historicism*, xiv–xxiii. This aversion or disinclination to generating a theory does not necessarily imply a covert theory, though Dunn and Haddox argue that it may.

24. Bernstein shows how Adorno goes about exposing the "pretense of autonomy" embedded in the aesthetic ideal and its "*promesse de bonheur*." The claim to autonomy, which Bernstein defines in part as the effort to "secure a space free from the interference of social or political utility," is "a consequence and so an expression of the fragmentation and reification of modern life" (*Against Voluptuous Bodies*, 3).

25. Bernstein lays out the nature of the dilemma or contradiction that Adorno targets. He argues that art wars against the breakup of cultural value into supposedly autonomous spheres in which fact and value, or empirical truth and ethical purposes, have their own domain. Yet aesthetic experience is not necessarily in the position to garner the authority necessary to challenge the dominant organizations of reason:

> [the contestation that art offers] is aporetic since no value sphere has been historically empowered to engage in a reflection on reason in its state of dispersion. What distinguishes art from other domains of culture is that such a reflection on reason in its dispersion is a precipitate of its rationalization; but a non-discursive precipitate, and hence not immediately recognizable as a reflection. Art's cognitive dimension appears as non-cognitive; this is another aspect of its resistance to enlightened rationality, its presumptive unintelligibility. (*The Fate of Art*, 232)

26. Bernstein follows Adornian lines in using Kant's aesthetic or "reflective" judgment (or what Adorno thinks of as nondiscursive cognition) as "the crux of my defence of the primacy of practical reasoning" (*Adorno*, 34). He then suggests that Adorno would argue for the dialectical power and ineffectuality of such judgment. See chapter 6 of *Adorno*.

27. For Adorno, capitalism's aggressive expansion into new realms of experience mirrors its explanatory role as a social logic—with immediate causal effects as well as highly

mediated ones. Even if the development of capitalism is unpredictable, one can be sure that it will return before too long in his writings to define both the dilemmas of ethical life and the development of artistic movements. Adorno and Horkheimer posit a force of nature at work both within history and within ourselves, and they align this experience of nature with a principle of heterogeneity or "non-identity" (*Dialectic of Enlightenment*, 12–18) that human beings attempt to tame out of fear of the unknown or of what resists social categories. He argues that capitalism is the chief instrument for conquering nature (whose potential chaos threatens us) by imposing its own rationality and order, establishing a technical logic of development. Adorno's thesis in *Aesthetic Theory* is that art undermines the telos that governs this logic by reminding us of experiences that are novel, heterogeneous, and resistant to the means-ends rationality that dominates social life. It can thus evoke the power of novelty within history. Thus, he calls art "the unconscious writing of history, [an] anamnesis of the vanquished, of the repressed, and perhaps of what is possible" (*Aesthetic Theory*, 259).

28. Adorno argues that art generates critique: it stands in need "of an aesthetics that will provide the capacity for reflection" (*Aesthetic Theory*, 341). Yet he is dialectical in his mode of thought, and he is capable of saying that art's critical function consists in its way of being noncritical, of doing just what I have been arguing that art does: create novelty. Nevertheless, Adorno returns to the critical function of art, or more generally, to its power to negate, as part of a recurring strategy of justifying its value (*Aesthetic Theory*, 21).

29. Berman rehearses Adorno's claim that art becomes politically engaged through its exile from reality and its monadic "opposition, at the level of artistic form, to the existing world" (quoted in *Modernist Commitments*, 25) and then argues that rather than accepting the supposed disengagement of art from the social and political world, in literary modernism "the world becomes the problematic to be addressed, transformed, configured, and reconfigured" (26).

30. For an account of modernists' commitment to public life and their way of parlaying their own celebrity into unpredictable spectacles of eccentricity, see Nieland's *Feeling Modern*. Nieland tends, however, to focus on a public sphere that unfolds in dance halls and circus rings rather than in more discursive political arenas.

31. Vrettos is interested in showing that "habits do not function, for Dickens, in an entirely self-enclosed system" ("Defining Habits," 19). She mines the tensions and contradictions in any alignment between "habit as eccentricity and habit as routine": "Whereas eccentricity involves a form of repetitive behavior that defines individuality in opposition to social conformity, routine implies the objectification, mechanization, or mass production of character as a result of conformity" (20).

32. In his *Critique of Judgment*, Kant differentiates aesthetic forms of judgment and artistic agency from empirical tastes and behavioral penchants—the gratifications of a purely passive subject laying claim to his or her knee-jerk preferences—and, ever since Kant, a subject defined by mere inclination has had the taint of pathology. He or she has no capacity for free decision-making and his or her judgments are without "claim to necessary validity for everyone" (*Critique of Judgment* 2.57.339). For Kant, empirical proclivities are not willed by the subject, so unlike aesthetic judgments, which are determined in accordance with the free lawfulness of the imagination or other strictly moral freedoms, they are liable to be felt as constraints.

33. As Crary says, "I am developing the issue of attention in order to question the relevance of isolating an aesthetically determined contemplation or absorption" (*Suspensions of Perception*, 7). For this reason and others, he concludes: "Attention finally could not coincide with a modern dream of autonomy" (46).

34. Crary concludes that Cézanne came to "the creative discovery that looking at any one thing intently did *not* lead to a fuller and more inclusive grasp of its presence, its rich immediacy. Rather, it led to its perceptual disintegration and loss, its breakdown as intelligible form" (*Suspensions of Perception*, 288–289).

35. "A body is docile," suggests Foucault, when it "may be subjected, used, transformed, and improved" (*Discipline and Punish*, 136). From an empirical point of view, the obsession with improving attention enables measurements of performance aptitude. Foucault suggests that projects for making the body docile, which begin in the eighteenth century, break it down into "its elements, its gestures, its behaviour" (138), thus subjecting it to control: "it was a question not of treating the body, *en masse*, 'wholesale', as if it were an indissociable unity, but of working it 'retail', individually; of exercising upon it a subtle coercion, of obtaining holds upon it at the level of the mechanism itself—movements, gestures, attitudes, rapidity: an infinitesimal power over the active body" (136–137).

36. Kant's rationalism offers a good example. What he calls the "taste of sense" rather than of reflection (the empirical inclination explained by more general laws) is bound up with a fixed attraction or desire for it as an object. But this model of attraction assumes an excessively rigid conception of how one acts on desires—that is, as an urge to consume or use an object, to gratify the lust it creates: "This is why we say of the agreeable not merely that we *like* it but that it *gratifies* us. When I speak of the agreeable, I am not granting mere approval: the agreeable produces an inclination" *Critique of Judgment*, 1.3.207). The object generates an impulse that is conceived in quasi-causal terms—a predisposition to act by means of a fixed set of behaviors. But vitalism puts pressure on this way of understanding an impulse; it is more malleable and less causally defined.

37. Critics often misread Bergson on this score, understanding him to valorize "pure memory" as the state in which one is most singularly oneself, as opposed to the habitual self, in which one takes on a generalized attitude. For a more intricate reading, which refuses simply to reverse terms and align habit with activity and pure memory or dream life with passivity, see Guerlac, *Literary Polemics*, 165. To a certain degree, Bergson himself encourages false impressions by seeming at times to imply that complexity is a feature of mental life occurring at its richest in states tending toward pure memory, while excluding habit, which is not memory at all but just mechanical action keyed to the present. Significantly, Bergson thinks that personality's wholeness inheres at all levels of mental functioning from habit to the nonintentional states of pure memory: all are "always whole and undivided." This means that memory and habit may be more or less contracted, but not—as aspects of the person—more or less credible as expressions of one's individuality. I prefer, following William James, to see habit as existing alongside and even enabling our higher powers, in his terms by "set[ting them] free for their own proper work " (*Principles of Psychology* 1:122).

38. Crary thinks that Bergson dismisses "pure memory" and its correlative states of dreaming as a sign of deficiency or weakness of will: "Departures from a normative consciousness, in particular experiences of dissociation in trance, dreams, and other states,

Bergson dismissed as having no revelatory, affirmative, or creative power. *Matter and Memory* is his attempt to reconceive dissociation in a form that would preserve a unified ego and a consciousness grounded in a world of action" (*Suspensions of Perception*, 326). But Crary oversimplifies Bergson's point by presuming that he celebrates industrious, workmanlike, practically instrumental behavior (what Crary calls "normative consciousness"). I would argue that Bergson thinks that actions, even when useful, can be creative and open ended in how they envisage what counts as advantageous or expedient. Attention is for that matter not action at all but a suspension of action or movement to set a course for virtual actions that have not yet been conceived of or settled on. "To call up the past," Bergson remarks, "in the form of an image, we must be able to withdraw ourselves from the action of the moment, we must have the power to value the useless, we must have the will to dream" (*Matter and Memory*, 82–83).

39. Bergson's complex understanding of personality did not stop T. S. Eliot from objecting to its excessively humanistic and progressive description of character. Indeed, as Ellmann argues, Eliot's reaction against "personality" coincided with his turning against Bergsonism. See her chapter "The Loop of Time" in *The Poetics of Impersonality*, 23–61. Nonetheless, as I will argue in Chapter 4, Eliot imported many Bergsonian concepts into his theory of impersonality.

40. Deidre Lynch accepts the structuralist mode that treats character as a textual effect but refuses to neglect the conventions of reading "generated in specific milieux" (*The Economy of Character*, 16) of market culture from which renderings of character emerged in the eighteenth century. Rather than reproducing the ahistoricism of structural approaches to character, she describes literary character as the expression of property relations and consumption practices. Among other things, characters helped readers track social distinctions in newly commercialized relationships.

41. Charles Altieri uses Kant's account of aesthetic experience to think about how we construct imaginative identifications. The mind's powers to reflect on the expressive activity of others make it possible, as he puts it, "to shift from an emphasis on producing concepts about the self to one devoted to how agents handle the range of attunements that such processes demand of them" (*Subjective Agency*, 123). As Kant would say about demonstrations of beauty, we discover rules in those instances that "allow us to perceive in the relation of our mental powers an inner purposiveness"; what matters is not what "[beauty's] nature is, nor even what purpose it has for us, but how we receive it" (*Critique of Judgment* 1.58.350).

42. Moran concedes that in a fictive setting one might wonder why one feels fear on behalf of another character, but "one's reaction may be similar, for example, to the extreme discomfort most people feel who are witnessing surgery for the first time, even if they are aware that no one is currently feeling any pain" ("Expression of Feeling in Imagination," 80).

43. For a more elaborate and, in some ways, a more skeptical account of Wollheim, see Altieri, *Particulars of Rapture*. Altieri takes Wollheim to task for a harboring a psychoanalytic account of emotional functioning concerned with an individual's "characteristic history" or past that fails to appreciate "the full range of the imagination's activities" (82).

44. Bergson speaks of duration as an unrolling unity, a "multiplicity of expanding states" through which "consciousness passes from one shade to another" (*Introduction to Metaphysics*, 27).

45. For the centrality of aesthetic feelings and emotions to vitalists' overall account of affects, see Bergson's *Time and Free Will*, 11–18, and William James on the "subtler emotions" in *The Principles of Psychology* 2:468–472.

46. For example, in *Studies in Hysteria*, Freud and Breuer describe the affective conversion of Fräulein Elisabeth von R. that is at the basis of their understanding of symptom formation: "She repressed her erotic idea from consciousness and transformed the amount of its affect into physical sensations of pain" (164).

47. Sedgwick cites Sylvan Tompkins, a psychologist who argues that Freud confuses affect with drive and "smuggles" some of the properties of the one system into the other. According to Tomkins, Freud focuses on the sexual drive (libido), as opposed to the drive to eat, breathe, excrete, or sleep, choosing the least imperious system, which is to say, least constrained in terms of object choice and aim, and therefore most like an affect system capable of fashioning its own ends. As Tomkins asserts, "Had Freud not smuggled some of the properties of the affect system into his conception of the drives, his system would have been of much less interest than it was" (*Shame and Its Sisters*, 49). However, even if libido or drive behaves much like an affect system (because it is labile in aims and objects), it gains its force and effectiveness not from the determinants of a situation but from infantile complexes and formative experiences.

48. The historical connection between William James, for instance, and Bergson is a complicated matter. James had an extensive correspondence with Bergson, whom he knew personally. Witness his passionate appreciation for Bergson's work:

> [*Matter and Memory*] is a work of exquisite genius. It makes a sort of Copernican revolution as much as Berkeley's Principles or Kant's Critique did, and will probably, as it gets better and better known, open a new era of philosophical discussion. It fills *my* mind with all sorts of new questions and hypotheses, and brings the old into a most agreeable liquefaction. I thank you from the bottom of my heart. . . . The *Hauptpunkt* acquired from me is your conclusive demolition of the dualism of object and subject in perception. I believe that the 'transcendency' of the object will not recover from your treatment, and as I myself have been working for many years past on the same line, only with other general conceptions than yours, I find myself most agreeably corroborated. (William James, *Correspondence*, December 14, 1902)

Bergson, in turn, hung up a picture of William James in his office for many years. Bergson also professed his admiration for Emerson (see Soulez and Worms, *Bergson*, 145), and James wrote several testimonials in honor of him. For an account of the philosophical relationship between James, Bergson, and Emerson, see Anna Nieddu, "Individuality."

49. See Teresa Brennan, who argues that " the transmission of affect means . . . that we are not self-contained in terms of our energies. There is no secure distinction between the 'individual' and the 'environment'" (*The Transmission of Affect*, 6).

50. Richard Poirier locates a pattern of metaphor that unites "Emersonian writers to the pragmatism defined by James" but accuses T. S. Eliot, for instance, of transferring "his never-admitted debts [to them] to figures who to him seem less provincial, as in his early expressions of admiration for Bergson" (*Poetry and Pragmatism*, 66). This implies that Bergson is an afterthought, and other critics have shared his contention. Stephen Meyer associates Bergsonian vitalism, quite misleadingly, with models of organicism that succumb to "temptations to totalization (aesthetic and political)" (*Irresistible Dictation*, 56). Joan Richardson also refers to William and Henry James's elaborations of "interest"

as a form of "non-vitalist organicism" (*A Natural History of Pragmatism*, 67), though she does not elaborate. As an exception, Patricia Rae in *The Practical Muse* seems more open to considering Bergson's role in the formation of Imagism as a movement of modernism, though she privileges a pragmatist framework. Scholars' focus on the nativist pulse of American philosophy needlessly distorts what was a two-way exchange between the central figures of pragmatism and the Europeans from whom they learned and with whom they felt kinship.

51. For Bergson's complementary view of William James's pragmatism, see "On the Pragmatism of William James: Truth and Reality." Cf. William James's review Bergson's work in "Bergson or Bradley?"

52. William James, I presume, would regard Rorty's conception of truth as excessively anthropocentric and parochial because it denies any access to it on the part of beings without language. Rorty does not look at life in its broader contours. If, as he grants, truth is a way of "enabling us to cope" (*Consequences of Pragmatism*, xvii) as agents in the world, then there must be a form of truth appropriate, say, to squirrels scattering from overplayful dogs. Rorty's bid to make all truth hang on the contingent circumstances of a given culture—his suggestion that one has no recourse to an "extra-historical Archimedean point" (xl)—certainly jibes with James's sense that truth presents a practical claim on the part of a self-interested agent in a specific milieu, in a specific moment in time. But this amounts to no more than saying that any truth matters within a circumstantial and relational context. As a concern, it emerges for a specific form of life, which in human terms might be described as a culture. If the universe consists of things that act on each other, then what one calls truth may simply be a way of measuring how parts work together and thereby intervening into those actions by adding to the balance of connections.

53. See Brian May's *The Modernist as Pragmatist* for an account of E. M. Forster as a pragmatic liberal ironist in the Rortian tradition. See also Günter Leypoldt's "Uses of Metaphor" for a discussion Rorty's ideas of world making and his position within literary criticism; and Ulf Schulenberg, who understands James Baldwin's claims of political self-making in the context of Rorty's left-liberal tradition of pragmatism ("Speaking Out of the Most Passionate Love").

54. Cavell complains: "Pragmatism seems designed to refuse to take skepticism seriously" (*Emerson's Transcendental Etudes*, 221). Emerson has a skeptical attitude that extends to language itself, retaining "stretches of the vocabulary of philosophy but divest[ing] it of its old claim to mastery" (219), while William James and Dewey claim as an inheritance of philosophy one "that gives back life to the words it has thought its own" (219). Poirier, however, does not agree that James's brand of pragmatism has a transparent or unproblematic relation to language, because he insists on the rhetorical and intellectual power of vagueness (*Poetry and Pragmatism*, 138–139).

55. Pragmatist critics sometimes fail to locate the effects of chafing contingency, discord, or conflicts of interest among different elements and strata of life, human and nonhuman. Surprisingly enough, this includes Joan Richardson, who forcefully defends Darwinism as an intellectual lens. One might expect Darwin to provoke an appreciation for struggle and competition, but as Martin Jay observes, Richardson's thesis in *The Natural History of Pragmatism*, "unlike many of the earlier descriptions of the American experi-

ence . . . is not primarily a conflictual, dialectic, or paradoxical one" (review of *A Natural History of Pragmatism*, 506). Richardson argues that developments in natural history, associated with Charles Lyell, Darwin, and others, inform the distinctively American genesis of pragmatism. She argues that American thinkers and writers such as Jonathan Edwards, Emerson, and William and Henry James thresh out their revised conceptions of the natural world by recourse to their vision of the vast expanses and frontiers of the American continent. But the organic order that she sees both in nature and in writing—the accretions, action potentials, anamorphoses, mutations, homeostatic balances, and repetitions—do not capture well the agonistic side of any evolutionary process. That said, Richardson's intellectual history usefully locates a profound exchange of ideas between European language theorists, comparative philologists, and science writers on the one hand, and American writers on the other.

NOTES TO CHAPTER 2

1. For an earlier and much fuller version of this argument, see my essay, "Henry James's Suspended Situations."

2. As a typical instance, see William McMurray, who argues that James's realism offers us "a dramatic illustration of pragmatism. Reality in the novel is such that all absolutisms, when tested by experience, either must yield their claims to sanctity or fall in disaster. . . . A pragmatism that would free us of these things by keeping life 'open' is what James urges" ("Pragmatic Realism in *The Bostonians*," 344).

3. See Carrie Tirado Bramen, who uses William James's pragmatism as a touchstone for exploring Henry James's realism, specifically as a practical attitude toward emotional difficulty, "a strategy of adaptability" (Bramen, 305). Pragmatist theory tends to enforce a practical attitude toward everyday practices, whether in legal theory or in practical reasoning more generally. For legal theory, see Richard Posner, who argues that legal reasoning should require "no special analytical procedure that distinguishes legal reasoning from other practical reasoning" (Posner, *Law, Pragmatism, and Democracy*, 73). See also E. W. Thomas, who argues that realism is a mood or attitude that "shuns abstract theories and a doctrinaire approach; it is alert to the practical consequences and impact of the law" (Thomas, *The Judicial Process*, 20).

4. Vitalists consider it possible that our preference for practical explanations (or intellectual ones that have their origin in practical thought) has a blind spot when it comes to mental processes that, in Bergson's terms, "striv[e] to transcend the conditions of useful action" (*Matter and Memory*, 15).

5. For critics who tie Jamesian renunciation to moral life, see Stevens, *Henry James and Sexuality*, 54, and Priest, "A Secret Responsive Ecstasy," 163–168. In *The Ordeal of Consciousness*, Dorothea Krook reads *The Wings of the Dove*, for instance, as a parable of moral transformation that elevates Milly as she renounces instrumental calculation, calculation incompatible with her own sacrificial nature. Krook states: "The Jamesian moral passion seems here to reach a pitch, the Jamesian vision of human possibility to acquire a depth and a breadth, which brings it to the edge of the religious" (221). She goes on to suggest that the tragic conflict is answered by Milly's "forgiveness, loving-kindness, and sacrificial death" (221). These critics pick up a line of reasoning from those among James's earliest readers who identified renunciation as a central motif in his work. See,

for instance, Conrad, "Henry James: An Appreciation," 365. Cf. Van Wyck Brooks, *The Pilgrimage of Henry James*, 32.

6. As Vermeule argues, disinterestedness became "the first requirement of the liberal polity" (*Why Do We Care about Literary Characters?*, 107). As a value, it arose in the eighteenth century to enforce public norms more consistently and discipline departures from those norms. From Kant to John Rawls, the rationalist tradition of liberal thought privileges disinterested, universal, and need-blind judgments to weigh questions of moral right and social equity more consistently.

7. According to Albert O. Hirschman, the very concept of an interest emerged historically to secure material acquisitiveness as a value from the vagaries and instability of the passions at large—thus isolating a predictable complex of motivations that, properly embedded within a uniform view of human nature, could provide an anchor for social life (*The Passions and the Interests*, 31–40). The idea is that the pursuit of self-interest could protect people from the uncertainty and inconstancy of passions that threatened to subject them to the arbitrary will of others.

8. As Hirschman points out, the concept of an interest was originally conceived of as one passion vying with other passions (*The Passions and the Interests*, 13). Francis Bacon, an early theorist of "interest," differentiated it from the passions at large by offering it as "a countervailing passion," one that could regulate human aspiration by checking and restraining the chaos of impulses that threaten the political order (27–28). By the time that it became the centerpiece of Adam Smith's theory of *homo economicus*, the concept became an all-encompassing motive-force, grounding social life in the pursuit of economic advantage (100–113). In Smith's haste to put the science of human motivation on a universal footing, he lost the sense of variability that the earlier discourse granted to interests. This claim to variability depended on locating an affective basis for interests rather than treating them as secure, incontrovertible benefits. Spinoza, for instance, tends to regard the acquisitive impulse as one passion among others. His *Ethics* specifies how "gluttony and greed," vying species of love, "pull a man" in different directions (*Ethics* IV.II.209 in *A Spinoza Reader*). The advantage of treating the interests as a multiplicity of passions that vie with other passions is at least twofold, I would suggest: it allows for much more mutable grounds for human motivation, and it gives greater flexibility in deliberating about what counts as an interest.

9. This would include Jürgen Habermas, who valorizes a rational public sphere that encourages public conversation and debate about competing interests (*Theory of Communicative Action*, 10–18), and Selya Benhabib who wants to ensure that the procedures that allow communities to negotiate competing interests are "radically open and fair to all" (*Situating the Self*, 6). She privileges public conversations as a demonstration of people's willingness to seek understanding.

10. What I am calling "superficial" is a specifically psychological quality of character and not a tendency to foreground the objects of the concrete material world (the subject of Otten's *A Superficial Reading of Henry James*).

11. For Bersani, the self-inventiveness that James dramatizes ultimately empties out all personal identity, resolving social discord by transforming personal motives into depersonalized art, therefore liberating the novel from any worry about strictly human-centered need. A reality that is resistant to easy forms of resolution—for example, the shocked

discovery of betrayal that lays the dramatic foundation for *The Golden Bowl*—succumbs at the end to the "artistic manipulation of life's materials" (*A Future for Astyanax*, 146) as Maggie turns her marriage into a superior fiction. Maggie creates a new reality by absorbing everything and everyone into her artful vision and, it would seem, by recasting herself in the same way that her fictive vision recasts the lives of others.

12. For examples of such character criticism, see Matthiessen, *Henry James: The Major Phase*, and Holland, *The Expense of Vision*. To see the recurrence and remobilization of claims about the aesthetic nature of James's novelistic resolutions, see Freedman, *Professions of Taste*. See also Leavis, who argued that our sympathy ought to lie with Charlotte and Adam Verver and that James, who clearly weighs the case otherwise, may have lost his moral sense in his elaborate oversubtlety (*The Great Tradition*, 159–163).

13. Bersani's position has parallels with that of Todorov, who suggests that the elaborations of talk in James's novel *The Awkward Age* (1899), filled with indirect speech and increasingly far-flung circumlocutions, liberate language from its reference to reality. See Todorov, *Genres in Discourse*, 125, 126. I would suggest, however, that the conversations about conversations that Todorov finds everywhere in *The Awkward Age* do not insulate fiction from reality but are in fact for James a form of reality. Our relations to the world, our impressions of it derived from banter and casual talk, simply construct the mode of being-in-the-world of those in "society."

14. Because James depicts characters whose identity is not dependent on any solid, interior foundation, Cameron simply concludes that James releases consciousness from empirical constraint, as he putatively does in *The American Scene* (1904–1907) by evacuating all other persons from the scene described, or as Maggie does in *The Golden Bowl* by her all-encompassing consciousness (Cameron, *Thinking in Henry James*, 95–111).

15. See Cameron's summary arguments:

> a poststructuralist account (the dominant critical alternative [to one that takes consciousness as psychologized and therefore centered]) critiques and dismisses the idea of such a center, conceptually replacing the structure of consciousness with the structure of the sign and then proceeding to deconstruct that. . . . I read James against the traditional account of consciousness as psychologized, arguing that consciousness in James's novels is not internal, not centered, not associated with subjectivity. (*Thinking in Henry James*, 170–171)

Cameron suggests that consciousness in late James exerts "magical claims" (41), implying that James disconnects power from any realistic exercise of it. By this account, one could only conclude that James succeeds in hypostatizing the imagination, presenting a consciousness that is little short of delusional because it ignores at great peril what Freud would call the "reality principle."

16. Critics have underestimated the relevance of vitalism to William James's philosophy. James writes to Bergson that *Pragmatism* is "jejune and inconsiderable" but so "congruent with parts of your system, fits so well into interstices thereof, that you will easily understand why I am so enthusiastic. I feel that at bottom we are fighting the same fight" (*The Correspondence of William James* 11:377). Bergson responds after reading *Pragmatism*: "For my part, I never understood better the affinity that exists between our two methods of thinking" (11:531; translation mine).

17. For an account that regards William James as a protophenomenologist, appraising him as a conceptual and historical forerunner of Husserl, the philosopher

who formalized phenomenology as a branch of philosophy, see Edie, *William James and Phenomenology.*

18. James's sympathy with and approval of key elements of his brother's philosophy does not prevent them from parting company on aesthetic grounds, an issue that dominates quite a number of their letters. "Philosophically, . . . I am 'with' you, almost completely" (*William and Henry James: Selected Letters*, 467), Henry writes to him, though he also dismiss his brother's complaints about the "twilight or mustiness" in his plots, the "fencing in the dialogue," and the lack of "straightness in the style" (463). For a fuller exploration of the complicated relationship between William and Henry James, see Posnock, *The Trial of Curiosity.*

19. Pippin thinks that James leaves the core of character or its heart "too weak to do much pumping, too endlessly qualifiable, to serve any real moral, judgmental purpose" (*Henry James and Modern Moral Life*, 127).

20. Pippin tends to treat beliefs as important stepping-stones on the way to action. Beliefs about other people's motives do this work: they introduce a "normative dimension of meaning and intelligibility" into everyday discriminations and enable rituals of interaction and communication (*Henry James and Modern Moral Life*, 66). These beliefs therefore confer trust and conviction in the institutions, practices, and traditions that convey meaning. They allow one to assess "the rightness of actions" (66) by confirming or envisaging realistic interpretations of them. Like many other James scholars, Pippin is not a strict cognitivist who always demands a clear discursive basis for assessing intentions, and he readily accepts the possibility that the novelty of certain experiences may make evaluation of them difficult, but he focuses on the particular understandings that James's characters come to have or fail to have of each other rather than on the social world they build or the forms of relationship they set in motion. In Bergson's and James's view, to give primacy to beliefs or fixed assessments of a situation is to live at an intellectual distance from the world.

For examples of other critics who display a similar anxiety about the lack of determinate guideposts for meaning, see Levin, who turns to "gaps in [characters'] communication," things left "unsaid" (*Poetics of Transition*, 144), and Cameron, who describes the impossibility in James of having "shared reference" (*Thinking in Henry James*, 95).

21. In *Creative Evolution*, Bergson posits a "universal vital impulsion" from which an organism gets its impetus to act, using "this energy in its own interest. In this consists *adaptation*" (50). But rather than presuming harmony, Bergson draws out the unpredictable development of forms of life. What he calls "radical finalism" is "unacceptable" because the doctrine "implies that things and beings merely realize a programme previously arranged." He concludes that if "there is nothing unforeseen," then "no invention or creation in the universe" (39) can happen, a possibility that does not accord with the nature of time itself.

22. James, like Bergson, thinks that people's beliefs about their motives are not always able to track the variegated relations to the world that cause them to act. Because people's actions are sensitive to a greater variety of relations than they can appreciate cognitively, their actions and doings are more revealing of the situation they are figuring out than any available cognitive form of assessment. This is what is implied when Bergson gives primacy to intuition over intellect, reason, or understanding. See Bergson's *Introduction to Metaphysics*, 31–39.

23. The force of an interest is to determine what one pays attention to. And the function of attention, in turn, is not to gather more data on a given object but to subtract all the other relations that distract from it. As Bergson puts it, "The reality of matter consists in the totality of its elements and of their actions of every kind. Our representation of matter [by this Bergson means our consciousness] is the measure of our possible action upon bodies: it results from the discarding of what *has no interest for our needs*, or more generally, for our functions" (*Matter and Memory*, 38; emphasis mine). Bergson's is a theory of how to deal with superabundant relations, with plenitude. The goal is to bring to the light of consciousness that which helps one's body to act.

24. Bergson suggests that our interests vary tremendously; some are keyed to immediately instrumental aims, while others appeal to objectives rather distant from our most direct needs (*Matter and Memory*, 100). The more distant the interest, the less automatic are our tendencies to act. Organisms that are more complex delay the interval between stimulus (or perception) and response, allowing more relations to come into view perceptually, which increases the repertoire of possible actions they might execute: "in the measure that the reaction becomes more uncertain, and allows more room for suspense, does the distance increase at which the animal is sensible of the action of that which interests it"; with this lag or suspense, we enter "into relation with an ever greater number of things" (32).

25. It may be useful to think of an affection as a threshold between perception and action, one that occurs in the passage from a virtual action to a real action. In other words, for Bergson, an affection helps the body to understand its own possibilities of action: if in daily life things impinge on us with "the greater or less imminence of a danger, the nearer or more remote fulfillment of a promise," affection tends to appear at the moment of the danger or the promise's proximity to us; "[b]ut the more distance decreases between this object and our body (the more, in other words, the danger becomes urgent or the promise immediate), the more does virtual action tend to pass into *real* action." This moment of convergence "is exactly what affection is" (*Matter and Memory*, 57).

26. British Aestheticism often flirted with aesthetic definitions focused on the cultivation of sensations. Walter Pater, for instance, speaks of a susceptibility to impressions, each of which has the "property . . . of affecting one with a special, a unique, impression of pleasure" (*The Renaissance*, xx). Still, this conception of the aesthetic is only a reductive starting point for aestheticism's more complex social and ethical aims.

27. For the relationship between character and moral action, see Williams, *Ethics and the Limits of Philosophy*, 56. Williams thinks that the Kantian account of morality ignores the relationship. Kant's account fails to bridge its reasons for justifying specific lines of action from the motivating reasons of specific agents.

28. Žižek argues that "[a]t a deeper, properly Hegelian, dialectical level," James manages to "*de-substantialize*" Kate as a subject, reducing subjectivity to "a formal, empty space in which the multitude of agents interact" ("Kate's Choice, or the Materialism of Henry James," 289). He celebrates Kate, not Densher, because she is willing to see her and Densher's fantasies, and the ethical acts they spur, as profoundly compromised.

29. James does not insist that Densher's pained conscience should assert itself apart from his concern over himself. In this respect it is, as Williams would say, "formally egoistic." Williams means that the decision-making process has "to show to each person that he has good reason to live ethically; and the reason has to appeal to that person in terms

of something about himself, how and what he will be if he is a person with that sort of character. But [the] outlook is not egoistic in the sense that [it tries] to show that the ethical life serves some set of individual satisfactions which is well defined before ethical considerations appeal" (*Ethics and the Limits of Philosophy*, 32).

30. See Richard P. Blackmur, who argues that "Densher comes out not with a bad conscience or a good conscience . . . [but] with created conscience . . . and the assertion of conscience is his form of action. He struggles with his own odium and discovers his own self, longing to embrace Kate but unable to do so" (*Studies in Henry James*, 172). See also Pippin, who argues in *Henry James and Modern Moral Life* that a number of James's protagonists, presumably characters like Densher, have to yield their desires and their bid for happiness to ultimate moral claims: "Violating or ignoring such claims [of the other as distinct and free] might or might not make one's life better or happier (it usually will), but, apart from that, the characters come to experience some unmistakable 'call of conscience' in such cases. . . . Such a claim, understood as a moral claim, is not conditional" (29–30) on the pursuit of a flourishing or happy life.

31. Kant's account of moral judgment excludes any consideration apart from the rational dictates of the categorical imperative (*Critique of Practical Reason* 5:32). He stresses the transcendent capacity for human freedom, exaggerating the open-endedness of agency by casting such freedom as unconstrained by habits or empirical dispositions.

32. Spinoza treats suicide as a decomposition of the body by causes ultimately external to it, which, in effect, renders one incapable of having interests. For an explication, see Deleuze, *Spinoza*, 34–43. But James grants Hyacinth Robinson's fatal resolution a psychological dimension in much the same vein that Nietzsche would. For Nietzsche's account of an individual willing her or his own repression or unfreedom, see *On The Genealogy of Morals*, 87.

Hyacinth is caught between profoundly unwelcome choices: whether to fulfill his mission as an assassin in the service of radical political causes or to renounce the effort, at the cost (deliberately left ambiguous) of the revolutionary Muniment's lethal retaliation against him. Hyacinth's will, consumed by self-denying affects that tug at him from opposing directions, demands the annihilation of his self-determination.

33. Mark Seltzer, Jonathan Freedman, Cameron, and Pippin all think that Maggie consciously succeeds in manipulating and dominating those around her by betraying no knowledge of her grievance as she orchestrates behind the scenes. See Seltzer, *Henry James and the Art of Power*, 63; Freedman, *Professions of Taste*, 237; Cameron, *Thinking in Henry James*, 100; and Pippin, *Henry James and Modern Moral Life*, 67–78.

34. Like Bersani and Cameron, Levin would rather not situate this unfolding perception in any specific locus of consciousness (*The Poetics of Transition*, 121). His investment in James's formal alignments and dénouement stop him from focusing on the psychological texture of the thoughts he presents. He looks for moments that exceed any character's understanding of events. By foregrounding James's commitments to realism, I am diverging from this approach to examine how James anchors these thoughts and experiences in his characters.

35. Clearly, James makes distinctions between his central protagonists, say, Maggie Verver or Lambert Strether, and his "ficelles" and minor characters, Fanny Assingham or Sarah Pocock. The latter do not display the exceptional open-endedness of the former.

James portrays Fanny fondly in *The Golden Bowl*, but her overbearing imagination remains a comically degraded version of that of his principal characters, while Pocock's excessively interested perspective and narrow imagination in *The Ambassadors* prevent her from achieving the vital incompleteness that marks James's more notable personages. For James's explanation of his use of "ficelles," see James, "The Preface to *The Ambassadors*" in *The Art of the Novel*, 322. His shorter works as well often parody the exacting psychology he bestows on the characters of his longer novels.

36. Indeed, James uses the interests of central characters as a way of consolidating narrative investment. James speaks of selecting "centres" for the narrative: "From the moment we proceed by 'centres'—and I have never, I confess, embraced the logic of any superior process—they must *be*, each, as a basis, selected and fixed; after which it is that, in the highest interest of economy of treatment, they determine and rule" (preface to the *The Wings of the Dove*, 11).

37. Freedman suggests that Maggie finds a way of disciplining Charlotte and policing her behavior by refusing to disclose her knowledge of the affair: "By the end of the novel, then, Maggie has fully invested herself with absolute punitive authority, and her infliction of punishment through the delineation of withheld knowledge is identified as the only ordering principle available in the resolutely demystified world of this novel" (*Professions of Taste*, 239).

38. According to Freedman, Maggie's coldness leaves Charlotte unconvinced as to whether she in fact still considers any wrong done to her, but she cannot say anything without admitting to her affair: "Maggie's counter-counter-responses range from indirection to outright prevarication, and they are neatly and cruelly calculated to present Charlotte with a façade of disingenuous ignorance and feigned innocence so perfect that it can never be penetrated or parted" (*Professions of Taste*, 237). She checks in Charlotte any immediate possibility of protest or maneuvering, any command of the latter's nearly superior self-composure.

39. See Seltzer: "The well-policed character of the 'world' of *Golden Bowl* is at once readily apparent and difficult to assess, apparent in that the novel everywhere displays the nexus of seeing, knowing, and exercising power that, I have argued, defines the politics of the Jamesian text, problematic in that police work and supervision in the novel are so thoroughly inscribed in gestures of compassion, care, and love" (*Henry James and the Art of Power*, 63). Maggie uses such gestures to assume "a position of power without hazarding that power by putting her knowledge in exchange" (78).

40. In *The Antitheatrical Prejudice*, Jonas Barish argues that "in Henry James . . . we find a defense not only of theater, but of theatricality and all it implies, the more telling in that it comes from a fastidious artist whose own temperament contains so much that is untheatrical" (381). Mark McGurl suggests that, for James, to "read a novel, to be immersed in its space, is to enter a sort of theater" ("Spatial Geometries," 68). He argues that the spatial figurations of *The Princess Cassamassima* (1886) constitute a response to Walter Besant's 1884 speech to the Royal Institution, which compares the novel to "a great theatre accessible to all of every sort, on whose stage are enacted, at our own sweet will, whenever we please to command them, the most beautiful plays" (quoted in "Spatial Geometries," 69). See also Christopher Greenwood, who explores theatrical form and its implications for Jamesian character (*Adapting to the Stage*, 27).

41. Litvak's criticism of Seltzer makes it clear that he does not understand theater to be an unequivocal instrument of social regulation, one that merely assimilates all spectacles into forms of disciplinary surveillance: "In neither case, I have suggested, does this self-doubling have to signify self-defeat; yet in neither case, I would add, should it be assimilated too quickly to what Mark Seltzer calls the 'double discourse' of power, whereby power is at once disavowed and ironically reinscribed" (*Caught in the Act*, 214). The "double discourse" to which Litvak is referring comes from Seltzer's reading of Foucault and concerns a paradigm of disciplinary formation in which power insidiously structures both the position of actor and spectator. Occupying each position simultaneously, this discourse leaves only an undifferentiated field in which there are scarcely alternatives to dominant regimes of power. Seltzer speaks of a "criminal continuity between the techniques of the novel and the social technologies of power that inhere in these techniques" (*Henry James and the Art of Power*, 57) that invariably places the novel on the side of law and order.

42. The claim that Bersani ignores circumstantial understandings applies mainly to his later writings. In *A Future for Astyanax*, a book written well before *The Freudian Body*, Bersani speculates that Maggie's actions suggest a thoroughly circumstantial mode of dealing with the world, her aspirational aims being too incidental to be considered within the terms of a global desiring structure: the forms of marriage "are, I think, merely the convenient social envelope for desires imagined as too original to be contained or expressed by any established form of social life" (*A Future for Astyanax*, 153). In *The Freudian Body*, which imposes a more clear-cut psychoanalytical framework, Bersani shifts terms somewhat, trying to assimilate the "improvisational psychology" that he describes in his early work into a denarrativized masochistic sexuality *within* psychoanalysis, which resists being placed in an oedipal framework at all. Even in *The Freudian Body*, one wonders whether the choice Bersani sets up between teleological desire and an unstructured (i.e., non–ends driven), decreative desire need be so stark (85–87). Maggie clearly wants to uphold marriage, but only according to her improvised and highly particular vision of it.

43. Regarding the masochistic position of the fantasizing subject, Silverman suggests that it leads to forms of self-abnegation, understood as a capacity to identify with the vulnerable or marginal position of others that is at antipodes to normative heterosexual masculinity. She discusses the particular case of Strether in *The Ambassadors*, a paradigmatic "man without means." The litany of characters she names who encounter a primal scene also includes a number of girls and women (*Male Subjectivity at the Margins*, 158, 166–170).

44. The primal scene, as a fantasy, recalls the subject to a moment in her own childhood development prior to the knowledge of sexual difference, one in which identifications proscribed by the oedipus development have not yet taken effect (*Male Subjectivity at the Margins*, 164–165). The immaturity of the child allows amorphous identifications, elicited by the imagined or remembered sexual act of the parents, which do not necessarily correspond to her socially sanctioned gender (180); thus, she might want to *be* the father as well as to love him. At such a moment, "father" is diffuse, extensible, and potentially continuous with other objects of desire or identification.

45. According to Silverman, those characters in James who perceive themselves as disappointed and undeceived, like Maggie, are able to reenact their own fantasies, not by carrying them out necessarily, but by repeating their own painfully pleasurable voyeur-

ism, including themselves in the scenes of passion; or else, like Strether and Longdon, by making love *through* other people (*Male Subjectivity at the Margins*, 166–167). The adult may be able to tap into the mobile identifications of childhood, but with this distinction: she knows that her erotic life is in a manner curtailed, having long since measured it by its accommodations with reality, even or especially the reality of oedipal normativity. For Silverman, the adult's capacity to construct mobile identifications is a retrospective construction of fantasy—that is, an identification from infancy as it is interpreted or activated from a later position, spun in response to a current trigger. See her discussion of Freud's concept of deferred action (164). Silverman is especially invested in the frame of fantasy, access to the variable identifications of infantile sexuality, particularly as they recur to memory within adult life. She emphasizes the shifts between adult identifications (late) and infantile ones (early) (179).

46. Fantasy, for psychoanalysis, is always more or less in the imaginary, in the realm of distorted wishes, projected ideas, and displaced memories. Freud's conceptual paradigm is built around a distrust of claims to lucidity. Thus, as a defense mechanism, projection stands as the "operation whereby qualities, feelings, wishes or even 'objects', which the subject refuses to recognize or rejects in himself, are expelled from the self and located in another person or thing" (Laplanche and Pontalis, *The Language of Psychoanalysis*, 349).

47. Bergson thinks that objects that interest us project virtual images that represent to us our possible action upon them: "every *attentive* perception truly involves a *reflection*, in the etymological sense of the word, that is to say the projection, outside of ourselves, of an actively created image, identical with, or similar to, the object on which it comes to mold itself" (*Matter and Memory*, 102). Virtual actions are stamped on the object or, as it were, "photographed upon the object itself" (103), which allows us to perceive the object within "ever widening systems with which it may be bound up" (105).

48. For the relationship between Bergsonian intuition and psychic identification, see Bergson's *Introduction to Metaphysics*. Bergson discusses intuition by analogy to the forms of "intellectual sympathy" with fictional characters: "The author may multiply the traits of his hero's character, may make him speak and act as much as he pleases, but all this can never be equivalent to the simple and indivisible feeling which I should experience if I were able for an instant to identify myself with the person of the hero himself" (22). Bergson may be as guilty as Freud of ignoring second-order feelings of the observer's difference from the object with which he or she identifies, but his account has a very specific agenda: to describe the primitive unity of experience that allows individuals to experience states of mind all at once rather than as separate snapshots.

49. For demonstration of the limits of Freud's model of identification, see his case study, "A Child Is Being Beaten." Freud argues that the ways his patients position themselves within their fantasies often paint false appearances. On a libidinal level, it does not matter that the women who are his patients produce outwardly sadistic fantasies of people other than themselves being beaten; nor does it particularly make a difference that they may be positioned as spectators in their own fantasy: "only the form of this phantasy is sadistic; the gratification which is derived from it is masochistic" ("A Child Is Being Beaten," 109). The implication is that underlying these relational permutations is a quite definite—and unconscious—psychic equivalence being made between the female patients and the boys in the fantasy they indulge in, summarized by the phrase "Some

boys are being beaten." For Freud, identification is a psychological process that seems to have no friction, that assimilates the object by a mental act of substitution or equivalence regardless of the relational differences that may seem to be a part of the operation, part of a scene of fantasy.

50. Maggie does not succumb to a psychoanalytic process of identification "whereby the subject assimilates an aspect, property or attribute of the other and is transformed, wholly or partially, after the model the other provides" (Laplanche and Pontalis, *The Language of Psychoanalysis*, 205). Instead she grants other people their differences in point of view as basic to the act of identification. Psychoanalysis is so determined to find the psychic identities underneath relational differences that it ends up offering an impoverished language for describing the distinctions and relevant situations that matter in any act of identification. To be fair to Freud, he tends to see identification split into two discrete regimes. In early life, the child can realize fluid identifications because its existence presupposes a different ontology from the adult's. It lives in a state where being and possessing are indistinct, having not yet formed decisive bodily boundaries. The adult, however, does not have the same capacity for identification because the ego's own structural position limits the variety of perspectives it is capable of entertaining. For an adult to identify with another person, the same primitive assimilations must be measured against the "reality" of separately socially coded egos. The adult's identifications no longer take in a polymorphous variety of parts but are informed by whole structures, which, Freud tells us, come about in the crystallization of the oedipus complex, with its comprehensive incorporations and introjections. In the course of development, the subject moves from identifications that accommodate local and provisional similarities and differences to a molar organization of imaginary resemblance.

51. Nietzsche avoids the psychological framework of guilt and self-censorship that marks Freud's psychological conception of repression. He construes "forgetting" in psychological terms according to two different constituent elements or aspects. On the one hand, it is a process that presumes latency: forgetting "is responsible for the fact that what we experience and absorb enters our consciousness as little while we are digesting it . . . as does the thousandfold process, involved in physical nourishment" (*A Genealogy of Morals*, 57). It is therefore a form of deferral or digestion, a way of paying no heed to what one knows to make room for new ways of thinking about things. On the other hand, forgetting may be construed as something far more absolute, a case of perfect and unqualified disappearance. One can, for example, forget one's grudges. Forgetting according to this understanding is a kind of cutting-off or simplifying, an act of summarizing, paring away, or disregarding.

52. The idea of performance, deployed most consistently by gender theorists, underscores how much people's identities are derived from the socially constructed functions and positions they take on in concert with others. See Butler, *Gender Trouble*, 25. Drawing on Nietzsche, Butler argues that identities do not precede their performance, which suggests, among other things, that they are relational in nature.

53. Leland Person, like Litvak, stresses how fluid, tractable, and open-ended social and gender roles are. According to Person and Litvak, James's theatricality works against domesticated closure and coherent, stable subjectivity. Obviously, the fact that social roles are contingent and in many cases situation-specific—not to mention that they allow for

self-conscious forms of disengagement from them—means that they enable some degree of suspension from their claims, especially to the degree that the role-playing is acknowledged by others. Person explores this concept of suspension "in favor of the improvisational freedom to construct a masculine self from a range of possibilities" (*Henry James and the Suspense of Masculinity*, 20). Much of his book concerns James's "suspense of masculinity," which allows James to defer making any choice about the sexual identity he confers on himself or his characters. As regards *The Golden Bowl*, Person is careful to say that Maggie and Amerigo's "gender identities [do not seem to] end in a state of suspense" (172). He implies, on the contrary, that despite the performance that Maggie "commissions" from her husband, which leads him to experience his "manhood at second hand," he has to own up to the balance of tasks and responsibilities that are his to assert. Person suggests compellingly that at the end of the novel the Prince has brokered a compromise with Maggie that allows him to keep his manhood intact while still deferring to her as a "phallic woman" (173). Thus, ironic self-distance must give way to an acceptance of the role he has accepted for himself, both in its limitations and in its possibilities of response.

54. Vermeule is right to suggest that this conception of knowledge as a form of exposure, which began as an instrument of Enlightenment reason in the eighteenth century, tends to mangle and distort the object under scrutiny. According to her, it "is closely related to tropes of dissection ('dissecting reason') and anatomy" (*Why Do We Care about Literary Characters?*, 109); the preferred metaphors—laying bare, flushing out, uncovering, stripping out—underscore just how *dead* the object under such scrutiny would be.

55. Berman claims that "community might grow even within the private sphere . . . emerging from an imagined set of contingent relations between subjects who always already exist both in common and separately" (*Modernist Fiction, Cosmopolitanism, and the Politics of Community*, 6). Even so, she tends to presume that such community building is always political. I would argue, however, that the move from an ethics to a politics is not inevitable or straightforward. In her second book, *Modernist Commitments*, she insists on "bridging the gap between ethics and politics, connecting ethical attitudes and responsibilities—ideas about what we ought to be and do—to the active creation of political relationships and just conduct—what is right and possible within the power structures and discourses of our social life and institutions" (6). Politics is, of necessity, conducted within the public sphere, and the suspensions that James promotes in his novels are sometimes meant to distance characters from the public perspectives and discourses demanded by a specifically political vision. That said, the need for such shelter from public life may itself lead to political reflection.

56. Butler has a point when she observes that desires come in multiples and sometimes express themselves in fantasies wherein permutational differences of position are only implicit and quite variable. She argues, for instance, that Charlotte is for Maggie a source of identification as her husband's lover, and through her jealous passion for him perhaps even a source of vicarious desire ("Capacity," 118).

NOTES TO CHAPTER 3

1. Schoenbach argues that Stein situates herself in opposition to a bellicose shock aesthetic whose claim to iconoclasm or originality is based in heroic opposition to convention. Stein, she thinks, establishes a pragmatic stream of modernism, producing work

committed to "gradualism, accretion, continuity, and recontextualization" ("Peaceful and Exciting," 240).

2. Olson thinks that, although habits prevent psychic trauma, they do so at the cost of concealing from individuals the suffocating uncertainty and violence occurring around them: "habits, as defense, . . . enable a dangerous blindness to what, especially in retrospect, demanded action" ("Gertrude Stein, William James, and Habit in the Shadow of War," 350). Habit would seem to prevent people from engaging in political resistance or assuming wider political agency. Because she understands it as a kind of pleasure-principle, the sensuous enjoyment in maintaining constancy and resisting change, she is forced to jettison the conception of habit defined "in terms of productive action" (330). Schoenbach argues that habits "create an environment in which innovations can take place" ("Peaceful and Exciting," 254) but tends to see their capacity to transmit important, sometimes unconscious, collective customs and dispositions of national life in a state of "push and pull" with the perceptive capacities of the mind, which alone distinguish novelty. Both Olson and Schoenbach think that habits threaten to deaden feeling.

3. Bergson, for instance, engaged Darwin explicitly and at length in his most famous book, *Creative Evolution*, while James consistently used Darwin as a reference point and wrote early reviews of his work. See James, *Essays, Comments, and Reviews*, 231.

4. Ann Charters, for instance, alleges in her introduction to *Three Lives* that Stein does away with psychological development: her method of composition "is also a reflection of her view of human character as static and unchanging, basically falling into one of two types, either aggressive or passive" (xiv).

5. Critics have debated the relative balance of progressivist politics and racial determinism in Stein's presentation of race. A great deal of critical ink has been spilled on the question of how the three portraits, especially the "Melanctha" section, exploit or finesse racist modes of typologizing. Critics who see Stein in some form or another as racist include Bridgman, "Melanctha"; Saldivar-Hull, "Wrestling Your Ally"; Cohen, "Black Brutes and Mulatto Saints"; and Doyle, "The Flat, the Round, and Gertrude Stein." Paul Peppis, who emphasizes the inconclusiveness of the approach to race in "Melanctha," puts the matter this way: "Yet while the progressive model promises growth and liberation from determinism, the novella treats it as ambiguously as the determinist model it opposes" ("Thinking Race in the Avant Guerre," 387).

A number of critics emphasize the difficulty of mapping Stein's political views and give reasons that include the shifting vocabulary of racial description over the course of the novella, the use of elaborate masking techniques, the strange discrepancies between narrative voice and authorial perspective, and the complicated combinations of blood inheritance, white upbringing, and social identifications with race. See Blackmer, "African Masks and the Arts of Passing in Gertrude Stein's 'Melanctha' and Nella Larsen's *Passing*," and Hovey, "Gertrude Stein: *Three Lives*."

6. Massumi is among most trenchant critical voices today arguing for the "mutual involvement" and "dynamic unity" of nature and culture. His arguments are consistent with some of the vitalist implications of Darwinism: "The point is that the 'natural' and the 'cultural' feed forward and back into each other. They relay each other to such an extent that the distinction cannot be maintained in any strict sense. It is necessary to theorize a nature-culture continuum" (*Parables for the Virtual*, 11).

7. Much of the discourse about the passions, since the earliest theorizing about them, has downplayed their connection to habits. It is true that habits, like passions, involve longstanding dispositions, but passions tend to erupt in "episodic moments of vehement feeling," as Philip Fisher notes (*The Vehement Passions*, 23–24). He argues that reliance on momentary experience, singular and often quite unprecedented, is what makes vehement passion distinctive and also makes literature central to the examination of it (22). In other respects, as Stein was certainly aware, habits overlap with passions. Neither of them renders one's actions quite involuntary, but in both cases one is being acted upon. This, as I noted in the introduction, is the etymological implication of passion (*passio*). Stein makes a firm connection between habits and passions because she regards any state to be in moving relation to the states that came before it. The same mental dispositions formed by habits also allow us to see passionate departures from them; continuity works in concert with difference. Stein, then insists that literature extend the scale in which it is willing to treat passionate experience.

8. Obviously, some human groupings are more provisional and less universal than others across the spectrum of human societies, and biologists and anthropologists argue about the merits of treating race as a useful biological category. If, however, we don't treat social and biological definitions as radically distinct, then perhaps we can agree that even historically limited ways that people find to categorize each other have biological effects on such things as mating patterns and resource allocations. Darwin, for his part, thought that racial variation is, in evolutionary terms, the product of differentiated tastes or sexual preferences within the human species. See especially his "On the Races of Man" in *The Descent of Man*, 194–240.

9. Aristotle ranks habit as a "state of character" ("Nichomachean Ethics" in *The Basic Works of Aristotle*, 1106a) whose virtue lies in its claim to being "firm and unchangeable" (1105a). His account reveals how much a particular interpretation of habit determines the models of character that one settles on. Stein also focuses on habit's practical nature, which involves not just knowing what should be done but actually doing it frequently and consistently.

10. Stein amuses herself with ordinary words that play on the distinction between durable designations and differences of stress. In her essay "Portraits and Repetitions," she dismisses repetition conceived as an exact reproduction: "Is there repetition or is there insistence. I am inclined to believe there is no such thing as repetition" (288).

11. Stein says that narrative "is a thing that has to be done since any one since every one inevitably has to tell something" (*Narration*, 31), but she distinguishes the repetitive act of telling, the narration that is the source of her interest, from the narrative content, the excitements of the thing told. For an explanation of her narrative strategy of "constant recurring and beginning," see Stein's "Composition as Explanation," 498.

12. Darwin's account of fitness, as laid out in his theory of natural selection, refuses to specify a defined goal for life, as Elizabeth Grosz points out: "Darwin describes natural selection as a 'principle of preservation,' but this preservation is quite ambiguous and multilayered. . . . Fitness carries with it the notion of an openness to changing environments; it is not necessarily the best adapted to a fixed and unchanging context" (*The Nick of Time*, 47).

13. The legacy of Darwin is constantly being reassessed as biological science advances. In recent decades, biologists have concentrated with renewed appreciation on the com-

plexity of his ideas. The rise of evolutionary psychology in the early 1970s and the dual-inheritance theory, which considers the interactions between genetic and cultural evolution, are clear examples. The reconsideration, inevitable with any paradigm-shifting theory, ensures that Darwinists have an array of competing perspectives to present. Yet the remarkable tenacity with which a large number of scientists and cultural theorists have insisted on the mindless and inevitable results of natural selection is belied by many key Darwinian observations. For an example of an influential contemporary exponent of Darwinism who treats the biologist's theory of evolution as speaking to a blind, predictable mathematical algorithm of genetic variation, see Dennett, *Darwin's Dangerous Idea.* For a Bergsonian critique of Dennett's mechanistic assumptions, see Pearson, *Philosophy and the Adventure of the Virtual*, 79–86.

14. See, for example, *The Descent of Man*, in which Darwin puts forth his account of sexual selection, specifying biological changes that result at least in part from the unpredictable sexual preferences individuals display rather than through biological inheritance alone (227–230, 245–246).

15. Paul Ekman speculates that Darwin's acceptance of the Lamarckian "use-inheritance" model is a signal reason why *The Expression of the Emotions in Man and Animals* has been neglected (introduction to *The Expression of the Emotions*, xxxii).

16. Wilson argues that Darwin did not consider psychological modes of inheritance as radically distinct from biological (genetic) transmission: "Every one of Darwin's texts attests that the stuff of evolution is radically heterogeneous; certainly it is biological, but it is also psychological, cultural, geological, oceanic, and meteorological" ("Trembling, Blushing," 69).

17. Clive Bush faults Darwin for relying on a chauvinistic ideology that allies marginal subaltern subjects"—representatives of "primitive" cultural phenomena—with the order of nature, in the process blurring the difference between social constructions of power and natural forms of expression. He cites Darwin's example of workmen in the botanical gardens at Calcutta whose kowtowing expressions before their superiors count as evidence of the naturalness of such behaviors (*Halfway to Revolution*, 273). Clearly, the discursive context for Darwin's use of decontextualized anthropological examples is important. Bush, however, neglects one surprising repercussion of Darwin's argument. One might just as well say that Darwin is providing an instance of acculturated nature as he is the naturalization of a cultural network of power relations.

18. For an account of eugenics during the period and its entanglement with discourses of Social Darwinism, see English, *Unnatural Selections.* English's book refers to the paradox, as the exponents of eugenics understood it, that the less fit succeed in reproducing more and therefore thriving better. This, for any number of figures whom she quotes, is "unnatural selection," and it is the result of the perverse intrusion of misguided social institutions such as the welfare state or the modern factory, which work against nature and lead to a degradation of the stock.

19. Bergson spends a fair amount of time distinguishing his position from Darwin's mechanistic interpretations. See especially *Creative Evolution* 56, 62–65.

20. Bergson emphasizes contradictory tendencies within evolution, not just harmonious forms of coordination: "In communicating itself, the impetus [of life] splits up more and more. Life, in proportion to its progress, is scattered in manifestations which

undoubtedly owe to their common origin the fact that they are complementary to each other in certain aspects, but which are none the less mutually incompatible and antagonistic" (*Creative Evolution*, 103).

21. Stein speaks of her indebtedness to James's brand of thinking in many contexts, stating plainly that he was one of "the strongest scientific influences I had" (*Wars I Have Seen*, 63–64).

22. The experiments do not specifically react against a psychoanalytic conception of the unconscious. Freud had not yet finished *The Interpretation of Dreams*, published in German in 1900. Stein was addressing the sources and antecedents from which psychoanalysis emerged. She directed her criticism at theories that hypothesized the existence of an irrational secondary personality susceptible to suggestion. Arguably, she does not address central features of hysteria as Freud understood them, including the conflict of wishes, the repression of the less acceptable ones, and their somatic conversion.

Stein's reference to "subconscious" response recalls turn-of-the-century models of hypnotic suggestion, which to a certain degree Freud set out to modify if not to challenge outright. Freud replaces the "magic, incantations, and hocus pocus" of suggestion with his conception of transference, which presupposes a theory of unconscious libidinal identifications ("Lecture XXVII," 449). Nevertheless, by the time Stein had disavowed subconscious aims in her writing in *The Autobiography of Alice B. Toklas* (published in 1933), she had already been introduced to Freudian theory by her brother and sometime housemate, Leo, who in 1909 developed an obsession with it. (For an account, see Ruddick, *Reading Gertrude Stein.*) Therefore, one presumes that her hostility to subconscious reactions eventually extended to psychoanalysis rather than limiting itself to her earlier sources.

23. The experiments throw out a set of models that admit the potential for involuntary social conditioning—those of unconscious suggestibility—but open the door to other techniques of social control. Though psychologists were not prone to examining social conditioning per se until Frederick Winslow Taylor published his *Principles of Scientific Management* in 1911, this is at least one implicit undercurrent of Stein's analysis.

24. Following the connection made by Barbara Will in "Gertrude Stein, Automatic Writing and the Mechanics of Genius," I apply the metaphor of the human motor to Stein's psychology experiment. For the nineteenth-century framework that gave rise to the study of the body as a machine that works apart from consciousness, see Rabinbach, *Human Motor*. Rabinbach cites interlaced discourses in physics, medicine, biology, and psychology directed at investigating the body's ideal working capacity. There are interesting parallels between the discourses that investigated the mechanical functioning of the body, which Rabinbach explores, and the vitalistic discourses I have cited, which are concerned specifically with the plasticity of life processes.

25. Stein was, as she noted in *Everybody's Autobiography*, younger than Solomons, who was a graduate student. She distinguished her own view of the experiment from that of her coauthor, suggesting that she believed the procedures they followed did not succeed in casting consciousness aside. A kind of consciousness, she thought, crept into the experiment by virtue of a familiarity that she and Solomons, as the two initial subjects of the study, had with the pragmatic operations and procedures of the laboratory. See *Everybody's Autobiography*, 274–275. In her later comments Stein may have conveniently attempted to rewrite an experiment whose emphasis she came to regret, but it seems just

as likely that her collaboration with Solomons was itself, like many of her later collaborations, the product of a sympathetic exchange. Stein's resistance may not have found an adequate avenue to express itself, being an intuitive resistance embedded in a habit of mind rather than an explicit and conscious difference of opinion.

26. In 1934, Skinner, who would become the most famous behaviorist psychologist of his generation, treated Stein's published experiments as methodological models for her "advanced" compositions, contending that they duplicated her later structure and style (Skinner, "Has Gertrude Stein a Secret?," 54).

27. Stein contests the word "automatic," associated as it was at this point with surrealist practice and Freudian thought: "I did not think it was automatic I do not think so now, I do not think any university student is likely certainly not under observation is likely to be able to do genuinely automatic writing" (*Everybody's Autobiography*, 275).

28. In a letter to her friend Lindley Hubbel, Stein rebuffed Skinner's insinuation that she had a secret to maintain about the origins of her writing practices (quoted in Meyer, "Writing Psychology Over," 141). Will, in her account of the mechanics of Stein's automatic writing, argues that the extra consciousness to which Stein refers is bound up with the effort not to take charge of movement, "resembling something like *attentive inattentiveness*" ("Gertrude Stein, Automatic Writing and the Mechanics of Genius," 173). The exact nature of the "xtra consciousness" aside, Stein thinks that the boundary that separates habit from will and attention is difficult to specify. The processes involved in writing are heterogeneous, requiring inferences, motor impulses, and regulating memories set down through a long practice of repetition. The meaning or intelligibility of all speech and writing relies to some degree on patterns of thought, learning, and sedimented history.

29. Stein and Solomons speak of the motor impulse entailed in dictation as involving "a mélange of visual and kinaesthetic material—whatever ordinarily innervates our writing—as well as other elements not easily described" ("Normal Motor Automatism," 498).

30. Habit in James's account tends to move one toward an increasingly determinate path, allowing one—as he says—to overcome inertia more readily, to do the same thing with less effort and a lower level of excitation: "*habit simplifies the movements required to achieve a given result, makes them more accurate and diminishes fatigue*" (*The Principles of Psychology*, 1:112). Habit itself, however, is part of a changing constellation of behaviors. New neural paths may be formed "by the sort of *chances* that in nervous material are likely to occur" (1:109).

31. Stein even proposes that certain predominant biases in habit formation differentiate people according to types. "Cultivated Motor Automatism" classifies types of people according to their particular reactions to the planchette. Stein draws a direct line from this insight to her experimental writing (*Everybody's Autobiography*, 274).

32. Bergson was giving weekly philosophical lectures at the Collège de France to packed crowds, including a fair number of modishly hatted ladies (see Grogin, *The Bergsonian Controversy in France*, 122–126). The link between Bergson and Stein was to be made more than once in the course of Stein's career. See Rogers, "*Tender Buttons*, Curious Experiment of Gertrude Stein in Literary Anarchy," 31, and Lewis, *Time and Western Man*, 49–51.

33. See also Joan Richardson, *A Natural History of Pragmatism*, and Levin, *The Poetics of Transition*. Curiously, such contemporaries as Wyndham Lewis were more likely to cite Stein as a "time-child" within the vitalist "time cult" (*Time and Western Man*, 55).

Innumerable studies have assessed James's distinctively "American" brand of philosophy but not the internationalist theories that he contributed to under the diffuse prerogatives of vitalism. Even those who examine the cosmopolitan climate of the period tend to adopt the disciplinary preoccupations of American Studies. See Posnock, *The Trial of Curiosity*, and Kuklick, *The Rise of American Philosophy*. Joseph Riddell is one outlier; he considers Stein in the context of Bergson's time philosophy ("Stein and Bergson" in *The Turning Word*).

34. Habit "demands first a decomposition and then a recomposition of the whole action" (Bergson, *Matter and Memory*, 80) and in the process would seem to reorganize itself every time a person receives new perceptions. What goes by the name of habit is only one part of a multiply jointed process in which the details of our senses are ordered. Objects are recognized and tied to a memorial precedent, and the past is made use of in the present. The body navigates objects by sweeping them up into patterns of engagement and movement. Sensations that are not yet organized or methodically integrated into our perceptual schema are constantly being inputted, and they solicit new actions on the part of the body and petition it to make decisions.

35. A number of critics have tended to accentuate a favorable rather than an antagonistic attitude to habit on James's part. Renée Tursi describes the "modernist paradox of James's richly processive and canny narrative of habit" ("William James's Narrative of Habit," 10), which gives a stabilizing consistency to the operations of spontaneous will, thus preventing experience from overwhelming agents. In "Gertrude Stein, William James, and Habit in the Shadow of War," Olson relies on Joseph Thomas's argument that James considers habit a way to make people feel "at home" in an experience that otherwise remains uncanny (Thomas, "Figures of Habit in William James"). The position that James stakes out is analogous to Bergson's. Their alternating valuation is probably typical of the larger discourse, which oscillates between an appreciative and a critical relation to the phenomenon.

36. Not all critics trump William James's psychological influence on Stein over Freudian psychoanalysis. Ruddick, for example, argues in *Reading Gertrude Stein* that Stein discarded Jamesian pragmatism and submitted to Freud's intellectual influence, which she incorporated unconsciously. In my opinion, though, her evidence is sufficiently scant for one to be skeptical. Stein may have been resistant to certain of James's theoretical commitments, and her writing may also have displayed preoccupations with such Freudian themes as childhood experience, sexuality, and parricide, but the preponderance of evidence suggests that Stein was searching for alternatives to Freudian psychological models throughout her long career as a writer.

37. Derrida links wandering to the experimental attitude associated with aesthetic pursuit. He stresses that the search for beauty in Kant's account requires an "errant" or undelimited purposiveness (a paraphrase of Kant's Latin translation of free beauty, "pulchritudo vaga"), a harmoniousness that is not grounded or explained in a preconceived concept or teleology, hence one that "wanders": "*Vague* [i.e., 'wanders, roams'—Trans] is a movement without its goal, not a movement without goal but without its goal. Vague beauty, the only kind that gives rise to an attribution of pure beauty, is an indefinite errance, without limit. . . . It does not arrive itself at its destination" (Derrida, *The Truth in Painting*, 93). One might say that the search for beauty in sexual partners itself requires errancy.

38. As Stein theorized her practice, portraiture refused to present her subjects "as they were doing anything"; it refused to tell "a story as a story" ("Lectures in America," 297). Instead, it aimed to tell "everything that was inside [everybody] that made them that one" (271) by replicating, as Charles Carmello puts it, "in the movement of words, sentences, and paragraphs the psychological and physical movements of her subjects" ("Reading Gertrude Stein Reading Henry James," 190).

39. Stein describes the development of her portrait practice in "Portraits and Repetition," one of the pieces in "Lectures in America": "I was gradually finding out listening and talking at the same time that is realizing the existence of living being actually existing did not have in it any element of remembering and so the time of existing was not the same as in the novels that were soothing" (297).

40. Stein claims in *The Autobiography of Alice B. Toklas* that despite her regarding Henry James "quite definitely as her forerunner," she only began reading him in later years and "was not interested in him" (78) before. Like a number of anecdotes she delivers, the timeline she presents turns out to be misleading. Stein refers to James's *Wings of the Dove* in her unpublished novel *Q.E.D.* (254), written in 1903, very early in her writing career. For other examples of misrepresentation or outright distortion in *The Autobiography*, see Morgan, "The Embryography of Alice B. Toklas," 315. Despite the possible fact-bending, we might regard Stein's claim to "read" James "only very lately" metaphorically, as a reference to an increasingly conscious and deliberative process that commenced when she began to recognize him as a "father." For an account of the rhetorical difficulties of construing the claims in *The Autobiography* as fact, see Johnson, "Narratologies of Pleasure," 590. See also Galow's "Gertrude Stein's *Everybody's Autobiography* and the Art of Contradictions," which details Stein's cultivation of textual contradiction in her lesser-known autobiographical work, *Everybody's Autobiography*.

41. In "Transatlantic Interview," Stein explains that Shakespeare's sonnets do not express his own thoughts; they recreate the opinions of others: "Shakespeare never expressed any feelings of his own in those sonnets. They have too much smoothness. He did not feel 'This is my emotion, I will write it down.' If it is your own feeling, one's words have a fullness and violence" (19). I take her to be suggesting that Shakespeare is working through subject matter that is in a sense already written. The thematic focus is on certain typical situations.

42. We might note how much recognizing a coincidence has an affinity in its structure to the appreciations associated with aesthetic experience. Judgments of taste are also hard to anticipate and can only be determined a posteriori, after the object or exhibition has been experienced. As Kant says, natural beauty emerges *as if* it were ordered, but the harmonies that it presents cannot be treated as ordered: "we do not posit the causes of this form in a will" (*Critique of Judgment* 1.10.220). It is no wonder that Stein uses the concept of a coincidence to explore the potential harmonies or purposive structure of James's aesthetic compositions.

43. In Bergson's terms, each action is embedded in a larger whole, which may be invisible to the eye but which makes itself felt in the vector or directionality of the action and its subsequent iterations. Actions emerge from serial patterns or habits, as well as other, more intangible elements of our past, such as the potentialities or spiritual force at work in our own duration. Some of these patterns and potentialities may be extremely old. A person's actions reveal not only the individual history of the actor, but her or his

species history as well, whether it is registered consciously or unconsciously. As he says, "Doubtless we think with only a small part of our past, but it is with our entire past, including the original bent of our soul, that we desire, will and act," and he argues that our impulses have within them "the condensation of the history that we have lived from our birth," as well as "prenatal dispositions" (*Creative Evolution*, 5).

44. In her portrait of Henry James, Stein refers several times to an experimental translation she had attempted of the French poet Georges Hugnet, "Before the Flowers of Friendship Faded Friendship Faded," describing it as a "coincidence" ("Henry James," 149). The title references the very act of anticipation or presentiment that she experienced when translating his work. Indeed, the looseness of her rendering and her desire for equal billing with Hugnet caused the souring in her relationship to him to which her title alludes. For a fuller account of this episode, see Watson, *Prepare for Saints*, 116–121. Before the overt signs of a subsiding friendship come into sight, some rearrangement of forces has already taken place that invisibly prepares the ground for its waning.

45. Stein was disposed to reference Emerson "casually," revealing a suggestive familiarity with his ideas about character. In *The Autobiography of Alice B. Toklas*, for instance, she refers to Emerson apropos of the "american system of education" (152) at a dinner table conversation she reported having with Bertrand Russell. Emerson's point in the essay "Fate," in which he comments on the "oblique and causal" way that accidents unfold, is that even painful and significant events—the loss of his son, for example—do not necessarily draw him closer to experience. The avenues of access to all experience, grief included, are indirect. "In specifying his inability to get something nearer," Stanley Cavell suggests by way of commentary, "he is leaving a direction open" (*Emerson's Transcendental Etudes*, 244). In the essay from which I take Cavell's remark (whose own title "Henry James Reading Emerson Reading Shakespeare" presents notable coincidences with Stein's writings on James), he goes on to argue that for Emerson the revelations of a text are indirect expressions of character. In this context, we might note Stein's own indirections. Although her mention of Emerson is en passant, an accidental turn in a conversation, in another respect it is fateful. It underscores the multiple indirect connections that draw Emerson into the orbit of Stein's other vitalist influences. For the very encroachments of fate on character that obsess Emerson resonate with Henry James, whose treatment of language and character Stein also calls "abstract."

46. Stein uses comedy to create paradox, which helps her undermine her own claims. Her effort to treat James's literary trajectory as a "coincidence" or to refer to the relation between her translation of George Hugnet's poetry and its original as a "coincidence" is equally question begging. As regards James, it is well known that he pursued a career as a writer by studiously avoiding an enlistment in the Civil War. More to the point, his own métier hardly seems an apt demonstration of a latent masculine doughtiness and martial intelligence. His writing tends rather to the urbane, polished, and *raffiné*, and focuses principally on female protagonists and unengaged men. For that matter, the conflicts he stages in his novels seem rather like elaborate examples of conflict avoidance. For an account of Stein's humor in another difficult experimental piece, *Tender Buttons*, see Schmitz, *Of Huck and Alice*.

47. Gallagher argues that the form of speculation to which military historians were prone presents the possibility that skill and planning can change events, taking for granted

that history does not obey rule-based prescriptions but rather hinges on the genius of an individual who can "bring great forces to bear in unexpected ways" ("The Formalism of Military History," 29).

48. Critics have not necessarily ignored what I am calling the "liveliness" of Stein's characters. But they tend to link her characters' expressions of animation to Stein's primitivist values, which offer black experience as a vital antidote to the mundane routines of civilization. See Michael North, who suggests that Stein's "identification with Africa replaced identification with countries and families whose traditions seemed stifling," thus enabling her to enjoy "the freedom of living outside the law" ("Modernism's African Mask," 278). See also Susanna Pavloska, who argues that Stein's primitivism does not seek a return to "an earlier form of life" but rather, in dialectical fashion, chases after a corrective to modernity: primitivism is "the antithesis of such nostalgia, as a way to force a revolutionary rupture with the past" (*Modern Primitives*, 18). I would suggest, however, that Stein treats routines and habits as themselves conduits of primitive experience.

49. In the beginning, the narrator provides a description of Melanctha's friend Rose: "the sullen, childish, cowardly, black Rosie grumbled and fussed and howled and made herself to be an abomination and like a simple beast" ("Melanctha," 59). Dark skin brings associations of stupidity and beastliness, or else aggressiveness, in Melanctha's especially dark-skinned father, who is described as virile and fierce. The baseline characteristics that Stein associates with African American racial types deserve scrutiny. Even determining that normative average, however, is not easily done given her emphasis on the exception. The narrator frequently makes racial generalizations only to qualify or undermine them: "Rose was never joyous with the earth-born, boundless joy of negroes. Hers was just ordinary, any sort of woman laughter" (60).

50. Taylor grants comedy critical power as a literary form and suggests that Stein fabricates a story that delights in its defeated heroine's "tenacious resistance to coopted discourses, both her own and those of the narration" (*The Tragedy and Comedy of Resistance*, 169). Even so, she thinks 'Melanctha' compares unfavorably with Stein's later novella, *Ida*, which succeeds in revealing a "fearful critique of what ["Melanctha"] leaves out: the tragically divided social world hovering behind a comically unfulfilled utopian mode" (169).

51. McCabe recounts Chaplin's own encounter with Stein in the 1930s, in which she lauded his early gestural films. This is Chaplin telling the story: "She would like to see me in a movie just walking up the street and turning a corner, then another corner, and another" (quoted in Sitney, *Modernist Montage*, 153). The remark makes clear how closely Stein understood the connection between repetition and comedy.

52. It is worth acknowledging Stein's risky and disconcerting alignment between comic form and racial typology. There is more than a hint of minstrelsy in what I am calling a "comic representation." Indeed, the story itself, based on an earlier autobiographical story about a lesbian triangle, is a symbolic form of blackface. For a larger context concerning modernist racial masquerade, see North, *The Dialect of Modernism*; Pavloska, *Modern Primitives*; and Torgovnick, *Gone Primitive*.

As Sianne Ngai points out, the comedy at stake in depictions of racialized subjects has all too often conjoined expressions of animation with a correlative inference of the characters' automation. The trait or feeling that she names "animatedness" and defines as an "'agitation' that is quickly stilled" (*Ugly Feelings*, 90) serves to empty out the black subject's agency, autonomy, and control. Clearly, Stein does not simply abandon the racial stereotypes and clichés around animated bodies, but perhaps one can count her among Ngai's examples of writers and artists who "generate unanticipated social meanings and effects" (125), principally by recognizing a surplus of animation that undermines racist representations. I propose that expressions of animation on the part of Stein's characters present eruptions of "unaccounted-for autonomy" (117) that emerge out of nature itself and modify existing power relations. For an account of the complexity and ambiguity of minstrelsy as a social form, see also Lott, *Love and Theft.*

53. As Nieland argues, Bergsonian comedy corrects and normalizes eccentric or mildly deviant social behavior to preserve a "vitally human" social order over and against the "fixity, and slumbering habits" of animals (*Feeling Modern*, 230). Nieland makes much of Bergson's assertion that "the comic does not exist outside the pale of what is strictly *human*" ("Laughter," 62), which implies that any comic representation that impresses on us a resemblance to animals or machines is merely apparent and illusory. Nieland refers to the work as "a sort of modernist biopolitics of comedy" (*Feeling Modern*, 239) and casts Bergson as a sentinel of the humanist tradition. He suggests that, like Aristotle, Bergson makes a claim for laughter as a sign of a distinctively human capacity for reflection, thus separating man as a political animal (*bios*) from the larger or more general ambit of life (*zo*).

54. For an account of modernist deadpan, specifically in the work of Nathaniel West and Djuna Barnes, see Nieland, *Feeling Modern*, 195–249.

55. For Bergson, any mechanism is just the piecemeal organization of matter set up so that it cannot change without destroying some essential function that it performs. In this respect, it does not differ from the organization of living substances. See Bergson's *Creative Evolution*, 10, 302. The real difference is that when matter changes, it can be changed back, while life does not have this luxury and disperses into nonlife the moment its singular organization breaks apart in any significant way. I would argue that complex living organisms do not pass away because they mime a matterlike state doggedly arranged to perform a mechanical task. After all, the machinery of matter, though vulnerable to malfunction, can be said to have a certain inward transposability that allows it to be repaired: one can substitute one part for another malfunctioning part. When matter changes into another form, it can also change back. Life, however, ceases precisely because it cannot do this—because, despite its plastic nature, it is susceptible to irretrievable decomposition.

56. Bergson suggests that matter has its own duration, "almost vanishing, but not nothing" (*Creative Evolution*, 201), which means, in part, that it betrays liveliness comparable to what is found in psychic and living systems.

57. For a philosophical exposition that traces Bergson's evolution away from dualistic claims and toward monism in his late work, granting duration to both matter and life, see Deleuze, *Bergsonism*, 35.

58. In *Creative Evolution*, Bergson clarifies that "individuality admits of any number of degrees and that it is not fully realized anywhere, even in man" (12). Life may tend toward variation without repetition, but this is just one aim or tendency, thwarted by an obverse necessity, to maintain and reproduce certain structures.

59. Darwin, incidentally, does not regard laughter as wholly distinct from animal behavior. See *The Expression of the Emotions in Man and Animals*, 356. Of all the expres-

sions, Darwin thinks of blushing "to be the most strictly human" (358) because it requires self-consciousness.

60. Carole Anne Taylor suggests that Stein disrupts the melodramatic mode with a "flatly assertive description of [Melanctha's] actual death [that] avoids any reference at all to how Melanctha feels beyond her clinical symptoms. From a perspective brutally outside Melanctha, it relates the action of melodrama without any of its characteristically affective layer" (*The Tragedy and Comedy of Resistance*, 164).

NOTES TO CHAPTER 4

1. Deleuze refutes the claim that Bergson's concern with the ontological foundation of language was not "particularly important in [his] work" (*Bergsonism*, 57). Instead, he suggests that "Bergson analyzes language in the same way as memory" (57).

2. Eliot uses the word "relations" to refer to the number of aspects under which a thing may be viewed or experienced. See, for instance, the following statement from Eliot's dissertation, referring to the identity of objects: "the reality of the object does not lie in the object itself, but in the extent of the relations which the object possesses without significant falsification of itself. These relations are all different points of view upon the object—i.e. they relate different aspects to a single point of reference" (*Knowledge and Experience in the Philosophy of F. H. Bradley*, 91).

3. See, in particular, Derrida's preface to the volume *Dissemination*, called "Outwork, Prefacing," in which he analyzes the "dispersal" of meaning that occurs as one of the effects of dissemination (17).

4. For Eliot, a speaker appropriates other people's voices (or at least components and elements of their voices) for certain pragmatic and expressive uses, relying on their associative linkages when they are imported into a new context. David Chinitz tracks the fabric of allusions to popular songs in Eliot's work, which, he suggests, offer the poet a "usable reservoir of phrases, symbols, and situations" to represent emotional events in his life and, crucially, to anticipate them before they happen in the flesh. Through the use of such material, Eliot reveals that emotions are "themselves a part of culture—not 'timeless givens which sprout from the soil of an eternal "inner" self'" ("In the Shadows," 462). By appropriating certain prescribed conventions for expressing feeling, Chinitz by no means "impl[ies] that Eliot falsified his feelings, for the creation of feeling is a *function* of culture—to which Eliot, like anyone else, was subject" (462). For Chinitz, the question is not why he makes use of such voices and material at all, because such appropriation is inevitable, but which patterns he selects and for what reason.

5. Habib suggests that Eliot's laughter is a "self-distancing gesture which knows its own futility. . . . Laughter is the visible apex of irony, compelled to stand as a spectator over its own complicity with what it rejects" (*The Early T. S. Eliot and Western Philosophy*, 69).

6. Lewis links the cult of personality to democratic politics: "When people are encouraged, as happens in a democratic society, to believe that they wish 'to express their personality,' the question at once arises as to what their personality *is*. For the most part, if investigated, it would be found that they had none" (*The Art of Being Ruled*, 164).

7. Lewis excoriated the logic of expression that touted the self's authentic emotional core because, according to Justus Nieland, its contours were already, to a greater or lesser degree, mediated by the public sphere. He feared the standardized social reflexes that

structured sympathetic emotional response along contagious and all too predictable lines. Nieland proposes that we should look for expressions of public feeling, especially in Lewis's early work, that are capable of producing surprise by virtue of their "eccentric" character: "To ascribe Lewis's fear of eccentric feeling and the nondifferentiation it entails to fascist paranoia, aristorcratic disdain, or the hysteria of one of modernism's many besieged masculinities is a powerful temptation and no doubt merited in part. Such claims, though risk overlooking Lewis's prescient hunch that eccentric feeling is, finally, the affective reflex of a mediated public sphere and its transformations of the human personality" (*Feeling Modern*, 64). Nieland suggests that Lewis seeks out an emotionally rich experience of life-in-public when—because of the emergent strangeness of certain social settings—the affective bonds at issue succeed in disorganizing discursive constructions of identity (*Feeling Modern*, 51–66) and thus allowing a measure of freedom from what he calls elsewhere "modernity's ossified political formations" (25). By this account, Lewis and other modernists do not celebrate privacy or interiority, which at best offers "meager compensations of freedom and authenticity" (28).

8. Lewis exploits a metaphor akin to the marionette in *The Art of Being Ruled*, where, following Goethe, he makes a distinction between two types of people, "Puppets" and "Natures," the former reserved for "machines, playing a part" (135) and the latter for the individuals whom they imitate. He asserts that the majority of people are empty siphons, the average mind conditioned by a response to stimulus much as J. B. Watson's behaviorism contends. Ophir offers an account of Lewis's complex relationship to behaviorist psychology. In the twenties, he "had embraced behaviorist psychology as an adequate account of the majority of human beings" ("Toward a Pitiless Fiction," 99), but he was alarmed at the ideological uses to which its ideas were put as behaviorism was co-opted by industry to fashion exemplary workers. In principle, I would suggest, *The Art of Being Ruled* preserves the possibility that human beings can disrupt the chain between stimulus and response by inserting words and speech, which are the "enemy of behaviour" with its dogma of mere action (394–395).

9. Eliot is riffing off of Arthur Symons, whose inspired characterization of Alfred Jarry's symbolist farce, *Ubu Roi*, gives this poem its provocation: "a generation which has exhausted every intoxicant, every soluble preparation of the artificial, may well seek a last sensation in the wire-pulled passions, the wooden faces of marionettes, and by a further illusion, of marionettes who are living people; living people pretending to be those wooden images of life which pretend to be living people" (*Studies in Seven Arts*, 374–355; cited in *Inventions of the March Hare*, 103).

10. In Zamir's account, expressions of seeming spontaneity do not result from a self-enclosed subject's authentic yearnings. Dolls bring us back to a rudimentary sense of self "in which animation and personalization are momentarily put on and then suspended" ("Puppets," 397).

11. Eliot occasionally mixes metaphors. He states, for instance, that the mind is a "receptacle for seizing and storing up numberless feelings, phrases, images" ("Tradition and the Individual Talent" in *Selected Essays*, 8), but he also refers to it as a medium whose function is to digest and transmute such relations—hence, as an organizing agent. Whether the mind does or does not contain such images, it gets its singularity from its rearranging and connecting particulars, exerting itself in an ongoing act of making. In *Matter and*

Memory, which Eliot might have been thinking of, Bergson explicitly rejects the view of the mind as a receptacle that stores or represents images at second hand (25). Perhaps, in this respect, Eliot is arguing against Bergson, though one sees Bergson's influence on his conception of the mind as an organ for the selection of images, which is explicit in the metaphor of a medium. "Of the Selection of Images" is, not by accident, the first section of *Matter and Memory*, in which Bergson argues that the brain selects images rather than reexhibiting and storing them in some putatively interior space.

12. See Eagleton, *Literary Theory*, 34–39. For a deflationary account of Eliot's antiliberal political commitments, see Morrison's chapter, "The Poetics of Failure," in *The Poetics of Fascism*.

13. For Du Bois, double consciousness is bound to a logic of social recognition: "After the Egyptian and Indian, the Greek and Roman, the Teuton and Mongolian, the Negro is a sort of seventh son, born with a veil, and gifted with second-sight in this American world,—a world which yields him no true self-consciousness, but only lets him see himself through the revelation of the other world. It is a peculiar sensation, this double-consciousness, this sense of always looking at one's self through the eyes of others, of measuring one's soul by the tape of a world that looks on in amused contempt and pity" (*The Souls of Black Folk*, 215). He implies that blacks, wishing to receive acknowledgment of their humanity or social claims from whites, accept instead an image of their own degraded or deidealized selves, which they are forced to identify with. They may have "second sight," and, with it, the capacity to see further into the social world than whites do because they can anticipate the predictable character of the responses to them and because they intuit the contradictions in the myth in which their social status is shrouded; because, however, they lack social recognition, they can only live in a fragmented or divided state. Du Bois's desire for social recognition for African Americans requires that they need to stake their claim to equality on the already established grounds of the majority, their ostensible betters.

14. The marionettes' apparent unawareness of their status as marionettes, their absorption in their role (understood in Michael Fried's sense as a self-forgetting that is associated with the beholder's own erasure) is an indication not of their authenticity but of their meager and reduced existence. In this respect, Eliot violates the normative values behind Fried's apparent contrast between absorption and theatricality. See Fried's *Absorption and Theatricality*, 31, 103–104. As Robert Pippin understands the difference, absorption consists in the "complete identification of a subject with the role or activity undertaken," while theatricality entails the performance of "an activity controlled and directed by an anticipation of what others expect to occur" ("Authenticity in Painting," 578) and is linked to a form of inauthenticity and mannered behavior. But while Eliot might accept that such pretense, in which one plays for effect and is less than fully committed to one's role, is a false mode of being, theatricality is always a great deal more unstable and open-ended than Fried allows. See my section "Theater of Affirmation" in Chapter 2 for a further account.

15. According to David Rosen, Eliot uses superannuated figures in his early poetry to suggest "knowledge without illusions" ("T. S. Eliot and the Lost Youth of Modern Poetry," 493), gaining authority from such world-weary attitudes. Rosen criticizes Eliot for his spurious attempt at sophistication while still a young man. By doing so, he charges, Eliot's early poetry rejects "a developmental understanding of self" that requires "both a force-

ful insistence on the poet's own maturity and a concealment of his past" (493). I would suggest, all the same, that the refusal to explore personal history is not aimed at negating developmental models of psychology; rather, it gives central place to the situationally responsive aspects of character.

16. See Bergson, *The Creative Mind*: "stating the [philosophical] problem is not simply uncovering, it is inventing. Discovery, or uncovering, has to do with what already exists, actually or virtually; it was therefore certain to happen sooner or later. Invention gives being to what did not exist; it might never have happened" (51). For an account of Bergson's theory of intuition as a creative method, see Deleuze, *Bergsonism*, 15–17.

17. For the relation between what William James calls "transitive thought" and feeling, see his *Principles of Psychology* 1.243–245.

18. Eliot to Eudo C. Mason (19 April 1945): "I am surprised to think that any indications of Christian tradition were present in *Prufrock*. I was certainly quite ignorant and unconscious of them myself, and at the time, or at least before the poem was finished, was entirely a Bergsonian" (quoted in *Inventions of the March Hare*, 411).

19. Eliot's lyric models tend to separate themselves from the narrative and dramatic forms of writing associated with the novel and the theater respectively. Some of Eliot's postmodern critics presume that Eliot did not give much credence to such distinctions. For instance, Jennifer Sorensen Emery-Peck suggests that Eliot was more interested in narrative modes than scholars have tended to foreground, which is important because it confirms his incorporation of popular genres and female or working-class voices into his work, disturbing the picture of Eliot as a genteel high modernist. She cites the pub scene in *The Waste Land* as an example, "mixing genres, genders, classes, and cultures in the production of the poem" ("Tom and Vivien Eliot Do Narrative in Different Voices," 332). It seems to me, though, that the pub section of the poem is not concerned with the depiction of ongoing action that gives narrative its importance for presenting character. If at all, the episode presents analogues in drama (always a perennial interest of Eliot's), though I would suggest that it is still best thought of within a lyric framework. Eliot juxtaposes the voices that emerge in such episodes with other voices in the poem, providing emotional analogues in corresponding scenes.

20. Emery-Peck cites James Phelan, who suggests that lyric modes are "less invested in character and event than in thoughts, attitudes, beliefs, emotions, and specific situations" ("Rhetorical Literary Ethics and Lyric Narrative," 635). I would like to suggest, in contrast, that lyric for Eliot is implicitly or explicitly intent on presenting eventlike situational facets of experience to reference psychological dispositions that flesh out character in distinctive ways.

21. Although he rejects the possibility that the self is constructed by an accumulation of points of view, Bergson, like Eliot, valorizes sympathetic states of mind, intuitive efforts to "identify myself with the person of the hero himself." This is an "indivisible feeling" that "cannot be perceived from without, being internal by definition" (*Creative Mind*, 160).

22. For an account, see the volume of essays, Burwick and Douglass, eds., *Crisis in Modernism*, and Grogin, *The Bergsonian Controversy in France*.

23. See especially Douglass, *Bergson, Eliot, and American Literature*; Gillies, "Virginia Woolf"; and Habib, *The Early T. S. Eliot and Western Philosophy*. For a broader context, see Ellmann's *The Poetics of Impersonality* and Levenson's *Genealogy of Modernism*.

24. On the question of whether Eliot had met T. E. Hulme, see Schuchard, "Did Eliot Know Hulme?"

25. The critics who foreground Eliot's growing rift with Bergsonism in a purely cultural or political context do not capture the full dimensions of his disaffection. It is true that Bergson was at the time of Eliot's initiation into his philosophy being taken into the camp of anarchist leftists such as George Sorel as well as liberal humanists. See Grogin, *The Bergsonian Controversy in France*, 88–93. But as Sanford Schwartz points out, there was a vitalism of the right as well as the vitalism of the left; the former emphasized spiritualism over the materialist values of an industrial society, while the latter promoted the overthrow of anachronistic institutions ("Bergson and the Politics of Vitalism," 278). For instance, the Catholic Revival movement adopted Bergson as an icon, though this obviously did little to endear him to Eliot. Eliot was clearly preoccupied by the company that Bergson kept; his paper responding to the "Relation between Politics and Metaphysics" testifies to that fact. But he would also have been averse to classifying highly speculative matters within any simple political chart.

26. For an account of the complexities of Eliot's philosophical positions, specifically his unorthodox engagement with pragmatism, see Brazeal, "The Alleged Pragmatism of T. S. Eliot." Brazeal offers a useful genealogy of critics' efforts to pin down Eliot's philosophical positions.

27. James would probably agree with the argument Eliot derives from Bradley: that "'a psychological event' can not be torn from its context and be set in a context of other purely psychological events" (*Knowledge and Experience*, 76). In other words, there is no delimited sphere of the psychological that does not gain its consistency from a connection to something beyond the psychological.

28. William James claims that nonsense words or phrases mean because they rely on our prior intimacy with words and grammatical structures. They meld into contexts that we may not be able to specify but which we feel as a vague frame of reference or penumbra of sense surrounding them: "Certain kinds of verbal associate [sic], certain grammatical expectations fulfilled, stand for a good part of our impression that a sentence has a meaning and is dominated by the Unity of one Thought" (*The Principles of Psychology* 1:264). James cites an "aching gap" within our thought that "we cannot yet fill with a definite picture, word, or phrase, but which . . . influences us in an intensely active and determinate psychic way" (1:259). Thus, the associations between our thoughts or memories do not have to be explicit. The gap leads to a variety of psychic effects, such as the feeling of irritation or strain over what has been left unarticulated.

29. Like Virginia Woolf, Eliot insists on an analogical and associative structure of meaning in poetry rather than a strictly referential basis for sense making (where reference defines a formal system of differences). As Woolf notes of *Twelfth Night* (a play Eliot also admired immensely), Shakespeare writes "not with the whole of his mind mobilized and under control but with feelers left flying that sort and play with words so that the trail of a chance word is caught and followed recklessly. From the echo of one word is born another word, for which reason, perhaps, the play seems as we read it to tremble perpetually on the brink of music" ("Twelfth Night at the Old Vic," 45).

30. For a similar effort to shift focus from the human experience of things to the agency or emotional qualities of things themselves, see Bennett, *Vibrant Matter*.

31. Eliot makes a distinction between two kinds of intensity, one emerging from the narrative and more or less capable of being named within it (emotion), and the other, a more evanescent aspect of the poetic rendering (feeling): "The episode of Paolo and Francesca employs a definite emotion, but the intensity of the poetry is something quite different from whatever intensity in the supposed experience it may give the impression of. . . . The difference between art and the event is always absolute" ("Tradition and the Individual Talent" in *Selected Essays*, 8–9).

32. Eliot suggests that the work of art "may be formed out of one emotion, or may be a combination of several; and various feelings, inhering for the writer in particular words or phrases or images, may be added to compose the final result" (9). He holds in special reverence poetry that cultivates feelings rather than emotions, such as in the Bruno Latini section of Dante's *Inferno*: "The last quatrain gives an image, a feeling attaching to an image, which 'came,' which did not develop simply out of what precedes, but which was probably in suspension in the poet's mind until the proper combination arrived for it to add itself to" (8).

33. For a contemporary version of Eliot's distinction between emotion and feeling, see Massumi, *Parables for the Virtual*. For Massumi, an affect or feeling is an emergent intensity, while "an emotion is a subjective content, the sociolinguistic fixing of a the quality of an experience which is from that point onward defined as personal. Emotion is qualified intensity, the conventional, consensual point of insertion of intensity into semantically and semiotically formed progressions, into narrativizable action-reaction circuits, into function and meaning" (28).

34. Even Rives, who presents a sophisticated account of Eliot's distinction between feeling and emotion, offers, to my mind, an unsatisfying formulation of the difference. She aligns feeling with subjective response, "enter[ing] the poet's mind and aid[ing] the creative process" and emotion with the "end" of the "artistic process itself" ("Things That Lie on the Surface," n.p.).

35. For Eliot, a feeling registers multiple implications and effects of any cause. In this respect, it amplifies knowledge. He thinks of such multilevel awareness in theatrical terms: "To say that one part of the mind suffers and another part reflects upon the suffering is perhaps to talk in fictions. But we know that those highly-organized beings who are able to objectify their passions, and as passive spectators to contemplate their joys and torments, are also those who suffer and enjoy the most keenly" (*Knowledge and Experience*, 23).

36. Eliot uses the concept of point of view in ways that are analogous to his use of other terms, such as feeling and tone, as an awareness of how one's observations stand in relation to other implicit frameworks of reference, to sensations, ideas, judgments that hover in the background. Feeling and tone both describe forms of relationality that remove us from the axis that refers exclusively to our position as selves. Centered around one pole (the position that pertains specifically to our body), the outlook we adopt has the capacity to bring into play other poles. Every internal relation we maintain and every point of view we occupy have in principle another context or perspective outside us. Bradley, though an idealist, did not subscribe to the crude schema that asserts that everything is "in" the mind. Nonetheless, he believed that in principle the mind could grant meaning to what is beyond it.

37. For Eliot, perspectivism does not just denote any particular clash of perspective resulting from variations in information, knowledge, or acquaintance with a thing, or disputes about values. The concept implies that the self is necessarily limited in its way of viewing the world because of something private within it—a content, not just a context. In Browning, for instance, the dramatic monologue form presents the psyche as a lockbox. Although the speakers are placed in a distinct social setting, the dramatic monologue fails to depict actual exchange or vocal interaction. The Duke in "My Last Duchess" cannot or will not exceed the purview of his own perspective, while Andrea del Sarto declares that "A man's reach should exceed his grasp" (Browning, *Selected Poetry*, 97), though he remains confronted with an addressee (Lucrezia) just out of his reach, whom he cannot quite make see. The monologue form mirrors this by presenting the speakers themselves only from the outside. Nonetheless, even in Browning, the privacy of a perspective is in some ways factitious. His speakers give away intimations of their character, despite their indifference or insensibility to their audience.

38. For Lacan's account of the Imaginary and its relationship to the "mirror stage" of infant development, see "The Mirror State as Formative of the Function of the I as Revealed in Psychoanalytic Experience" in *Écrits: A Selection*, 1–7.

39. Despite the façade he projects of having an ironic grasp of the elderly woman's seductions, the speaker in "Portrait of a Lady" cannot encapsulate the point of view of the lady he observes without acknowledging it as a reaction against his aloofness. She throws the masklike smile he clings to back at him in a form that makes it excruciatingly awkward to use should he wish it as a defense: "' . . . And youth is cruel, and has no remorse / And smiles at situations which it cannot see.' / I smile, of course, / And go on drinking tea" (*Complete Poems and Plays*, 9). Out of habit, discomfort, or willfulness, it is not clear which, the speaker falls back on his smile, even as it cannot maintain the objectifying distance from her that he wants. Neither the speaker nor the lady can encompass the other's point of view without accepting their mutual vulnerability to the other's interpolations and assessments, even as they stand in a defiant relation to it. Nonetheless, each of their attitudes is dependent on their counterpart's attitude and cannot be separated from it.

40. Ellmann says, for instance, that "we can only really know the self through intuition, and when we pass from intuition to expression we have already compromised with space" (*The Poetics of Impersonality*, 28). Bergson's concern is not principally with the limits of our knowledge but with the kinds of distortion (spatial thinking) that prevent us from recognizing the productive undercurrent of our own personality.

41. Bergson treats the intellect as a faculty whose origin lies in practical life. It, therefore, wishes to impose a practical order on the universe by immobilizing it as a picture, and when does not succeed in finding the order it seeks, it leaves one prone to blaming the universe for one's resulting consciousness of disarray. By Bergson's account, the anomie of modern life—like all practical ideas of disorder—is a "disappointment of a certain expectation, and it does not denote the absence of all order" (*Creative Evolution*, 274). As Deleuze notes, Bergson claims that the appearance of lack comes when we project a false prescriptive schema, imposing a "psychological motive" that guides our interpretation, testifying only that the disorder we perceive corresponds to "the absence of what interests us" (Deleuze, *Bergsonism*, 17). Bergson never wavers from his conviction that the universe

is nascently ordered, with each facet tending toward an immanent state of increasing synchronization and complexity. If we cannot perceive this order, he thought, the deficiency lies with us and not with the universe (*Creative Evolution*, 274). Eliot took to calling this Bergson's "Romanticism" and equated it, in however slapdash a way, with a belief in progress (see Schwartz, "Bergson and the Politics of Vitalism," 295–297). Despite this reductivism, Eliot has a point. Bergson's account says nothing about why we seem to have such vital interest in this projection. He dismisses such ideas as illusions or distortions that we correct for through intuition, and in so doing he ignores their sustained effects. In other words, he places what he calls "practical" beliefs on a different psychological plane from the impersonal events that transpire elsewhere in the universe, disregarding the former and refusing to speak about their consistency as a reality, with its own feedback effects.

42. Bergson does not offer any overt critique of the normative status of values, but one presumes that he would treat such claims with great skepticism, exposing any fixed picture of the world to the same flux that characterizes all purely relational structures. Because Bergson spent very little time speaking about social life as such, with the exception of his book *The Two Sources of Morality and Religion*, which came out in 1932, long after Eliot had written such lyrics as "Prufrock," one must, like Eliot, extrapolate his positions on the basis of his other writings. Even *The Two Sources of Morality and Religion* does not refer to fixed social perspectives, exploring instead mythical structures (the consolidation of past "forms of life") and dynamic forces. This book received a positive review in the *Criterion* while Eliot was editor of the journal. See Thorold's review of *Les Deux Sources de la Morale et de la Religion.*

43. Bradley thought that our social experiences (the accumulation of communal perspectives and relations) themselves construct a kind of reality. In other words, he differs from Bergson in that he treats any subjective alteration of perception or imposition of consciousness as itself "real." Bergson objected to this on several fronts. To borrow a phrase used by Richard Wollheim in a different context, such a view monstrously overpopulates reality. It gives just about any minor delusion or pragmatic mental shortcut some purchase on the real. Bergson also opposed any conception of virtuality conceived of as a dialectic process. Dialectical thinking relies on a specious conception of temporality that constantly evokes the momentary. It also ties the concept of potentiality to the engine of negation, thus distorting the positivity of the virtual. And, finally, Bergson objected to Bradley's idealist commitments. Bradley considers reality a function of the subject's experience—or, to be fair, many subjects who "intend" upon the same object. Bergson is much closer to a kind of realism. He describes his via media between realism and idealism in the introduction to *Matter and Memory*. Bradley, in turn, could accuse Bergson of being a poor psychologist because he treats the intellect as a token aspect of the real.

It is this last, I believe, that finally precipitated Eliot's defection and Wyndham Lewis's jibing contempt for Bergson. Eliot thought that the intellect in all of its aspects must be given a vital, if contained, public function; hence, his inversion of the Bergsonian hierarchy: "It is that the follies and stupidities of the French, no matter how base, express themselves in the form of ideas—Bergsonism itself is an intellectual construction, and the mondaines who attended lectures at the College de France were in a sense using their minds" ("Imperfect Critics" in *The Sacred Wood*, 45–46).

44. Bradley believed that, in principle, the mind could make comprehensive order of the relations beyond it. His account flirts with a totalizing vision of cultural knowledge that, properly incorporated, can come to an endpoint that he called "the Absolute." In his philosophical work, Eliot remained skeptical of such claims, but occasionally his own writings betray a similar fantasy of interpretive control and artistic domination over cultural materials. In "Tradition and the Individual Talent," he suggests that the mind of the poet, more capacious than any private mind, undergoes a development "which abandons nothing *en route*, which does not superannuate either Shakespeare, or Homer, or the rock drawing of the Magdalenian draughtsman" (*Selected Essays*, 6). The idea that these monuments ensure the conformity or coherence of the present with perspectival touchstones from the past constructs history, according to John Zilcosky, as an "endless accumulation" ("Modern Monuments," 29), an "economy" that recoups all forms of loss "without any 'expenditure'" (29). Yet for the most part, Eliot is aware that perspectives do not seamlessly build on one another. One cannot have an impersonal point of view without encompassing other people's resistances to it.

45. Cf. Bergson: "Every image is within certain images and without others; but of the aggregate of images we cannot say that it is within us or without us, since interiority and exteriority are only relations among images" (*Matter and Memory*, 25).

46. Eliot's intellectual premises are, as Richard Wollheim mentions in passing, indebted to William James's neutral monism ("Eliot and F. H. Bradley," 177–178). James's idea is that the difference between consciousness and what consciousness is *of* depends solely on how it functions or is used in a given context. There is no aboriginal difference between what philosophers sometimes (misleadingly) call a mental image and the thing outside the mind to which it points (James, *Essays in Radical Empiricism*, 9–11). Consciousness simply consists of the world that it experiences; it does not add any representation, any additional mental image or conception, that is not already "there." If the resulting perspective appears delusional—if it is distorted or exaggerated—that is because the perspective has lost track of some of the relations that situate it. Nonetheless, the resulting vision is, as Hugo Münsterberg would put it, "out there" in a distorted world, not in the mind. William James reverts to Münsterberg to flesh out his own ideas: "The objects of dreamers and hallucinated persons are wholly without general validity. But even were they centaurs and golden mountains, they still would be 'off there,' in fairy land, and not 'inside' of ourselves" (quoted in *Essays in Radical Empiricism*, 20).

47. As Levenson has argued, *The Waste Land* goes to great lengths to suggest discrete voices that cohere across syntactic and contextual elements, only to disrupt them and have them infiltrated by other voices. "In any given line," from the first verse paragraph, he comments, "we may find a stylistic feature, which will bind it to a subsequent or previous line, in this way suggesting a continuous speaker, or at least making such a speaker plausible. But we have no single common feature connecting all the lines. . . . And these overlapping principles of similarity undermine the attempt to draw boundaries around distinct speaking subjects" (*Genealogy of Modernism*, 170–171). In so doing, Eliot signals that he is not interested in dramatizing narratively sustained fictional individuals.

48. For some of the ways that literature retains the importance of sound in its own sense-making, see Garrett Stewart's phonemic analyses of poetry in *Reading Voices*, which he refers to as phonotexts.

NOTES TO AFTERWORD

1. For treatment of the intricate intellectual context within which the two brothers operated, see Posnock's *The Trial of Curiosity*. Posnock examines the relationship between William and Henry James through the prism of literary pragmatism.

2. For the full history of Bergson's attraction for the Syndicalist left and its tug of war with Catholics over the consequences of Bergsonism, see Grogin, *The Bergsonian Controversy in France*.

3. Hulme, like many of the modernist critics and writers most interested in Bergson, was attracted by the tendency of the later Bergson to emphasize the "impersonal" forces of duration that run like a current through all life and enable "creative evolution" (*Speculations*, 212).

4. For an account of Lewis's fascination with the body as a mechanical prosthesis, see Burstein, "Waspish Segments." As evidence of Lewis's attitude toward the organic constitution of public life, see Nieland, *Feeling Modern*, 51–52.

5. Burstein quotes Roger Caillois on insect mimicry and applies it to Lewis's celebration of frozen life ("Waspish Segments," 154–156).

6. For Lawrence's debt to nineteenth-century physiological psychology, see Ryan, *Thinking without Thinking in the Victorian Novel*, 175–178. For an account of the connections Lawrence draws between the unconscious and nondeliberative movement associated with occult psychic energy, see Cowan, "Lawrence's Myth of the Body."

7. See Bergson's *Duration and Simultaneity*.

8. See Wittgenstein: "If you are led by psycho-analysis to say that really you thought so and so or that really your motive was so and so, this is not a matter of discovery, but of persuasion. In a different way you could have been persuaded of something different. Of course, if psycho-analysis cures your stammer, it cures it, and that is an achievement. One thinks of certain results of psycho-analysis as a discovery Freud made, as apart from something persuaded to you by a psycho-analyst, and I wish to say this is not the case" (*Lectures and Conversations on Aesthetics, Psychology, and Religious Belief*, 27).

9. See Deleuze, *Cinema 1: The Movement Image* and *Cinema 2: The Time Image*.

10. Hansen argues that "the body, in conjunction with the various apparatuses for rendering information perceptive, gives form to or *in-forms* information" (*New Philosophy for New Media*, 10).

11. Fredric Jameson wonders whether Bergsonian time is a precursor to contemporary posthistorical systems, arguing that Deleuze's version of posthistorical thought succeeds in replicating "one of the most fundamental rhythms of capitalism, namely its reduction to the present, rather than constituting a critique of it" (*A Singular Modernity*, 194). He goes on to assert that Deleuze's concept of the virtual (which he inherits from Bergson) is a "new and different way of making the present self-sufficient and independent from those dimensions of the past and future from which the earlier concept of the schizophrenic also wished to escape" (194).

12. For the larger context of this debate, see Jones, "The Eleatic Bergson," 22–23.

13. For an account of some of the philosophical ambiguities surrounding the ontological status of the virtual in Deleuze and its relation to actualization, we might consult Žižek's *Organs without Bodies*. Žižek sees Deleuze's concept of virtuality as straddling two models that are mutually incompatible. Each has its own corresponding conception

of what constitutes a productive condition. I would suggest that Deleuze inherits the ambiguity from Bergson. On the one hand, for Deleuze the proper transcendental space is [conceived of as] the virtual space of the multiple singular potentialities, of 'pure' impersonal singular gestures, affects, and perceptions that are not yet the gestures-affects-perceptions *of* a preexisting, stable, and self-identical subject" (19–20). And on the other hand, "The proper site of production is *not* the virtual space as such, but, rather, the very *passage* from it to constituted reality, the collapse of the multitude and its oscillations into one reality—[where] production is fundamentally a limitation of the open space of virtualities, the determination and negation of the virtual multitude" (20).

14. For Bergson's exploration of telepathy, see his "'Phantasms of the Living' and Psychical Research" in *Mind-Energy*, 75–103. For an account of paramnesia or what we now commonly call "déjà vu," see his "Memory of the Present and False Recognition" in *Mind-Energy*, 134–185.

15. For this provocative history, see Thrailkill, *Affecting Fictions*, 225–234. For a full record of William James's experiments in psychical research, see his *Essays in Psychical Research*.

16. Still, the distance between W. B. Yeats and more secular modernists may be less than is commonly thought. For an account that examines Yeats's interests in fairies as evidence of a larger belief in the vital or animistic state of the world, see Mattar, "Yeats, Fairies, and the New Animism." Mattar suggests that Yeats developed his animism as a means of combatting scientific materialism and giving central place to astonishment and reverence in human encounters with the lifeworld.

BIBLIOGRAPHY

Ackroyd, Peter. *T. S. Eliot.* London: Hamish Hamilton, 1984.

Adorno, Theodor. *Aesthetic Theory.* Ed. Gretel Adorno and Rolf Tiedemann. Trans. Robert Hullot-Kentor. Minneapolis: University of Minnesota Press, 1997.

———. *Minima Moralia: Reflections from Damaged Life.* Trans. E. F. N. Jephcott. London: New Left Books, 1974.

Adorno, Theodor W., and Max Horkheimer. *Dialectic of Enlightenment.* Trans. John Cumming. New York: Continuum, 1982.

Allen, Garland E. "Mechanism, Vitalism and Organicism in Late Nineteenth and Twentieth-Century Biology: The Importance of Historical Context." *Studies in History and Philosophy of Biological and Biomedical Sciences* 36 (2005): 261–283.

Allport, Gordon. *Personality: A Psychological Interpretation.* New York: Henry Holt, 1937.

Altieri, Charles. *The Particulars of Rapture: An Aesthetics of the Affects.* Ithaca, N.Y.: Cornell University Press, 2003.

———. *Subjective Agency: A Theory of First-Person Expressivity and Its Social Implications.* Oxford, UK: Blackwell, 1994.

American Heritage Dictionary. 5th ed. New York: Houghton Mifflin Harcourt, 2011.

Antliff, Mark. *Inventing Bergson: Cultural Politics and the Parisian Avant-Garde.* Princeton, N.J.: Princeton University Press, 1993.

Aristotle. "Nichomachean Ethics." In *The Basic Works of Aristotle*, ed. Richard McKeon, 935–1126. New York: Random House, 1941.

———. "Poetics." In *The Basic Works of Aristotle*, ed. Richard McKeon, 1455–1487. New York: Random House, 1941.

Barish, Jonas. *The Antitheatrical Prejudice.* Berkeley: University of California Press, 1985.

Batson, Daniel, and John Darley. "From Jerusalem to Jericho: A Study of Situational and Dispositional Variables in Helping Behavior." *Journal of Personality and Social Psychology* 27 (1973): 100–108.

Benhabib, Selya. *Situating the Self: Gender, Community, and Postmodernism in Contemporary Ethics.* New York: Routledge, 1992.

Benjamin, Walter. *Illuminations: Essays and Reflections.* Ed. Hannah Arendt. Trans. Harry Zohn. New York: Schocken, 1968.

Bennett, Jane. *Vibrant Matter: A Political Ecology of Things.* Durham, N.C.: Duke University Press, 2010.

Bergson, Henri. *Creative Evolution.* Trans. Arthur Mitchell. Mineola, N.Y.: Dover, 1998.

———. *The Creative Mind: An Introduction to Metaphysics.* Trans. Mabelle L. Andison. New York: Citadel Press, 1992.

———. *Duration and Simultaneity: Bergson and the Einsteinian Universe.* Trans. Leon Jacobson. Manchester, UK: Clinamen Press, 1999.

———. *An Introduction to Metaphysics.* Trans. T. E. Hulme. Indianapolis: Hackett, 1999.
———. "Laughter." In *Comedy*, ed. Wylie Sypher, 60–190. Baltimore: Johns Hopkins University Press, 1986. Originally published as *Le rire: Essai sur la signification du comique.* Paris: Félix Alcan, 1900.
———. *Matter and Memory.* Trans. N. M. Paul and W. S. Palmer. New York: Zone, 1991.
———. Mind-Energy. Trans. H. Wildon Carr. Greenpoint, Conn.: Greenwood Press, 1920.
———. "On the Pragmatism of William James." In *Creative Mind: An Introduction to Metaphysics*, 209–219. New York: Carol, 1992.
———. *The Two Sources of Morality and Religion.* Trans. R. Ashley Audra and Cloudesley Brereton. Notre Dame, Ind.: University of Notre Dame Press, 1986.
———. *Time and Free Will: An Essay on the Immediate Data of Consciousness.* Trans. F. L. Pogson. Mineola, N.Y.: Dover, 2001.
Berman, Jessica. *Modernist Commitments: Ethics, Politics, and Transnational Modernism.* New York: Columbia University Press, 2011.
———. *Modernist Fiction, Cosmopolitanism, and the Politics of Community.* Cambridge: Cambridge University Press, 2001.
Bernstein, J. M. *Adorno: Disenchantment and Ethics.* Cambridge: Cambridge University Press, 2001.
———. *Against Voluptuous Bodies: Late Modernism and the Meaning of Painting.* Stanford, Calif.: Stanford University Press, 2006.
———. *The Fate of Art: Aesthetic Alienation from Kant to Derrida and Adorno.* University Park: Pennsylvania State University Press, 1992.
Bersani, Leo. *The Freudian Body: Psychoanalysis and Art.* New York: Columbia University Press, 1986.
———. *A Future for Astyanax: Character and Desire in Literature.* New York: Columbia University Press, 1984.
Blackman, Lisa. "Affect, Relationality and the 'Problem of Personality.'" *Theory, Culture & Society* 25:1 (2008): 23–47.
Blackmer, Corinne E. "African Masks and the Arts of Passing in Gertrude Stein's 'Melanctha' and Nella Larsen's *Passing.*" *Journal of the History of Sexuality* 4:2 (October 1993): 230–263.
Blackmur, Richard P. *Studies in Henry James.* New York: New Directions, 1983.
Bonney, William W. "Suspended." In *Conrad in the Twenty-First Century: Contemporary Approaches and Perspectives*, ed. Carola M. Kaplan, Peter Lancelot Mallios, and Andrea White, 175–194. New York: Routledge, 2005.
Bramen, Carrie Tirado. "James, Pragmatism, and the Realist Ideal." In *The Cambridge History of the American Novel*, ed. Leonard Cassuto, Clare Virginia Eby, and Benjamin Reiss, 304–321. Cambridge: Cambridge University Press, 2011.
Brazeal, Gregory. "The Alleged Pragmatism of T. S. Eliot." *Philosophy and Literature* 30:1 (2006): 248–264.
Brennan, Teresa. *The Transmission of Affect.* Ithaca, N.Y.: Cornell University Press, 2004.
Bridgman, Richard. "Melanctha." *American Literature* 33 (1961): 350–359.
Brooker, Jewel Spears. "Writing the Self: Dialectic and Impersonality in T. S. Eliot." In *T. S. Eliot and the Concept of Tradition*, ed. Giovanni Cianci and Jason Harding, 41–57. New York: Cambridge University Press, 2007.

Brooks, Van Wyck. *The Pilgrimage of Henry James.* New York: Dutton, 1925.

Brown, Wendy. *States of Injury: Power and Freedom in Late Modernity.* Princeton, N.J.: Princeton University Press, 1995.

Browning, Robert. *Selected Poetry.* Ed. Daniel Karlin. New York: Penguin, 1990.

Burstein, Jessica. "Waspish Segments: Lewis, Prosthesis, Fascism." *Modernism/Modernity* (1997): 139–164.

Burwick, Frederick, and Paul Douglass, eds. *Crisis in Modernism: Bergson and the Vitalist Controversy.* New York: Cambridge University Press, 1992.

Bush, Clive. *Halfway to Revolution: Investigation and Crisis in the Work of Henry Adams, William James and Gertrude Stein.* New Haven: Yale University Press, 1991.

Butler, Judith. "Capacity." In *Regarding Sedgwick: Essays on Queer Culture and Critical Theory*, ed. Stephen M. Barber and David L. Clark, 109–121. New York: Routledge, 2002.

———. *Gender Trouble: Feminism and the Subversion of Identity.* New York: Routledge, 1990.

Cameron, Sharon. *Impersonality: Seven Essays.* Chicago: University of Chicago Press, 2007.

———. *Thinking in Henry James.* Chicago: University of Chicago Press, 1989.

Carmello, Charles. "Reading Gertrude Stein Reading Henry James, or Eros Is Eros Is Eros Is Eros." *Henry James Review* 6:3 (Spring 1985): 182–203.

Cavell, Stanley. *Emerson's Transcendental Etudes.* Stanford, Calif.: Stanford University Press, 2003.

Charters, Ann. Introduction to *Three Lives*, by Gertrude Stein, vii–xx. New York: Penguin, 1990.

Chinitz, David E. "In the Shadows: Popular Song and Eliot's Construction of Emotion." *Modernism/Modernity* 11:3 (2004): 449–467.

Church, Margaret. "The Birth of an Idea: Bergson and Proust." Chapter 1 in *Time and Reality: Studies in Contemporary Fiction.* Chapel Hill: University of North Carolina Press, 1949.

Clarke, Edwin, and L. S. Jacyna. *Nineteenth-Century Origins of Neuroscientific Concepts.* Berkeley: University of California Press, 1987.

Cohen, Milton. "Black Brutes and Mulatto Saints: The Racial Hierarchy of Stein's 'Melanctha.'" *Black American Literature Forum* 26 (1986): 119–121.

Connor, Steven. *Dumbstruck: A Cultural History of Ventriloquism.* New York: Oxford University Press, 2000.

Conrad, Joseph. "Henry James: An Appreciation." In *Henry James: Critical Assessments*, vol. 4., ed. Graham Clarke. Mountfield, UK: Helm Information, 1991.

———. *Lord Jim: A Tale.* New York: Bantam, 1965.

Cowan, James C. "Lawrence's Myth of the Body: The 'Biological Psyche' in Illness and Healing." In *D. H. Lawrence and the Trembling Balance*, 115–134. University Park: Pennsylvania State University Press, 1990.

Crary, Jonathan. *Suspensions of Perception: Attention, Spectacle, and Modern Culture.* Cambridge, Mass.: MIT Press, 1999.

Darwin, Charles. *The Descent of Man.* New York: Penguin, 2004.

———. *The Expression of the Emotions in Man and Animals.* 3rd ed. Ed. Paul Ekman. New York: Oxford University Press, 1998.

———. *On the Origin of Species by Means of Natural Selection, or, the Preservation of Favoured Races in the Struggle for Life.* Mineola, N.Y.: Dover, 2006.

Dawkins, Richard. *The Ancestor's Tale: A Pilgrimage to the Dawn of Evolution.* New York: Mariner's Books, 2005.

Dean, Tim. "T. S. Eliot, Famous Clairvoyante." In *Gender, Desire, and Sexuality in T. S. Eliot*, ed. Cassandra Laity and Nancy K. Gish, 43–65. Cambridge: Cambridge University Press, 2004.

Delbanco, Andrew. *Melville: His World and Work.* New York: Knopf, 2005.

Deleuze, Gilles. "Bartleby; or, the Formula." In *Essays Critical and Clinical*, Michael A. Greco and Daniel W. Smith, 68–90. Minneapolis: University of Minnesota Press, 1997.

———. *Bergsonism.* Trans. Barbara Habberjam and Hugh Tomlinson. New York: Zone Books, 1988.

———. *Cinema One: The Movement-Image.* Trans. Barbara Habberjam and Hugh Tomlinson. Minneapolis: University of Minnesota Press, 1986.

———. *Cinema Two: The Time-Image.* Trans. Barbara Habberjam and Hugh Tomlinson. Minneapolis: University of Minnesota, 1989.

———. *Difference and Repetition.* Trans. Paul Patton. New York: Columbia University Press, 1994.

———. *Spinoza: Practical Philosophy.* Trans. Robert Hurley. San Francisco: City Lights, 1988.

Deleuze, Gilles, and Félix Guattari. *Anti-Oedipus: Capitalism and Schizophrenia.* Trans. Robert Hurley, Mark Seem, and Helen R. Lane. New York: Viking, 1977.

Dennett, Daniel. *Darwin's Dangerous Idea: Evolution and the Meaning of Life.* New York: Touchstone, 1996.

———. *Kinds of Minds: Toward an Understanding of Consciousness.* New York: Basic Books, 1997.

Derrida, Jacques. *Dissemination.* Trans. Barbara Johnson. Chicago: University of Chicago Press, 1981.

———. *The Truth in Painting.* Trans. Geoff Bennington and Ian McLeod. Chicago: University of Chicago Press, 1987.

Dodge, Mabel. "Speculations, or Post-Impressionism in Prose." *Arts and Decorations.* March 1913: 172–174. Reprinted in *Critical Essays on Gertrude Stein*, ed. Michael Hoffman, 27–31. Boston: G. K. Hall, 1986.

Doris, John M. *Lack of Character: Personality and Moral Behavior.* New York: Cambridge University Press, 2002.

Douglass, Paul. *Bergson, Eliot, and American Literature.* Lexington: University Press of Kentucky, 1986.

Doyle, Laura. "The Flat, the Round, and Gertrude Stein: Race and the Shape of Modern(ist) History." *Modernism/Modernity* 7:2 (April 2000): 249–271.

Du Bois, W. E. B. *The Souls of Black Folk.* In *Three Negro Classics.* New York: Avon, 1965.

Dunn, Allen, and Thomas F. Haddox. Introduction to *The Limits of Literary Historicism.* Ed. Allen Dunn and Thomas F. Haddox. Knoxville, University of Tennessee Press, 2011.

Eagleton, Terry. *Literary Theory: An Introduction.* Minneapolis: University of Minnesota Press, 1983.

Edie, James M. *William James and Phenomenology.* Bloomington: Indiana University Press, 1987.

Ekman, Paul. Introduction to *The Expression of the Emotions in Man and Animals*, by Charles Darwin. 3rd ed. Oxford: Oxford University Press, 1998. xxi–xxxvi.

Eliot, George. *Middlemarch*. New York: Oxford University Press, 1997.

Eliot, T. S. *The Complete Poems and Plays: 1909–1950*. New York: Harcourt, 1967.

———. "Draft of a Paper on Bergson." Unpublished essay, 1913–1915. Ms Am 1691 (132). Houghton Library, Harvard University.

———. *Inventions of the March Hare: Poems 1909–1917*. Ed. Christopher Ricks. New York: Harcourt, 1996.

———. *Knowledge and Experience in the Philosophy of F. H. Bradley*. New York: Columbia University Press, 1964.

———. *On Poetry and Poets*. London: Faber and Faber, 1957.

———. "The Relation between Politics and Metaphysics." Unpublished essay, 1913. Ms Am 1691 (25). Houghton Library, Harvard University.

———. Review of *Reflections on Violence*, by Georges Sorel. *Monist* 27:3 (July 1917): 478–479.

———. *The Sacred Wood: Essays on Poetry and Criticism*. London: Methuen, 1950.

———. *Selected Essays*. New York: Harcourt, 1950.

Ellmann, Maud. *The Poetics of Impersonality: T. S. Eliot and Ezra Pound*. Cambridge, Mass.: Harvard University Press, 1987.

Emerson, Ralph Waldo. *Emerson's Prose and Poetry: Authoritative Texts, Contexts, Criticism*. Ed. Joel Porte and Saundra Morris. A Norton Critical Edition. New York: Norton, 2001.

Emery-Peck, Jennifer Sorensen. "Tom and Vivien Eliot Do Narrative in Different Voices: Mixing Genres in *The Waste Land*'s Pub." *Narrative* 16:3 (2008): 331–358.

English, Daylanne K. *Unnatural Selections: Eugenics in American Modernism and the Harlem Renaissance*. Chapel Hill: University of North Carolina Press, 2004.

Faulkner, William. "1952 Interview with Loïc Bouvard." In *Lion in the Garden: Interviews with William Faulkner 1926–1962*, ed. James B. Meriwether and Michael Millgate, 68–73. New York: Random House, 1968.

Fisher, Philip. *The Vehement Passions*. Princeton, N.J.: Princeton University Press, 2002.

Foucault, Michel. *Discipline and Punish: The Birth of the Prison*. Trans. Alan Sheridan. New York: Vintage, 1979.

———. "On the Genealogy of Ethics: An Overview of Work in Progress." In *Michel Foucault: Beyond Structuralism and Hermeneutics*, ed. Hubert Dreyfus and Paul Rabinow, 229–252. Chicago: University of Chicago Press, 1982.

Freedman, Jonathan. *Professions of Taste: Henry James, British Aestheticism, and Commodity Culture*. Stanford, Calif.: Stanford University Press, 1990.

Freud, Sigmund. "'A Child Is Being Beaten': A Contribution to the Study of the Origins of the Sexual Perversions." In *Sexuality and the Psychology of Love*. Trans. Alix Strachey and James Strachey, 97–122. New York: Simon and Schuster, 1997.

———. "Lecture XXVII." *Introductory Lectures on Psychoanalysis*. Trans. James Strachey, 431–437. New York: Norton, 1966.

Freud, Sigmund, and Josef Breuer. *Studies in Hysteria*. Trans. James Strachey. New York: HarperCollins, 1994.

Fried, Michael. *Absorption and Theatricality: Painting and Beholder in the Age of Diderot*. Chicago: University of Chicago Press, 1988.

Gallagher, Catherine. "The Formalism of Military History." *Representations* (Fall 2008): 24–33.

———. "War, Counterfactual History, and Alternate-History Novels." *Field Day Review* 3 (2007): 53–65.

Galow, Timothy W. "Gertrude Stein's Everybody's Autobiography and the Art of Contradictions." *Journal of Modern Literature* 32:1 (2008): 111–128.

Gidley, Mick. "The Later Faulkner, Bergson, and God." *Mississippi Quarterly* 37:3 (1984): 377–383.

Gillies, Marie Ann. "Virginia Woolf: Bergsonian Experiments in Representation and Consciousness." In *Henri Bergson and British Modernism*, 107–131. Montreal: McGill-Queen's University Press, 1996.

Goldie, Peter. *On Personality*. London: Routledge, 2004.

Gordon, Lyndall. *T. S. Eliot: An Imperfect Life*. New York: Norton, 1999.

Greco, Monica. "On the Vitality of Vitalism." *Theory, Culture & Society* 22:1 (2005): 15–27.

Greenberg, Jonathan Daniel. *Modernism, Satire, and the Novel*. New York: Cambridge University Press, 2011.

Greenwood, Christopher. *Adapting to the Stage: Theatre and the Work of Henry James*. Burlington, Vt.: Ashgate, 2000.

Grogin, R. C. *Bergsonian Controversy in France, 1900–1914*. Calgary: University of Calgary Press, 1988.

Grosz, Elizabeth. *The Nick of Time: Politics, Evolution, and the Untimely*. Durham, N.C.: Duke University Press, 2004.

Guerlac, Suzanne. *Literary Polemics: Bataille, Sartre, Valéry, Breton*. Stanford, Calif.: Stanford University Press, 1997.

———. *Thinking in Time: An Introduction to Henri Bergson*. Ithaca, N.Y.: Cornell University Press, 2006.

Habermas, Jürgen. *The Theory of Communicative Action*. Vol. 1, *Reason and the Rationalization of Society*. Trans. Thomas McCarthy. Boston, Mass.: Beacon Press, 1984.

Habib, M. A. R. *The Early T. S. Eliot and Western Philosophy*. New York: Cambridge University Press, 1999.

Haney, C., C. Banks, and Philip Zimbardo. "Impersonal Dynamics in a Simulated Prison." *International Journal of Criminology and Penology* 1 (1973): 69–97.

Hansen, Mark. *New Philosophy for New Media*. Cambridge, Mass: MIT Press, 2004.

Harpham, Geoffrey Galt. "Beyond Mastery: The Future of Conrad's Beginnings." In *Conrad in the Twenty-First Century: Contemporary Approaches and Perspectives*, ed. Carola M. Kaplan, Peter Lancelot Mallios, and Andrea White, 17–38. New York: Routledge, 2005.

Hertz, Neil. *George Eliot's Pulse*. Stanford, Calif.: Stanford University Press, 2003.

Hirschman, Albert O. *The Passions and the Interests: Political Arguments for Capitalism before Its Triumph*. Princeton, Princeton University Press, 1977.

Hochman, Baruch. *Character in Literature*. Ithaca, N.Y.: Cornell University Press, 1985.

Holder, Alan. "T. S. Eliot on Henry James." *PMLA* 79:4 (September 1964): 490–497.

Holland, Laurence B. *The Expense of Vision: Essays on the Craft of Henry James*. Baltimore: Johns Hopkins University Press, 1982.

Hollis, Martin. "The Shape of a Life." In *World, Mind, and Ethics: Essays on the Ethical Philosophy of Bernard Williams*, ed. J. E. J. Altham and Ross Harrison, 170–184. Cambridge: Cambridge University Press, 1995.

Hovey, Jaime. "Gertrude Stein: *Three Lives*." In *Companion to Modernist Literature and Culture*, ed. David Bradshaw and Kevin J. H. Dettmar, 450–458. New York: Blackwell, 2006.

Horkheimer, Max. "On Bergson's Metaphysics of Time." *Radical Philosophy* 131 (May/

June 2005): 9–19. Translation of "Zur Bergsons metaphysik der Zeit." Zeitschrift für sozialforschung 3:3 (1934): 321–43.

Hulme, T. E. *Speculations: Essays on Humanism and the Philosophy of Art.* London: Routledge, 1958.

Isen, Alice, and Paul Levin. "Effect of Feeling Good on Helping: Cookies and Kindness." *Journal of Personality and Social Psychology* 21 (1972): 384–8.

Jacobson, David. *Emerson's Pragmatic Vision: The Dance of the Eye.* University Park: Pennsylvania State University Press, 1993.

Jain, Manju. "Eliot, Babbitt, and Paris." In *T. S. Eliot and American Philosophy: The Harvard Years,* 40–59. Cambridge: Cambridge University Press, 1992.

James, Henry. *The Ambassadors.* New York: Penguin, 1986.

———. "The Art of Fiction." In *The Critical Muse: Selected Literary Criticism,* ed. Roger Gard, 186–206. Harmondsworth, UK: Penguin, 1987.

———. *The Art of the Novel: Critical Prefaces.* 50th anniversary ed. Boston: Northeastern University Press, 1984.

———. *The Critical Muse: Selected Literary Criticism,* ed. Roger Gard. Harmondsworth, UK: Penguin, 1987.

———. "Emerson." In *Emerson's Prose and Poetry: Authoritative Texts, Contexts, Criticism,* ed. Joel Porte and Saundra Morris, 615–628. A Norton Critical Edition. New York: Norton, 2001.

———. *The Golden Bowl.* Ware, UK: Wordsworth Editions, 1995.

———. "Is There a Life After Death." In *In After Days: Thoughts on the Future Life,* ed. W. D. Howells, 199–233. New York: Arno, 1977.

———. *The Letters of Henry James.* Ed. Percy Lubbock. New York: Scribner's, 1920.

———. *What Maisie Knew.* In *What Maisie Knew and the Pupil.* New York: Vintage, 2007.

———. *The Wings of the Dove.* Ed. J. Donald Crowley and Richard A. Hocks. A Norton Critical Edition. New York: Norton, 2002.

James, William. "Bergson or Bradley?" *The Journal of Philosophy, Psychology, and Scientific Methods* 7:2 (January 20, 1910): 29–32.

———. *The Correspondence of William James.* Ed. Ignas K. Skrupskelis and Elizabeth M. Berkeley. 12 vols. Charlottesville: University Press of Virginia, 2002.

———. *Essays in Psychical Research.* Cambridge, Mass.: Harvard University Press, 1986.

———. *Essays in Radical Empiricism.* Lincoln: University of Nebraska Press, 1996.

———. *Pragmatism: A New Name for Some Old Ways of Thinking. Writings, 1902–1910.* Ed. Bruce Kuklick. New York: The Library of America, 1987.

———. *The Principles of Psychology.* 2 vols. Mineola, N.Y.: Dover, 1950.

———. *Essays, Comments, and Reviews.* Vol. 17, *The Works of William James,* ed. Frederick H. Burkhardt, Fredson Bowers, and Ignas K. Skrupskelis. Cambridge, Mass.: Harvard University Press, 1987.

James, William, and Henry James. *William and Henry James: Selected Letters.* Charlottesville: University Press of Virginia, 1997.

Jameson, Fredric. *A Singular Modernity: Essay on the Ontology of the Present.* New York: Verso, 2002.

Jay, Martin. "Modernism and the Specter of Psychologism." *Modernism/Modernity* 3:2 (1996): 93–111.

———. Review of *A Natural History of Pragmatism: The Fact of Feeling from Jonathan Edwards to Gertrude Stein*, by Joan Richardson. *Hopkins Review* 1:3 (Summer 2008): 505–509.
Johnston, Georgia. "Narratologies of Pleasure: Gertrude Stein's The Autobiography of Alice B. Toklas." *Modern Fiction Studies* 42:3 (1996): 590–606.
Jones, Donna. "The Eleatic Bergson." *Diacritics* 37:1 (Spring 2007): 21–32.
———. *The Racial Discourses of Life Philosophy*. New York: Columbia University Press, 2010.
Jones, Ernest. *Hamlet and Oedipus*. New York: Norton, 1976.
Jung, C. G. *Psychological Types*. Trans. H. G. Baynes. Princeton, N.J.: Princeton University Press, 1971.
Kant, Immanuel. *Critique of Judgment*. Trans. Werner S. Pluhar. Indianapolis: Hackett, 1987.
———. *Critique of Practical Reason*. Ed. and trans. Mary Gregor. New York: Cambridge University Press, 1997.
Kenner, Hugh. *The Invisible Poet: T. S. Eliot*. New York: Ivan Obolensky, 1959.
———. *T. S. Eliot: A Collection of Critical Essays*. Englewood Cliffs, N.J.: Prentice-Hall, 1962.
Knights, L. C. "How Many Children Hath Lady Macbeth?" In *Explorations*, 1–39. London: Chatto & Windus, 1965.
Krause, S. R. "Bodies in Action: Corporeal Agency and Democratic Politics." *Political Theory* 39:3 (2011): 299–324.
Krook, Dorothea. *The Ordeal of Consciousness*. Cambridge: Cambridge University Press, 1967.
Krupat, Arnold. "Antonymy, Language, and Value in Conrad's *Heart of Darkness*." *Missouri Review* 3:3 (1979): 63–85.
Kuklick, Bruce. *The Rise of American Philosophy*. New Haven: Yale University Press, 1977.
Kumar, Shiv. *Bergson and the Stream of Consciousness Novel*. New York: New York University Press, 1963.
Lacan, Jacques. *Écrits: A Selection*. Trans. Alan Sheridan. New York: Norton, 1977.
Laplanche, J., and J. B. Pontalis. *The Language of Psychoanalysis*. Trans. Donald Nicholson Smith. New York: Norton, 1973.
Lash, Scott. "Lebenssoziologie: Georg Simmel in the Information Age." *Theory, Culture & Society* 22:3 (2005): 1–23.
Lawrence, D. H. *Psychoanalysis and the Unconscious, and Fantasia of the Unconscious*. New York: Viking, 1960.
———. *Studies in Classic American Literature*. Cambridge: Cambridge University Press, 2003.
Leypoldt, Günter. "Uses of Metaphor: Richard Rorty's Literary Criticism and the Poetics of World-Making," *New Literary History* 39:1 (2008): 145–163.
Leavis, F. R. *The Great Tradition: George Eliot, Henry James, Joseph Conrad*. London: Chatto and Windus, 1948.
Lee, Brian. *Theory and Personality: The Significance of T. S. Eliot's Criticism*. London: Athlone, 1979.
Levenson, Michael H. *A Genealogy of Modernism: A Study of English Literary Doctrine, 1908–1922*. Cambridge: Cambridge University Press, 1984.
———. *Modernism and the Fate of Individuality: Character and Novelistic Form from Conrad to Woolf*. New York: Cambridge University Press, 1991.
Levin, Jonathan. *The Poetics of Transition: Emerson, Pragmatism, and American Literary Modernism*. Durham, N.C.: Duke University Press, 1999.
Lewis, Wyndham. *The Art of Being Ruled*. New York: Haskell House, 1972.

———. *Rude Assignment: An Intellectual Autobiography*. Ed. Toby Foshay. Santa Rosa, Calif.: Black Sparrow, 1984.

———. *Time and Western Man*. Santa Rosa, Calif.: Black Sparrow, 1993.

Litvak, Joseph. *Caught in the Act: Theatricality in the Nineteenth-Century English Novel.* Berkeley: University of California Press, 1992.

Lobb, Edward. *T. S. Eliot and the Romantic Critical Tradition*. London: Routledge & Kegan Paul, 1981.

Lott, Eric. *Love and Theft: Blackface Minstrelsy and the American Working Class*. Oxford: Oxford University Press, 1993.

Lynch, Deidre. *The Economy of Character: Novels, Market Culture, and the Business of Inner Meaning*. Chicago: University of Chicago Press, 1998.

MacIntyre, Alasdair. *After Virtue: A Study in Moral Theory*. 3rd ed. Notre Dame, Ind.: University of Notre Dame Press, 2007.

Massumi, Brian. *Parables for the Virtual: Movement, Affect, Sensation*. Durham, N.C.: Duke University Press, 2002.

Mattar, Sinéad Garrigan. "Yeats, Fairies, and the New Animism." *New Literary History* 43:1 (Winter 2012): 137–157.

Matthiessen, F. O. *Henry James: The Major Phase*. Oxford: Oxford University Press, 1944.

Matz, Jesse. *Literary Impressionism and Modernist Aesthetics*. Cambridge: Cambridge University Press, 2001.

———. "T. E. Hulme, Henri Bergson, and the Cultural Politics of Psychologism." In *The Mind of Modernism: Medicine, Psychology, and the Cultural Arts in Europe and America, 1880–1940*, ed. Mark S. Micale, 339–351. Stanford: Stanford University Press, 2004.

May, Brian. *The Modernist as Pragmatist: E. M. Forster and the Fate of Liberalism*. Columbia: University of Missouri Press, 1997.

McCabe, Susan. "'Delight in Dislocation': The Cinematic Modernism of Stein, Chaplin, and Man Ray." *Modernism/Modernity* 8:3 (2001): 429–452.

McGurl, Mark. "Spatial Geometries: Taking Place in Henry James." *Representations* 68 (1999): 59–83.

McMurray, William. "Pragmatic Realism in *The Bostonians*." *Nineteenth-Century Fiction* 16:4 (1962): 339–344.

Meisel, Perry. "Decentering *Heart of Darkness*." *Modern Language Studies* 8:3 (1978): 20–28.

Melville, Herman. *The Confidence-Man: His Masquerade: An Authoritative Text, Contemporary Reviews, Biographical Overviews, Sources, Backgrounds, and Criticism*. A Norton Critical Edition, ed. Hershel Parker and Mark Niemeyer. 2nd ed. New York: Norton, 2006.

———. *Moby-Dick*, ed. Tony Tanner. Oxford: Oxford University Press, 1988.

Meyer, Steven. *Irresistible Dictation: Gertrude Stein and the Correlations of Writing and Science*. Stanford, Calif.: Stanford University Press, 2001.

———. "Writing Psychology Over: Gertrude Stein and William James." *Yale Journal of Criticism* 8:1 (1995): 133–163.

Milgram, Stanley. "Behavioral Study of Obedience." *Journal of Abnormal and Social Psychology* 67 (1963): 371–378.

———. *Obedience to Authority*. New York: Harper and Row, 1974.

Mill, John Stuart. "What Is Poetry." In *Art in Theory: 1815–1900: An Anthology of Changing Ideas*, ed. Charles Harrison, Paul Wood, and Jason Gaiger, 185–189. New York: Blackwell, 1998.
Miller, J. Hillis. *Poets of Reality*. Cambridge, Mass.: Harvard University Press, 1965.
———. "Heart of Darkness Revisited." In *Conrad Revisited: Essays for the Eighties*, ed. Ross C. Murfin, 206–220. Tuscaloosa: University Alabama Press, 1985.
Miquel, Paul-Antoine. "Evolution of Consciousness and Evolution of Life." *MLN* 120 (2005): 1156–1167.
Mitchell, Robert. *Bioart and the Vitality of Media (In Vivo: The Cultural Mediations of Biomedical Science)*. Seattle: University of Washington Press, 2010.
Moran, Richard. *Authority and Estrangement: An Essay on Self-Knowledge*. Princeton, N.J.: Princeton University Press, 2001.
———. "The Expression of Feeling in Imagination." *Philosophical Review* 103:1 (1994): 75–106.
Morgan, Lynn M. "The Embryography of Alice B. Toklas." *Comparative Studies in Society and History* 50:1 (2008): 304–325.
Morrison, Paul. *The Poetics of Fascism: Ezra Pound, T. S. Eliot, Paul de Man*. New York: Oxford University Press, 1996.
Moses, Omri. "Henry James's Suspended Situations." *Modern Philology* 108:1 (2010): 116–150.
Mularkey, John. "Life, Movement and the Fabulation of the Event." *Theory, Culture & Society* 24:6 (2007): 53–70.
Murphet, Julian. *Multimedia Modernism: Literature and the Anglo-American Avant-garde*. Cambridge: Cambridge University Press, 2009.
Ngai, Sianne. "Merely Interesting." Critical Inquiry 34:4 (2008): 777–817.
———. *Ugly Feelings*. Cambridge, Mass.: Harvard University Press, 2005.
Nieddu, Anna M. "Individuality: The Emersonian Background of the Bergson-James Controversy." *European Journal of Pragmatism and American Philosophy* 3:1 (2011).
Nieland, Justus. *Feeling Modern: The Eccentricities of Public Life*. Urbana: University of Illinois Press, 2008.
Nietzsche, Friedrich. *Beyond Good and Evil*. Trans. Walter Kaufmann. New York: Vintage, 1989.
———. *On the Genealogy of Morals*. Trans. Walter Arnold Kaufmann. New York: Vintage, 1967.
———. *The Will to Power*. Trans Walter Kaufmann and R. J. Hollingdale. New York: Vintage, 1968.
North, Michael. *The Dialect of Modernism: Race, Language, and Twentieth-Century Literature*. Oxford: Oxford University Press, 1997.
———. *Machine-Age Comedy*. Modernist Literature and Culture. New York: Oxford University Press, 2009.
———. "Modernism's African Mask: The Stein-Picasso Collaboration." In *Prehistories of the Future: The Primitivist Project and the Culture of Modernism*, ed. Elazar Barkan and Ronald Bush, 270–289. Stanford: Stanford University Press, 1995.
Olson, Liesl M. "Gertrude Stein, William James, and Habit in the Shadow of War." *Twentieth Century Literature* 49:3 (Fall 2003): 328–359.
Ophir, Ella Zohar. "Toward a Pitiless Fiction: Abstraction, Comedy, and Modernist Antihumanism." *Modern Fiction Studies* 52:1 (Spring 2006): 92–121.

Oser, Lee. *The Ethics of Modernism: Moral Ideas in Yeats, Eliot, Joyce, Woolf, and Beckett.* Cambridge: Cambridge University Press, 2007.

Otten, Thomas. *A Superficial Reading of Henry James: Preoccupations with the Material World.* Columbus: Ohio University Press, 2006.

Otter, Samuel. *Melville's Anatomies.* Berkeley: University of California Press, 1999.

Oxford English Dictionary. 2nd ed. Oxford, U.K.: Clarendon, 1989.

Pater, Walter. *The Renaissance: Studies in Art and Poetry*, ed. Donald L. Hill. Berkeley: University of California Press, 1980.

Pavloska, Susanna. *Modern Primitives: Race and Language in Gertrude Stein, Ernest Hemingway, and Zora Neale Hurston.* New York: Routledge, 1999.

Pearson, Keith Ansell. *Philosophy and the Adventure of the Virtual: Bergson and the Time of Life.* London: Routledge, 2002.

Peppis, Paul. "Thinking Race in the Avant Guerre: Typological Negotiations in Ford and Stein." *Yale Journal of Criticism* 10:2 (1997): 371–395.

Person, Leland. *Henry James and the Suspense of Masculinity.* Philadelphia: University of Pennsylvania Press, 2003.

Petruso, Thomas. *Life Made Real.* Ann Arbor: University of Michigan Press, 1991.

Phelan, James. *Reading People, Reading Plots: Character, Progression, and the Interpretation of Narrative.* Chicago: University of Chicago Press, 1989.

———. "Rhetorical Literary Ethics and Lyric Narrative: Robert Frost's 'Home Burial.'" *Poetics Today* 25:4 (2004): 627–51.

Pilkington, Antony. "Proust." *Bergson and His Influence.* Cambridge: Cambridge University Press, 1976.

Pippin, Robert. "Authenticity in Painting: Remarks on Michael Fried's Art History." *Critical Inquiry* 31 (Spring 2005): 575–598.

———. *Henry James and Modern Moral Life.* Cambridge: Cambridge University Press, 2000.

Poirier, Richard. *Poetry and Pragmatism.* Cambridge, Mass.: Harvard University Press, 1992.

Posner, Richard A. *Law, Pragmatism, and Democracy. Cambridge, Mass.: Harvard University Press, 2005.*

Posnock, Ross. *The Trial of Curiosity: Henry James, William James, and the Challenge of Modernity.* New York: Oxford University Press, 1991.

Pound, Ezra. "Henry James." In *Literary Essays of Ezra Pound*, 295–338. New York: New Directions, 1968.

———. "A Retrospect." In *Literary Essays of Ezra* Pound, 3–14. New York: New Directions, 1968.

Priest, Ann-Marie. "'A Secret Responsive Ecstasy': James and the Pleasure of the Abject." *Henry James Review* 22:2 (2001): 163–179.

Quirk, Tom. *Bergson and American Culture: The Worlds of Willa Cather and Wallace Stevens.* Chapel Hill: University of North Carolina Press, 1990.

Rabinbach, Anson. *The Human Motor: Energy, Fatigue, and the Origins of Modernity.* New York: Basic Books, 1990.

Rae, Patricia. *The Practical Muse: Pragmatist Poetics in Hulme, Pound, and Stevens.* Lewisburg, Pa.: Bucknell University Press, 1997.

Renker, Elizabeth. "'A _______!': Unreadability in *The Confidence Man.*" In *The Cambridge*

Companion to Herman Melville, ed. Robert S. Lavine, 114–134. New York: Cambridge University Press, 1998.

Richards, I. A. *Practical Criticism: A Study of Literary Judgment.* New York: Harcourt Brace, 1929.

Richardson, Joan. A *Natural History of Pragmatism: The Fact of Feeling from Jonathan Edwards to Gertrude Stein.* Cambridge: Cambridge University Press, 2007.

Richardson, Robert D. *William James: In the Maelstrom of American Modernism.* New York: Houghton, 2006.

Riddell, Joseph. "Stein and Bergson." In *The Turning Word: American Literary Modernism and Continental Theory*, ed. Mark Bauerlein, 84–123. Philadelphia: University of Pennsylvania Press

Rives, Rochelle. "'Things That Lie on the Surface': Modernism, Impersonality, and Emotional Inexpressibility" *disClosure* 16 (2007): n.p.

Rogers, Robert E. "*Tender Buttons*, Curious Experiment of Gertrude Stein in Literary Anarchy." *Boston Evening Transcript*, July 11, 1914, 12. Reprinted in *Critical Essays on Gertrude Stein*, ed. Michael Hoffman, 31–33. Boston: G. K. Hall, 1986.

Rorty, Richard. *Consequences of Pragmatism.* Minneapolis: University of Minnesota Press, 1982.

Rosen, David. "T. S. Eliot and the Lost Youth of Modern Poetry." *Modern Language Quarterly: A Journal of Literary History* 64:4 (2003): 473–494.

Ruddick, Lisa. *Reading Gertrude Stein: Body, Text, Gnosis.* Ithaca, N.Y.: Cornell University Press, 1990.

Russell, Bertrand. *The Philosophy of Bergson.* Cambridge, UK: Bowes and Bowes, 1914.

Ryan, Vanessa L. *Thinking without Thinking in the Victorian Novel.* Baltimore: Johns Hopkins University Press, 2012.

Saldivar-Hull, Sonia. "Wrestling Your Ally: Stein, Racism, and Feminist Critical Practice." In *Women's Writing in Exile*, ed. Mary Lynn Broe and Angela Ingram, 182–195. Chapel Hill: University of North Carolina Press, 1989.

Schmitz, Neil. *Of Huck and Alice: Humorous Writing in American Literature.* Minneapolis: University of Minnesota Press, 1983.

Schoenbach, Lisi. "'Peaceful and Exciting': Habit, Shock and Gertrude Stein's Pragmatic Modernism." *Modernism/Modernity* 11:2 (Fall 2004): 239–259.

Schuchard, Ronald. "Did Eliot Know Hulme? Final Answer." *Journal of Modern Literature* 27:1 (2003): 63–69.

Schulenberg, Ulf. "'Speaking Out of the Most Passionate Love': James Baldwin and Pragmatism." *European Journal of American Studies* 2 (2007): 2–16.

Schwartz, Sanford. "Bergson and the Politics of Vitalism." In *Crisis in Modernism: Bergson and the Vitalist Controversy*, ed. Frederick Burwick and Paul Douglass, 277–305. New York: Cambridge University Press, 1992.

Sedgwick, Eve Kosofsky. *Touching Feeling: Affect, Pedagogy, Performativity.* Durham, N.C.: Duke University Press, 2003.

See, Sam. "The Comedy of Nature: Darwinian Feminism in Woolf's *Between the Acts.*" *Modernism/Modernity* 17:3 (September 2010): 639–666.

Seltzer, Mark. *Henry James and the Art of Power.* Ithaca, N.Y.: Cornell University Press, 1984.

Sitney, P. Adams. *Modernist Montage: The Obscurity of Vision in Cinema and Literature.* New York: Columbia University Press, 1990.

Silverman, Kaja. *Male Subjectivity at the Margins.* New York: Routledge, 1992.

Skinner, B. F. "Has Gertrude Stein a Secret?" *Atlantic Monthly* 153 (January 1934): 50–57.

———. *Science and Human Behavior.* New York: Free Press, 1953.

Smith, Grover. "T. S. Eliot and the Fragmented Selves: From 'Suppressed Complex' to *Sweeney Agonistes.*" *Philological Quarterly* 77:4 (1998): 417–437.

Soulez, Phillippe, and Frederic Worms. *Bergson: Biographie.* Paris: Flammarion, 1997.

Spinoza, Benedictus de. *A Spinoza Reader: The Ethics and Other Works.* Ed. and trans. E. M. Curley. Princeton, N.J.: Princeton University Press, 1994.

Stein, Gertrude. *Autobiography of Alice B. Toklas.* New York: Vintage, 1961.

———. "Composition as Explanation." In *A Stein Reader*, ed. Ulla E. Dydo, 495–503. Evanston, Ill.: Northwestern University Press, 1993.

———. "Cultivated Motor Automatism: A Study of Character in Its Relation to Attention." *Psychological Review* 7 (May 1898): 295–306.

———. *Everybody's Autobiography.* Cambridge, Mass.: Exact Change, 1993.

———. "Henry James." In *Writings: 1932–1946*, 147–189. New York: Library of America, 1998.

———. "Lectures in America." In *Writings: 1932–1946*, 191–336. New York: Library of America, 1998.

———. *Narration: Four Lectures.* Chicago: University of Chicago Press, 1977.

———. "Portraits and Repetition." In *Writings: 1932–1946*, 287–312. New York: Library of America, 1998.

———. *Q.E.D.* Appendix to *Three Lives.* New York: Penguin, 1990.

———. *Three Lives.* New York: Penguin, 1990.

———. "Transatlantic Interview." In *A Primer for the Gradual Understanding of Gertrude Stein*, ed. Robert Bartlett Haas, 15–35. Los Angeles: Black Sparrow Press, 1971.

———. *Wars I Have Seen.* New York: Random House, 1945.

Stein, Gertrude, and Leon M. Solomons. "Normal Motor Automatism." *Psychological Review* 3:5 (September 1896), 492–512.

Stevens, Hugh. *Henry James and Sexuality.* Cambridge: Cambridge University Press, 1998.

Stewart, Garrett. *Reading Voices: Literature and the Phonotext.* Berkeley: University of California Press, 1990.

Susman, Warren. *Culture as History: The Transformation of American Society in the Twentieth Century.* New York: Pantheon, 1984.

Symons, Arthur. *Studies in Seven Arts.* New York: E. P. Dutton, 1906.

Sypher, Wylie. "The Meanings of Comedy." In *Comedy*, 193–255. Baltimore: Johns Hopkins University Press, 1980.

Taylor, Carole Anne. *The Tragedy and Comedy of Resistance: Reading Modernity through Black Women's Fiction.* Penn Studies in Contemporary American Fiction. Philadelphia: University of Pennsylvania Press, 2000.

Taylor, Frederick Winslow. *The Principles of Scientific Management.* New York: Harper and Brothers, 1911. Reprint, New York: Norton, 1967.

Thacker, Eugene. "Thought Creatures." *Theory, Culture & Society* 24:7/8 (2007): 314–316.

Thomas, E. W. *The Judicial Process: Realism, Pragmatism, Practical Reasoning and Principles.* Cambridge: Cambridge University Press, 2005.

Thomas, Joseph M. "Figures of Habit in William James." *The New England Quarterly* 66:1 (March 1993): 3–26.

Thorold, Algar. Review of *Les Deux Sources de la Morale et de la Religion*, by Henri Bergson. *Criterion* 12 (1932): 124–131.

Thrailkill, Jane F. *Affecting Fictions: Mind, Body and Emotion in American Literary Realism.* Cambridge, Mass.: Harvard University Press, 2007.

Todorov, Tzvetan. *Genres in Discourse.* Trans. Catherine Porter. Cambridge: Cambridge University Press, 1990.

Tomkins, Silvan. *Shame and Its Sisters: A Silvan Tomkins Reader.* Ed. Adam Frank and Eve Kosofsky Sedgwick. Durham, N.C.: Duke University Press, 1995.

Torgovnick, Marianne. *Gone Primitive: Savage Intellects, Modern Lives.* Chicago: University of Chicago Press, 1991.

Tursi, Renée. "William James's Narrative of Habit." *Style* 33:1 (Spring 1999): 1–13.

Vermeule, Blakey. *Why Do We Care about Literary Characters?* Baltimore: Johns Hopkins University Press, 2010.

Vrettos, Athena. "Defining Habits: Dickens and the Psychology of Repetition." *Victorian Studies* 42:3 (1999): 399–426.

Walkowitz, Rebecca L. *Cosmopolitan Style: Modernism beyond the Nation.* New York: Columbia University Press, 2006.

Warshick, Bonnie, and Elizabeth Wingrove. "Politics That Matter: Thinking about Power and Justice with the New Materialists." *Contemporary Political Theory.* Forthcoming, 2014.

Watson, Steven. *Prepare for Saints: Gertrude Stein, Virgil Thomson, and the Mainstreaming of American Modernism.* Berkeley: University of California Press, 1998.

Wientzen, Timothy. "Automatic Modernism: D. H. Lawrence, Vitalism, and the Political Body." *Genre* 46:1 (Spring 2013): 33–55.

Will, Barbara. "Gertrude Stein, Automatic Writing and the Mechanics of Genius." *Forum for Modern Language Studies.* 37:2 (2001): 169–175.

Williams, Bernard. *Ethics and the Limits of Philosophy.* Cambridge, Mass.: Harvard University Press, 1985.

———. "Nietzsche's Minimalist Moral Psychology." *European Journal of Philosophy* 1:1 (April 1993): 10–11.

———. "Replies." In *World, Mind, and Ethics: Essays on the Ethical Philosophy of Bernard Williams*, ed. J. E. J. Altham and Ross Harrison, 185–224. Cambridge: Cambridge University Press, 1995.

Wilson, Elizabeth. "Trembling, Blushing: Darwin's Nervous System." In *Psychosomatic: Feminism and the Neurological Body*, 63–77. Durham, N.C.: Duke University Press, 2004.

Wittgenstein, Ludwig. *Lectures and Conversations on Aesthetics, Psychology, and Religious Belief.* Ed. Cyril Barrett. Berkeley: University of California Press, 1972.

Wollheim, Richard. "Eliot and F. H. Bradley: An Account." In *Eliot in Perspective*, ed. Graham Martin, 169–193. London: Macmillan, 1970.

———. *On the Emotions.* New Haven: Yale University Press, 1999.

Woloch, Alex. *The One vs. the Many: Minor Characters and the Space of the Protagonist in the Novel.* Princeton, N.J.: Princeton University Press, 2003.

Woolf, Virginia. "Modern Fiction." In *The Common Reader*, 146–154. London: Mariner, 2002.

———. "Twelfth Night at the Old Vic." In *The Death of the Moth and Other Essays*, 45–50. New York: Harcourt, 1974.

Zamir, Tzachi. "Puppets." *Critical Inquiry* 36 (Spring 2010): 386–409.

Zilcosky, John. "Modern Monuments: T. S. Eliot, Nietzsche, and the Problem of History." *Journal of Modern Literature* 29:1 (Autumn 2005): 21–33.

Zimbardo, Philip. "Prison Life Study: General Information" [Stanford prison experiment]. August 1971. www.prisonexp.org/pdf/geninfo.pdf.

Žižek, Slavoj. "Kate's Choice, or the Materialism of Henry James." In *Lacan: The Silent Partners*, ed. Slavoj Žižek, 288–311. New York: Verso, 2006.

———. *Organs without Bodies: Deleuze and Consequences.* New York: Routledge, 2004.

———. *Tarrying with the Negative.* Durham, N.C.: Duke University Press, 1998.

INDEX

Adorno, Theodor, 44–47, 51, 223nn24, 25, 26, 27, 224nn28, 29
Aesthetic experience, 4, 43, 68, 75, 226n42; in Adorno, 44–47, 223n25; in Kant, 95–96, 226n41
Affect, 4, 20, 32, 47, 60–65, 204, 206, 223n21, 227nn45, 46, 47,49, 250–251n7; in Adorno, 44–45; and formation of interests, 77–78, 86–87, 89–94, 100–101, 104, 230n8; in Gertrude Stein, 148–50, 250n60; in Herman Melville, 13–17; in neo-vitalist theory, 204–7; in T. S. Eliot, 155, 168, 170–71, 178–79, 185–86, 194, 198, 255n33. *See also* Emotion; Feeling; Tone
Affection, 60, 63, 91, 233n25
Allport, Gordon, 35, 221n6
Altieri, Charles, 96, 155, 226n41, 226n43
Aristotle, 35, 38, 41–42, 45, 122, 215n1, 241n9, 349n53
Attention, 36, 43–44, 47–55, 59, 70, 78, 84, 90–91, 225nn33, 35, 38, 233n23; in Gertrude Stein, 119, 129–30, 150, 244n28; in T. S. Eliot, 164, 177–78. *See also* Crary, Jonathan
Automatism, 49, 51, 162, 168, 222n18, 233n24; in Gertrude Stein, 128–30, 134, 136, 147–48, 244nn27, 28, 248n52
Autonomy, 27, 35, 41, 44, 46, 50, 76, 96, 103, 116, 145, 162, 164, 223nn24, 25, 249n52; in Joseph Conrad, 11, 13

Behavior, 2, 4–6, 13, 17, 19, 26, 30, 34–41, 45, 49, 52, 57–61, 64, 75–76, 202, 209, 215n1, 219n31, 221n8, 222nn11, 17, 224nn31, 32, 225n36, 226n38, 242n17, 244n30, 249nn53, 59; in Gertrude Stein, 22, 117–26, 128–29, 131, 135, 138, 142–43, 147, 152; in T. S. Eliot, 155, 163, 179, 185
Behaviorism, 4, 34, 37–38, 222n12, 251n8
Benjamin, Walter, 51, 118
Bergson, Henri, 3–4, 19–20, 46, 53–54, 60–67, 74, 82, 128, 152, 172–177, 199–213, 218nn23, 24, 25, 26, 27, 226nn39, 44, 227nn45, 48, 50, 229n4, 231n16, 232nn20, 21, 22, 249nn55, 56, 57, 58, 250n1, 254n25, 256nn40, 41; and attention, 53–54; and biopolitics, 208–209; and comedy, 145–150, 249nn53; *Creative Evolution*, 74, 82, 138, 174–75, 188, 203, 209, 222n18, 232n21, 240n3, 242nn19, 20, 246n43, 249nn55, 56, 58, 256n41, 259n3; and duration, 62, 82, 124, 131, 135, 203, 207, 226n44, 246n43, 249nn56, 57, 259n3; on feeling and affection, 60–64, 89, 159, 163, 168, 172–177, 189–190, 233n25; and habit, 128, 132–138, 142, 152, 222n18, 240n3, 242nn19, 20, 245nn34, 35, 246n43; *Introduction to Metaphysics*, 163, 173–74, 218n24, 226n44, 232n22, 237n48; *Matter and Memory*, 23, 53, 64, 86, 89, 91, 133–34, 157, 210, 225n38, 227n48, 229n4, 233nn23, 24, 25, 237n47, 245n34, 251n11, 257n43, 248n44; and media theory, 204–206; and organic evolution, 202–203, 242nn19, 20, 249nn55, 58; and pragmatism, 64–67, 69, 227n50; and psychoanalysis, 201–202; and "pure memory," 53, 210–211, 225nn37, 38, 251n11; and self-interest, 74, 82, 86, 89, 91–94, 110, 232nn20, 21, 22, 233nn23, 24; and time, 20, 23, 132–134, 136, 149, 188, 200, 202–203, 207, 210–212, 232n21, 244n33, 259n11; and virtuality, 23, 110, 119, 157, 168, 184, 187–89, 210–13, 237nn47, 48, 246n43,

253n16, 257n43, 259nn11, 13; and voice, 25, 46, 155, 157, 159, 163, 168, 172–77, 207, 226n39, 253nn16, 21; and William James, 3–4, 19, 53, 60–67, 82, 84, 86, 91–92, 119, 128, 133–34, 172, 174–76, 199, 207, 211–12, 225n37, 227nn45, 48, 228n51, 231n16. *See also* Duration (durée); Élan vital; Eliot, T. S., and Bergson; Intuition; James, Henri, and Bergson; Stein, Gertrude, and Bergson; Virtuality, Vitalism

Berman, Jessica, 18, 47–49, 113–14, 224n29, 239n55

Bernstein, J. M., 41, 45, 94, 223nn21, 24, 25, 26

Bersani, Leo, 9, 81–82, 85, 107–108, 110, 220nn34, 35, 230n11, 231n13, 234n34, 236n42

Biopolitics, 208, 249n53

Blackman, Lisa, 20, 207

Body, experience of, 26, 93, 201, 217n13, 225n35, 234n32, 255n36, 259n4; in Bergson, 23, 54, 89, 91–93, 133–134, 149, 210–211, 233nn23, 25, 245n34; in Darwin, 126–128; and digital media interface, 206, 259n10; in Gertrude Stein, 130, 243n24; in William James, 62, 91–92

Bradley, F. H., 34, 155, 159, 161, 172–74, 177, 179–82, 184–85, 188–91, 193, 222n12, 228n51, 250n2, 254n27, 255n36, 257n43, 258n44

Brown, Wendy, 113–115

Butler, Judith, 115, 238n52, 239n56

Cameron, Sharon, 32, 81–82, 85, 231nn14, 15, 232n20, 234nn33, 34

Cavell, Stanley, 68, 228n54, 247n45

Character: context dependent vs. context independent, 20, 33–34, 80, 154–60, 163–66, 170, 189–190, 192–94, 456n37; deep vs. superficial, 10–11, 31, 80–81, 112–113, 153, 162, 164, 179, 191–92, 217n13, 230n10; erratic or eccentric, 13–15, 49–50, 138, 144, 167, 224n30, 249n53, 251n7; literary-critical methodologies for, 24, 55–59; passive vs. productive, 32, 49–54, 128, 137, 224n32, 240n2; pre-modernist literary approaches to, 1–2, 5–19, 24, 29, 215nn1, 2; process-oriented versions of, 6, 12, 19, 22, 26, 54, 83, 92, 104, 113; relation between literary and moral concept of, 1–2, 4–5, 215nn1, 2; repsychologizing of, 20, 55–60; scripted/prescripted, 105–109, 111, 126, 145, 147; subordination to formal imperatives, 7, 25, 81–82, 231n14; substantialist models of, 5–6, 26, 33, 74, 81, 124; typologies of, 30, 35, 41, 55, 120–21, 144–152, 182, 221n6, 240nn4, 5, 244n31, 248n49, 249n52. *See also* Consistency, of character; Impersonality; Morality, and relation to character; Personality

Circumstances: changing 2–5, 20, 32, 36, 43, 60, 73, 131, 219n33, 228n52; responsiveness to, 36, 40–41, 43, 50, 54, 60, 124, 199, 219n33, 221n7; and "situational self" 73–75, 78, 94

Cognitive understanding, 4, 12, 32, 45, 57–60, 62, 74, 88, 95, 134, 163, 202, 204, 223n25, 232n22

Coherence, *see* Character, and ideal of consistency; Consistency, of character

Communal norms, 13, 42–43, 104, 223n21, 230n9

Community, formations of, 3, 9, 34–35, 47, 77, 113–114, 171, 239n55; community life, 18, 21, 27, 41, 77, 193

Conrad, Joseph, 5–6, 10–14, 80, 216, 230n5

Consistency, of character, 1–2, 5–6, 24–25, 32, 35, 38–41, 49, 66, 215nn1, 2, 230n6, 241n9; in Gertrude Stein, 117, 131–132, 135–136, 138–139; in Henry James, 73–74, 76, 80–83, 97, 114–115; in modernist precursors, 10, 13–18; in social psychology, 38–41, 222–23n19; in T. S. Eliot, 155, 166, 180, 182, 198, 254n27, 256–57n41; in William James, 19, 83–4, 245n35, 254n27. *See also* Inconsistency

Consciousness: in Bergson, 61–62, 91, 134, 172–73, 176–177, 203–4, 210, 225n38, 226n44, 233n23, 256n41 (*see also* Intuition); in Darwin, 125, 128; in Emerson, 67–68; in F. H. Bradley, 257n43; in Freud, 227n46; in Gertrude Stein, 124, 130, 243n25, 244n28; in Henry James, 81–82, 84, 231nn14, 15, 234n34; and modernist character, 26, 70, 201, 204, 243nn24; in Nietzsche, 238n51; stream of, 82–84, 176; in T. S. Eliot, 159–60, 172–73, 176–178, 181, 192, 196 (*see also* Double consciousness; Self-consciousness); in William James, 82–84, 176, 258n46. *See also* Unconscious

Contingency, 9, 16, 20–21, 25, 36, 46, 54–55, 74, 77, 81, 94, 102, 114–115, 137, 140, 142–143,

191, 204, 211, 218n29, 219n33, 228n52, 228n55, 238n53, 239n55
Cosmopolitanism, 47–49, 114, 239n55
Crary, Jonathan, 50–54, 225nn33, 34, 225–26n38

Darwin, Charles, 4, 20, 60, 64–65, 69, 124–129, 131, 133–34, 137–138, 149–50, 152, 199, 209, 216n6, 228–29n55, 240n6, 241nn8, 12, 13, 242nn14, 15, 16, 17, 18, 19, 249n59; and Bergson, 4, 19–20, 60, 64–65, 69, 119, 128, 240n3, 242nn19, 20; *The Expression of the Emotions in Man and Animals*, 64, 118, 124–26, 152, 242n15, 249n59; *On the Origin of Species*, 118, 137. *See also* Emotion, in Darwin; Evolution, Darwin's theories of; Habit, in Darwin; James, William, and Darwin; Stein, Gertrude, and Darwin; Vitalism, and Darwinism
Deleuze, Gilles, 14, 17, 193, 203–204, 206–207, 211, 217n15, 218–19n29, 234n32, 249n57, 250n1, 253n16, 256n41, 259n9, 11, 259–60n13
Derrida, Jacques, 138, 157, 245n37, 250n3
Disinterestedness, 13, 76, 87, 94, 96, 100–101, 175, 230n6
Doris, John, 38–41, 222n19
Double consciousness, 169–170, 252–53n13
Du Bois, W. E. B., 169, 252n13
Duration (durée), 19, 37, 62, 82, 124, 131, 135, 203, 207, 226n44, 246n43, 249nn56, 57, 259n3

Ego psychology, 4, 35–36
Élan vital, 53, 65, 74, 128, 138, 152, 201, 209
Eliot, George, 5–10, 13, 216nn7, 8
Eliot, T. S.: and Bergson, 19, 23, 25, 29, 32, 34, 36, 40–41, 43, 45–47, 53, 155, 157, 159, 163, 168, 172–77, 179–80, 184, 187–89, 218nn21, 22, 253nn18, 21, 254n25, 257n42; "Convictions, Curtain Raiser," 164–72, 195; exploring points of view, 34, 41, 53, 156–161, 167, 170, 173, 178–83, 185, 187–90, 192–94, 197–98, 235n21, 250nn2, 4, 256n39, 257n43, 258n44 (*see also* Double consciousness); historical connection to vitalism, 2–3, 19, 22, 25, 155–56, 159, 172–76, 179, 188–90, 200, 218nn21, 22, 226n39, 227n50, 253nn18, 23, 254nn25, 26, 257nn41, 42, 43; and the Imaginary, 182–84, 194, 196; on imagination, 43, 50–51, 53, 190–91, 196; "The Love Song of J. Alfred Prufrock," 153, 158, 162, 172, 181–185, 190, 253n18, 257n42; lyrical and non-narrative formal effects in, 23, 25, 36, 159–60, 173, 175, 177, 179, 195, 197–98, 253nn19, 20, 253n19, 254n29, 255nn31, 36, 258n49 (*see also* Lyric); and personae, 25, 153–54, 168; philosophical orientation and training, 19, 25, 157, 159–61, 163, 169, 171–76, 180–81, 188–89, 200, 218n21, 222n12, 227n50, 253n18, 254nn25, 26, 258n44; "Portrait of a Lady," 158, 172, 185–88; "Tradition and the Individual Talent," 33–34, 49–50, 155, 159, 162–63, 167, 178–79, 190, 220n3, 251n11, 255n31, 258n44; *The Waste Land*, 34, 45–46, 154, 166, 196–97, 205, 253n19, 258n47; and William James, 3, 60, 169, 172, 174–77, 199, 258n46. *See also* Affect, in T. S. Eliot; Bradley, F. H.; Emotion, in T. S. Eliot; Ethics, in T. S. Eliot; Feeling, in T. S. Eliot; Impersonality; Lyric; Modernism; Personality, in T. S. Eliot; Theatricality; Tone; Vitalism; Voice, in T. S. Eliot
Ellmann, Maud, 34, 188, 220n3, 226n39, 253n23, 256n40
Emerson, Ralph Waldo, 1, 16, 27, 64–70, 119, 142–143, 170, 227nn48, 50, 238nn54, 238–39n55, 247n45
Emotion: in Bergson, 61–63, 146, 227n45; in Freud, 63–64; in Darwin, 64, 125–27; distinction between emotion and feeling, 60–61, 178–79, 255nn33, 34; in Gertrude Stein, 118, 126, 145, 148, 246n41; in Henry James, 22, 73, 77, 91–92, 99, 103, 229n3; and literary texts, 57, 59–60; psychological accounts of, 36, 61–62, 221n8, 226n43; in T. S. Eliot, 25, 33, 155, 158, 160–61, 167–171, 173, 177–179, 181, 189, 193–196, 198, 220n4, 250n4, 253n19, 255nn31, 32, 33, 34; in William James, 61–63, 227n45, 229n3; in Wyndham Lewis, 250–51n7. *See also* Affect; Affection; Feeling; Intuition;Tone
Ethics: 2–5, 9, 12–13, 18–20, 24, 26, 37, 41–43, 47–50, 69–71, 199 (*see also* individual authors for more specific references); in Adorno, 44–47, 223nn 25, 26. 223–34n27; and aesthetics, 4, 43–47, 50, 86, 94, 233n26; in Aristotle, 35–36, 38, 41–42, 215n1, 241n9; and attention, 47–50; and behaviorism,

37–38; and cosmopolitanism, 47–49; in Gertrude Stein, 12, 26, 40–41, 241n9; in Henry James, 12, 24, 26, 40, 45–47, 50, 69, 75–78, 80–81, 86–88, 94, 98–104, 109, 115–16, 233n28, 233–34n29, 239n55; in Herman Melville, 13, 16–18; and impersonality, 30, 35, 154–155, 160, 168, 197, 220–21n5; in Joseph Conrad, 10–13; in neo-vitalists, 20–21; and self-interest, 26, 75–78, 80–81, 86–88, 94, 98–101, 104, 115–116, 230n8, 233–34n29; and social psychology, 37–41, 222n17; in T. S. Eliot, 12–13, 45–47, 49–50, 69–71, 104, 154–55, 160, 168, 197, 220n5. *See also* Communal norms; Consistency, of character; Judgment, ethical; Modernism, ethical commitments; Morality; Rationalism, and ethics; Suspension, of ethical judgment; Time, necessary for ethical judgment

Evolution: Bergson's theories of, 89, 128, 149, 203, 242n20, 249n57, 259n3; Darwin's theories of, 4, 20, 60, 65, 201, 208–209, 228n55, 241n8, 241n13, 242n16; Gertrude Stein's interest in, 118, 122, 124–125, 137, 152; and media theory, 205–206. See also Darwin, Charles

Feeling: aesthetic, 4, 58–63, 94–95, 227n45; in Bergson, 60–64, 89, 146, 159, 163, 168, 172–77, 189–90, 233n25, 237n48; in Darwin, 150; distinction between feeling and emotion, 61–62, 178–79, 255nn33, 34; and formation of interests in Henry James, 79, 89–93, 95, 99, 101, 103, 109–110, 112; in Freud, 63–64, 237n46; and intuition, 4, 67, 174; and modernist literary character, 26, 48, 52, 58–60, 79, 90, 201, 226n42; in Nietzsche, 93; psychological accounts of, 30, 35, 37–38, 59–60, 67, 89–90; and relation to habit, 121, 123, 131–32, 136, 240n2, 241n7, 246n41, 248n52; in T. S. Eliot, 154–56, 159–61, 168–74, 176–81, 186, 189–90, 194–95, 250n4, 255nn31, 32, 33, 34, 35; and "ugly feelings," 103, 168 (*see also* Negative agency); in William James, 60–63, 84, 92, 172, 174. *See also* Affect; Affection; Emotion; Intuition

Fixity, 14, 32, 99, 114, 131, 145–146, 249n53

Foucault, Michel, 51, 104, 208, 222n10, 225n35, 236n41

Fragmentation, social, 29, 43–44, 47, 52, 55, 196, 207, 223n24

Freedman, Jonathan, 104–106, 219n32, 231n12, 234n33, 235nn37, 38

Freud, Sigmund, 11, 35, 107, 136, 201–202, 220n5, 227n46, 227n47, 231n15, 236n45, 237nn46, 48, 49, 238nn50, 51, 243n22, 244n27, 245n36, 259n8; and affect, 63–64. *See also* Libido; Primal scene; Psychoanalysis; Unconscious

Fried, Michael, 252n14

Goldie, Peter, 31, 36, 222n9

Grosz, Elizabeth, 3, 216n6, 241n12

Guerlac, Suzanne, 203, 218n17, 225n37

Habermas, Jürgen, 43, 230n9

Habit, 49–54; 130–133, 199, 203, 224n31, 234n31, 240n2, 241n7, 241n9, 244n30; in Bergson, 132–135, 148–150, 222n18, 225n37, 244nn28, 31, 245n34, 246n43, 248n48, 249n53; in Darwin, 4, 118–119, 124–129, 137, 149–150, 152; in Gertrude Stein, 10, 12, 22, 25–26, 117–124, 129–140, 143–145, 148–152; and vitalism, 4, 52–53, 117, 119, 128, 130, 133, 136–137, 139, 144, 152, 243n24, 244n30, 245n34

History: Frankfurt School accounts of, 46, 223n27; historicist and materialist approaches to, 43–44, 46–47, 51–52, 54–55, 207–208, 223n23, 223–24n27, 259n11; literary and intellectual, 9, 23, 157–58, 196–97, 211, 223n23, 228n55, 247n47, 258n44; vitalism's provisional view of, 52, 54–55, 208–209

Horkheimer, Max, 207, 210, 224n27

Hulme, T. E., 20, 175, 200, 218n24, 220n4, 254n24, 259n3

Idealism, philosophical: Deleuze's opposition to, 203, and F. H. Bradley, 155, 172, 177, 255n36, 257n43

Impersonality, 22, 29–30, 32–34, 53, 154–156, 159–163, 167–68, 172, 178, 180, 188, 190–91, 197, 200, 220nn3, 4, 226n39, 258n44. *See also* Personality

Improvisation, 2, 4, 10, 42, 46, 49–50, 96, 142, 205; in Henry James, 23, 40, 50, 73, 75, 78–79, 105, 107–8, 110, 112, 236n42, 239n53; in Herman Melville, 13, 17–18

Inconsistency, 6, 13–18, 24, 115, 132, 135, 215n1. *See also* Consistency
Instinct: in Bergson, 174–75; in Darwin, 126, 138
Instrumentality, 17, 36, 49, 52, 54, 87, 98, 100–101, 138, 175, 225n38, 230n5, 233n24; aesthetic resistance to, 4, 44, 47, 58, 79, 95
Interests, of self, 13, 25–26, 122, 199, 227n50, 228n55, 230nn7, 8, 9, 233nn23, 234n32; in Henry James, 73–81, 84–87, 89–106, 108–116, 227n50, 234n32, 235n36. *See also* Disinterestedness
Intimacy: in Herman Melville, 14–18; intimate sphere in modernist writers, 22, 47–49, 105–106, 184–86, 197, 205. *See also* Relationality
Intuition, 4, 23, 36, 67, 110, 159, 212, 218n23, 256n40; in Bergson, 23, 46, 133, 172–76, 207, 212, 232n22, 237n48, 253n16, 257n41; and feeling, 4, 67, 174

James, Henry: aesthetic experience in, 4, 43, 68, 75, 79–81, 86–87, 94–96; *The Ambassadors*, 73, 77, 79, 84, 86–97, 99, 101, 169, 216n9, 234–35n35, 236n43, 236–37n45; and Bergson, 23, 46, 74, 82, 86, 89, 91–94, 99, 110, 199, 232nn20, 22; and disinterestedness, 76, 87, 94, 96, 100–101; *The Golden Bowl*, 24, 73, 78–79, 82, 84–85, 92, 102–116, 230–31n11, 231n14, 234–35n35, 235nn37, 38, 39, 236n42, 238n50, 238–39n53; and liberal politics, 77, 113–114; and life, 3, 27, 41, 75–77, 86, 95, 100–101, 115, 199, 229n2; and novel form, 78–81; relation between perception and action in, 89–92; theatrical metaphors in, 78, 105–112, 235n40; and vitalism, 2–3, 5, 19–23, 27, 69–70, 75–77, 81–82, 86, 96, 103–104, 110, 199–200, 202, 205, 211–13, 227–28n50, 247n45; and William James, 19, 82–84, 92, 199–200, 211–12, 227–28n50, 229nn55, 3, 232n18, 259n1; *The Wings of the Dove*, 73, 77, 79, 86, 97–101, 229n5, 235n36, 246n40. *See also* Bergson, Henri, and Henry James; Consistency, of character, in Henry James; Disinterestedness; Emotion, in Henry James; Ethics, in Henry James; Feeling, and formation of interest in Henry James; Improvisation, in Henry James; Interests, of self, in Henry James; Modernism; Morality, and relation to character in Henry James; Motivation, in Henry James; Suspension, of ethical judgment; Vitalism
James, William: and Darwin, 3–4, 60, 64–65, 69, 118–19, 124, 126, 128–29, 199, 228–29n55, 240n3; on emotion and feeling, 4, 60–64, 67, 84, 92, 172, 174, 176–77, 227n45; *The Principles of Psychology*, 62, 82–83, 92, 124, 126, 130, 134–35, 176, 225n37, 227n45, 244n30, 253n17, 254n28; "stream of consciousness," 82–84, 176; and vitalism, 3–4, 19, 53, 60–68, 70, 82, 92, 118–19, 133–137, 172, 175, 199–200, 207, 211–212, 228n51, 231n16. *See also* Bergson, Henri, and William James; Consistency of character, in William James; Eliot, T. S., and William James; James, Henri, and William James; Pragmatism; Stein, Gertrude, and William James; Vitalism
Jones, Donna, 207–208, 259n12
Judgment, 30, 63, 77, 114, 130, 170, 189, 193–94; aesthetic/reflective, 44, 58, 94–95, 171, 173, 223n26, 224n32, 225n36, 230n6, 246n42; ethical, 4, 42, 47, 59, 80 87, 94, 97, 219n31, 234n31
Jung, C. G., 35, 221n6

Kant, Immanuel, 11, 41, 84, 94–96, 100, 171, 223nn21, 26, 224n32, 225n36, 226n41, 227n48, 230n6, 233n27, 234n31, 245n37, 246n42

Lacan, Jacques, 182, 221n7, 256n38
Levenson, Michael, 11, 92, 196, 216nn9, 11, 253n23, 258n47
Levin, Jonathan, 27, 66, 84, 104, 232n20, 234n34, 244n33
Lewis, Wyndham, 19, 117, 127, 162–64, 200–201, 218n23, 244nn32, 33, 250n6, 250–52n7, 251n8, 257n43, 259nn4, 5
Libido, 64, 227n47
Life processes: and pragmatism, 228nn52, 54, 55, 229n2; and vitalist philosophy, 3–4, 18, 20–23, 41, 53–54, 60, 65, 67, 74–75, 77, 83, 86, 118–119, 121, 131, 133, 137, 148–50, 174–175, 196, 199, 204, 207–209, 218n29, 232n21, 241n12, 242n20, 243n24, 249nn55, 57, 58,

257n42, 259n3. *See also* Gertrude Stein, and life; Henry James, and life; Liveliness
Liveliness, 117, 119, 128, 138–39, 145, 149, 151–2, 165, 199, 248n48, 249n56
Lyric, 19, 22, 159–60, 173, 175, 195–97, 253nn19, 20

Massumi, Brian, 121, 204, 240n6, 255n33
Materialism, 44, 54, 64, 77, 202, 216n5, 254n25, 260n16. *See also* New Materialisms
Media theory, 205–6
Melville, Herman, 5–6, 13–19, 103, 216–17n12, 217nn13, 14, 15, 16, 17, 217–18n18
Memory: in Bergson, 53–54, 132–134, 136, 210, 225n37, 225–26n38, 250n1, 252n11; in Freud, 63, 236n45, 237n45. *See also* Pure memory
Milgram, Stanley, 38–40, 222n17
Modernism: and aesthetic experience, 4, 43–46, 75, 79, 94–97, 171, 175; and affect, 47, 60, 64–65, 149–50, 204 (*see also* subheadings for Affect for more specific references in modernist figures); criticism by Adorno, 43–47, 224n29; criticism by Jessica Berman and Rebecca Walkowitz, 47–49; criticism by Jonathan Crary, 50–52; historical influence of vitalism on, 2–5, 19–23, 25, 27, 64–66, 199–202, 204–205, 207–209–213, 218nn22, 23, 227–28n50, 244–45n33, 259n3 (*see also* individual authors for more specific references to vitalism); models of character within, 2–6, 9, 12–13, 19–36, 40, 50, 52–53, 55, 57–58, 60, 64–65, 70–71, 199–202, 204–205, 213 (*see also* individual authors for more specific references); and politics, 18, 46–49, 77, 106, 113–114, 162, 167, 175, 200, 205, 208, 218n23, 224nn29, 30, 235n39, 239n55, 240nn2, 5, 250n6, 252n12, 254n25; and psychoanalysis, 5, 23–24, 201–202 (*see also* Psychoanalysis). *See also* Eliot, T. S.; James, Henry; Stein, Gertrude
Moral psychology, 16, 39, 85, 219n31
Morality, 2, 5, 31, 38–39, 42–47, 57, 96, 113, 215n1, 219n31, 223–4n19, 224n32, 230n6, 233n27, 257n42; and relation to character in George Eliot and Joseph Conrad, 7–12, 216nn9, 11; and relation to character in Gertrude Stein, 122, 146–149, 151; and relation to character in Henry James, 22, 76, 81, 84–87, 94, 96–98, 100, 112–114, 229n5, 230n30, 231n12, 232nn19, 20, 234nn30, 32, 33; and relation to character in Herman Melville, 16–17. *See also* Nietzsche, and morality
Moran, Richard, 59, 221–22n8, 226n42
Motivation, psychological and behavioral, 2, 5–6, 35–37, 41–42, 143, 221n6, 223n21, 230nn7, 8, 232n22, 233n27, 256n41, 259n8; in Joseph Conrad, 6, 10–13; in Herman Melville, 14, 16; in Henry James, 12, 22, 36, 73, 76–77, 79–81, 86–87, 96, 100, 113, 220n35, 230n11, 232n20; in Gertrude Stein, 119, 143; in T. S. Eliot, 190, 220n5
Mutability, 2, 3, 27, 47, 138, 159, 230n8

Negative agency, 70, 76–77, 101–103
Nervous response, 125–30, 147, 201
Nervous system, 125, 127
New materialisms, 20–21, 204, 219n30
Ngai, Sianne, 94–95, 103, 160–161, 168, 186, 217n16, 248–49n52
Nietzsche, Friedrich, 3–4, 19, 37, 60, 64–65, 67, 70, 76, 92–94, 112–13, 199, 216n6, 218n20, 218n23, 234n32, 238nn51, 52; and morality, 22, 39, 96–97, 219n31, 222n18

Open-endedness, 4, 26, 36, 46, 75, 80, 121, 142, 182, 192, 199, 234n31; of character, 155, 190, 196, 198, 234n35, 239n53; of habit, 122, 138; of interests, 77, 79, 85, 93, 99, 114
Openness, as a value, 2, 4, 10, 32, 241n12
Organicism, 1, 133, 151, 227–28n50, 229n55; and evolution, 203. See also Life

Performance, 81, 105–107, 111–14, 159–61, 164–66, 197, 238n52, 238–39n53, 252n14
Personality, 2, 19–20, 22, 24, 29–38, 41, 207, 221nn6, 7, 250n6, 250–51n7; in Bergson, 53–54, 82, 148, 225n37, 226n39, 250n40; in Gertrude Stein, 117, 120, 124, 129, 243n22; in Henry James, 50, 80; in Joseph Conrad, 11–13; in T. S. Eliot, 36, 49–50, 154–155, 158, 162–164, 166, 183, 188, 191, 193–194, 198, 226n39. *See also* Character, Impersonality
Personality psychology, 35, 37, 221n6
Pippen, Robert, 84–85, 232nn19, 20, 234n30, 252n14
Plasticity, of response, 41, 76, 97, 99, 101,

123, 132, 243n24; in Bergson, 53, 82, 148, 249n55; in William James, 124, 130
Politics, 76–77, 223n24, 240n2; and modernist literature, 18, 46–49, 55, 106, 113–114, 162, 167, 175, 224nn29, 30, 235n39, 239n55, 240nn2, 5, 250n6, 252n12, 254n25; and vitalism, 175, 200–201, 204–205, 207–208, 249n53, 254n25
Poststructural criticism, 4, 24, 56, 82, 203, 231n15
Pragmatism, 64–71, 75–77, 104, 133, 176, 227–28n50, 228nn51, 52, 53, 54, 228–29n55, 229nn2, 3, 231n16, 239–40n1, 244–45n33, 245n36, 254n26, 259n1
Primal scene, 106–107, 109–110, 236nn43, 44
Psychoanalysis, 5, 23–24, 78, 105–110, 112, 115, 129, 136, 201–202, 220nn34, 35, 226n43, 236nn42, 43, 44, 236–37n45, 237n46, 238n50, 243n22, 245n36, 256n38, 259n8
Psychological content, 5, 62–63, 66, 80, 83, 221n7; as conceptualized by T. S. Eliot, 33, 162, 189, 192–96, 256n37
Psychological history of the individual, 60, 117, 153, 193, 226n43, 246–47n43, 252–53n15; as manifested in habit, 123–24, 137, 142–143, 244n28
Psychology: behavioral, 4, 37–38, 222n12, 251n8; ego, 4, 35–36; moral, 16, 39, 85, 219n31; personality, 35, 37, 221n6; social, 38–40
Public sphere: in Herman Melville, 14, 16, 18; and modernism, 207, 224n30, 230n9, 239n55, 250–51n7
Pure memory, 53, 210, 225nn37, 38

Rationalism: and aesthetics, 44, 223n25, 224n27, 225n36; and ethics, 40–42, 76, 87, 96, 100, 230n6, 234n31; and psychology, 4, 14, 40, 53–54, 60, 62, 65
Realism: in literature, 6–7, 14, 17–18, 22, 29, 32, 75, 80–81, 229nn2, 3, 231n15, 234n34; philosophical and political, 67, 76, 173, 257n43
Reflex action, 125, 128–129, 147, 152, 204
Relationality, 1, 14, 27, 34, 77, 158–9, 162, 182, 255n36; self defined by, 2, 46, 64, 70, 73, 80–86, 102, 154, 159–60, 162–64, 172, 188, 191
Repetition, 4–6, 24, 37, 49, 55, 105, 127–128, 152, 224n31, 228–29n55, 249n58; in Gertrude Stein, 22, 25, 117–119, 122–124, 127, 131–133, 135, 137, 140, 145–152, 241nn10, 11, 244n28, 246n39, 248n51. *See also* Habit
Rorty, Richard, 67, 228nn52, 53

Science, cognitive, 57. *See also* Cognitive understanding
Science, evolutionary. *See* Evolution
Sedgwick, Eve Kosofsky, 64, 227n47
Self-consciousness, 84, 155–56, 169, 177, 181, 187, 238–39n53, 250n59, 252n13
Silverman, Kaja, 107, 109, 236nn43, 44, 236–37n45
Situational. *See* Character, situational models of
Social psychology, 38–40
Spinoza, Baruch, 27, 64, 76, 101–102, 104, 230n8, 234n32
Stein, Gertrude: and Bergson, 23, 119, 128, 132–38, 142, 145–50, 152, 240n3, 241n13, 242nn19, 20, 245n32, 245nn34, 35, 246n43, 249nn53, 55, 56, 57, 58; and comedy, 121, 143–51, 247n46, 248nn50, 51, 248–49n52; "continuous present" in, 12, 131–132, 246n39; and Darwin, 19, 118–121, 124–129, 131, 133–34, 137–138, 149–50, 152, 218n26, 241nn8, 12, 13, 242nn14, 15, 16, 17, 18, 19, 249n59; and life, 118–119, 121, 131, 133, 139, 142–146, 148–151; "Melanctha," 24, 119–123, 131–132, 135–138, 141, 144–151, 240n5, 248nn49, 50, 250n60; and portraiture, 120, 139–40, 143–44, 246nn38, 39; and race, 120, 122, 144–146, 151, 240n5, 248nn48, 49; and repudiation of consistency of character, 2, 5, 13, 24–25, 40–41, 117, 131–132, 135–136, 138–139; and science, 19, 118–19, 126–28, 209, 243nn21, 24; and situational models of character, 2, 5, 9, 19–20, 23, 40, 127–129, 131–132, 135, 140, 205; *Three Lives*, 117, 119–120, 128, 131, 133, 136–137, 139–140, 240n4; and typology, 120, 144–152, 240nn4, 5, 244n31, 248n49, 249n52; and William James, 19, 118–19, 124, 126, 128, 130, 133–136, 243n21, 245n36. *See also* Affect, in Gertrude Stein; Automatism, in Gertrude Stein; Emotion, in Gertrude Stein; Ethics, in Gertrude Stein; Evolution, Gertrude Stein's interest in; Habit, in Gertrude Stein; Liveliness; Modernism; Morality, and relation to character in Gertrude Stein; Personality,

in Gertrude Stein; Repetition, in Gertrude Stein; Vitalism
Stream of consciousness, 82–84, 176
Suspension: of ethical judgment, 42, 49, 76, 79–80, 84–86, 97–99, 102–4, 106, 114, 173, 183, 226n38; of identity or character, 19, 23, 55, 73–74, 90, 112, 164, 239n53
Sympathy, 15, 150, 163, 168, 173–75, 191, 201, 237n48, 244–45n25, 250–51n7, 253n21; and the sympathetic nervous system, 126–27, 130–31, 152

Theatricality, 78, 105–112, 155, 165, 168–70, 189–90, 195, 235n40, 236n41, 238–39n53, 252n14
Time: in Bergson, 20, 23, 82, 132–134, 136, 149, 188, 200, 202–203, 207, 210–212, 232n21, 244–45n33, 245n34, 259n11; and evolution, 120, 125, 136; as a feature of narrative, 123–124, 131–132, 142, 220n3, 246n39; and Gertrude Stein's "continuous present," 12, 131–132, 246n39; and mutability of character, 3, 12, 18–19, 35, 37–38, 40–41, 43, 55, 58, 82, 104, 123, 131–134, 136, 142–143, 154, 159, 222n17; necessary for ethical judgment, 12, 86, 88, 91, 99, 102, 222n17; and social relationships, 18, 123, 218n29; suspended in, 23, 26, 55, 73–74, 79–80, 109. *See also* Consistency; Continuity; Duration (durée)
Todorov, Tzvetan, 11, 231n13
Tone, 25, 153, 155–56, 159–61, 164, 168–69, 171, 176–79, 185–187, 195–197, 255n36

Unconscious, 11, 24, 63, 67, 201–202, 210, 221n8, 224n27, 237n49, 247n43, 259n6; in Gertrude Stein, 125, 129–132, 134–137, 152, 243nn22, 23; in Henry James, 108–110, 113
Unpredictability, 3, 18, 149, 199, 203–4, 224nn 27, 30, 232n21; of behavior, 1, 13, 40, 44, 52, 54, 58, 106, 119–120, 125, 127–128, 142, 149, 157–158, 161, 177, 180–181, 186, 188, 190, 195, 197, 204; of interests, 25, 79
Vermeule, Blakey, 57–59, 113, 215n2, 230n6, 239n54
Virtuality, 23, 26, 46, 110, 119–121, 144, 157, 168, 173, 176, 181, 187, 194–95, 203–204, 206, 210–212, 218n29, 253n16, 257n43, 259n11, 259–60n13; and "virtual action," 26, 91, 93–94, 110, 142, 225–26n38, 233n25, 237n47
Vitalism, 2–5, 14, 18–23, 27, 40, 44, 53–55, 65, 136–37, 199–213, 215–16n4, 216n5, 218n23, 218–19n29, 225n36, 231n16, 243n24, 254n25; and affect, 61–64, 172, 89–90, 176–177, 227n45; and attention, 53–55; and continuity of character, 80–82; and Darwinism, 118–19, 128, 137, 149, 152, 240n6; on the formation of interests, 75–77, 86, 89, 96, 100, 102, 232n21; historical emergence of, 2–5, 19–20, 64–66, 200, 215–16n4, 216n5, 218n23, 227–28n50, 231n16, 244n33, 247n45, 254n25; and impersonality, 53, 155–56, 162, 172, 200; and the occult, 211–212; and pragmatism, 64–70, 76–77, 104, 133, 227–28n50, 229n4; and racial theories, 120–121, 208. *See also* Bergson, Henri; Darwin, Charles; Eliot, T. S., and historical connection to vitalism; Emerson, Ralph Waldo; Habit, and vitalism; James, Henry, and vitalism; James, William, and vitalism; Nietzsche, Friedrich; Spinoza, Baruch; Stein, Gertrude
Voice: in Bergson and F. H. Bradley, 25, 155, 161, 176, 181, 189–190; and literary character, 20, 46, 153–154, 197, 240n5; in T. S. Eliot, 25, 45–46, 60, 153–158, 160–162, 164–165, 167–169, 176, 181, 183, 185–190, 195–198, 250n4, 253n19, 20, 258n47; and ventriloquism, 167–168, 197. *See also* Double consciousness; Eliot, T. S.; Tone
Walkowitz, Rebecca, 47–49, 114
Will, faculty of, 4, 21, 36, 41, 43, 52–53, 67, 202, 224n32, 225n38, 246n42, 245–46n43; in Gertrude Stein, 128, 131, 134, 136, 152, 244n28, 245n35; in Henry James, 45, 75, 97, 112, 234n32; in Nietzsche, 19, 22, 93, 112, 218n20, 219n31, 222n18, 234n32; in T. S. Eliot, 164, 166, 183
Williams, Bernard, 40–41, 219n31, 223nn20, 22, 233n27, 233–34n29
Wilson, Elizabeth, 127, 242n16
Wollheim, Richard, 59–62, 192–93, 226n43, 258n46